The Eunuchs in the Ming Dynasty

明代宦官

蔡石山 著

The Eunuchs in the Ming Dynasty

Shih-shan Henry Tsai

STATE UNIVERSITY OF NEW YORK PRESS

Cover illustration, a eunuch holding tight the emperor's horse, mid-sixteenth century (courtesy of National Palace Museum of Taiwan)

SUNY series in Chinese Local Studies
Harry J. Lamley, editor

Published by
State University of New York Press, Albany

©1996 State University of New York

For information, address State University of New York Press,
State University Plaza, Albany, N.Y., 12246

Production by Dana Foote
Marketing by Fran Keneston

Library of Congress Cataloging-in-Publication Data

Tsai, Shih-shan Henry.
    The eunuchs in the Ming dynasty / Shih-shan Henry Tsai.
       p. cm. — (SUNY series in Chinese local studies)
    Includes bibliographical references and index.
    ISBN 0–7914–2687–4 (alk. paper). — ISBN 0–7914–2688–2 (pbk. :
alk. paper)
       1. Eunuchs—China. 2. China—History—Ming dynasty. 1368–1644.
I. Title. II. Series.
HQ449.T73 1996
951'.026—dc20
                                     95-22265
                                         CIP

10 9 8 7 6 5 4 3 2 1

To Rocky, who helped to ease the pain of my *alexia* during the course of writing this book.

CONTENTS

MAPS AND FIGURES

MAPS

FIGURES

ACKNOWLEDGMENTS

I am indebted to my artist brother Wen–ching and my student Jiang Jin for their assistance in gathering materials for this book. I also want to acknowledge my gratitude to Professors Edward L. Farmer, Denis Sinor, and Willard Gatewood, Jr., for reading all or part of the manuscript and giving me their generous suggestions. Five anonymous reviewers have provided many constructive comments that not only save me from embarrassing errors but also help me improve the manuscript. To these Ming specialists as well as to Harry Lamley, editor of the SUNY Series in Chinese Local Studies, I would like to express my most sincere appreciation.

Several able scholars on both sides of the Pacific have at different stages of my research provided assistance and encouragement. They include Paul S. Holbo, Theodore Foss, Edward J. Malatesta, S.J., Father Jean Charbonnier, S.J., John E. Wills, Jr., Fred W. Drake, William N. Harrison, Liu Shih–ji, Hsing Yi–tien, and Xu Hua. I owe much to Mary Kirkpatrick for typing the manuscript from its draft form to its final version and Gary Shepard for doing most of the illustration reproduction. I should also thank Sonia and Shirley for helping me acquire my initial computer literacy and showing me how to be patient.

I am also grateful to the National Palace Museum of Taiwan for permission to use several of its Ming illustrations. The final version was written with the aid of a Fulbright College of Arts and Sciences Research Assignment from the University of Arkansas, and by a grant from the Academia Sinica.

Successive Reigns of the Ming Emperors

No.	Reign Titles	Reign Dates	Age at Enthronement	Age at Death	Total Tenure	Influential Eunuchs
1.	Taizu, Hongwu	1368–1398	40 sui*	71 sui	31 years	Wu Cheng
2.	Huidi, Jianwen	1399–1402	22	Unknown	4	
3.	Chengzu, Yongle	1403–1424	42	65	23	Zheng He, Hou Xian
4.	Renzong, Hongxi	1425	47	48	1	
5.	Xuanzong, Xuande	1426–1435	27	37	10	Liu Ning, Jin Ying, Wang Jin
6.	Yingzong, Zhengtong	1436–1449	9		14	Wang Zhen, Xi Ning
	Yingzong, Tianshun	1457–1464	30	38	8	
7.	Jingdi, Jingtai	1450–1456	23	30	7	Cao Jixiang, Yishiha
8.	Xianzong, Chenghua	1465–1487	18	41	23	Wang Zhi, Huai En, Niu Yu
9.	Xiaozong, Hongzhi	1488–1505	18	36	18	Li Guang, Jiang Cong
10.	Wuzong, Zhengde	1506–1521	15	31	16	Liu Jin, Zhang Yong
11.	Shizong, Jiajing	1522–1566	15	60	45	Xiao Jing, Mai Fu
12.	Muzong, Longqing	1567–1572	30	36	6	Chen Hong
13.	Shenzong, Wanli	1573–1620	10	58	47	Feng Bao, Chen Ju, Zhang Jin
14.	Guangzong, Taichang	1620	39	39	1 month	Wang An
15.	Xizong, Tianqi	1621–1627	16	23	7	Wei Zhongxian
16.	Sizong, Chongzhen	1628–1644	17	34	17	Cao Huachun

*In Western society a baby would not be considered one year old until it had lived 12 months but a Chinese baby was counted one sui at birth.

I

꙰

Introduction

THE SCHOLAR AND THE EUNUCH

In the late sixteenth century when Protestants and Catholics were opposing one another across the length and breadth of Europe, two baby boys, Yang Lian and Wei Zhongxian (also known as Li Jinzhong), entered the world in the mountain-girded Hubei of central China and in the arid Hebei near the Beijing area, respectively. They were destined to play significant roles in the political arena of the Ming dynasty. Like many others of their time, both tried desperately to work through narrow and tortuous paths that led to position and wealth. Yang chose the civil service examination system that tested how well a scholar could write bagu or eight-legged essays, became a literati-official, exerted a great influence on the people, and before his death in 1625, rose to the rank of senior vice censor in chief. Wei, on the other hand, by choosing castration and because of a streak of cunning in his nature, worked his way to be the powerful managing grand eunuch in the Ceremonial Directorate of the Ming court. By traditional accounts, Yang had done good deeds for the country, retained his sterling qualities by upholding Confucian ideals and convictions. In vivid contrast, Wei was a wily, unprincipled scoundrel, who having no means for education, took a shortcut to position and power. As a palace eunuch, he cheated and fawned on his superiors in order to swindle them and win advantages. Whether or not such accounts, mostly written by Confucian scholars in the seventeenth and eighteenth centuries, are reliable, both Yang and Wei, in winning riches and power, had to endure unbearable hardships and make enormous sacrifices. For Yang to pass the extremely difficult examinations, he dedicated away his young life in working on bagu composition and mastering the myriad of words and mechanic syntax of the classic language. In such an endeavor, Yang had to restrict his learning, suppress freedom of thought, and stifle his creativity. For Wei, needless to say, he lost forever his "manhood" and had to live an abnormal life as a deficient man, worrying about wetting his bed every night.

Born in 1571 in Hubei's Yingshan county, Yang began to learn Confucian classics when he was very young. Through perseverance and industry, he passed both a county test and a prefectural test and became one of a dozen people from his area to hold a Xiucai (flowery talent) or a bachelor degree, which not only brought him respectability, but entitled him to receive a meager stipend from the government. Even though he continued to struggle, his villagers no longer despised him and no one dared to trample his family under. Also, by earning his first degree, Yang no longer was required to kneel to a magistrate. More important, even if he ran out of luck or failed all else in life, he could at least tutor village youngsters for a living. But he also realized that he was only a novice in the realm of the scholars and that he was far from being a learned person. Consequently, he persevered and studied day and night for yet another competitive examination, which was held only once every three years in his provincial capital city of Wuchang.

A chief examiner and a number of vice examiners, all appointed by the emperor, presided over his provincial examination. Good fortune once again smiled on him for he passed the second examination and was bestowed a Juren (recommended person) or licentiate degree. Of the few dozen licentiates who took the examination with him, many failed several times in previous attempts; some had gray hair, and a few indeed led miserable lives before passing the examination. By becoming a licentiate, however, Yang, like most other fellow degree holders, now enjoyed fame and also frequently received pigs, porcelain, housewares, and possibly land and a house from his neighbors, admirers, and people who needed political clout. But he was never allowed to forget even for a moment that the duty of a scholar was to become a government official. So he could not relax as he had one more very difficult stair to climb to earn an official position; that is, to pass the final metropolitan examination.

There is no record as to how many times Yang Lian had to take the metropolitan examination to earn the highly prized Jinshi (advanced scholar) degree or a doctorate. Directly supervised by the Ministry of Rites, the metropolitan examination was held once every three years in Beijing and each time awarded between 200 to 300 doctorates among the thousands of qualified licentiates from all over the country. In preparing for the examination, many candidates injured their health, ranging from bleeding ulcers, insomnia, indigestion, tuberculosis, to depression, nervous breakdown, and other mental illnesses. Several hanged themselves in the examination cells. But Yang Lian survived, for in 1607 he passed the metropolitan examination and completed this most tortuous journey to officialdom. Following another palace test, plus a brief interview with the Emperor Wanli (1573–1620), Yang Lian, now thirty-six years of age, was officially given a doctor degree and a government post.

Yang Lian began his career as a magistrate of Changshu county in the coastal Jiangsu province. He reportedly listened to the voice of the people, avoided bringing shame to himself or getting involved in bribery scandals, and steadily rose through the ranks. He was duly promoted to be a supervising secretary in Beijing, in charge of scrutinizing revenue and military affairs. In the Confucian lexicon, fealty, courage, and uprightness were the qualities that a virtuous official should possess. Yang seemed to personify all of such virtues and was therefore made a censor near the end of Wanli reign.[1] However, Yang Lian was not among those flowers born to blush unseen and waste their sweetness on the desert air. Within the bounds of Ming political collegiality, Yang clashed vigorously with powerful ministers, infuriated prestigious grand scholars, and condemned sleazy eunuchs. Then came the eventful year of 1620. China had three different emperors on the throne within only two months and, because of frequent changes of leadership, the functioning of the government was seriously disrupted, and Yang Lian was involved in the thick of political manipulations.

Emperor Wanli died on August 18, 1620, and the Emperor Taichang, the fourteenth Ming sovereign, ascended to the throne, already a dying man. After taking several "red pills," Taichang died on September 26, 1620. Soon a pall was cast over Beijing as factional strife in the Ming court intensified while three major scandals shattered even the confidence of the cabinet. Amid the general confusion, Yang Lian, who was also known for his rash judgment, and Wang An, the dead emperor's favorite eunuch, kidnapped the sixteen-year-old crown prince from his foster mother's quarters and had him installed as Emperor Tianqi on October 1, 1620. But the enthronement of the fifteenth Ming emperor also catapulted the eunuch Wei Zhongxian from obscurity into the limelight of power. Finally, in the summer of 1624, Yang confronted the powerful Wei and brought about an acrimonious standoff that flared the politics of Ming court between the literati-bureaucrats and the palace eunuchs.

If Yang's scholarly and political journey was one of mental anguish and emotionally drained experience, Wei's rise to power was physically vexatious and psychologically tumultuous. Wei started as the son of a decent but poor man on February 27, 1568, in Hebei's Suning county, an area that served as one of the major regions that supplied eunuchs. Constantly struggling just for mere subsistence, Wei grew up illiterate and a habitual gambler. Wei was briefly married to a peasant girl who gave him a daughter. But when treated brutally by the hooligans who relentlessly badgered Wei to pay off his gambling debts, Wei decided to make a radical change in his life by voluntarily having himself emasculated. Such a decision, as peculiar as it seemed to any rational modern man, was not a matter of inconsequence in Chinese history.

This is because Wei, as our story unfolds, was to help accelerate the downfall of the Ming dynasty.

Various methods of castration were used in China. According to the French writer Richard Millant, Japanese scholar Jitsuzo Kuwabara, and the British researcher Garter C. Stent, a volunteer like Wei, would first have to seek a specialist for the risky operation. Accompanied by a guarantor, who witnessed the operation and also was responsible for the volunteer's payment and recovery, Wei met his surgeon in a small hut. Before the specialist performed the operation, he ritually asked the young volunteer if he would regret it or not. If the answer was negative and firm, the specialist would immediately flash his blade and, in a few minutes, the castration was completed. In addition to excruciating pain, many would-be eunuchs died of excessive bleeding, urine blockage, or other complications.[2] Wei survived; however, it took him several months to heal from the surgery.

Emotionally scarred and physically deformed, Wei was later thoroughly examined by the palace head eunuch who made sure that Wei's "treasure parts" had been permanently severed from his body. He was about twenty-one years old, and through a relative of his mother, Wei entered the palace service. He was now a novice, surrounded daily and closely watched by hundreds of fellow eunuchs, who had chosen the same tortuous method to gain employment in the emperor's harem. In the ensuing months and years, Wei was to discover that he had joined a group of peculiar people who were neither men nor women. With his natural male forces abated, the fundamental process of biological change occurred in his body cells, evidenced in changed functions and in appearance. There was an apparent loss of height and beard, his nose became broader and his ear lobes thicker. Decreasing hormone levels caused loss of elasticity: his skin wrinkled, his joints stiffened, and his muscle strength gradually weakened. His nails had a dull yellow appearance, the halfmoons disappeared, and the nails developed ridges. He quickly underwent a change of voice. He now sounded a bit more shrieking and evidently more feminine than masculine. His body weight increased, mainly because of reduced physical activity in an environment where food was plentiful. Although not readily visible to him, perhaps the most important changes occurred in the lungs and the cardiovascular systems. These led to a decrease in his body's ability to gather oxygen from the air and a decreased ability to pump adequate blood with its essential components to all parts of the body. He soon became soft and fat.[3]

According to a famed Chinese physican, Chen Cunren (1909–1990), who treated eunuchs in his Shanghai clinic in the 1930s and early 1940s, physical and physiological changes after castration were much easier to detect than psychological changes. However, based on available literature and historical records, including the eunuch Liu Ruoyu's memoir, a castrated man like Wei Zhongxian tended to have a chip on his shoulder, that is to say, he was extremely sensitive about his "deficiency" and the fact that he rose to power by way of a "shortcut." He was often paranoid, petty, and took trivial matters very seriously. He also became peevish, vindictive, and capable of quick and ruthless decisions; but gentle and loyal to his friends and generous to his relatives. Accordingly, he needed to align with powerful eunuchs and collaborate with influential palace women. Above all, he always stood by his autocrat employer like a faithful dog and would come to the defense of his emperor even when the emperor flouted with the wishes of the people by acts of tyranny.[4] Stories about the eunuchs' intimacy with both the palace women attendants and the imperial family are abundant, and the following chapters will provide a few typical examples.

For the next thirty-odd years, Wei Zhongxian worked in the imperial stable, palace construction, and various inner court storehouses. In the taxonomy of Ming eunuchism, Wei was neither fish nor fowl; he held no office. He was reported to enjoy profane forms of entertainment and love dog meat, flowers, fancy clothes, and flattery. During this long time of service Wei also acquired a cursory knowledge of the written Chinese language. Then, by a stroke of luck, he was assigned to cook for Emperor Wanli's grandson, who was later to become Emperor Tianqi (1620–1627). Wei served the young prince diligently, not only creating a strong bond with the future emperor, but also establishing a close relationship with the prince's wet nurse, Mistress Ke, to whom Tianqi was deeply attached. Ke was a very attractive woman and Tianqi, then a teenager, felt something more than just childlike devotion to a former wet nurse. In fact, it was on the recommendation of Ke that Wei was appointed in 1622 to be a managing grand eunuch in the most powerful Ceremonial Directorate, which handled the flow of imperial documents. The official Ming history says that, together with Mistress Ke, Wei exerted an unhealthy and improper influence over the young emperor, introducing the emperor to a life of profligacy while consolidating his power bases. Wei even received the emperor's approval to train a eunuch army within the palace and had the chief grand eunuch Wang An, Wei's former patron, demoted and then murdered. By the end of 1623, now fifty-five years old, Wei was also made the director of a secret police establishment, known as the Eastern Depot.[5] It was said that Wei effectively utilized this position to harass or remove persons he deemed undesirable and begin a reign of terror.

While the young emperor indulged in archery contests, water works, carpentry, opera, and led a life of idleness and debauchery, Wei was said to have caused the death of an imperial concubine, dismissed numerous honest officials, stolen precious jewelry from imperial treasury, and acquired riches and highest honors for himself and his relatives. It was against this background that the Censor Yang Lian decided to risk his life by impeaching Wei and remonstrating with the emperor. Yang listed twenty-four heinous crimes allegedly committed by Wei. Even though some 100 other officials also denounced Wei, Emperor Tianqi stood by his eunuch confidant. Consequently, Wei had Yang and a dozen high ranking officials thrown into jail and later flogged to death or executed. During this show of power, more than 700 literati-bureaucrats were also purged.[6] The year was 1625, when Charles I took the throne of England, but less than a decade later, the last Ming emperor Chongzhen, Tianqi's brother, flew even more brazenly in the face of his people than did Charles I. But before Chongzhen committed suicide in 1644, on the approach of rebels, he saw to it that Wei and his cronies were eliminated.

Wei's patron and protector, Emperor Tianqi, unexpectedly died on September 30, 1627, at the age of twenty-three. After nearly three months of tense waiting, an imperial rescript came to remove Wei from Beijing and ordered him confined in Fengyang, a special Ming penitentiary for convicted imperial clansmen and high ranking eunuchs not far from Nanjing. Wei left Beijing with a guard of 800 eunuchs, 1,000 horses, and 40 wagonloads of jewelry. About halfway between Beijing and Fengyang, Wei took his own life, and his guards were also arrested. Worse still, in early 1628 Wei's corpse was sadistically dismembered and displayed in Wei's native village as a warning to the public. Wei's closest ally, the Mistress Ke was beaten to death, six of his coconspirators suffered immediate execution, nineteen officials who were associated with Wei, were marked for execution in the winter of 1628, thirty-five of Wei's relatives were banished to the frontier and nearly 200 other people received various degrees of punishment.[7] The counterpurge of 1628 was indeed as bloody and malicious as that of the purge that took place three years early, but the Ming dynasty was about to run its course.

NEW THEMATIC APPROACHES

The turmoil of the 1620s in general and the tragic deaths of the scholar Yang Lian and the eunuch Wei Zhongxian have generated enormous interest among Chinese historians. With their emphasis on the importance of Confucian ethics and propriety, they tend to downplay, if not grossly neglect, the shortcomings of China's traditional social and political organizations. According to this line of interpretation, the problems of the 1620s were caused primarily by the shortcomings of individuals, such as Wei Zhongxian and the Mistress Ke, instead of the ritualistic and absolutist imperial system. By their so-called praise and blame standard, this is a black and white case, a struggle between the eunuch who had a malevolent touch on imperial system and the scholar who adhered to strict Confucian morals. So far as these historians are concerned, the event bodes well. However, by cutting loose from traditional Chinese moorings and carefully studying the rise and fall of hundreds of Ming personages, one can easily find that no individuals or groups, except the emperors, could maintain an unchallenged and durable hold on power for more than a decade. This is because the Ming institutional framework, which lasted for 276 years, was so well established that even the handful of eunuchs that had occasionally risen to powerful positions found themselves constantly subject to institutional restraints and traditional restrictions. In the final analysis, both the literati-officials and the eunuchs were really the pawns of the colossal Ming institutions and absolutism.

Chinese historians who condemn the evil influence of the Ming eunuchs often cite such notorious eunuchs as Wang Zhen in the 1440s, Wang Zhi in the 1470s, Liu Jin in the early 1500s, and Wei Zhongxian in the 1620s. But had the eunuchs' rise to power in the Ming dynasty resulted in "one profit but hundreds of damages," as proclaimed by the chroniclers of the *Ming shi*, the standard history of the Ming? It is true that at times of intense power struggle, as in the case of 1625 when eunuchs had the upper hand, hundreds of their rival literati-bureaucrats were tortured, disgraced, forced to leave positions or even put to death. However, of the estimated 1 million eunuchs employed by the Ming emperors throughout the dynasty, only a small number actually rose to power and influence. And among the powerful castrati were many laudable generals and admirals, skillful diplomats and explorers, talented architects and hydraulic engineers, noteworthy financiers and exemplary administrators.

Although a few secret police chiefs and eunuch political bosses at one time or another enjoyed riches and power and basked in adulation, the lives of ordinary eunuchs, who were servants and slaves of the emperor, his consorts, and relatives, were restricted, routine, and boring. They worked year in and year out in the imperial quarters, in the frontiers, and in the princely establishments all over the Ming empire. But, although their hard labor and long subservience provided the emperor and his relatives—their number estimated at 20,000 in 1550 and over 80,000 at the end of the Ming—with luxury, beauty and safety, and political intelligence, the eunuchs also represented a threat to the scholar-officials' cherished role as the instrument of imperial government. After the office of premiership was abolished in the 1390s, Ming state affairs were divided among six ministries or boards; namely, Personnel, Revenues, War, Punishment, Rites, and Public Works. Each ministry had a minister but the ministries were really under the direct control of the emperor, who frequently used his trusted eunuchs to run the state.

The grim irony in Chinese historiography is that the Chinese intelligentsia somehow felt that they were charged with a mission to build an ideal society and, if the system derailed, they were responsible for mending it to meet the criteria as prescribed by legendary sage-kings in ancient times. Unfortunately, cruel political realities often defeated such idealism. Failing to implement their utopian ideology, many intellectuals felt powerless, impotent, and ultimately disappeared from the historical scene. Others utilized their writings to continue to promote the politics of the sage-kings. Constantly locked into an adversary position against the eunuchs, these highbrow bureaucrat-scholars had a tendency to portray their arch rivals as rapacious, wicked, and unscrupulous. They attributed all the evils to the despised and hateful eunuchs when in fact the cause of the ills of the society was the very imperial institution that Chinese intelligentsia gleefully served. The two groups collided, interacted, and conflicted throughout the Ming period and for nearly 250 years vied with one another for control of the imperial apparatus. Corresponding to such idealism and rivalry was the timidity and lack of revolutionary tradition of the Chinese intelligentsia. Consequently, Chinese historians rarely openly and persistently criticized the autocratic political system and the tyranny spawned from it. Instead, they singled out the eunuchs as the scapegoats and refused to treat this lowbrow group as a social and political complex.

The cliches that too often were recorded—the weak and lazy emperors, the sly and cynical eunuchs—should now be viewed as unsympathetic reverberations from idealistic and timid traditions of Chinese intelligentsia. Should twentieth century historians continue to condemn eunuchs as palace termites, blame them for corruption in imperial court, and accuse them of being usurpers and terrorists; or should we treat them as needed hewers of wood and drawers of water, themselves the victims of a tyrannical system? It is high time that eunuchs be allowed to speak for themselves and be seen as the subjects rather than the objects of Ming history. It is important that eunuchs be studied in the context of the emperor's immediate environment, his court, and the bureaucracy that the emperor headed and which received its power from him. Our investigation has already yielded evidence that there were many loyal talents among eunuchs and that their contributions to the Ming society were indeed very significant.

In the past century a few Western scholars have deviated from orthodox Chinese ideological abettors and tried to give eunuchs a more balanced treatment. For example, Paul Pelliot and Wolfgang Franke, while sharing the view that the eunuch system was a disturbing and irrational element in China's imperial past, also saw it as a necessary cement that held imperial institutions together and made China's polygamous society work. Other scholars, who were attracted to this subject matter, utilized modern methodological tools for examining political and social behavior of the eunuch group. In 1908, Richard Millant of France wrote *Les Eunuques: A Travers Les Ages*, detailing the castration techniques and processes by which young boys were brutalized and forced to trade their manhood for jobs in imperial courts. Robert B. Crawford in 1961 wrote an article, "Eunuch Power in the Ming Dynasty," in the Dutch journal *T'oung Pao*, briefly analyzing eunuch political activities in Ming period. Two years later, Japanese popular writer Taisuke Mitamura completed his best seller, *Chinese Eunuchs: The Structure of Intimate Politics*. More recently, a German scholar Ulrike Jugel wrote a laborious Ph.D. dissertation, studying the social-political role and the development of the eunuch group in the Later Han dynasty (25–220 A.D.). And in 1968, Ulrich Mammitzsch wrote a thesis defending the controversial eunuch Wei Zhongxian.[8]

It is evident that a more objective and in-depth study of Chinese eunuchs in general and the roles of Ming eunuchs in particular is needed for the topic to break free from the traditional framework in which it has been studied. The thematic stress of usurpation of power by the eunuchs and the conceptual framework of historical harm and damage done by the eunuchs should be balanced with an attempt to look at the eunuchs' social backgrounds and their ways of life. Horrid stories and high-handed power games need to be discussed in the context of Chinese despotic political traditions. And individuals and their behavior also should be reexamined in the light of institutional tyranny. The following chapters will present a comprehensive picture of the eunuchs as a central, constituent element of the imperial government equally as significant as the civil and military hierarchies. They will also demonstrate that the eunuchs were not just household servants meddling in affairs of state, but made up a third administrative hierarchy through which emperors could, and did, exercise their power in all areas of government.

Map A. Fifteenth Century China

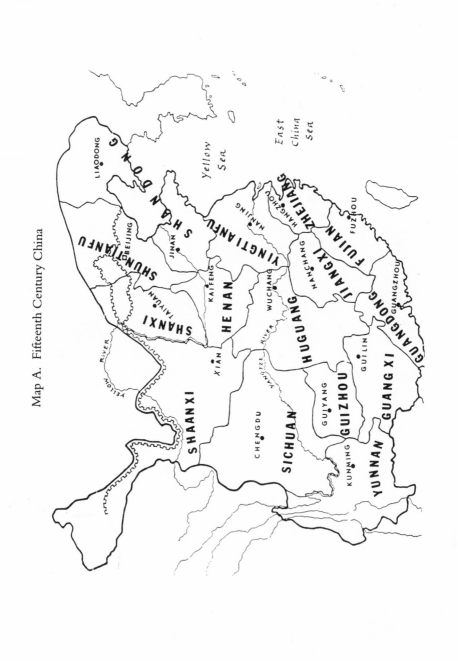

II

汧

The Demand and Supply
of Ming Eunuchs

HISTORIC ORIGINS

The presence of eunuchs is in no way limited to Chinese society. In the 1700s as many as 4,000 boys were castrated each year in Italy and 70 percent of all opera singers were castrati.[1] In China, at the end of the fifteenth century, there were approximately 10,000 eunuchs in the Forbidden City and in various Ming princely establishments. At the time of the establishment in 1644 of the Qing dynasty it was estimated that the total number of eunuchs in China had reached 100,000 in a total population of about 130 million people.[2]

Castration and eunuchism appeared not only in ancient Egyptian, Persian, Greek, and Roman literature, but was condemned in the Bible. For several centuries, the Arabs, the Indians, and the Turks widely used castrated men for a variety of assignments in palaces. Nobody knows when and how eunuchs were first institutionalized in China except that castration was frequently used as a substitute for the death penalty. In China, palace eunuchs were called *huanguan* which was a recognized official title during the Shang dynasty (1765–1222 B.C.) as it appeared on the Shang oracle bones. *Zhouli* (Rites of the Zhou) also used a variety of terms when it referred to this group of castrated men. Other literature confirmed that the Zhou kings had in fact employed eunuchs as chamberlains in the palaces, assigning them to supervise royal chambers and guard the king's harem. Confucius (551–479 B.C.) was said to have been so irked by the evil example of a prominent eunuch named Yun Chu of the state of Wei that, after staying only for a month, he decided not to serve the duke of Wei. The first notorious eunuch who drew the attention of ancient chroniclers was Pei, who, according to the historian Zuo Qiuming, served under three mutually hostile dukes during the sixth century B.C. Pei was to become a stereotype eunuch—a person of sycophancy, ruthlessness, treachery, greed, and luxury. Such prejudice was also reflected in the *Book of Odes*, which said,

Not heaven but women and eunuchs
Bring misfortunes to mankind.
Wives and those without balls
Bleat with similar voices.

During the Qin dynasty (221–207 B.C.), more eunuchs were employed to serve the ambitious empire builder Qin Shihuangdi, who established a new agency called Zhongchangshi for the sole purpose of managing the ever-increasing number of court eunuchs. In the succeeding dynasties, court eunuchs continued to grow in number and influence and ultimately became an important part of China's imperial apparatus. Although Chinese society generally viewed these people as anathema, their status had by the beginning of the Christian era been firmly established. During the Eastern Han dynasty (25–220 A.D.), six dowager empresses subsequently promoted court eunuchs to powerful positions and inevitably sowed the seeds for the dynasty's downfall. Before the rebels entered the Eastern Han capital in Luoyang, an ambitious eunuch murdered the chief minister, He Jin, whose deputies in turn put to death more than 2,000 eunuchs as means of retribution, and brought down the dynasty. The next major dynasty that was to be constantly plagued with eunuch problems was the prosperous and culturally brilliant Tang dynasty (618–906). During the Tang rule, eunuchs were appointed commanders of palace guards and supervisors of the army and allowed to participate in the decision-making process. It is no exaggeration to say that high officials of the central government in Xian and the provinces were reduced to ingratiating themselves with the favorites of chief eunuchs to maintain their power and positions. Near the end of the dynasty, Tang eunuchs became virtual king makers, because they were instrumental in selecting seven of the last eight Tang emperors. But once again, the eunuchs had to pay a heavy price for wielding such enormous power. In 903, the warlord Zhu Quanzhong arrived in Xian and executed 162 court eunuchs and their collaborators. He later arrested and killed 300 more and ordered every eunuch who had been involved in military affairs to commit suicide. With most of the eunuchs gone, so went the Tang dynasty.

During the next fifty-four years of the so-called Five Dynasties, China witnessed political division and chaos, but very few eunuchs rose to prominent positions. Upon ascending the throne, the founder of the Song dynasty (North Song 960–1126, South Song 1127–1279), fully aware of the eunuch problems in previous dynasties, took measures to keep his castrated servants under control. During the first hundred years of the Song dynasty, which governed then the largest nation on earth, China enjoyed the reign of a succession of emperors who were conscientious and able administrators, as well as the general absence of any notorious perfidy on the part of the eunuchs.

However, several eunuchs were given military command and, in fact, a very influential eunuch by the name of Tong Guan, who at one time commanded an army of 800,000 men, was later blamed for causing the downfall of the North Song. When China was under the Mongol rule, 1279–1368, eunuchs were rarely active in the political arena. Nevertheless, Kublai Khan (1216?–1294) commissioned a eunuch named Guo Shoujing to construct a section of the Grand Canal near Beijing. And in 1348, Jia Lu was appointed a Taijian, or grand eunuch, to manage flood control and maintain China's hydraulic infrastructure. Taijian, a unique eunuch title in China's officialdom, was thus created and henceforth became an important element in Chinese history.

When Zhu Yuanzhang (known as Emperor Hongwu) founded the Ming dynasty in 1368, he was keenly aware of the potentially pernicious eunuch problems and decided to limit the number of court eunuchs to fewer than 100. Even though he was later to increase the number of palace servants to more than 400, he reportedly also decreed that no eunuch be permitted to learn books or to give advice on political matters. Even the few eunuchs with whom Hongwu might chat were kept dutifully awed and never allowed to discuss politics. In 1384 he had the following inscription engraved on an iron tablet in front of the palace: "Eunuchs are forbidden to interfere with government affairs. Those who attempt to do so will be subjected to capital punishment."[3] Shortly before his death he ordered that eunuchs should no longer be allowed to wear the uniform of government officials and that their rank should not exceed the fourth grade. Officials of all departments were forbidden to communicate with eunuchs by written documents.

The commands of the founder of the dynasty were disobeyed soon after his death. When Yongle (1402–1424) usurped the throne of his nephew, Emperor Jianwen (1398–1402), he had to rely on the help of the eunuchs because the court ministers had remained loyal to his nephew. After his successful coup d'état, Emperor Yongle rewarded the eunuchs by giving them high ranks and showing them special favor, even putting some of them in charge of military affairs. In the ensuing years, Emperor Xuande, Yongle's grandson, established a classroom known as Neishutang, or Inner Court Study, and appointed four scholars from the Hanlin Academy to teach some 200 to 300 young eunuchs whose average age was about ten. Some of these educated eunuchs were to become secretaries of the emperor and often had communication with court officials. As the eunuchs were becoming literate, they became a dominant group to be reckoned with. Not only did they secure power bases in the court, their number also grew steadily.

FOREIGN SUPPLY OF EUNUCHS

The eunuch system victimized not only the Chinese population but also non-Chinese peoples who lived in China's peripheral regions. At the time when the Romans were building their empire in the West, China produced the dominant civilization in the East, from which her neighbors derived much of their culture. In Chinese eyes, states adjacent to China were civilized only to the extent that they accepted Chinese ideas, customs, and institutions and agreed to use the Chinese lunar calendar to date their official documents. As a consequence, eunuchism possessed a pan-Asian character long before Genghis Khan's armies swept China proper.

The ninety years of Mongol rule ended in the summer of 1368 when the Ming forces from the south occupied Beijing and captured at least six Mongol princes and their families. Together with their eunuchs, these prisoners of war remained south of the Great Wall as hostages while the fleeing Mongols journeyed northward across the barren and brown wasteland. In 1371, a grandson of the last Mongol emperor, by the name of Mai-de-li-ba-la, was taken prisoner. Accompanied by hundreds of Mongol officials, women, and eunuchs, he was detained in Nanjing under close surveillance. Ten years later, Ming generals Lan Yu and Fu Youde led an army into China's southwestern province of Yunnan and took 380 Mongol and Muslim prisoners of war. Among them were many young castrated boys, including possibly the future great Ming maritime explorer Zheng He, who was then ten or eleven years old. There is no record of how many Mongol captives were castrated as a means of punishment; nevertheless, it is known that during the early reign of Emperor Hongwu (1368–1398), there was an increasing population of Mongol eunuchs in Nanjing.[4]

While the Ming forces were pushing the Mongols to the north, they also reestablished influence over China's neighboring states. From its very advent, Ming China was able to attract foreign embassies and tributary missions from all of the lands in East Asia. Korean, Japanese, Annamese, and Champan missions arrived in Nanjing in 1369. Later, tributary missions came from Cambodia, Ryukyu Islands, Siam, Borneo, and from kingdoms of the Malayan peninsula. At a time when castration was performed as a symbol of conquest and a method of revenge, rulers throughout East Asia, with the exception of those in Japan, also adopted eunuchism and often used castrati as tributes. Likewise, in addition to luxury products from their native lands, most tributary missions also included young handsome castrated boys and virgin girls. Numerous Ming documents testify to such practices. In 1383, for example, a Siamese king sent 30 elephants, various native products, and 61 servants; in 1380 the ruler of Champa presented many elephants and 125 young servants. It was not clear whether the Siamese and Champan servants were all castrated, but most of the servants from Korea, Annam (northern part of present-day Vietnam), and Ryukyu Islands were meant to be used as imperial eunuchs. In 1408 when the king of Borneo visited the Ming court, he was ushered in by a gaggle of eunuchs from China's various ethnic tribes as well as castrated men from Mongolia, Korea, Annam, Cambodia, Central Asia, Siam, and Okinawa.[5]

The two neighboring states that provided Ming emperors with the largest number of foreign eunuchs were Annam and Korea, due undoubtedly to their geographical proximity, similar written ideographs, earlier Sinicization, and frequent contacts. Relations between Ming China and Annam were in general more precarious and volatile than those between China and Korea. Consequently, Korean eunuchs enjoyed more power than any other foreign group in the Ming court. With the enthronement of Emperor Hongwu, the Tran dynasty of Annam seemed to have found a reliable "big brother" to its north and was quite willing to perform its obligations as a vassal state by regularly paying tributes to Nanjing. In 1383, Tran Wei, the king of Annam, sent a mission to the Ming court, and among its tributes to Emperor Hongwu were twenty-five beardless castrated boys, most of whom bore the last name of Nguyen. Similar missions were undertaken every two years as Tran presented thirty eunuchs to the emperor in 1384 and again nineteen castrati in 1385.[6]

The event that turned China and Annam against one another was the successful coup d'état by Yongle against Emperor Jianwen who disappeared mysteriously after being routed by his uncle's forces. A persistent rumor had it that the deposed Jianwen was hiding in Southeast Asia and that he was secretly under the protection of the Tran regime. Whether it was for this reason or because Tran, a vassal of Jianwen, openly defied Yongle, a war broke out between China and Annam less than four years later. In 1406 a Chinese army of 200,000 men marched across the border of Annam, bringing down the Tran dynasty. The resilient Annamese, however, continued to resist Chinese invasion in the Red River basin and, beginning in 1418, rallied under the banner of a new leader, Le Loi, driving the Chinese out of their country by 1427.

During the long period of hostilities both sides inflicted frightening casualties upon one another. Hundreds of thousands of prisoners of war were either executed or castrated. In 1427, Le Loi invaded a border town inside of China but suffered a crushing defeat. According to a Ming report, the Chinese slaughtered more than 10,000 Annamese, including Le Loi's chief eunuch named Le Mi.[7] Other reports condemned Annamese alleged violation of an Asian "diplomatic protocol" as they killed and enslaved several Southeast Asian envoys who carried tributary missions to China in 1469. Older members of the mission were all killed while younger members were castrated and sold into slavery by their Annamese captors.[8] Castration as a means of punishing prisoners of war became a legacy of Ming-Annamese relations.[9]

While China and Annam waged a war of attrition, Korea appeared to have a reasonably good rapprochement with the Ming government as she gleefully recognized Ming suzerainty and dutifully complied with demands from Ming emperors. At first, Korean tributary missions were sent to the Ming court once every three years, but they gradually increased in frequency, often as much as three times a year. No one knows how many Korean castrati and virgin girls were included in these missions, but Ming documents suggest that, after working for a certain period of time, Korean eunuchs were allowed to return home with honor and pensions. A few of them gained favor with their Chinese masters and became confidants of Ming emperors. One such person was Shin Guisheng who was to become Emperor Hongwu's "ears and eyes." Other Korean-born eunuchs were entrusted with such important assignments as managing fiscal and monetary affairs for the emperor's inner court. Between 1370 and 1634, the Ming government sent a total of twenty-eight eunuch-led missions to Seoul, primarily for the purpose of installing new Korean kings. More than half of the eunuch-ambassadors were Korean-born.[10]

There were compelling reasons for placing eunuchs from outside races and tribes in positions of trust, because one of the major concerns of the emperor was the security of the imperial line. The best way to preserve it and keep court secrets was to use foreign-born eunuchs such as Shin from Korea and Wang Zhi, a captured Yao tribesman.[11] In the frontier provinces of Sichuan, Guizhou, Yunnan, and Huguang, there existed large numbers of aboriginal tribes, who had not been assimilated into the Chinese culture and were thus considered barbarians (see map A). They were generally suspicious of the Han Chinese and were often hostile to the Ming regime. But the Ming used force, appeasement, or guile in dealing with these tribes. Whenever punitive expeditions were launched and conquests made, the supply of eunuchs became abundant. In 1460, a Miao tribe in southwest China capitulated and the victorious Ming commander ordered the castration of 1,565 Miao boys. Of these unfortunate souls, 329 died during the brutal operation. News of the tragic proportion and unusual number of casualties reached Beijing, and Emperor Tianshun (1457–1464) was reported to have upbraided his governor in Guizhou province for arbitrarily undertaking such a large-scale operation.[12] Not all the castrated war prisoners were brought to the capital; many in fact were given to local officials as rewards. In 1453, for example, the regional commander of Guangxi province, after subjugating a rebellious aboriginal people, was faced with a surplus of castrated persons. Consequently, the emperor ordered him to distribute the young castrati among the royal family members and the meritorious government officials in the region.[13]

DOMESTIC SUPPLY OF EUNUCHS

In addition to tributes and prisoners of war from peripheral states and frontier tribes, Ming eunuchs also came from various domestic sources. Several Ming documents indicate that local officials were often required to offer a certain number of castrated men to the imperial palace. In 1449, a regional commander presented 108 men, who had already been castrated, to Emperor Zhengtong. In 1451, a Fujian proctor presented fifty-nine castrati to the Directorate of Ceremonial, and a year later, the commander of Nanjing sent to the capital four emasculated persons.[14] Many officials, however, performed castration without imperial authorization and kept such castrated men for their own use. In 1599, for instance, a high ranking Beijing official, on a mission to purchase steeds in Shaanxi province, ordered castration of several dozen boys without prior approval of the throne. He was later punished for this act.[15]

When the Ming dynasty was first founded, extremely severe forms of punishment were used against the political enemies of the regime. Near the end of the Hongwu reign, however, the emperor abolished the tattooing, severing body organs, and castration as forms of criminal justice. As substitute for such baneful punishment, he introduced corporal punishment and various forms of flogging.[16] A similar proclamation was issued in 1425 by the fourth emperor Hongxi, in which Confucian filial piety was cited as a reason for prohibiting the pernicious castration punishment. According to this rationale, a son who could not produce a male heir to carry on the family name committed a serious transgression against Confucian doctrine. But in spite of repeated imperial proclamations, Ming monarchs in the later period often disregarded such prohibitory decrees and resorted to castration for punishing major political criminals and their young male relatives.[17]

It is obvious that castration remained a savage weapon readily available for the Ming autocrats when and if they or their surrogates chose to use it against their enemies. Such inconsistent legal practice engendered abuses in the years to come. Although the first Ming emperor deemed castration an ineffective and unnecessary deterrent against criminals, the third emperor condoned it and, in fact, might have actually encouraged his henchmen to do likewise. During the civil war against his nephew, Zhu Di trusted a self-seeking opportunist named Ji Gang and made him a battalion commander. Ji castrated several hundred people and trained them as new recruits to bolster Zhu Di's strength.[18] The Ming penal code, the embodiment of centuries of previous penal codes, was frequently misused and misinterpreted by Ming emperors. But that could also mean life or death for hundreds of common people and fortunes or misfortunes for those who executed the law. In 1566, for instance, a criminal justice official, by the name of Wang Xiang, castrated three suspects before he could prove their culpability. Upon hearing the news, the emperor reportedly went into a rage and ordered Wang Xiang into exile.[19]

The misuse and misinterpretation of the penal code had a pervasive impact on the Ming society as a whole. Many privileged nobles and wealthy landlords also practiced castration on their own hired hands. Owners of large manors, who loved to imitate the lifestyle of the emperor and always maintained concubines in their households, naturally found castrated men the most practical servants and personal retainers. Indeed, throughout most of the Ming period, castration remained a common practice in the southeastern provinces of Fujian and Guangdong. Some landlords required their tenants to cut off their penes and scrotums before taking them as household servants. In 1372, upon hearing of such a practice in Fujian province, Emperor Hongwu threatened to castrate those who castrated their servants.[20] But in spite of repeated stern warnings, well-to-do landlords continued to abuse, castrate, and even murder their tenants and hired laborers with little or no fear of being punished by the state.

It is then a canard that only emperors used castrati for servile work in their harems. As a matter of fact, a significant number of the Ming castrated men were hired by nobles and members of the imperial family who were enfeoffed throughout the empire. Ming emperors, as a rule, had many wives and concubines and produced many sons and daughters. But apart from the crown prince, all others were sent away from the capital as soon as they were grown up. They were given territorial titles, manors, and retainers and servants ranging from 3,000 to 19,000 persons.[21] Since the status of imperial princes was hereditary, the oldest sons of the imperial princes and the sons of each new emperor exponentially added to their number. Moreover, the younger sons of every imperial prince became princes of the second degree and successive generations of their sons were granted noble titles in descending ranks. Such hereditary privileges continued until after the eighth generation when the imperial descendants were no longer ranked as nobles. Nevertheless, with polygamy as a general practice, after a period of 250 years, the number of imperial clansmen had grown to an estimated 100,000 and demand for castrated servants appeared to be insatiable.[22]

In addition to the male descendants of the Ming emperors, women of imperial families were also made nobles and given retainers, eunuchs, and lands. The paternal aunts of a reigning emperor, the sisters, and daughters were all named imperial princesses, and their husbands were given privileges of nobility. Although the ranks and salaries accorded to relatives of the empresses and concubines were purely personal and were not inherited by their descendants, they undoubtedly helped create a bigger market for eunuch service. Finally, meritorious officials and victorious generals also added to the noble ranks of duke (*gong*), marquis (*hou*), and earl (*bo*). They were generally granted territorial designations and, in addition to receiving annual stipends of varying amounts, were also allowed to retain varying numbers of eunuchs.[23]

Even though these princes and princesses were nothing more than salaried dignitaries and had no administrative or judiciary functions, they were not only a perpetual drain on state revenues but also eager employers of castrati. Here the simple economic theory of supply and demand came into play, as Ming society became more polarized between landowners and the proletariat. Destitute men castrated themselves or their children so that they could find employment in the princely establishments. And as social and economic conditions deteriorated, castration of one's own volition grew increasingly popular. For a commoner, unable to climb into the gentry class by either passing the difficult civil service examinations or purchasing a degree, the only means of gaining access to privileges and influence was by means of eunuchism. Consequently, voluntary castration became epidemic.

Ironically, the Ming government prohibited such practice. In the previous dynasties self-castration was permitted if closely monitored by the officials, who recorded the day of emasculation, examined the wound, and checked every detail during the healing process. However, since the establishment of the Ming dynasty, self-castration had been forbidden and several emperors had in fact issued decrees to ban such a practice. In 1424, Emperor Hongxi received a report from the city of Changsha that a man had cut off his own genital organ and offered himself to serve in the palace. The emperor considered this person a lazy vagabond who had failed to observe the Confucian principle of filial piety and had him banished to the frontier as a soldier. One month later, an elderly guard from a princely manor cut off his son's genitals before asking for a eunuch position for his son. Emperor Hongxi rebuked the father and made his son a soldier.[24] During the decade after the death of Emperor Hongxi, virtually all persons involved in self-castration were either drafted as soldiers or exiled to the frontier regions or both.

No sooner had Emperor Xuande been enthroned than several low-ranking military and civilian personnel castrated themselves and applied for jobs in the palace. The new monarch reiterated his father's policy and ordered the Minister of Rites to send all such men to the border of Annam. A few months later, the Ministry of Rites again reported a case of self-emasculation in Shandong province. Without hesitation the emperor ordered the man banished and then warned the village heads not to conceal any information of wrongdoing or acts that were clearly in violation of Confucian filial piety.[25] Nevertheless, the practice of self-emasculation continued into the reign of Emperor Xuande's successor. In 1436, a Buddhist monk performed his own emasculation. The new emperor Zhengtong not only annulled the monk's corvée exemption but also exiled him to southern Manchuria.[26]

Even though several emperors had repeatedly prohibited self-castration, members of the imperial clans did not always heed such proclamations, because they regarded themselves superior elements within the state and the emperors often bent the rule when dealing with their relatives. During Emperor Xuande's first year on the throne, nine civilian and military personnel in Shanxi province practiced self-castration and then presented themselves to the princely establishment of Jin. As soon as the news reached Beijing, a censor impeached the Shanxi authorities. The emperor, after a brief deliberation, ordered that all nine persons be punished according to the penal code. The senior administrator of the princely establishment of Jin, who presumably failed to admonish the prince, was arrested and tried in the capital.[27]

Of course, not all hereditary nobles were as arrogant and reckless as Prince Jin of Shanxi province who dared to ignore imperial proclamations. Usually when princes and princesses needed eunuchs they first sought the permission of the emperor. Some asked the emperor to supply their needs directly; others received imperial approval for accepting castrated servants from other sources. Prudent princes who maintained cordial relations with the reigning monarch usually had no problems in securing castrated servants.[28]

The custom of using eunuchs in the princely establishments appears to have started with the third emperor, Yongle, who always had a special political relationship with castrati during his career. After taking the crown away from his nephew in 1402, Yongle wanted to make sure that his triumph, which had sapped the vitality of the country, would not in any way create further perilous resonances. Although answerable only to Heaven and his ancestors, he was careful not to alienate further his surviving brothers and relatives. At the same time, he wanted to make sure that there was no effective opposition to his legitimacy and no encroachment of the local magnates; he therefore took measures to strengthen the bond between the emperor and the princely establishments. One such measure was that of giving regular royal presents to the princes and princesses who had demonstrated their loyalty to him during the stormy civil war. The list of royal gifts included silks, fabrics, tapestry, silver and gold bullion, and peculiarly enough, eunuchs who were professionally trained to work as "ears and eyes" of the emperor in the provinces. In the Ming official history, there are numerous records of such gifts.[29] In the winter of 1425 when a prince in Shaanxi got married, Emperor Xuande gave him twenty-five palace women and twenty eunuchs; three years later this same monarch sent as wedding gifts seven women and five eunuchs to a prince enfeoffed in southern Manchuria. In 1445, Emperor Zhengtong bestowed on a prince in Datong four eunuchs, five cooks, and forty guards.[30]

But as the number of nobles multiplied, by the mid-fifteenth century there appeared to be an increasing shortage of eunuchs as more and more requests for castrated servants arrived in the capital. In 1449 alone, Ming records show a total of thirty-four requests by the princes and princesses for the supply of eunuchs. Of the thirty-four requests, Emperor Zhengtong granted fourteen, denied one, but placed the other nineteen requests in limbo. What happened was that at the time the requests were made, the emperor had no more eunuchs to be spared. Consequently, he chose to condone a new practice by allowing his relatives to purchase self-castrated men from private sources.[31] But the fact that the emperor acquiesced to such a practice actually encouraged some of his relatives to methodically stock up on castrated servants.[32]

During the reign of Emperor Jingtai (1449–1457), the problem of self-castration had worsened and the new monarch was obviously annoyed by the fact that many of his trusted relatives did not seem to heed the ban on acquiring self-castrated men from private sources. In an attempt to arrest this practice, he adopted two measures, but neither of them brought any immediate tangible results. One measure was to exile the entire family of a self-castrated man to a frontier military colony if such a person was a soldier. If, on the other hand, the self-castrated man was a civilian, he was to be charged with a violation of filial piety and his village heads and neighbors would also be punished if they concealed knowledge of his act. Undoubtedly, the emperor was trying to restore some credibility to an established policy. But he soon realized that he was running short of carrots as he was constantly under traditional obligation to send eunuchs to his cousins' weddings or his aunts' birthdays or to reward his meritorious ministers. Consequently, later in his reign, whenever he discovered illegal eunuchs who had practiced self-emasculation, he literally confiscated them, took them to the capital and put them under the supervision of the Directorate of Ceremonial. In other words, the emperor was forced to stockpile his own "inventory" of eunuchs so that whenever the occasion was called for, he could easily draw on his "commodities." Eunuchism had by the mid-fifteenth century become a political and social tool of the Ming emperor.

MORE SUPPLY THAN DEMAND

Eunuchism, like other political games in Ming China, rose and fell according to the imperial whim. Critics may say that this is too simplistic a view of

Ming institutional and political history. But emperors like Hongwu, who were stern and serious about limiting the number and influence of the eunuchs, kept the castration problem under control. On the other hand, emperors like Chenghua (1464–1487), who were inconsistent and lenient toward the practice of self-castration in fact encouraged fortune seekers to risk their lives or punishment by performing self-emasculation. Prior to the enthronement of Emperor Chenghua, self-castrated men were either sent to work in agro-military colonies or were confiscated by the central government for future royal presents. Such punishment was obviously too mild to have any deterrent effect as self-castrated men had become more numerous and more obnoxious by the 1470s. In the winter of 1474–1475, fifty-four self-emasculated men presented themselves to the Ministry of Rites, requesting employment. As they grew into a boisterous mob, Emperor Chenghua ordered his imperial embroidered-uniform guards to restore order. They were arrested and paraded in public as a form of humiliation.[33] But the problem would not go away. In the early summer of 1476, Emperor Chenghua had to send seventy-six self-castrated men to Nanhaizi and, in the spring of 1477, had 900 such persons beaten with whipping clubs, thirty strokes each, before ordering them to agro-military colonies in the frontier provinces.[34]

Two years later, 2,000 self-castrated men once again invaded the Ministry of Rites. It took the imperial guards nearly ten days to have all of them rounded up. This time, the emperor ordered that each receive a hundred strokes and wear a particularly cumbersome cangue for a month.[35] The cangue was a heavy wooden board, three feet square with a hole in the center, weighing approximately 100 pounds. The punishment of wearing the cangue consisted in having the culprit's neck locked in the round hole and since the culprit was unable to feed himself nor to attend to other necessary functions, he relied completely on the help of others. Though he was not jailed and was allowed to pursue a normal life, he was required to stand for so many hours a day in public. Such public degradation was meant to impress upon the victim the mistake of his conduct and to cause the victim to lose "face" in a shame-oriented society. Nevertheless, many of these people later changed names, adopted new identities and repeatedly tried their luck; a few of them ultimately were selected to work in the palaces and rose from rags to riches in only a few years. The problem of an excessive supply of castrati clearly surfaced as nearly 1,000 such people once again knocked at the gates of the imperial city in Beijing in 1480. Again, in 1487, more than 2,000 such peculiar job seekers invaded the capital city.[36] Self-castrated men had indeed become a political headache and social nuisance.

Emperor Chenghua, perplexed and apparently annoyed by such a problem, attempted to demonstrate his opposition to the practice of self-castration. In the summer of 1484, a scoundrel by the name of Li An operated on four teenage boys at the request of their fathers. The emperor believed that Li had committed a crime of venality and had him whipped thirty strokes before sending him to a Manchurian military colony. The fathers of the four young boys were ordered to work in an iron foundry for three years while the castrated boys were all confiscated by the central government.[37] But the way Emperor Chenghua handled this case suggested that a window of employment opportunity was opened to the castrated young boys. And indeed several Ming documents reveal that the monarch often broke his own word by waiving prosecution against his favorites and by selecting his eunuchs from among the numerous confiscated castrated men. As a consequence, any punishment short of death would not effectively deter desperate people from taking a chance. After all, in the squalid and brutal system, it was still an easier way to get a job from the emperor than by studying Confucian classics, writing eight-legged essays, and competing endlessly in the difficult civil service examinations.

During the reign of Emperor Hongzhi (1487–1505), the central government continued to "appropriate" castrated servants for the princely households. Recruitment of eunuchs by nobles was strictly prohibited, and for a while self-castration seems to have subsided. This was primarily the result of a more emphatic measure taken by Emperor Hongzhi who not only repeatedly denied requests by princes to acquire their own eunuchs but actually put to death a few of the self-castrated men. He even chastised his ministers for failing to execute the anticastration laws. In 1493, some 300 self-castrated men from Ansu county, Hebei province, hit the so-called attention drum of the Ministry of Rites and asked for employment. They were arrested en masse and referred to the Ministry of Punishment for trial. When Emperor Hongzhi learned that neither beatings nor exile were recommended against them, he angrily reprimanded Minister of Punishment Peng Shao and withheld the salary of the Chief Minister of the Court of Judicial Review Feng Guang for five months. Feng's two vice-ministers were also to forfeit their salaries.[38]

Obviously, Emperor Hongzhi abhorred castration and resolved to put an end to the practice. Hongzhi Veritable Record, completed in 1509, leaves no doubt that, during his eighteen-year rule, this emperor consistently stuck to his tough policy against the practice of self-castration and kept a very close eye on the potentially explosive problem of eunuchs. For instance, he periodically confiscated properties of deceased eunuchs and gave them to the victims of drought, locusts, earthquake, or flooding. To demonstrate his determination against self-castration, he even had the mother of a self-castrated boy brought to justice.[39]

Unfortunately, in a state ruled by men instead of laws, the death of an old emperor and the accession of a new one often saw drastic changes in policy, style, and personnel. Soon after Emperor Zhengde (1505–1521) ascended the throne, he reversed his father's policy on both the practice of self-castration and the means by which the power and wealth of palace eunuchs were brought under control. As a result, all that his father had striven for was flung to the wind. Emperor Zhengde promoted eight eunuchs, known as "the eight tigers" in his lax and generally corrupt court. Among them was Liu Jin whose well-publicized activities and power had greatly tarnished the image of Ming eunuchs. Many of these people received dragon robes and jade belts, symbols of imperial patronage. As a consequence, a clear signal was sent to the populace that there were good opportunities for self-castrated men and that previous bans on such a practice had now become dead letters.

The first quarter of the sixteenth century witnessed an acceleration of Mongol hostilities against the Chinese and an increase in domestic uprisings throughout the realm of Ming China. Wars, coupled with natural calamities in such regions as Shandong, Henan, Nanjing, and Shaanxi, aggravated the already impoverished population. Many peasants lived in destitution. In 1505, in the province of Hubei alone, an estimated number of 730,000 people lost their homes and were forced to wander around the country. It was against this background that desperate males took the "shortcut," while officials who were supposed to enforce the bans could not help but condone the practice of self-castration. By the early sixteenth century, excessive numbers of castrated men formed long lines at public agencies and waited for the government dole. In 1507 one village alone produced several hundred recalcitrant self-castrated men who tried their luck with Emperor Zhengde.[40]

By 1516, the excessive number of self-castrated men had become a serious problem as several thousands of them appeared in the capital. In that year alone, the central government had to accept 3,468 such persons, each of whom received three piculs (about 400 pounds) of rice monthly. However, many thousand others were either driven away or secretly hiding in or near Beijing. Zhengde Veritable Record, completed in 1535, reports that in the year 1517 Emperor Zhengde took in more than 5,030 castrated men who consumed some 24,148 piculs of highly polished grain annually.[41] It seems safe to assume that before Emperor Zhengde's death in 1521, the total number of eunuchs, who were on the government payroll, had exceeded 10,000. In fact, as soon as Emperor Jiajing (1521–1566) was enthroned, he had to adopt a policy of retrenchment, since the government could no longer afford an extravagant expenditure of 137,000 piculs of highly polished grain to feed the eunuchs. In his retrenchment campaign, the emperor attempted to halve the number of his imperial servants but later was forced to retreat from such a policy.[42] As much as he deplored the practice of self-castration and desired to reduce government expenditures, he soon realized that many of these poverty-stricken, miserable people actually practiced cannibalism. Reluctantly, between 1536 and 1566, he took in thousands of new eunuchs to fill in sinecure offices and positions. By so doing, he at least could keep these people from starving to death.[43]

It is difficult to argue that the rise in numbers of eunuchs was caused primarily by the increased misery of the common people toward the end of the dynasty. One can say that a great deal of economic expansion was attended by structural changes that seemed to have resulted in a larger pool of nonagricultural labor. The economic expansion also resulted in increased imperial revenues and lavish spending by the court, particularly in Wanli times (1572–1620). Thus, one might see the situation as one of increased attraction to the largesse of the court on the part of men who otherwise would have gotten ordinary nonagricultural jobs. During the reign of Emperor Wanli, the Ming government willingly and unwillingly accepted many more thousands of self-castrated men. In 1572, the emperor selected 3,250 such persons and assigned them to different bureaus and directorates of the imperial household. In the summer of 1578, the Directorate of Ceremonial screened 3,570 castrated men for imperial employment; and in the winter of 1588, over the objection of his minister of rites, Zhu Geng, Emperor Wanli added 2,000 more eunuchs to the government payroll.[44] This particular emperor appeared to have a genuine sympathy for eunuchs. He lavishly and indiscriminately provided his relatives with them. In 1601, Emperor Wanli picked 4,500 castrated men off the streets of Beijing. He kept 3,000 for his own use and gave 50 to each of the territorial princes, 20 to every imperial prince (his own sons), and 10 to each prince of second degree (the sons of every imperial prince).[45]

As eunuchism was considered by many people as their only safety net, the practice of self-castration had grown out of control by the early seventeenth century. In 1620, some 20,000 such people swarmed into the capital, begging for whatever jobs the government could give them. When their petitions and requests were rejected, the job seekers became angry and turned into a rowdy and militant mob. Supervisors from both the Ministry of Rites and the Ministry of War were undoubtedly alarmed as they began to take measures against any possible uprising.[46] Many of these people, after failing to gain employment and having been driven back to their villages, took their own lives because they felt that they had "lost face" with their relatives. This sort of disturbing news often rendered good excuses for such eunuch patrons as Emperor Tianqi (1620–1627) to acquiesce to the practice of self-castration. In 1621, for example, he placed 1,500 castrated men in his already cumbersome governmental apparatus, and in 1623, he accepted 4,000 more such persons.[47] This, indeed, was the heyday of the Ming eunuchs, when the chief eunuch Wei Zhongxian wielded enormous power and virtually stifled the voice of eunuch opponents. But one may wonder if the Ming government was truly a government of men or merely a government of half-men.

THE PROBLEMS OF EXCESSIVE CASTRATI

Orthodox Chinese historians almost universally attribute the downfall of the Ming dynasty to the lascivious conduct and the insolent power of the eunuchs, a power derived from their intimacy with the monarch, from access to offices inside and outside the Forbidden City, and from a passive government beset with corruption, fear, and inept leadership. But should twentieth-century historians continue to overlook Ming economic and social complexities that contributed to such a political phenomenon? An immediate question one needs to address is what caused the sharp increase of the castrated male population from a mere hundred at the beginning of the dynasty to approximately 10,000 in the 1520s, eventually reaching the astonishing figures of 100,000 near the end of the dynasty? A possible answer to this question may lie in the increasing pressure of a Chinese population whose figures had risen from 70 million to 130 million between the end of the fourteenth century and the middle of the seventeenth century. Such an answer is obviously unconvincing because throughout the entire Ming period, the Chinese population increased only twofold while the number of castrated men had jumped by a staggering thousandfold. Of course, there were constant demands for castrated servants by the concomitant rising number of the imperial relatives and the rich families who owned huge manors, but the fact remains that there was far more supply than demand for eunuchs and that, since the second half of the sixteenth century, hundreds of thousands of young Chinese boys from the least favored classes willingly or unwillingly joined the rank of castrati. To solve this puzzle, one should take a careful look at the economic and social "revolution" in sixteenth century China.

For a century or so after the founding of the dynasty, there was no upsurge in the Ming economy, but by the early sixteenth century several factors drastically changed the Ming economic and social framework. First, the discovery of new silver mines, coupled with the inflow of silver from abroad, resulted in an increase in the circulation of silver ingots. Second, beginning in 1552, the traditional taxes on land and labor were undergoing a gradual reform that commuted them to payments in silver and consolidated the many small taxes into one "single whip." At the same time, a technological breakthrough in agriculture led to the cultivation of commercial crops such as cotton, sugar cane, indigo plant, peanuts, and tobacco. There was an increase in iron and steel production, and the manufacture of lacquer was expanding. Easy access to silver and the ensuing growth of commerce and industry led to the emergence of a new mercantile class. An economic "revolution" was in fact taking place as evidenced in the growth of urban population, commercial crops, volume of foreign trade, handicraft and industrial goods, area of cultivated land, and the popular use of money.

Although economic changes of the sixteenth century had brought prosperity to a great number of enterprising Chinese, they also worsened the economic problems of the lowest strata of the peasantry. The generalization of silver as means of payment, which often induced an inflationary economy, had an unpredictable effect on struggling peasants. Whenever the price of silver soared, the peasant, whose income came solely from the land and its taxable produce, had great difficulties. Previously, he needed one-third of his harvest to pay off the taxes; now since the price of silver had gone so high, two-thirds of his crops would not be sufficient to pay for the taxes. Moreover, as capital shifted from land to commerce and craft, land prices fell steadily and collapsed near the end of the sixteenth century. In only a few years, his resources were reduced from inadequate to nothing. At the turn of the seventeenth century, rural China was sinking like a stone tossed in a hog wallow.

In the meantime, there was a financial crisis at the court. The Korean War from 1593 to 1598 (against the Japanese invasion) cost the treasury some 26 million silver taels while sumptuous allowances paid to imperial relatives and the ever-increasing expenses of the court led to the rise in taxes and duties.[48] In the end, the ever-increasing price of silver and crushing taxes drove hundreds of thousands of peasants from their land either by desertion or foreclosure. They ran like lemmings into the sea, hoping they would revitalize and recover from their dire straits. But they drowned! Many sought protection by transferring the ownership of their land to the large household who used bribery and various sanctimonious scams to escape the tax burden. Others moved to the mines or the towns to work for meager pay. But the more militant often opted to fight the establishment and engaged in piracy, banditry, or smuggling. In the meantime, a new social malaise was slowly gnawing the moral fiber of a Confucian society, where the buying and selling of slaves became commonplace.

Even though the Ming Code did not sanction slavery, it allowed people to employ servants. By collusion with officials and falsifying the records, daring people openly made a travesty of legal integrity. When wealthy families purchased slaves, they put in the bond such words of euphemism as *adopted sons* or *adopted daughters* or simply called them *employed servants*. As economic and social dislocations worsened and hard-pressed peasants had to sell their children to whomever could provide for them, slaves became abundant and cheap. One writer reported that in a single county the number of slaves amounted to 20 to 30 percent of the whole population.[49] It was indeed a buyer's market. The patriotic Ming scholar Gu Yanwu said that as soon as anyone was appointed to a position in the government, numbers of the people, sometimes a thousand or more, offered to serve him and were willing to be regarded as slaves.[50] Military commanders, public officials, wealthy merchants, and affluent landlords universally practiced concubinage and kept large numbers of slaves. Of course, the biggest slave owner of the Ming period was the emperor himself, and although ordinary slaves could be bought and sold, castrated eunuchs were an imperial monopoly. Excessive castrati, like the telling numbers of slaves, were not so much a consequence of a faltering economy as of a decadent and polarized society. But the deeds of Ming eunuchs, for good or bad, had added to the complex political texture of China's imperial legacy.

III

米

Institutionalization of
the Eunuch Agencies

EARLY EUNUCH ESTABLISHMENTS

No sooner had Zhu Yuanzhang ascended the dragon throne in 1368 than he recruited some sixty eunuchs to staff the imperial household in Nanjing in the beautiful surroundings along the southern banks of the Yangtze River. While bestowing honors on 20,000 wealthy families who had contributed to the prosperity and expansion of his newly established capital and organizing his government on the base of previous dynasties, he made sure that his eunuchs were restricted to do only the sprinkling and sweeping jobs. In a highly touted instruction to the Ministry of Rites, Emperor Hongwu had some harsh words to say about his castrated servants. "Not one or two of these people out of thousands are good. Those who are evil frequently number thousands. If they are employed as ears or eyes, then the ears and eyes are covered. If they are employed as the heart and bowels, then the heart and bowels will be sick. The way to control them is to make them fear the laws and not permit them to have merit. If they fear the laws then they will be attentive to their conduct. If they have merit, then they will be arrogant and lustful."[1]

The apparently unfavorable image the dynasty founder had of the castrati also meant that he would not be disposed to their blandishments, nor would he tolerate any eunuch peccadillos or conniving in the Inner Court. In such a rigid and unpromising atmosphere, the Ming eunuchs embarked on a course that was wretched, squalid, and brutal. At the outset, more than thirty castrated men were assigned to take good care of imperial seals, keys, books, headgear, footwear, ceremonial robes, belts, and everyday palace apparel while twenty others were to prepare such daily necessities as court meals, dried foods, wine, vinegar, noodles, and the like. Seven eunuchs were in charge of medicine, drugs and surgery, while eight people managed incense supplies and maintained the imperial sacrifice temple. The emperor also had six castrati taking care of his horses, three guarding the palace granary, and three others keeping an eye on the palace treasury. In the household of his Heir Apparent, he placed a dozen eunuchs to take care of the Prince's seals, books and stationery, meals, clothing, vehicles, and medicine. In addition, each of the seventeen palace gates were guarded by two eunuchs.[2]

Ming eunuchs' salaries were skimpy and fixed; they were required to live within the palace and not permitted to correspond with officials or become literate. All of these regulations were, however, to be violated in the ensuing reigns. According to the Ming Zhiguanzhi, or Treatise on Officialdom, eunuch's ranks were generally limited to between 8a and 5a.[3] But as the imperial household grew bigger and the lifestyle of the royal family became more sophisticated, more and more eunuchs were needed to handle the ever-increasing palace chores, even though the first emperor constantly waged a campaign against prodigious government waste. One document reveals that only fifteen years after his accession, Emperor Hongwu brought 361 additional eunuchs into his harem and, in late 1383, added 76 more castrated servants to work in his Inner Court. Notwithstanding his pronounced distaste for the eunuchs, he in fact selected two literate eunuchs to watch over the flow of information from government agencies and pasteurize and homogenize palace events before recording them for posterity.[4]

The legend of the first emperor's rise from pauper to prince was well known in Chinese folklore. Coming from an extremely poor, humble background and gaining power by having to overcome tremendous odds, Emperor Hongwu possessed a deep mistrust of all persons, including those who helped him attain supreme power. In particular, he bore a pathological prejudice against scholar-officials, generally treating them with contempt and frequently having them flogged during imperial audiences.[5] As Emperor Hongwu approached his declining years, he had become a hubristic and crotchety ruler. In 1380, when he was fifty-three years of age, he started a purge against his old comrade, Premier Hu Weiyong. As a result, over 15,000 innocuous scholars and officials were implicated, many of whom were either sentenced to die or to serve long prison terms. New purges took place five years later, once again bringing about the execution, exile, and disgrace of thousands of officials and their relatives. But every time the emperor put his spin on the scholar-officials, he consciously though grudgingly elevated the position of his eunuchs. By the 1380s, eunuchs not only had become imperial instruments for political purges and surveillance, but in fact also functioned as an embryo of Ming tyranny!

It was no coincidence that a new eunuch agency called Silijian, or the Directorate of Ceremonial, was established in 1384, the very year when the seemingly paranoid autocrat was growing edgy over the security of his imperial line and was unrelentingly purging potential threats to his absolutist power. Originally, the Directorate of Ceremonial was charged to take care of palace ceremonies and protocol, codify imperial etiquettes and precedences, supervise eunuch behavior and attire, and scrutinize any eunuch misconduct or violation of palace rules. A director ranking 7a, and a deputy ranking 7b, were initially the only appointees to this agency. But as succeeding emperors failed to put a crimp in the growth of eunuchs, more deputies and assistants were needed to police the palace castrati and to help ease the emperor's burdens. Each week, hundreds of documents that flowed throughout the complex Ming bureaucracy often had to be issued in the emperor's name. By tradition only the emperor himself wrote in red while his people wrote in black. Some lazy emperors were said to have frequently delegated the Director of Ceremonial to make important state decisions and pen state documents on their behalf. It was also from this agency that the emperor sicced his spies onto his officials and generals who were slated for surveillance. Ultimately, its director was to become the second most powerful person in the Ming court.

By the summer of 1384, the restructuring of imperial eunuch organizations was largely completed. In addition to the Directorate of Ceremonial, there was a Neiguanjian or Directorate of Palace Servants, which was to function as an inner court physical plant since it was responsible for all palace construction and repairs. Then, there was a Shengongjian, or Directorate of the Imperial Temples, whose duties included cleaning the imperial temples, burning incense, and preparing for seasonal sacrifices to the heavens. A most unique eunuch office, called Shangbaojian, or Directorate of Imperial Seals, was created to look after the emperor's rare books and authorization documents, and to safeguard day and night the seventeen Ming imperial seals, all made of precious stones. In this directorate, shifts changed between three and five in the afternoon, when the eunuchs on duty passed a small ivory tablet about one inch long to a new group of eunuchs who would work there for the next twelve hours. A director ranking 7a, and a deputy ranking 7b, were appointed to supervise this office. Other eunuch offices included the Shangshanjian, which prepared court meals and banquets; the Shanyijian, in charge of imperial headgear, clothing, and footwear; the Sishejian, providing palace draperies, cushion, canopies, raincoats, and outfittings for the imperial cortege and outings; and the Yumajian, an agency specifically charged to look after the emperor's horses, swords, elephants, and other exotic animals. Each one of these directorates had a 7a director and a 7b deputy, plus varying numbers of assistants, ranking from 9a to 9b.

In addition, there were a number of lesser Inner Court agencies functioning as integral parts of the eunuch bureaucracy. For example, the Zhidianjian, which was staffed at the outset with seventeen eunuchs, was responsible for cleaning all imperial structures and getting everything ready for official functions. There was also a department of messengers, an office of gatekeepers, an agency of key keepers, and an agency of imperial gifts which took care of gold, silver pieces, silk fabrics of imperial design adorned with pythons and flying fish, and other presents reserved for rare honors. Finally, Emperor Hongwu set up eight new eunuch bureaus in charge of manufacturing, producing, and managing, respectively: (1) headgear and scarfs; (2) all clothing in the Inner Court; (3) dyeing; (4) vegetables and fruits; (5) animal husbandry and meat; (6) leather works; (7) weaponry; and (8) metal works. Each of these bureaus was headed by a 9a chief and assisted by a various number of skilled artisans, who were all castrated before being employed.

For the next decade, eunuch institutions remained unchanged. Nevertheless, their functions expanded beyond the Inner Court and their numbers steadily increased as Emperor Hongwu's twenty-six sons and sixteen daughters also had begun to multiply the number of nobles. Consequently, in the fall of 1395, Emperor Hongwu decided to reorganize once again his eunuch bureaucracy by upgrading several Inner Court agencies and simultaneously promoting many eunuch officials. He then established eleven directorates under the supervision of 4a directors and 4b deputies, six bureaus, headed by 5a and 5b deputies, three agencies, and two departments. In addition, he appointed a personal attendant, ranking 6a, who would accompany the emperor wherever he went. Two years later, he added more of such attendants and finally created a new directorate called Duzhijian to staff his constant companions. Headed by a 4a director and two 4b deputies, members of this new office were to function as imperial shadows.[6]

With the establishment of this new office, the renowned twelve eunuch directorates, which survived until the twentieth century, were firmly institutionalized. Each directorate had a director ranking 4a, two deputies (4b), two assistants (5a), one recorder (6a), plus various numbers of attendants (6a). High-ranking eunuch officials wore specially designed uniforms that would distinguish their positions. For example, eunuchs with 4b rank and above wore red robes, while those with 5a and below attired in blue. Eunuchs under fifteen years of age, on the other hand, could dress only in plain robes and wear a small black hat. It is noteworthy to point out that during Emperor Hongwu's reign, he had twice promoted the directors of major eunuch offices from 7a to 6a and then to 4a. Moreover, his attitudes toward his castrated servants had gone through a wide gyration, belying the widespread impression that he never employed them as "the heart and bowels" and that he was not responsible for the rise of eunuch power in the Ming dynasty. But, of course, he could not foresee the days when several thousand castrated men would inundate the Ministry of Rites and ask for employment. Nor could he imagine that some of the eunuch directors would wield untrammeled powers later in the dynasty. In the long run, however, the absolutist embryo that he had cultured would inevitably require a substantial number of eunuchs to make it grow.[7]

Not all of the castrated men accepted by the court held official ranks or worked in the palaces. Many of them were either given to the numerous princely establishments throughout the country or assigned to temporary servile labor in or out of Beijing and Nanjing. But as eunuch services had to march in step with an imperial household that was expanding in both size and degree of sophistication, eunuch agencies proliferated and their staff membership multiplied—ultimately surpassing that of the state civil service.

By the early sixteenth century, each of the twenty-four eunuch agencies had a staff of at least thirty people, some even reportedly having over 100 people on the payroll. Moreover, each agency was allowed from time to time to hire additional artisans and workers for temporary work. For instance, in 1500, the eunuch Bureau of Garments took in 1,000 young tailors, the Armament Bureau employed 2,000 blacksmiths, while the Directorate of Outfittings hired a total of 1,000 workers.[8] In 1581, Emperor Wanli took a special interest in horses and soldiers and placed 2,000 new palace guards under the eunuch directorate in charge of the Imperial Stables. Ranking eunuchs were commissioned as officers while younger ones enlisted as soldiers or served as valets.[9] It was quite obvious that next to the army, eunuch agencies had become the biggest employers of Ming China. Wang Shizhen (1526–1590), a prominent Ming scholar and a doctoral degree holder of 1547, reported that in 1525 the Dyeing Bureau employed 2,164 new people, while the Directorate of Palace Servants—which was already staffed with 7,856 castrated men—added 1,500 new recruits. The employees of these two eunuch agencies alone consumed a total of 150,240 piculs of grain during that particular year.[10]

After running a course of over two centuries, one can now see an interesting dialectic evolution or revolution in the history of Ming eunuchs. Clearly, the eunuch system—the thesis—as first set up by Ming founders, had generated an antithesis, that is, a qualitative change in the eunuch status. Previously, a eunuch was merely a servant to the emperor and his family, but by the sixteenth century, practically every ranking eunuch had retained for himself the service of household managers, secretaries, personal couriers, and attendants. Eunuchs were no longer employed servants, they had become powerful bosses! According to Wang Shizhen, in the year 1532, when Holy Roman Emperor Charles V was at the height of his power, Emperor Jiajing (1522–1567) of China permitted the Seal Keeper of the Imperial Seals Directorate to retain sixty servants in his household; the director of each eunuch agency to keep fifty-five personal servants; deputy director, forty; assistant director, thirty; and the recorder to have twenty.[11] The thesis furthermore had produced a synthesis that involved a quantitative change. At the outset of the dynasty, the number of Ming eunuchs was limited to a few hundred, but by the early sixteenth century, it had increased to several thousands. And in 1643 when Louis XIV ascended the throne of France and European absolutism had not yet attained its zenith, the Ming Court kept an estimated 100,000 eunuchs. Let us pause a moment and consider some sobering figures. If each of the 100,000 eunuchs on average had retained two household servants and also adopted a son or supported a nephew, that would mean that the total eunuch personnel the Ming government had to feed would be around 300,000. This was indeed a new variable, and one that should be injected into the equation of all Ming historical discourses.

EUNUCH'S NEW HAVEN

Ming absolutism grew at a stronger pace during the reign of Emperor Yongle, when he moved the capital from Nanjing to Beijing and built a 9,000-room palace complex to house his family, consorts, officials, and eunuchs. It was from this walled and well-guarded imperial complex that the next fourteen Ming emperors ruled China with an absolute authority rarely paralleled in human history. Between 1406 and 1420, over 200,000 workers and artisans participated in the construction of the imperial complex, which covered an area of approximately 250 acres. The imperial complex was located at the center of Beijing, surrounded by the huge Taiyi Lake and a wide moat called the Jade River and protected by a wall, thirty-five feet high, marked off by towers at each corner. The center of the complex was the Forbidden City, which had six major palaces from south to north on a straight line and numerous structures that stood two stories high, roofed with yellow tiles and flanked by various shapes and sizes of courtyards. Most of these detailed works were designed and created by a eunuch named Nguyen An, presumably a tribute from the King of Annam. Inside these elegantly architectured buildings were the residential quarters of the emperor and his family, studies and libraries, temples, imperial gardens, and a park. In such a remarkable setting, the Ming emperors spent their time between official businesses and private pleasures, decided the life and death of their subjects while dallying with beautiful women and exotic games. They rarely, if ever, left the heavily guarded compound. This is why the Forbidden City, an area of a quarter of a square mile, was often derided as His Majesty's luxurious playground as well as his monotonous prison.

The construction of such an imposing architectural masterpiece was largely completed by 1420. In the ensuing years, however, artificial hills, bronze statues, adorned pavilions, and sculptured arts were added to embellish its splendor. Pines, cypresses, and rare flowers were planted to heighten its gorgeous landscape. By 1450, it had surpassed Constantinople, the capital of the Byzantine empire for a millennium, to become the most magnificent palace city of the world, and had certainly also replaced the capital of eastern Christendom as the leading eunuch center, where devious backstage political machinations and court intrigues reigned. Had the great conqueror Sultan Mehmet II of the Ottoman Empire visited the Forbidden City, he would certainly have envied the megalomaniac vastness and the pomp of the imperial Chinese structure. It had definitely impressed and dazzled an Annamese envoy who bore a tributary mission to Beijing in 1453, the very year the sultan won over Constantinople.

After studying detailed court decorum and rehearsing palace rituals for three days with a deputy from the Ministry of Rites, the Annamese envoy was led through one of the four tall crimson gates of the Imperial City for a scheduled imperial audience. His party traversed northward across a huge square before entering through the massive Wumen, or Meridian Gate, which was surrounded by five pavilions. A small group of eunuchs from the Directorate of Ceremonial, all in their embroidered robes, greeted his party at the gate. The envoy instinctively realized that he was inside the Forbidden City and that it was from the heights of the gate that the Ming emperor reviewed his armies. He was also told that in the square, prisoners were occasionally trooped past His Majesty so that the emperor could decide which were to be executed and which to be pardoned. Inside the Meridian Gate, the envoy saw five marble-balustraded bridges across the bow-shaped channel of the famed Golden Water River. He then trotted over an immense courtyard and crossed one of the bridges specifically designed for foreign envoys and barbarian chieftains. Right in front of him was the Huangjimen, or the Gate of Polar Convergence, a long building supported by huge red columns and guarded by two fearful looking bronze lions. Three stairs lead to three carved marble terraces. His eunuch escorts directed him through the left flight, as he was told beforehand that the central flight was reserved for the exclusive use of His Majesty. He also learned that the courtyard beyond the Polar Gate could accommodate several thousand people during auspicious state ceremonies.

Passing through the grandiose Polar Gate and trotting over another immense courtyard, the envoy approached the Fengtiandian or the Respect-Heaven Hall, the tallest palace building elevated on triple stairs. Outside this splendid hall, the Annamese envoy saw several bronze incense burners, many ornamental marble frames that enclosed its space, and two gigantic gilded copper caldrons containing water prepared in the event of fire. Inside the hall, the envoy saw, for the first time in his life, the imperial throne, lying in solemn intonation with a mystic dragon screen. Here he sensed the power and sacredness of the Ming emperor who was believed to be the Son of

Heaven and a medium between the heaven and earth. The seemingly nervous guest from the southern neighboring state was informed that before daybreak Emperor Jingtai had already conducted state affairs and met with his officials at the Polar Gate, but would receive the audience of the envoy and his protocol staff in the Respect-Heaven Hall at noon.

During the audience, the envoy practiced the kowtow ritual in front of his silent and motionless Ming overlord, who alone faced the south while his ministers faced the north, and was the only one seated during the entire proceeding. A ceremonial official shouted aloud a question to the envoy, "His Majesty wishes to know if your king was well when you left your country?" The envoy, while responding to the question, prostrated and knelt, stood up, then prostrated and knelt again. The ceremonial official then asked a second question, "His Majesty wishes to know if you feel tired after making such a long journey?" Once again, when the envoy was answering the question he knelt, stood up, and prostrated. Before the emperor left his dragon throne, a band played a certain series of court music while the envoy prostrated four more times. In addition to the three kneelings and nine prostrations in front of the emperor, the envoy was required to prostrate eight times to the crown prince before submitting tributary presents to the future Son of Heaven. After sweating through all these rituals, the envoy finally was allowed to present his credentials to the ranking grand-secretary who introduced him to other high officials of the Ming government.

The twenty-six-year-old Emperor Jingtai was keenly aware that the envoy was a feeler sent out by the new Annamese king who desired a rapprochement with China; likewise, he was quite pleased to receive the representative from his new vassal. Following the kowtow ceremony, His Majesty gave a state banquet in the envoy's honor in the Jinshendian, or Prudence Hall. After the banquet, a grand-secretary toured the Annamese envoy about the famed Wenhuadian, or Literary Flora Pavilion, where the emperor periodically held private and public study sessions and interviewed civil service officials. Overwhelmed by the awesome imperial pomp and dumbfounded by its ritualistic trappings, the envoy trudged across yet another large courtyard that was surrounded by exquisite bronze statues in the shapes of tortoise, crane, and elephant. But before he left the Forbidden City that day, he browsed through a number of anterooms, one of which displayed the gifts he just presented to the crown prince, and stood stunned after seeing another flight of marble steps known as the "dragon pavement."[12]

The envoy later learned that the "dragon pavement" was an unwritten demarcation line that separated the business quarters from the living quarters of the Forbidden City. Beyond the "dragon pavement" laid the Qianqinggong or the Palace of Heavenly Purity, the emperor's main residence and office, and an imperial museum where the emperor collected historic works of scientific inventions—in particular, devices for measuring time, such as the sundial and clepsydra or water clock. Behind the Palace of Heavenly Purity was Jiaotaidian or Union Hall where the emperor and empresses generally celebrated their birthdays. As for the Ming empresses, they lived in the Kunninggong or the Palace of Earthly Tranquility, but the rest of the royal family and imperial consorts were scattered around many living quarters of the East and West Palaces. For them, the places to escape the occasional quagmire of boredom included the intricate imperial gardens and the country-setting of Coal Hill, an artificial park of over fifty-six acres immediately adjacent to the gardens. On Coal Hill, which was the highest point in Beijing, young princes and princesses could play hide-and-seek, chase hares and foxes, and care not a whit which province or region was being beset by draught or locust.

During the next 150 years after the Annamese envoy left Beijing, several buildings in the Forbidden City were destroyed by fire, but they were always rebuilt and some of them were given new names. The Palace of Heavenly Purity, for example, was burned to the ground in early 1514, and it took seven and a half years, millions of silver taels and hundreds of huge, straight trees to restore this splendid structure. In 1557, all the three imperial halls between the Meridian Gate and the Palace of Heavenly Purity were also damaged by fire, but after their successful restoration in 1562, Emperor Jiajing changed their names from Fengtiandian to Huangjidian, Huagaidian to Zhongjidian, and Jinshendian to Jianjidian (see map B). These same three halls suffered fire damage again in 1597; moreover, the main residential palaces of the emperor and empress were also severely burned during Wanli's reign. But once again, all were repaired and refurbished, and the structure and beauty of the Ming nerve center remained miraculously intact until the twentieth century.

What the Annamese envoy had seen and learned in 1453 was only a small part of the larger capital city. Surrounding the Forbidden City was the Imperial City, which was also walled and restricted. An area of about three square miles, the Imperial City functioned like a maintenance plant for both the government and the imperial household as the two were in fact indivisible. In this exclusive place most eunuch agencies were located, and thousands of Ming eunuchs lived, worked, found honor or disgrace, and died. From here they managed imperial treasuries and warehouses; manufactured metals, papers, firearms and gunpowder, produced wine, noodles, candles, incenses, leatherworks, court apparel, and silver utensils; prepared food and drink for imperial weddings, birthday parties, and state banquets; and assisted the emperor in performing endless sacrificial ceremonies and court rituals. In this city of hustle and bustle the eunuchs and their artisans set up shops for dyeing, printing, tailoring, bakery, distillery, confectionery, and so on.[13] And in this peculiar setting the eunuchs rivaled with and spied upon ministers and

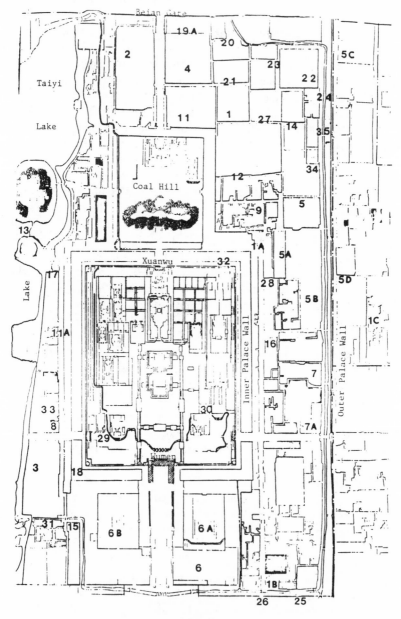

Map B.
Eunuch Agencies in the Ming Palace (from *Ming Qing Beijingcheng kao*)

Key to Map B
Layout of Eunuch Agencies

1. Silijian (Ceremonial)
2. Neiguanjian (Palace Servants)
3. Yuyongjian (Palace Carpentry)
4. Sishejian (Outfittings)
5. Yumajian (Imperial Stables)
6. Shengongjian (Imperial Temples)
7. Shangshanjian (Palace Foods)
8. Shangbaojian (Imperial Seals)
9. Yinshoujian (Document Filing)
10. Zhidianjian (Custodians)
    (No office Building)
11. Shangyijian (Royal Clothing)
12. Duzhijian (Entourage Guards)
13. Xixinsi (Fire and Water Dept.)
14. Zhonggusi (Entertainments)
15. Baochaosi (Toilet Paper)
16. Huntangsi (Bathhouse)
17. Bingzhangju (Armament Bureau)
18. Yinzuoju (Silverware)
19. Wanyiju (Nursing Home)
    (Beyond the Palace Wall)

19a. Anletang (Infirmary)
20. Jinmaoju (Headgear)
21. Zhengongju (Garments)
22. Neizhiranju (Dyeing)
23. Jiucumianju (Wine, Vinegar, and Noodle)
24. Siyuanju (Vegetables)
25. Shanglinyuanjian (Royal Farms)
26. Taiyiyuan (Academy of Medicine)
27. Neifu gongyongku (Inner Court Supplies Depot)
28. Neichengyunku (Imperial Treasury)
29. Yujiufang (Royal Wine Room)
30. Yuyaofang (Pharmacy Room)
31. Lingtai (Terrace of Spirits)
32. Genggufang (Night Drum Room)
33. Tianshifang (Bakery)
34. Hanjingchang (Buddhist School)
35. Fanjingchang (Lamaist School)

officials whose offices were located just outside the walls of the Imperial City. All told, their perfidy might know no limit, their conduct and abilities might become fodder for debate, but they were the creatures not the creators of Chinese absolutist monarchy!

The Imperial City clearly was the center of supply installations and service agencies for the imperial household and the imperial clan. It was also the center for state granaries, armaments, sports and recreation, arts and sciences, finance, and the like. But it was where the eunuch bureaucracy of the inner court and the civil bureaucracy of the outer court merged, sometimes following a course of collision but often in full cooperation. In Ming fiscal operation, the government budget and the palace budget were as a rule separately handled. On paper, all palace expenses, imperial household appropriations and accounting were under the jurisdiction of different governmental ministries. In practice, however, the emperor used his eunuchs to make the governmental machines tick. For example, in managing the warehouses in the Imperial City, the civil officials took care of the books while the eunuchs kept the keys.[14]

EUNUCH AGENCIES INSIDE THE IMPERIAL CITY

The most powerful eunuch agency was Silijian, or the Ceremonial Directorate, which was located northeast of Coal Hill and southwest of the Beian

Gate (1 of map B). The official title of its director was Sili zhangyin taijian, or the grand eunuch of the seal of the Ceremonial Directorate. Under him were four to five, sometimes eight to nine, Sili bingbi taijian, or managing grand eunuchs of the Ceremonial Directorate, who took turns daily in running the agency. An ivory tablet, a little more than one inch long, was passed on by the bingbi going off-duty to the next bingbi between three and five o'clock in the afternoon. The documents and memorials slated for imperial inspection were collected by the bingbi on duty, and documents considered particularly important were sent up to the zhangyin director. Occasionally, the bingbi on duty would call a conference to discuss the contents of the documents and arrive at a consensus. In general, every bingbi was authorized to deliberate on state documents and given the "red ink or pihong," which gave them official imperial sanction. Sometimes the most trusted bingbi was also made a concurrent director of the Eastern Depot, the Inner Court spy agency. And among the emperor's most favorite bingbi and zhangyin, there were those who frequently received the prestigious python silk gowns and were allowed to sit on a chair during an imperial audience and also to ride a horse in the palace courtyard. When a bingbi or zhangyin grand eunuch got a promotion, he almost always added 12 piculs of rice to his annual stipend, which was considered a modest increment as compared to a top Ming minister who drew an annual salary of 732 piculs of rice.[15]

Next to the zhangyin and bingbi was a eunuch intendant, tidu taijian, who actually "lived" in the office of the Ceremonial Directorate, and presumably no one in the court would ever question his trustworthiness and integrity. He was to safeguard all books and references in the office and make sure that all the files of records were in place. He was also responsible for providing and maintaining an adequate supply of various kinds of stationery, such as stone slabs, ink, papers, brushes, silks, and cloths that were used for writing. Materials for exclusive imperial use were kept in special store rooms and guarded by four, sometime six to seven, highly trained veteran eunuchs. In addition, the Ceremonial Directorate ran a number of service shops and depots. For instance, there was a printing shop on the west side of the Imperial City, whose charge was printing calendars, Confucian classics, and producing books on Buddhism, Daoism, astronomy, and so on.[16]

In addition to the half a dozen powerful grand eunuchs, the Ceremonials office was also staffed with numerous deputies and recorders to whom the emperor held the highest standard of service. One deputy was in charge of gathering materials pertinent to the history of the imperial family. Others were responsible for supervising such affairs as Inner Court etiquette, eunuch criminal conduct and palace gate curfew time. There were also deputies who functioned as liaison officials between the Inner Court and the six government ministries and the military establishment, both of which were located just south of the Imperial City. These people safeguarded letters of imperial appointment and dismissal and directed couriers who daily transmitted documents to and from the office of the Ceremonials. Another deputy was assigned to keep dossiers on all the court eunuchs, including such information as name, birthdate, job classification, rank, incident, desertions, and the like. Then there were deputies who were charged to supervise the twenty-four Inner Court offices, and recorders to copy imperial decrees and proclamations and to prepare for imperial awards and promotion certificates.

One source reveals that at the height of its operation, the office of Ceremonials employed more than a hundred eunuchs to perform a variety of chores and make the imperial machinery function smoothly. These people worked on a two-shift schedule; each shift had four teams and each team was further subdivided into various sections. The day shift began about five to seven o'clock in the morning and lasted until three to five in the afternoon when the night shift took over. Most of the eunuchs received four days off every month, but whenever the emperor attended the morning lecture, made a lengthy tour, or inspected a tomb or construction project, many of them had to work overtime. Occasionally, eunuchs from the Ceremonial Directorate were the recipients of imperial largesse, but they had also become the subject of jealousy and could not escape the prying eyes and constant scrutiny of their peers and enemies.

The office of Ceremonials, in the true sense of the word, functioned as the message center of the Ming government, as it processed all communications among the various agencies of the capital—in fact, since it coordinated policies between the central government and provincial authorities, it could be compared to the White House office of the United States executive branch. All incoming documents first reached the Office of Transmission, or Tongzhengsi, which was directed by a commissioner, rank 3a. The documents were then turned over to the palace at the Huijimen, where eight to ten eunuchs from the Ceremonial Directorate performed the first screening. There the eunuchs color coded the files to sort out documents from the six ministries or military agencies or the princely establishments. The eunuchs then decided whether to immediately send the documents to the zhangyin for special attention or to forward them through the normal channels to the Grand Secretariat or Neige, from which they would ultimately return to the office of Ceremonials for final imperial decision. Outgoing documents would travel the reverse route; needless to say, all decrees, edicts, notes and instructions written by the emperor or scribed by the zhangyin and bingbi on behalf of the emperor were recorded before being filed by the personnel in the Ceremonial Directorate.[17]

Directly attached to the office of Ceremonial Directorate was Neishutang, a palace school established by Emperor Xuande (1426–1435) for the education of eunuchs. Young castrati, numbering between 200 and 300, were selected to study in this school, and the instructors were usually chosen from among the grand secretaries, Hanlin compilers, and ministers of various departments. Liu Zhong, who was a secretary in the Ministry of Punishment and also a royal reading companion, taught there in the early days of the school. Chen Shan, a grand secretary, actually had taught hundreds of teen-aged castrati before he retired from his government post. Later it had become a common practice to select four scholars from the Hanlin Academy to teach promising young castrati. It is safe to conclude that, even though the majority of Ming eunuchs remained generally illiterate, many of them began to be literate by the mid-fifteenth century.

On the day the young castrato, usually around ten years old, was to be enrolled at the school, he first came through the Beian Gate and, after being introduced to all the faculty, he had to kowtow to his own "sage," a designated master who would guide him throughout his school years. He was required to pay his sage a white candle, a handkerchief, and a dragon-shaped incense stick as token tuition. Each pupil received a book that contained the 100 most popular Chinese surnames and another book that provided the 1,000 basic Chinese characters. After mastering such basics he would be gradually taught the *Filial Piety Classic*, the *Four Books*, poetry, and so on. He recited and copied the lines from the books hundreds of times, sometimes without understanding their meaning. If he was ambitious enough, he would hire a private tutor to teach him after the schoolday was over. Bright and more advanced pupils often could get part-time jobs in various scribe offices; slower pupils and those who violated school rules always received various degrees of punishment. In general, relationships between the sage teachers and their castrated pupils were cordial and warm. In addition to state holidays, the boys had the first day and the fifteenth day of the month off. Every afternoon, before they were dismissed, each one was required to read aloud a poem he had written. And when they left the schoolyard, the boys walked in droves and always received polite and respectable greetings from onlookers.[18]

Since the volume of correspondence was very heavy, the number of castrati attending this school remained high; and in fact there are reports that from time to time there were not enough learned eunuchs for all the twenty-four Inner Court offices. Learned eunuchs were usually assigned to copy documents, scribe imperial proclamations and decrees, and even to draft criminal prosecutions, convictions, and verdicts. They were trained to write with brevity and directness, and some of them could actually write in fine literary style. One such a learned eunuch was Liu Ruoyu, who had been studying for the civil service examinations when he got himself castrated in 1589. He was then fourteen years old but quickly found scribal work in the palace. In his autobiographical account, *Zhuozhong zhi*, Liu characterized himself as a dutifully awed and well-informed palace eunuch. Even though he became a victim of the power struggle during the 1624–1627 period, his book provides the most interesting insights into the vagaries of the eunuch life.[19]

Probably the most interesting subsidiary of the Ceremonial Directorate was the agency of Liyifang, or the Etiquette Room, a most unique palace institution given a misleading name. Located just east of the Dongan Gate and southeast of the Palace Pasturage (1c), the Etiquette Room provided the healthiest and best wet nurses for all the infants born of the emperor's wives and concubines. The eunuchs who worked in this agency were also responsible for cutting the hair of the prince and princess when they became one month old. The emperor customarily would give his children names when they survived the first 100 days of their young lives. At the "name-giving" ceremony, eunuchs once again cut the hair of the young prince or princess, but put the severed locks into a special exquisitely made sack. Eunuchs in this agency also carefully monitored and recorded all the activities of the young princes and princesses until they became teenagers. The meticulous recording of the life history of each royal male scion also included the date when the emperor officially conferred a princely title upon him, and the spouse or spouses his father chose for him.[20]

Of all the eunuch agencies, none has piqued more interest among non-Chinese readers than the one that dealt exclusively with the nocturnal relations between the emperor and his women. Several popular writers, including Taisuke Mitamura, the Japanese expert on Chinese eunuchs, have identified this agency as Jingshifang, or Respect the Affair Room, and the eunuchs in this agency were supposed to have taken care of all the activities of the imperial bedchamber. Mitamura provides an extremely juicy "ritual" by which the Ming emperor chose a woman for sex and the extent to which the Jingshifang eunuchs participated in the love life of the Son of Heaven. Mitamura, however, quickly uses a disclaimer by saying that "exactly when this system was made official in the Ming dynasty is not known."[21] But he gives neither sources nor credible references to substantiate such sensational descriptions of the eunuch's exotic duties. The upshot is that a number of modern-day movie and television makers have actually believed Mitamura's assertions and plagiarized Mitamura's anecdotal history. In his *Minggong shi* [History of the Ming Court], possibly the most authoritative source on the Ming eunuchs, Lü Bi, a seventeenth century eyewitness, listed and detailed some fifty eunuch agencies in the Ming palace, but included in that list was no such office as Jingshifang. Sex is such a private matter and so taboo that it is very unlikely that the Ming government would record it in any official form. However, when the empress or any imperial concubines became pregnant, their activities, such as their menstrual cycle, vomiting, and miscarriages, would be closely monitored and recorded by the eunuchs.

The second most important eunuch agency was Neiguanjian, or the Directorate of Palace Servants, which was located just inside the northern palace wall near the Beian Gate (2 of Map B). The largest of all the eunuch agencies in terms of personnel and office space, this directorate took charge of palace construction of all kinds, including mansions for princes and tombs for deceased emperors and empresses. Under a zhangyin grand eunuch were various numbers of managers, deputies, assistants, accountants, recorders, and so on. The personnel of this office was divided into three shifts, each taking turn to stay overnight inside the Imperial City. Each shift had a foreman and an artisan, who specialized in either the woodworking, stone and slate masonry, brick and clay masonry, or scaffolding and painting. This office also kept numerous warehouses and depots where rice, salt, and ice, as well as platforms for temporary use and other building materials were stored. In addition, its personnel had access to such metals as copper, tin, bronze, iron, and the like. Its many workshops and factories set up in the country were under the supervision of high ranking intendant eunuchs who, by custom, could serve only four years in one station. For example, it had a stone quarry in the West Lake of Hangzhou and a forest farm in Zhendingfu.[22]

Next to the Palace Servants Directorate was Yuyongjian, or the Palace Carpentry Directorate, which was established along the southern shore of the Taiyi Lake on the west side of the Imperial City (3). A zhangyin grand eunuch and two deputies—one managed affairs inside the palace and the other affairs outside the palace—commanded a team of the top cabinetmakers in the nation. They made palace screens, decorative room items and utensils, lamps and lanterns, hard wood and bamboo furniture of all sorts, and ivory works. Among the delicate things they made were artificial flowers, white and purple sandals, wooden toys of various sizes and shapes, chessmen, and playing cards. This office also manufactured such useful daily necessities as combs, lacquerware, dishes, cups, fans, buckets and canes. The office hired a dozen weavers to process woolen yarns sent from Central Asia and also make carpets and rugs of the highest quality. Finally, it was responsible for providing all the papers and written materials for the offices in the palace. Parallel to the Palace Carpentry was Sishejian, or the Outfittings Directorate (4), which was almost like an extension of the Palace Servants Directorate. Its duties included providing all of the required gear, costumes, and equipment during each and every imperial ceremony. It made the sheets, towels, cushions, and blankets used in every palace chamber. It also produced tents, bags, umbrellas, canopies, and other housewares and apparel for seasonal use. Eunuchs who worked in this agency learned how to deal with tedious and laborious chores and were frequently subject to inventory checks, since

Ming censors subscribed to the belief that tens of thousands of palace apparel items were stolen from palace warehouses by the castrated servants.[23]

The office of Yumajian, or the Imperial Stables (5), was constructed during the Zhengde reign (1506–1522) and was staffed with one zhangyin and four intendant grand eunuchs, plus many guards and assistants, and horse and elephant trainers. In addition to taking care of the nine elephant stables (5a), each of which maintained at least one female elephant, and numerous horse and exotic animal stables, Yumajian also ran a horse track, a circus arena, and three breeding and fodder farms (5b, 5c, 5d). Fodder generally consisted of rice or millet-straw and black or yellow beans. The standard amount of daily provision for a riding horse was three liters of beans and one sheaf of straw (grass). Rarely were the horses in the Imperial Stables fed low-quality substitute forage. Every year the horses were put to pasture during summer and fall, when the fields were covered with grass, and fed with fodder in the stables during winter and spring. Eunuchs in this agency also made saddles and horseshoes, but they fed the animals more like zookeepers than American cowboys, as some of them were also assigned to take care of His Majesty's cats.[24]

But whereas the eunuchs working in the stables were daily subjected to animal odors, the eunuchs serving in Shengongjian, or the Imperial Temples, constantly inhaled the pleasant aroma of incense sticks. Located right in front of the Changan Left Gate, only a few hundred feet from the Six Ministries, this agency (6) was responsible for maintaining the so-called nine temples south of the Meridian Gate. Of them, the two most sacred temples were the Ancestral Temple on the east side (6a) and the Altar of Earth and Grain on the west (6b). On the first day of the first moon, the fourth moon, the seventh moon, and the tenth moon, the emperor was required to make state sacrifices at these temples. But whenever there was a solar eclipse or a leap month, the sacrificial ceremony was changed to the fifth day of the month. Other state holidays and special occasions, like the emperor's personal pleading for rain, always resulted in the eunuchs' working day and night in the agency.[25]

One of the more desirable agencies for emperor's castrated servants was to be found in Shangshanjian, or the Palace Foods Directorate (7), which had to work hand in glove with Guanglusi, or the Imperial Kitchen (7a); both were centrally located on the east side of the Imperial City. The Palace Foods Directorate also ran a cattle farm, a lamb farm, and other food supply subsidiaries with a total personnel of more than 100 eunuchs; during extraordinary occasions, the two offices together could hire up to 6,300 cooks at one time. From these farms, the agency obtained meat, fish, flour, cooking oil, soy sauce, vegetables and condiments of various kinds. But routinely, they received supplementary tributes from Nanjing and other provinces and also frequently went to the market to purchase whatever was required to serve from 10,000 to 15,000 persons every day.

The meals for His Majesty, however, were prepared separately by the cooks of the Director of Ceremonial during odd months and by the cooks of the Director of the Eastern Depot during even months. These meals were served once every three hours. The emperor's tea, fruits, wine, and beverage were also provided by a special group of eunuchs.[26] A separate bakery, Tianshifang (33), hired the best eunuch confectioners and prepared cakes, sweets, candies (the most popular being the Tiger's Eyes), cookies, and fancy dishes with sugar, syrup and honey. These eunuch bakers also made exquisite boxes of cake and containers of delicacies that the imperial family frequently used as presents to their favorite officials and subordinates. But the Imperial Kitchen and Palace Foods Directorate provided food, fresh fruits, and delicacies for the rest of the palace personnel and were also in charge of preparing sacrificial offerings, ceremonial banquets, and distributing groceries and daily necessities to every member who worked or lived in the Imperial City. It was reported that these two agencies alone consumed 210,000 piculs of rice, 100,000 jars of wine, and 70 tons of salt every year. No wonder a Ming scholar calls these agencies "the world's largest grocery store and dining hall."[27]

Shangbaojian, or the Imperial Seals Directorate (8), located just outside the Sihua Gate on the west side of the Imperial City, and Yinshoujian (9), or the Document Filing Directorate, set up north of the elephant stables, were responsible for keeping the twenty-four imperial seals and safeguarding written appointments of peerage, passports, authorization papers, and identification documents. Eunuch participation in the management of official papers and palace documents is a crucial topic and will be discussed separately in Chapter IX. But the one eunuch agency that had no office building but had to provide all the janitorial service was Zhidianjian, or the Palace Custodians Directorate. Countless eunuchs in this directorate were assigned to clean the numerous halls and pavilions inside and outside the Forbidden City, to polish copperware, and to sweep the immense courtyard, among other menial work. They were among the lowest paid eunuchs, but they had the toughest chores to do, particularly during the cold winter season. Eunuchs in Shangyijian, or the Royal Clothing Directorate (11), on the other hand, utilized their skills primarily as tailors and shoemakers and made ceremonial robes, everyday apparel, headgear, and footwear for the emperor, his family, and other palace personnel. This exclusive group of artisans was housed in a place called Xizhifang (11a), centrally located on the west side of the Imperial City, just south of the Armament Bureau (17). Finally, Duzhijian, or the Entourage Guards Directorate (12), completed the well-publicized twelve eunuch major institutions. Approximately 100 well-built, husky eunuchs worked in this agency and were charged to carry imperial sedans and to bring canopies, fans, and umbrellas, for the emperor, the empress, or their family. When His Majesty went to practice shooting or hunting, these eunuchs carried bows and arrows, wine and snacks, and also boxes of presents for impromptu imperial awards on the spot. Some of them were used to deliver special foods and cakes from pavilion to pavilion and from chamber to chamber. These people, however, also had lower stature among their eunuch colleagues and could not easily get promoted or transferred to other agencies.[28]

In addition to the twelve directorates were four eunuch departments and eight bureaus that, after their institutionalization, had all become indispensable imperial service agencies. The first of these was Xixinsi, or the Fire and Water Department (13), located near the Xian Gate and quite far away from the other eunuch offices. It had several branch offices—the north factory, south factory, west factory, and new south factory—extending just outside the Imperial City. Its main duty was to provide the entire Imperial City with firewood for cooking, fuel for sacrificial and nighttime burning, and charcoal for winter use. On the fourth, the fourteenth, and the twenty-fourth days of each month, the zhangyin grand eunuch of the department and many of his deputies would open up the Xuanwu Gate, which was situated between the Imperial Garden and Coal Hill and direct their eunuchs to haul away garbage, trash, night soil, and also to clean up carts, charcoal piles, and waste dumps. And at the approach of early spring when the weather became warmer, they would command their staff to dredge the moat, dig the dirt from every ditch, and drain and repair the numerous wells inside and outside the Forbidden City. One of the most demanding chores was to prepare for the celebration of the Chinese Lunar New Year. To fight any possible fire, they had to fill every gigantic copper caldron and every available pail and bucket with water.

While the Fire and Water Department provided comfort for the entire Imperial City personnel, Zhonggusi, or the Department of Entertainments, provided amusement, fun, and pleasure for His Majesty and his family. Located not too far from the east side of the Ceremonial Directorate, this department (14) employed more than 200 talented actors, musicians, puppet masters, and dancers. Eunuchs from this agency hit the drums and bells before His Majesty initiated the morning audience, when he paid a filial visit to his widowed mother, and also when he returned to his residential palace. And if there was a solar eclipse or lunar eclipse, all the eunuch drummers and pipers would be summoned to play their instruments until they had "rescued" the sun or the moon. In addition to such professional musicians, the agency also kept a troupe of talented eunuch actors who periodically entertained the emperor, the crown prince, palace women, and royal guests.

Schoolchildren in China and Taiwan are always taught to remember the four great ancient Chinese inventions—the compass, paper, gunpowder, and printing—and that a eunuch by the name of Cai Lun, about 100 A.D., was the first person in the world to make paper. The technology of making paper was undoubtedly passed on to future eunuch generations, as the Ming eunuchs had to supply all the paper for the palace needs. Baochaosi, or the Department of Toilet Paper (15), was set up between the Altar of Earth and Grain (6b) and Lingtai, or Terrace of the Spirits (31), and annually manufactured millions of sheets of toilet paper, generally from two to three feet in width. Its factory, located outside of the Imperial City, was equipped with seventy-two ovens, and every month it processed tons of straw, shredded wood, lime, and plant oil. The finished products, after being stamped with red marks, were then transported on a small one-wheel cart and delivered to every room in the Forbidden City, as well as the Imperial City and other buildings that had lavatory facilities. The toilet paper used by His Majesty, however, was made separately by the Palace Servants Directorate. It was much thinner and felt very soft, like cotton; the materials for making this kind of paper were said to have come from the Hangzhou area.

Toilet paper and bathtubs probably should have been managed under the same agency, but the Ming emperor chose to have a separate service office called Huntangsi, or the Department of the Bathhouse (16), which was located northwest of the Imperial Kitchen. This agency was responsible for providing bathing water and equipment, as well as supplying all cleansing detergents for the palace women and ranking eunuchs. Ordinary eunuchs, however, took their baths in the nearby Buddhist temples, which generally offered washing facilities. A group of less fortunate castrati derogatorily called *wumingbai*, or "white without name"—implying that they had lost their sexual organs surgically but still could not work for the emperor—always dawdled about there and were ready and willing to scrub, rub, and massage their more fortunate counterparts for meager tips. It is to be reminded that not all of the castrati received imperial commissions and became eunuchs; but instead the vast majority of the eunuchs were viewed and treated as nothing but the emperor's slaves and servants.

Next on the list of the eunuch agencies was Bingzhangju, or the Armament Bureau (17), which was centrally located along the east shore of the Taiyi Lake, and from which the eunuch blacksmiths manufactured weapons and ammunition for the palace guards. This bureau was also in charge of making the deadly cannon balls and had a gunpowder arsenal attached to it. Located in southeastern Beijing, the arsenal hired some ninety engineers plus several dozen workers. From time to time these engineers tested the new cannon balls, often causing the deaths of both civilians and soldiers and the destruction of houses in the vicinity. On the seventh night of the lunar month of July, a festival in which the Chinese pay respect to ghosts and spirits, the eunuchs from this bureau displayed fireworks on top of Longevity

Hill. In addition, this bureau operated a smaller factory just outside of the Palace Wall, where the eunuchs manufactured such hardware tools as keys, locks, hammers, needles, screwdrivers, scissors, and the like. Finally, the drums, chimes and other ritual instruments for "rescuing" the sun and the moon during the eclipses also came from the Armament Bureau.

At the southeastern corner of the Palace Wall and neighboring the Palace Servants Directorate sat the palace mint, Yinzuoju, or the Silverware Bureau (18). The eunuchs in this bureau cut gold and silver bullion into various shapes and forms such as peaches, needles, and bean leaves (with each weighing from three or five fen to one jian) before setting them with gems and crystals. In the Ming monetary and weight system, a liang or tael (about 1.3 English ounces) was the most common denomination, with a tael equaling ten jian, a jian having ten fen, and a fen equalling ten li, the smallest denomination. These kinds of gold and silver jewelry were used primarily as imperial gifts. But this bureau also made the famed huayin, or floral silver, which was composed of 80 percent sterling silver, with each weighing ten taels. After the Xuande reign (1426–1435), as silver came into official use as currency, this bureau set up another mint, located in southwestern Beijing, and hired some sixty eunuchs to make the popular silver money called piaoeryin. The new silver money had denominations of ten taels, five taels, three taels, and one tael and were used for paying the salaries of officials. In addition, the bureau produced small square-shaped coins, each worth a jian, which contained roughly 60 to 70 percent sterling silver and became very convenient media for exchanges.[29]

When the eunuchs retired or became disabled, they would be sent to Wanyiju, or the Nursing Home Bureau (19), located several miles away from the northwestern corner of the Palace Wall and surrounded by a cluster of Buddhist temples. The Palace Servants Directorate provided these retirees with rice, salt, and daily necessities. They lived in a quiet, peaceful environment, but were totally isolated from the outside world, as they were absolutely forbidden to reveal the Inner Court secrets and its operational mechanism to anyone. And when the eunuchs got sick, they were treated in the Anletang, the eunuch infirmary (19a), located right inside the Beian Gate. If the invalid died, the Palace Servants Directorate would provide a copper tablet and a coffin for him, and the Fire and Water Department would send wood to have his dead body cremated in the Jingletang pagodas.[30]

The Ming court also established Jinmaoju, or the Headgear Bureau (20), in the northern part of the Imperial City to provide headgear, shawls, audience uniforms, and shoes for the imperial family as well as for the army of the eunuch servants. Every year before the summer season arrived, this bureau routinely prepared a list of all the eunuch names for the Ministry of Public Works, which normally appropriated more than 100,000 silver taels for the bureau's expenses. Also, when a new bingbi grand eunuch was commissioned, it was the bureau's responsibility to send him an entirely new set of gowns, headgear, and shoes that would clearly distinguish his rank and title. By the same token, when a eunuch envoy was accredited to a foreign state, the bureau would see to it that his uniforms, headgear, and the outfits of his grooms and guards were all provided for. Other such routine duties included providing official apparel for all the princes and husbands of the princesses who had just been conferred new titles. Finally, when an enfeoffed prince was about to depart for his princely establishment, this bureau had to take care of its designated flag and colors plus all the prescribed uniforms of the prince's staff.

Zhengongju, or the Garments Bureau (21), situated right between the Headgear Bureau and the Ceremonial Directorate, shared similar responsibilities, but it provided essentially all the summer and winter garments for all the court eunuchs. This bureau also gave each eunuch a small amount of New Year's money wrapped in a red envelope. And although the Headgear Bureau provided apparel for happy events, this bureau provided all the tablecloths, canvasses, and banners for imperial funerals and sacrificial rituals. Also, when a high-ranking bingbi grand eunuch died or was disgraced, his silk gowns, sometimes embroidered with pythons, had to be returned to this bureau for storage. But for ordinary eunuchs, their garments were to be periodically washed and dyed at Neizhiranju, or the Dyeing Bureau (22), which had one factory outside the Palace Wall and another located on the west side of Beijing suburb. The latter produced various indigoes and other materials for dyeing plain hemp clothes and silk fabrics into differing colors.[31]

Right in between the Garments Bureau and the Dyeing Bureau was Jiucumianju, or the Wine, Vinegar, and Noodle Bureau (23), which provided the imperial family and the entire Inner Court personnel with daily foodstuffs, including wine, vinegar, noodles, nuts, and the like. This bureau regularly obtained from Zhejiang and other provinces such items as sweet rice, flour, soy beans, and various brands of grains. The court's favorite white noodle was legendary, made by the eunuchs in this bureau. However, His Majesty's food supply was under the charge of Yujiufang, or the Emperor's Wine Room (29), a building adjacent to the Wuyingdian. Under the watchful eyes of an intendant grand eunuch, this agency prepared the best wine, the most delicious dry foods, and forever fresh pickles and bean curds for the emperor. The court's daily consumption of vegetables, tea, and fruits came under the supervision of yet another service agency, Siyuanju, or the Vegetables Bureau (24). But this bureau alone could not handle the many demands of daily food consumption in the court and indeed had to work with two other farm agencies, Nanhaizi and Shanglinyuan.

Located outside the Palace Wall on the southeast side of Beijing, the forty-square-li Nanhaizi was primarily an imperial hunting preserve, but also functioned as a reserve camp, where hundreds of thousands of castrati were temporarily detained, waiting to be interviewed for palace work. It is to be noted that all self-castrated males were carefully screened here and not every castrato was permitted to stay. Those who were allowed to stay would be under strict supervision of a eunuch director and four intendant grand eunuchs. These vagabond castrati were then assigned to work in twenty-four different laboring units in this huge complex. Whenever the Inner Court needed new eunuchs, the prospective castrati were brought to an auditorium in the Ministry of Rites, interviewed, and examined by high-ranking grand eunuchs from the Ceremonial Directorate. Those selected were then led out of a back door of the Ministry to spend a night in a vegetable depot in Nan-haizi. At dawn the next day, they were ushered through the Dongan Gate and again interviewed and carefully checked by the grand eunuchs in the Palace Servants Directorate. If they passed this test, they would then be given each a black wooden tablet and would be assembled in Coal Hill for job assignments and instructions. Under the circumstances, Nanhaizi might be compared to an earthly purgatory from which the self-castrated young volunteers could climb to the paradise and work for the emperor.[32]

Parallel to the Nanhaizi in terms of division of labor was Shanglinyuan-jian, or the Directorate of Imperial Farms (25), which had a central office right next to the Imperial Academy of Medicine (Taiyiyuan, 26) and a number of farms spreading beyond the Beijing metropolis. Products from the Imperial Farms were exclusively for the emperor's personal use, ancestral sacrifices, state banquets, and daily consumption in the palace. Immediately adjacent to the Beijing metropolis, the Imperial Farms extended east to the White River, west to the West Hills, north to the Great Wall at Juyonguan Pass, and southwest to the Huen River. In 1408, Emperor Yongle expanded the Directorate of Imperial Farms from four departments to ten departments, but Emperor Xuande later restored it to its original organization. During Emperor Zhengde's reign, ninety-nine eunuchs were reported to have staffed this food supply center, and despite subsequent changes in its personnel and functions, the Imperial Farms remained an indispensable eunuch service station throughout the Ming period. Nevertheless, it should be noted that time and again the Ministry of Revenues demanded to have this agency transferred to its direct supervision, but without success.[33]

According to Ming regulations, hunting for recreation and sport in the Imperial Farms was prohibited because exotic animals and birds—deer, elk, turtles, cranes—were kept for medicinal use. From the onset of the dynasty, the emperor and his family were well served by an Imperial Academy of Medicine (26) located right next to the Ministry of Rites. The academy had from four to six royal physicians who worked with some thirty to fifty eunuch herbalists. Trained to master all aspects of medical knowledge, these eunuchs kept commonly used herbs and drugs in the Yuyaofang, or the Emperor's Pharmacy Room (30), which was like an annex to the Wenhua-dian. When the emperor felt ill, the royal physicians donned on their special "lucky gowns," and rushed to the emperor's chamber, where they burned some incense before kowtowing to His Majesty. While kneeling, one physician felt the emperor's pulse on his left hand and another his right hand pulse. They then changed sides and felt still more pulses before consulting with one another. Together they prescribed a list of herbs and gave it to the emperor's eunuch attendants, who immediately went to the strictly guarded Pharmacy Room to fill the prescriptions.[34] After assembling all the prescribed herbs and ingredients, the eunuch herbalists put them into one big pot, where they were boiled with water. When the herb soup was done, a eunuch would pour the soup into two bowls and wait until it cooled. One physician and one eunuch would, as a rule, first drink one bowl of the herb soup, and after a long while, the emperor would drink the second bowl.[35] Indeed, every precaution was taken to safeguard the emperor's safety.

The eunuch herbalists seasonally grew and collected various kinds of herbs and animal organs. Among the most popular medicinal items were wild ginger, licorice, dried lilacs, milkwort, yam root, tree peony, lily flowers, seeds of wutung fruit, cinnamon heart, shining asparagus, pine oil, cypress seeds, walnuts, lotus seeds, almonds, and dried dates. They also collected such exotic items as pomegranate peel, sulphur, deer penis, elk horn, and bear paw, for preserving the vital forces of the emperor and his children.[36] Some emperors, particularly those who had personal idiosyncrasies and who listened to the teachings of the Daoist cult, believed that some of the herbs possessed aphrodisiac value and could improve their virility. Others who wanted to live forever often took elixir pills, which abounded in the Emperor's Pharmacy Room. Almost routinely the eunuch herbalists ground the prescribed herb ingredients into powder and used honey as the binding base to make pills for four seasons. It is believed that some emperors contracted mysterious and debilitating diseases by taking overdoses of aphrodisiac and immortal pills. When this happened, the eunuchs involved always became scapegoats. For example, the Grand Eunuch Zhang Yu, who was the director of the Imperial Academy of Medicine when Emperor Hongzhi died in 1505, was charged with negligence and was tried and convicted by the Censorate.[37]

In addition to working in the Imperial Farms and the Pharmacy Room, the eunuchs were entrusted with the guarding of all sorts of depots, storehouses, and treasury rooms. Neifu gongyongku, or the Inner Court Supplies Depot (27), hired more than 100 eunuchs, charged with distributing rice stipends to all of the eunuchs working in the twenty-four palace offices and to those who guarded the cavernous royal tombs and sacred hills on the outskirts of Beijing. On average, each eunuch received four dou (roughly 124 English liters) of rice monthly, plus some oil and candles. The unique function of this depot was to store large quantities of yellow candles, white candles, and various kinds of incense. At nighttime, eunuchs from this agency had to keep oil lamps burning in every street, alley, and gatewall in the Imperial City. Eunuchs from Suyaoku, or the Keys Storehouse, on the other hand, were responsible for locking and opening all the palace gates and halls. Every morning around three o'clock, they left the office and began to open the huge Meridian Gate, the Donghua Gate, the Heavenly Purity Gate, and so on. They usually returned the keys to the storehouse before dawn, but would use them to lock all the gates at dusk.[38]

Nei chengyunku, or the Imperial Treasury (28), located between the Imperial Stables and the Bathhouse Bureau, was the place for storing such precious items as gold, silver, jewels, satin silks, high-quality wool fabric, jade, ivory, pearls, gems, and other articles of value. Since the mid-fifteenth century, this treasury warehouse began to store millions of tax monies, including those from the gold and silver mines and foreign tributes. In the earlier reigns, the tax monies were sent to Nanjing to be used in paying the salaries of officials, but Emperor Zhengtong (1436–1450) ordered millions of taels worth of the grain taxes commuted into silver money and deposited in this agency. The money was called *jinhuayin*, or the gold flower silver, of which only about 10 percent was needed to meet the annual military payroll. As a consequence, the emperor kept the rest of such silver funds for his own use. During the second month of every tax season, hundreds of thousands of taels of such money were transported through the Changan Right Gate and deposited in this eunuch agency. A cluster of warehouses set up at the northwestern corner of the Imperial City (28a) was used to store these treasures and other articles of value and state monopoly.[39]

Ming eunuchs also served as the emperor's astrologers and geomancers, several dozens of them were assigned to work in a very special place called Lingtai, or the Terrace of Spirits, which was located at the southwestern corner of the Imperial City (31). Most of the Ming emperors took great interest in religion, and some even wanted to make contact with the preternatural and the unknown worlds. Others probably believed that cosmic omens were important harbingers of temporal affairs, and that the ruler should always heed the warnings of Mother Nature. Indeed, the observance of certain days and certain hours as good or bad, lucky or unlucky, in which to act or to refrain from acting was a very important Chinese tradition. The Terrace of Spirits, in a way, was an observatory where the trained eunuchs used a set of astronomical instruments to observe the heavens and reported good and bad omens to the ceremonial director. These eunuchs daily studied holy hymns, books on the yin-yang theory, and various religious scriptures. They also made planetary prognostications, drew up all sorts of horoscopes, and recorded and analyzed all meteorites, so that their emperor could take action or refrain from action to avert possible calamities. It was reported that their tidings and recommendations were always treated as the state's top secrets and that the public, even the ministers, were not allowed to know their tidings.[40]

Predicting what Mother Nature would do at that time was difficult enough, but measuring and keeping the time was also a challenge to the Ming eunuchs. Knowing that the future and fortune of the state depended upon the measurement of time, the ancient Egyptians, Greeks, and Romans all had learned how to use the clepsydra for the measurement of time, but the Ming eunuchs had truly become the experts of this device. Every day and every night, more than ten eunuchs worked in a water clock room behind the Wenhuadian, and as water flowed through a small orifice to a container, hours were measured according to the level of a float on the water (eight levels made an hour). At the end of every hour, eunuchs from the Directorate of Palace Custodians would bring the "hour tablet" to the Heavenly Purity Palace and exchanged it for a new one. The "hour tablet" was about a foot long, painted in green with golden words written on it. Any person who saw the tablet had to move to the side, and those who were seated had to stand up and show their respect for the tablet courier. At dawn, when the eunuchs heard the first drop of water at the ninth level, they had to announce the time outside the palace gate, and when they heard the second drop of the ninth level, they had to immediately report to the emperor's attendants.[41]

Other eunuch timekeepers worked at nighttime at Genggufang, or the Night Drum Room, located at the very northeastern corner of the Forbidden City (32). A team, usually of five eunuchs, some of whom were disgraced and serving light punishment, took turns climbing up the Xuanwu Gate, an extremely important location separating the imperial chambers from Coal Hill, and beating the night drums. Ming Chinese divided each night into five gengs and a geng into several dian, or points. The first geng ushered in the nightfall, the third geng indicated midnight, and the fifth geng signaled the daybreak. At the beginning of every new geng, the eunuchs in this agency had to hit the drum on top of the Xuanwu Gate, while between the gengs, they struck a bronze bell at certain dian intervals. This chore was among the toughest assignments, as the eunuchs were not allowed to bring lanterns or make mistakes. It was particularly unbearable during rainy or cold nights.[42]

North of the Imperial Stables was a special Buddhist school, Hanjingchang, where the court ladies learned Buddhist scriptures. On the emperor's birthday and other feasts during the year, such as the fifteenth day of the seventh moon, religious ceremonies were held in this place. Several emperors selected honest and pious palace women to perform Buddhist ceremonies, offer incense, and pray in front of the altar. In general, eunuchs who worked in this school had already been converted to Buddhism and functioned like Buddhist monks. Ming eunuchs, as a whole, believed deeply in the future life and made certain that when they died they would be buried in Buddhist monasteries. Some of them became patrons of the monks and contributed to the construction of Buddhist temples. Others even set up their own prayer room inside the Imperial City and offered up prayers periodically to the Buddha. Elderly eunuchs, who had demonstrated religious piety and mastery of Buddhist rituals, were assigned to burn incense in a number of Buddhist temples where His Majesty and his family occasionally visited and worshipped.[43]

A number of Ming emperors, such as Yongle, Chenghua and Zhengde, were also attracted to Tibetan Lamaism, and their adherence to the doctrine of cause and effect was so strong that they invited Tibetan lamas to the Ming capital. The Tibetan high monks were given the title *imperial teachers* and taught the emperor how to recite the Buddhist scriptures in the Tibetan language and dress himself in the robes of a Tibetan holy abbot. To maintain contact with Tibetan lamas and continue the study of this mystic religion, the Ming court established the Fanjingchang, or the School of Barbarian Religion (35), north of the School of Buddhism. Eunuchs who worked in this school donned Tibetan monk hats, wore red frock coats with yellow collars, and offered candles, oil lamps and incense to a huge black-faced, long-bearded idol.[44]

In addition to Buddhism and Lamaism, Ming emperors also worshipped native Chinese Daoism and set up various devotional statues. It was, however, not clear which sect of Daoism the Ming emperors patronized, though holders of the Zhang Tianshi (also called *Heavenly Teachers* and previously from the five-bushel-of-rice sect) were frequently summoned to the capital to perform religious functions, especially in times of calamity. The Daoist Heavenly Teacher was admitted into the most sacred chambers of the palace for ceremonies of exorcism, particularly when the emperor believed that his palace was bewitched by evil spirits. Eunuchs who studied with the Heavenly Teachers also performed the exorcism rituals, which often lasted three days and three nights, but sometimes as long as an entire week without cessation.

In China's syncretic religious tradition, other religions, such as Islam and Christianity, were tolerated and welcomed. During the early Ming reigns, several Islamic astronomers were summoned to the capital to reform the lunar calendar. However, although a great number of Moslems settled in Gansu and the northwestern provinces and several mosques were erected in Beijing and Nanjing, Islam did not appear to have attracted a significant percentage of the Ming eunuch population. Nor did the latecomer Christianity appeal to the spiritual needs of the Ming castrati. Twenty years after Francis Xavier died (1552) on a small island near the coast of Guangdong, the Italian Jesuit father Matteo Ricci, then not quite thirty years of age, came to Macao and set up his residence in Zhaoqing in southern China. Ricci's attempt to convert the emperor and his family and then work down to the common people found only very limited success. Certainly some high-ranking scholars in the Ming court were impressed with Ricci's mathematical and astronomical knowledge and skills, but most of the Mandarins took him as an alchemist and were more interested in learning the secret of transforming cheap metals into mercury than seriously studying the Christian gospels.

Nevertheless, the persistence of Ricci and his followers, such as Adam Schall, began to see notable results by the 1630s and 1640s. It was estimated that, by the end of the Ming dynasty, the Christian religion had spread to thirteen of the fifteen Chinese provinces and that the Chinese Christians numbered about 150,000. Among them included such influential eunuchs as Pang Tianshou, known to the Europeans as Achilles Pang, and Wang Ruoshe, or Joseph Wang. It was believed that the governor of Guangxi province, Qu Shisi or Thomas Qu, was also a devout Catholic. Through these people, the Prince Gui, leader of an exile Ming government, was well disposed to the Christian religion. When Prince Gui was at Zhaoqing, upon the advance of the Manchus, eighteen of his court ladies, including his wives, were baptized, bearing such Christian names as Helen, Anne, and Isabella. In fact, a scion of Prince Gui was baptized Constantine of China by the Jesuit father Andre Koffler. This small group of Christian elite, however, did not exert any significant influence on Chinese government or society. In fact, Prince Gui was driven out of China and, after a brief exile in Burma, was killed by General Wu Sangui in 1662.[45]

EUNUCH AGENCIES OUTSIDE THE CAPITAL CITY

While the eunuch bureaucracy tinctured every aspect of the capital city, eunuch activities also vividly colored the provinces and frontiers of the Ming empire. The nature of their activities ranged from guarding and managing imperial mausolea, countless supply depots, state granaries, and salt control projects to gathering intelligence, purchasing horses, and most unusually and importantly, directing military operations. Some eunuchs were permanently institutionalized while others were sent for temporary missions. Ming China was dominated by quaint rules and bizarre customs that every autocrat observed. The customs were often costly, rigid, and superstitious, but no one would dare to change them. One such wasteful custom was tomb building and maintenance. Ming emperors paid a great deal of attention to placing the tombs of their parents and themselves, and even their deceased children and wives, in the right position—an art known as *feng shui*, or geomancy. Tradition had it that tombs with favorable feng shui, which literally means "wind and water," brought good fortune to descendants as well as honor to the departed. In a culture where reverence of ancestors is a compelling emotion, feng shui exerted a powerful draw. For example, in Fengyang in present-day Anhui province, the ancestral home of the Ming founder Hongwu, a special administration, the central metropolis, was established, and eight guards under a eunuch commandant were assigned to protect the tombs of Hongwu's ancestors. Located some 300 li or 100 miles east of Nanjing, the central metropolitan area covered thirteen counties and had a population around a million by 1578. Eunuchs stationed in Fengyang took turns lighting incense and candles every day and kept the fires in the tomb temples burning all the time. On the anniversary of the deaths of Hongwu's parents, eunuchs dressed in smocks mourned and prayed for forty-nine days. As well as such duties, the eunuchs in the central metropolis were also in charge of a very special penitentiary. Ming princes and royal magnates, if convicted of crimes, were sent to the central metropolis for confinement.

But the most sacred and the most revered tomb, a prodigious feat of engineering and finance, was that of the founder of the Ming dynasty. Located at the Single Dragon Valley northeast of Nanjing and constructed in 1381, the Hongwu Filial Tomb was protected by a wall more than twenty-two kilometers long, where several thousand soldiers commanded by eunuchs were permanently stationed. Along the path leading to the tomb stood twelve pairs of stone animals in the courtyard and a ten-foot tall stone monument, all of which still remain. Another special city exclusively governed by eunuchs was Xingdu in modern-day Hubei province. It was the ancestral home of the eleventh Ming emperor, Jiajing (1521–1566) who renamed the city the *Flourishing Metropolis*. A special eunuch grand commandant was assigned to safeguard the tombs of Emperor Jiajing's parents and serve as an imperial commissioner responsible for the security and stability of Central China.[46]

This unique tradition required that each Ming emperor select the location and design of his tomb while still alive. It was very obvious that, while he was at his zenith, Emperor Yongle must have consulted with a number of geomancers before he selected the famed Tianshoushan, or Heavenly Longevity Mountain, as the gravesite for himself and his successors. The Heavenly Longevity Mountain is nestled in pockets between two dragon-shaped hillsides north of Beijing, supposedly possessing excellent feng shui and constituting an auspicious long home for the Son of Heaven. As such, thirteen of the sixteen Ming emperors chose this area for their burial ground, and a special eunuch commandant was created to protect and maintain the tombs.

The eunuchs assigned to this post realized that they not only were protecting the imperial coffins, but also safeguarding hundreds of chests of jewelry and antiques that were buried with the Ming emperors and empresses. Other permanent eunuch agencies were charged with supervising rare local products, manufacturing textile fabrics, and managing tributary trade with foreign states. In Hubei's Mt. Taihe, for example, a special eunuch agency was established to manage its incense, tea, bamboo, plum, and prune production. In Nanjing, Suzhou and Hangzhou, where high-quality silks—brocade, damask, gauze, and satin—were produced, trusted eunuchs were stationed so that the purity of the silk fabrics for palace use could be absolutely guaranteed. Also, in the three busiest coastal cities, Quanzhou in Fujian province, Mingzhou (Ningbo) in Zejiang province, and Guangzhou in Guangdong province, the Ming court established three Maritime Trade Superintendencies, which were all headed by eunuchs.[47] After 1522, partially because of the declining foreign trade, all but the Guangzhou office were closed.

It is amazing that the Ming emperor frequently sent his trusted eunuchs to the provinces to take over the jobs his civil bureaucrats, numbering from 10,000 to 15,000, were required to do and to check up on military commanders alleged with pusillanimous defense of the emperor's interest. Some of these designations overlapped provincial administration, and eunuch designees frequently stepped on the toes of local officials. But this was precisely what Ming autocrats wanted, as overlapping, duplication, and power sharing among their different subordinate cliques certainly would reduce the chances of rebellion and disloyalty. This clearly reflects the Ming regime's dualistic characteristics—a system evidently distinguishing the eunuchs from the civil and military bureaucracies and yet at the same time allowing the two different elements to check on and balance one another. For all its inefficiencies, follies, and problems, this carefully arranged overlapping and double-decked system might ironically be the reason why the Ming dynasty survived as long as it did, for two and three-quarter centuries.

IV

Eunuchs and the
Ming Military System

EUNUCHS AS MILITARY COMMANDERS

Speaking of duplication and overlapping, nowhere was it more evident than in the Ming military establishment, where the Ming autocrat appointed eunuchs as grand defenders and grand commandants throughout the empire and made the career commanders and the eunuch commandants rub elbows so that he could "sleep on the tall pillows without worries." The presence of eunuch commandants among career commanders should properly be considered one of the more mysterious phenomena of Ming history. And because of this security arrangement, a legend was created that there existed an aura of cunning and dark secrets pervading the innermost circle of the Ming court. Such rumors were indeed very astute, but they were also rough and vulgar, and they began at the turn of the fifteenth century.

During the civil war of 1402–1403, many a eunuch had exhibited a great deal of military acumen, and many had made significant contributions in the field of secret service toward the victory of Emperor Yongle. Yongle's ascent to the place of power had without a doubt occurred amid many tears and much blood, for he was a ruthless man who put down all opposition with an iron hand. Beginning in 1403, Yongle appointed tactically savvy eunuchs to deal with his virulent enemies in the border provinces, along the seacoasts, and in the areas of greatest military need. Those who sow the wind tend to reap hurricanes. Eight years later, Yongle made the eunuch Ma Jing a regional commander in the inland frontier region of Gansu, and Ma received the Ming equivalent of a Croix de Guerre for his outstanding service. Ma's title was *zhenshou*, or the grand defender, which normally ranked 1a in the Ming military establishment. Though Ma's appointment was only for "roving inspections," the involvement of eunuchs in the Ming military administration had nevertheless begun. By 1411 at least three other eunuchs—Wang An, Wang Yanzhi, and Sanbao tuotuo—were supervising the troop conditions in the various military units.[1]

59

When Yongle died at Yumuchuan, in present Chahar, during the summer of 1424, it was on the order of the powerful eunuch Ma Yun that the bad news be kept from the public until he could move the Ming expeditionary forces safely from Inner Mongolia to China proper. Then in the first moon of 1425, the Admiral Zheng He was named *shoubei*, or the grand commandant, of Nanjing; and one month later the eunuch Wang An, a sinicized Jurchen native, was appointed the grand defender of Gansu, hence the beginning of the eunuch zhenshou system. During the late summer of 1426, two more court eunuchs, Huang Rang and Chen Jin, were dispatched to the important Grand Canal city of Huaian to suppress a rebellion staged by the Prince Gao Xu of Han. In short, only two years since the death of Emperor Yongle, the eunuchs had become increasingly visible in the management of Ming military affairs. But the major appointments came in 1439 when Emperor Zhengtong flouted Ming tradition by naming the eunuchs Wu Cheng and Ji Xiang regional commanders and authorizing them to put down a rebellion in the mountains of Sichuan province.[2]

In the subsequent years, more and more eunuchs were given military assignments, in particular, in defending the northern border against the Mongols. The most notable ones included Cao Jixiang and Liu Yongcheng, both of whom were given the command to guard the Great Wall passes and beyond. Still, the most interesting appointment was Yishiha, another man of Jurchen stock, who was to become the first eunuch grand defender in Manchuria. From his office in Liaodong, Yishiha time and again sent expeditionary troops into Siberia, attempting to bring the tribes in that region into the Ming orbit.[3] It should be noted that when all of these appointments were being made the country was so accustomed to peace with the Mongols that the eunuchs seemed to have been given free hand to erode the power of the military professionals. Then came the 1449 disaster at Tumu, where Emperor Zhengtong was carried into captivity after listening to the advice of his trusted eunuch Wang Zhen to come in person to battle the Mongols. Wang Zhen, then the ceremonial director, took all the blame for the catastrophe.

Nevertheless, the eunuchs' inroads into the Ming military establishment continued unabated, because this was also the time when new types of firearms were being developed by the Ming armies and, as the method of manufacturing firearms was considered a state secret, they could be made only in the capital under the watchful eyes of the emperor's castrati. One type of crude cannon was made of brass or iron and cast in the shape of a quiver; an inside tube filled with gunpowder and stones was loaded through the muzzle, so that the soldiers could light the fuse to shoot forth the stones as if from a quiver. The second type of firearm was a prototype of modern artillery, and the soldiers used such an instrument to project iron arrowheads to a distance of a hundred yards. It is impossible to ascertain to what extent the eunuchs actually contributed to the development of this new technology, but the Ming records show that they were entrusted to set up cannons on the mountains surrounding Beijing and that by 1448 two grand eunuchs, Cao Jixiang and Wang Jin, had become the commanders of the capital's artillery regiments.[4] During the 1450s, Cao's star was on a steady rise, until finally he was made the ceremonial director and one of his nephews, an earl. Ultimately, however, Cao fell victim to his own ambition when he unexpectedly staged a mutiny in the early fall of 1461. The mutiny was crushed, and Cao and his relatives were put to death and their properties confiscated. Cao's misdeeds, nonetheless, did not significantly cause the waning of the eunuchs' power as a group, but it did adumbrate that the Ming military system had started to deviate from its original design.

Ming military officers, like their civil counterparts, were classified in grades, ranking from 1a down to 6b. A military district established within a county was called *suo*, or battalion, and had about 1,120 soldiers under a battalion commander who ranked 5a. A military district covering two counties was known as a *wei*, or guard, and theoretically had 5,600 soldiers under the command of a guard commander who ranked 3a. In the early fifteenth century, there were approximately 493 guards and 359 battalions in the country, but because of constant trouble along the borders, the wei-suo units increased substantially during the later years of the dynasty. In addition to the wei-suo troops, there were forty-two capital guards and thirteen imperial embroidered-uniform guards who were trained by special officials. The capital guards for both Beijing and Nanjing were later increased to seventy-two, and the imperial guards were augmented to twenty-six. According to Ming official accounts, troop strength in 1392 numbered 1,198,442, but had grown to 3.15 million in the 1440s, and was reported at a figure of 4 million in the late sixteenth century.[5] Before the seventeenth century, most of the soldiers were sons of hereditary military families; after 1600, however, recruitment took the place of conscription.

Moreover, the increase in number corresponded to a decline in the quality of soldiery as the mercenaries dominated the army near the end of the dynasty, while the military records were, for a long time, left unchecked. Commanders often exaggerated expenses and reported greater numbers of soldiers than had actually gone into battle. Worse still, many of the soldiers were employed in manual labor for the commander's personal service. And apparently because of incompetence, corruption, and the lack of rigorous training, these soldiers ultimately lost their valor. In 1550, when the Mongols attacked the capital, the Minister of War could muster only between 50,000 and 60,000 soldiers, and even these had to be forced to fight.[6] "All those under arms," wrote the Jesuit Father Matteo Ricci, "led a despicable life, for they have not embraced this profession out of love of their country or devotion to their king or love of honors and glory, but as men in the service of a provider of employment." Ricci said that Ming armies in the declining years of the dynasty were the refuse dump of society and consisted of idlers, rascals, jailbirds, and highwaymen.[7]

As with their civil bureaucracy, the Ming founders built into their military system several layers of security. All the wei and suo districts were combined in a hierarchy, the Five Chief Military Commissions, which had charge of all the military registers of the empire. Each of the Chief Military Commissions was headed by an unprescribed number of chief commissioners (rank 1a), deputy commissioners (1b), and assistant commissioners (2a). But while military commissioners controlled the tactical direction of the army and supervised the professional aspects of military administration, the Ministry of War, headed by a 2a minister and two 3a deputies, in Beijing originated basic strategy and decided personnel, supply, and troop mobilization. In short, the commissioners only executed the orders and policies of the Ministry of War and led the army in the battlefield. When there was a war, troops were mobilized from various wei-suo units on orders from the capital, and commanders were chosen from the Five Chief Military Commissions to lead them. But as soon as the war was over, troops returned to their respective wei-suo districts, and the generals surrendered their temporary tactical command. Such a system was created to avoid close relationships between the commanding officers and the soldiers. It created many coordinating and communication problems in times of an urgent military crisis, however.

As constant vigilance was required along the inland frontiers and in the immediate vicinity of Beijing, Ming autocrats often chose trusted eunuchs, instead of career military commissioners, to lead the troops. From the time of the Yongle reign, the imperial guards were closely associated with the eunuchs and so were not attached for supervision to the Five Military Commissioners. Even the capital guards in Beijing were not to be supervised by regular military commissioners, but were instead strictly under the command of the emperor's castrated servants. Beginning in 1425, more and more eunuchs were appointed grand defenders with tactical commands. Previously, such appointments were given only to dukes, marquises, earls, or other dignitaries. Over the next 200 years, castrated men were to become an integrated part of this military operation, supplementing rather than replacing career military officials. Once again, it underscores the dualistic nature of Ming government.

Eunuch grand defenders were, at the outset, assigned only to exposed towns, forts, stockades, ports, passes, barriers, and other frontier locations that required garrison forces. But as time went on, more and more eunuchs were dispatched to interior posts for one reason or another. The specially delegated grand defenders commanded troops from nearby wei-suo districts jointly with career officials. In 1445, for example, a eunuch grand defender worked closely with thirteen other officials in the southeastern provinces of Zhejiang and Fujian, where bandits were ravaging the population. Depending upon necessity, more than one grand defender could be stationed in a province. Shandong province was always under supervision of a grand defender, but in 1494, Emperor Hongzhi delegated his eunuch confidant Li Quan to specifically manage a civil disturbance then caused by the Yellow River flooding. Yunnan province also had a permanently stationed eunuch grand defender, but for the fear of an aboriginal uprising, Emperor Hongzhi sent another eunuch named Sun Xu to double his security forces in the southwestern frontier. Such a duplication was to be seen even more frequently in the Ming's nine most sensitive frontier areas. They included Liaodong in modern Manchuria, Jizhou in northeast Beijing, Xuanfu in northwest Beijing, Datong in northern Shanxi province, Taiyuan covering the central and western portions of Shanxi province, Yulin in northern Shaanxi province, Guyuan covering the western and central portions of Shaanxi province, Ningxia outside the Great Wall north of Shaanxi, and Gansu in the far west.[8] Throughout the Ming period, eunuch grand defenders were always stationed permanently or temporarily in these strategically crucial areas.

In the immediate vicinity of the capital, Ming emperors were particularly concerned about the security problems. Consequently, they built even thicker layers of garrison forces. By the early sixteenth century, twenty-four grand defenders were scattered about the northern edge of the Beijing metropolitan area. For example, a eunuch grand defender at Changping guarded the Juyongguan Pass and the Great Wall section at Badaling. He had to maintain the battlements at regular intervals so that they were good for use as beacon towers. In addition, there was a eunuch grand defender at Baoding and another one at Jizhou, whose responsibility was to safeguard the strategically important Shanhaiguan Pass near the Bohai Sea. By the mid-sixteenth century, every one of the 129 passes along the 3,750-mile Great Wall, every major city, many important stockades and barriers in the frontier region, and even mountains with sacred names or trading posts along the canals were all under the watchful eyes of His Majesty's cloistered eunuchs.

THE EUNUCH BATTALIONS

While the Ming emperor settled the greater part of the army along the Great Wall and maintained a formidable force throughout the empire, he also established a "praetorian guard" nearby the palace. When Emperor Yongle moved the capital from Nanjing to Beijing in 1421, he increased the capital troops to seventy-two guards (wei) and divided them into three services—

infantry, cavalry, and artillery. Beginning in 1465, the first year of Emperor Chenghua's reign, some 140,000 of the best soldiers were picked out of various military units and organized into the so-called twelve capital regiments, which were placed under the command of court eunuchs. The total number of these Ming praetorian guards was almost five times larger than that of the Roman elitist troops under Augustus Caesar, and they allowed the Ming autocrat to act from a position of strength against his enemies, domestic as well as foreign. During the next century—the reigns of Emperors Chenghua, Hongzhi, Zhengde, and Jiajing—the Ming military system underwent radical alterations, until finally the Directorate of Ceremonial had replaced the Ministry of War as the decision-making body concerning military affairs.

The twelve capital regiments were later reorganized into three divisions: the Five Armies (Wujunying) infantry, the Three Thousand (Sanqianying) cavalry, and a regiment of artillery (Shenjiying) that specialized in firearms.[9] The Five Armies infantry had one eunuch-commander and two career officials as deputy commanders, whereas the Three Thousand cavalry was supervised by two eunuchs and two career officials. The artillery regiment was under the command of a eunuch and a career military general and was in the vanguard of the cannon effort. Its four departments manufactured and maintained the deadly blunderbuss called *Folangji chong*. There were two types of blunderbusses: the smaller type weighted only twenty-seven pounds and could shoot iron arrows to a distance of 600 paces; the larger type weighted about ninety-three pounds and could shoot as far as two miles. In 1529, Emperor Jiajing ordered the casting of 300 cannon, and as they proved to be very effective weapons for guarding towers, he ordered the manufacture of a larger number of such weapons to be distributed to his capital guards. Massive production of this type of weapon followed suit, and the Ming court was able to distribute 2,500 blunderbusses to the soldiers defending the border in Shaanxi in 1536, plus 3,800 iron blunderbusses and 3,000 brass cannon to other frontier units.[10]

As more and more eunuchs were given military command, a feud slowly but inevitably developed between the castrati and the professional soldiers. By custom, all of the eunuch military personnel received their commissions from the Directorate of Ceremonial, generally ignoring the wishes of the Ministry of War. Worse still, during the review of the capital troops, which took place once every three years, the director of ceremonials instead of the minister of war had the honor of administering the most significant military rituals. It was reported that during the reign of Emperor Hongzhi (1488–1506), a fairly influential minister of war once asked to review the troops together with Li Rong, then director of ceremonials, but the request was brushed aside with a negative reply.[11] If this humiliation sounded the death knell for the Ministry of War, it needs to be reminded that the incident clearly reflects Ming's fundamental polity; that is, dualism and power sharing.

No sooner had Zhengde assumed the emperorship before he began to appoint a large number of eunuchs to each military unit, first around the capital city, then extending to the frontier and the interior. Early in 1506, he named Liu Jin, then director of palace servants, commander of the Five Thousand infantry; Zhang Yong, then director of palace carpentry, commander of the artillery regiment; and Wei Bin, then director of the imperial stables, commander of the Three Thousand cavalry. Each of these three eunuch commanders was assisted by 100 eunuch ranking officials. Within a year, more than a dozen prominent eunuchs also received military assignments to guard various strategically important locations. Most of these appointees held the titles of deputy director or assistant director in the twelve eunuch agencies at the time of their new assignments. For instance, a deputy director of the Entourage Guards was sent to Jizhou as its grand defender, and another deputy from the same eunuch agency became the grand defender of the Taiping Stockade. Other second-tier eunuchs became grand defenders at such famous places as Suzhou, Liujiakuo, Huanghuazhen, Ermie Mountain, Huaian, and so on. Moreover, an increasing number of lesser eunuchs were stationed permanently as army inspectors and instructors in and out of the palace.[12]

It would be a great mistake to stereotype this group of eunuch commanders, as there were both plums and lemons among them. However, a profile of an exemplary eunuch commander such as Zhang Yong might help shed some light on the caliber and character of the peculiar castrated generals. As Emperor Zhengde, a fun-loving man of blissful optimism, continued to promote eunuchs and delegate power to several of them, his policies and personal behavior ultimately angered a number of imperial princes who were accustomed to comfortable princely establishments, but now had to bribe eunuch bosses to maintain their special privileges. In the early summer of 1510, the Prince Zhen Fan of Anhua from the Gansu region raised a standard rebellion by occupying Ningxia, but was soon suppressed by some 30,000 "praetorian guard" soldiers commanded by the eunuch general Zhang Yong. A native of Baoding, in present-day Hebei province, Zhang worked his way up through the eunuch ranks, until he became the commander of the deadly artillery regiment in 1506. This grand eunuch put down the rebellion of Prince Anhua, and he later helped bring down the eunuch dictator Liu Jin.[13]

During his campaign in Ningxia and its vicinities, Zhang Yong used a melon-shaped gold seal, specially made for him by the Ministry of War, to issue orders and execute military plans. When he returned to the capital, Zhang was hailed a national hero, and Emperor Zhengde, dressed in his military uniform, personally went to the Dongan Gate to greet his eunuch commander. For his awards, Zhang received 48 piculs of rice as an increment to his annual salary, 500 silver taels, and 50 suits of silk. In the precarious Ming officialdom, however, no one could predict the vicissitudes of political fortune. Soon after his victorious return, Zhang was accused of taking bribes and temporarily stripped of all his many titles. But a renewed Mongol threat in the northern frontier in 1514 forced the emperor to reinstate Zhang Yong, making him director of the imperial carpentry and also the grand commandant of Datong and Xuanfu.[14]

Once again, Zhang Yong fought off the invaders and restored peace and tranquility in the region. Then a more serious rebellion, staged by another prince—Chen Hao of Ning—in Jiangxi province, began to threaten the Nanjing auxiliary capital. But before Zhang Yong's renowned cannon regiment, some 2,000 strong, could reach the scene, the great philosopher Wang Shoujen (or Wang Yangming, 1472–1528) had already captured the rebel leader. In the late spring of 1521 Emperor Zhengde died without issue, and while the dowagers and grand secretaries were still pondering who should be the successor, Zhang Yong and his elitist troops closely guarded all the nine palace gates and prevented any possible unrest. But when the new sovereign Jiajing took over the command of the realm, Zhang Yong was demoted to be only a common castrato and, indeed, was exiled to Nanjing. Even though Zhang was called out of his exile to command the Imperial Guards in 1530, the Ming system would allow him to go only so far, but no further.[15] Zhang Yong died of natural causes, his career being a mirror upon which the rise and fall of Ming eunuchs could be clearly seen.

By the early sixteenth century, an increasing number of eunuch commanders were making names for themselves, good as well as bad, in the Ming annals, but the most controversial and bizarre act of all was the formation of an exclusive eunuch battalion in the Inner Court. Beginning in 1508, Emperor Zhengde selected from among his castrated servants good riders and skilled shooters and organized them into an exclusive eunuch battalion. He chose Gu Dayong, then director of the Imperial Stables, to be the battalion commander, who drilled the eunuch soldiers early in the morning and late in the afternoon. He later managed to fully equip all these eunuch soldiers and provide each one of them with yellow armor. Occasionally, the emperor himself would put on his own military uniform and act like a field marshal. Ultimately, these eunuch soldiers were also taught other combat arts, as well as learning how to fire the cannon. One witness said that the cannon noise deafened the ears of every palace gatekeeper and its fire brightened the palace walls.[16]

It was not clear how many soldiers were in the eunuch battalion when it first started. It probably began with a few dozen and gradually increased to a few hundred and later reached the thousand mark. By 1552, it became necessary to construct an Inner Court facility to house and train these eunuch soldiers on a more regular and professional basis. No details about the facility are available, but the compound built by Emperor Jiajing in 1552 had apparently proven to be either insufficient or had become dilapidated because, fifteen years later, Emperor Longqing expressed his desire to have the facility refurbished. This idea, however, encountered vehement opposition from one of his grand secretaries.[17] Slowly and reluctantly, Longqing withdrew his support from the eunuch battalion, but when his third son Wanli grew into maturity, he gathered 2,000 new eunuch soldiers and resumed full-fledged training on the palace ground. That was the spring of 1583, but when the seventeen-year-old Wanli asked the Court of the Imperial Stud to deliver 3,000 horses to his eunuch battalion, the Minister of War, a righteous man by the name of Zhang Xueyan, refused to comply with the request. Zhang earned his doctorate in 1553 and had served with distinction as governor of Liaodong and minister of revenues. It is from his memorial of dissent that we have learned the extent of the imbroglio caused by the controversial "nei-cao," or the Inner Court drill.

The minister of war Zhang Xueyan time and again tried to persuade Wanli to stop the Inner Court drill but to no avail. During the autumn of 1583, Wanli made an inspection tour of imperial mausolea in the serene valley just north of Beijing. He was escorted by more than 100,000 regular troops, plus his newly formed eunuch battalion. According to Minister Zhang, the discipline of his regular troops was good and their conduct exemplary, but that of the eunuch soldiers was egregious and contrary to all military norms. He complained that, at the end of the inspection tour, when all the state-owned vehicles and carts had come back to the capital city, the eunuch soldiers refused to turn in their weapons to the storehouses. That, he said, was a violation of the Ming military code. The minister went on to warn the emperor that he was not just abstractly concerned but personally worried about His Majesty's security and the tranquility of the entire palace complex. He therefore strongly appealed to Wanli to rescind his recently formulated program and do away with the eunuch troops altogether.[18]

Minister Zhang Xueyan's admonition, however, did not win Wanli's sympathetic ears, because it was construed by the emperor partly as the War Ministry's attempt to protect its turf and partly as Zhang's own way of venting his frustration. In the end, Zhang Xueyan was asked to leave his position, but the issue of "the Inner Court drill" kept rumbling and bubbling as Wanli added 1,000 more soldiers to his eunuch battalion within a year and spent an invisible 20,000 silver taels to boost its morale. Rumors continued to spread that many a eunuch soldier had been injured and had died during the drill and that the emperor condoned, if not directed, the more nefarious conduct of his eunuch troops. Against this backdrop, another self-righteous official, Dong Ji, a doctorate of the class of 1580, filed new charges against the eunuch battalion. Dong found something deeply and wildly outrageous in the power exercised by the eunuch soldiers. These charges, written in a formal memorial, were submitted to Wanli in 1584, but the young monarch interpreted them as slander connived to defame his "private army" and had Dong Ji demoted two degrees and reassigned to a frontier post.[19]

Warnings, protests, and sharp criticism nevertheless continued to emanate from four corners of the empire. Among them was a reasonable and persuasive argument made by a highly respected grand secretary, Shen Shixing (fl. 1583–1591) to the director of ceremonials. The grand secretary said that the core of the problem had everything to do with the personal security of the emperor and the serenity of the entire Forbidden City. With so many armed soldiers coming and going, incidents were bound to happen, as wicked people would find it easier to infiltrate the security system. Knowing that this particular grand secretary was not a sniveling hypocrite and sensing the enormous responsibility thrust upon his office, the ceremonials director began to talk the emperor out of his highly controversial program. Indeed, Wanli temporarily ordered the Inner Court drills to stop.[20]

Years had gone by since this issue was heatedly debated in the 1580s, but after Wei Zhongxian rose to power, he advised the young emperor Tianqi (1621–1628) not only to resume the eunuch soldier battalion, but also to increase its number to nearly 10,000. The Inner Court drills started in the third moon of 1622, but by the spring of 1624, the matter was once again brought up by a Fujian circuit inspector, Li Yingsheng. The emperor, undoubtedly dominated by Wei Zhongxian, could not be persuaded to discontinue the drills. Such military training on the palace grounds continued unabated even after the execution of Wei in 1628 and, in fact, lasted until the fall of the dynasty.[21]

The intent of the Ming's military dualism in general and the creation of a special eunuch battalion in particular was to prevent sedition and conspiracy. But the downside of it was that the Ming military establishment gradually became an overlapping, cumbersome bureaucracy, and that was where the hamstringing occurred. On the other hand, one needs to be reminded that behind the staid Ming facades were constant intrigues; noblemen, local magnates, and desperados, drunk with power, not infrequently plotted against the Son of Heaven in dim rooms and damp cellars. On most occasions, the eunuchs managed to learn the best-kept secrets and pulled off coups that astounded their contemporaries. There is no question that numerous eunuchs earned high marks as commanders and substantially contributed to the internal peace of the Ming dynasty, particularly from the mid-fifteenth to the mid-sixteenth centuries. There is also no denial that many a eunuch commander became fat and lazy, too well-blessed and unwilling to sacrifice. *Ming shi* correctly points out that in 1644 several eunuchs surrendered at the

Beijing city gates and that the praetorian palace guards dispersed under the city walls. *Ming shi*, however, failed to mention that several other eunuchs continued to fight on with fitful gusto even after they were chased out of Beijing.[22]

THE NANJING GRAND COMMANDANT

Of all the eunuch military assignments outside the capital city, none was more important and carried more weight and responsibility than that of the command of Nanjing (known officially as Yingtian fu) and its metropolitan area, where we find the second largest eunuch population in Ming China. Since the Eastern Jin dynasty set up its court in this lower Yangtze valley city around 317 A.D., Nanjing had been the capital of six dynasties and had gone on for over a thousand years amid drama, crisis, and panic. But the city was indestructible! It was a center of great wealth and its silk and cotton industries achieved wide reputation. During the Ming period, it had become a national center of scholarship, astronomy, mathematics, and other sciences. In Nanjing some 2,000 Ming scholars gathered to compile the gigantic *Yongle Encyclopedia*, a collection of 11,095 juan of excerpts and entire works from the mass of Chinese literature. It was also a favored place of Bohemian literati and eremitical poets and artists. Wu Jingzi's highly acclaimed novel, *The Scholars*, was set in eighteenth century Nanjing. Its streets were narrow, sometimes labyrinthian, but all had wonderful names. Educated men in Nanjing were genuine experts on calligraphy and philosophy who liked to pose as dabbling dilettantes. It was and still is a microcosm of civilized China, where everything changed except appearances.

During the Ming period, Nanjing had two walls, an inner wall built with bricks and an outer wall built with clay and mud. The outer wall, which was approximately sixty kilometers in length, had eighteen gates. More than thirty kilometers in length and between fourteen and twenty-one meters in height, the inner wall was designed to be an impregnable barrier. Twenty-three arsenal depots were hidden inside the wall, and since the mid-fifteenth century, eunuchs were stationed at these sensitive posts.[23] A total of ninety-seven counties comprising the territory of modern Anhui and Jiangsu provinces were directly attached to the Nanjing metropolis. The city itself had a population ranging from 1.2 million in 1394—making it the largest city in the world at that time—to approximately 800,000 in 1578.[24]

Since Emperor Yongle moved the capital northward, Nanjing had lost some of its power and population, but none of its grandeur and delicacy. It preserved its mystique and remained an "auxiliary capital," and was staffed with six departments and nine ministers, a skeleton duplication of a national government bureaucracy. Emperor Yongle employed forty-nine capital guards, seven of which were designated imperial guards, to protect this sac-rosanct metropolis. At the outset, military command was vested in two or three specially designated nobles: a grand commandant or shoubei; usually a marquis or earl; and a grand adjutant or canzan jiwu, a title often granted to the Nanjing minister of war. In 1425, however, Emperor Hongxi appointed the internationally renowned navigator Zheng He to be a eunuch grand com-mandant of the Nanjing metropolis. In the ensuing years, more and more mer-itorious eunuchs were made commandants of Nanjing. They took orders directly from the emperor and the director of ceremonials and were awed as the "princes" of Nanjing, as they managed both civilian and military affairs of the auxiliary capital and maintained the tomb of the dynasty's founder.[25]

The establishment of a Nanjing grand commandant symbolized the most towering achievement of Ming eunuchism, because Nanjing not only func-tioned as the political and military command post of southern and central China, but it was also the nerve center of the Ming's transportation network, from which the empire's economic lifeblood was pumped to the capital city of Beijing. According to Da Ming huidian, the Great Ming Administrative Code of 1511, Nanjing had 525 government offices and employed some 1,551 civil officials. As the emperor's personal representative, the grand commandant enjoyed a broad scope of administrative powers, but at the same time was responsible for the governmental operations of Nanjing. He often had to insti-tute preventive, corrective, and punitive measures when they seemed war-ranted. He customarily presided over the official meeting of the Nanjing "court," while a marquis and an earl would sit below him and the Nanjing chief military commissioner at the rear. The dignity or indignity of his position, however, often depended upon the cooperation of the two chief censors of Nanjing, some of whom gave their approbation to the grand commandant's conduct, whereas others only gave their tepid endorsement. Even though the Ming emperors generally were quite enamored of their cloisonne servants, they did not always give their Nanjing grand commandants a free ride. Con-sequently, the history of the Nanjing grand commandants is a history of the struggle between the eunuchs and the censors—two important pillars that sus-tained the Ming dualistic structure.

At the outset, there was only one grand commandant, but this number was later increased to two, and by 1506 there were four eunuch grand com-mandants in Nanjing. From 1425 to the end of the Ming dynasty, there must have been hundreds of such grand commandants; some were gold but many were grit. The one shining grand commandant was Liu Ning, who served in this post throughout three early Ming reigns—Xuande (1426–1435), Zheng-tong (1436–1450), and Jingtai (1450–1457). Liu Ning's rise to prominence began as Emperor Xuande's entourage guard. Once, Xuande's boat capsized in a huge, deep lake; fortunately, Liu Ning's loyalty and courage saved His

Majesty's life. An illiterate but magnanimous man, Liu Ning was later made the powerful ceremonial director, and it was then that he hired another influential court eunuch, Wang Zhen, to be his ghost writer. After serving for several years as the grand commandant of Nanjing, Liu won almost universal praise; among his admirers was a chief censor of Nanjing, Wei Dan. In his report to Emperor Zhengtong in 1440, the censor said, "Of the many officials in Nanjing, the rich and the powerful often ganged together and worked for personal gain, while the lowly and the poor were isolated and hapless. . . . The grand commandant Liu Ning constantly kept his vigil alive and remained loyal, straightforward, and utterly fairminded."[26]

But, as the censors were charged with keeping under surveillance all personnel and operations of the governmental mechanism, they generally displayed the most limited enthusiasm for the eunuch leaders, and some would soon clash with the grand commandants. The fight between the censor Jiang Wan, a doctorate of the class of 1478, and the grand commandant Jiang Cong was a typically ugly one. In 1489, the censor charged that the grand commandant infringed upon the powers of other state officials, intimidated the Yangtze River supervisor, undermined the judiciary system by involving himself in legal litigation of private parties, extracted money from government workers, punished innocuous career bureaucrats, and above all, deceived the emperor by promoting and dismissing eunuchs without following regular procedures. The grand commandant, on his part, countered that the censor insulted time and again national university students in Nanjing and spent too much time priggishly picking at the peccadillos of other officials and finally that everything he spit out against him was untrue.[27] Both parties understandably claimed that the charges against them were preposterous and groundless.

After a lengthy investigation by the court, it found that most of the charges brought against the grand commandant were false. As a consequence, the censor Jiang Wan was arrested for committing perjury and, after a trial in the Censorate, was demoted one degree and reassigned to a remote post. But the victory of the grand commandant Jiang Cong proved to be only short-lived, as his reputed arrogance and sometimes reckless behavior were endlessly raked over in the Nanjing official circles. Jiang Cong had a quick mind and a sharp tongue and also had a tendency to treat his less intelligent peers with contempt. His problems began unexpectedly with a mining project in a Nanjing suburb hill when his enemies charged that the digging of the peat soil had undermined the yin-yang equilibrium of Emperor Hongwu's tomb. The upshot was that the entrance of the mine was refilled with dirt and forever sealed off, and Jiang Cong was demoted to tending a vegetable garden in Hongwu's tomb for the rest of his life.[28]

This episode represents just another chapter in the rancorous relationship between the eunuchs and the censors and once again demonstrates the fact that, even though the eunuchs were a cosseted lot and did the emperor's bidding, their positions remained precarious, no matter how high they had climbed. For example, between 1507 and 1513, all three eunuchs in the stewardship of Nanjing bore deep scars from personal attacks and official impeachments. A circuit censor charged the grand commandant Zheng Qiang with sloppy record keeping and allowing several government projects to wither under his hands-off style of management. A supervising secretary from the Ministry of War accused the grand commandant Peng Shu of pirating government coffers and condoning repeated misconduct by his staff members. Another supervising secretary from Nanjing actually impeached the grand commandant Liu Lang for launching a terrorist campaign against both the military personnel and civilians in the lower Yangtze valley.[29] Notwithstanding the debunking of credible evidence, the fate of eunuch commanders generally depended upon the personality and the age of the emperor. In these three cases, the young monarch Zhengde—who once said that, "out of every ten civil officials, only three or four of them were any good"—quickly dismissed the charges as frivolous.[30]

The story of the grand commandant Liu Lang did not end here, and his relationships with Emperor Zhengde and local magnates reveal that even a grand eunuch like Liu had to constantly keep vigil while parlaying a political career in the process. Apparently Liu had become friendly with an ambitious prince in Jiangxi named Chen Hao and occasionally revelled in the closest contact with the prince's staff. But in the summer of 1519, the prince started a feckless rebellion, which was put down within a month, and the grand commandant found himself in hot water. During a rebellion postmortem, Liu Lang was implicated in the crimes of taking bribes from the rebels and intending to let the Nanjing defense slide so that the prince could establish a foothold in the lower Yangtze. Fortunately, Emperor Zhengde did not take umbrage at the charges, but between conspiracy and complacency, chose to fault Liu Lang with the latter. Liu lost his job and had to serve time in a special penitentiary for political rehabilitation.[31]

It had become obvious that, to stay in his Nanjing office, a eunuch grand commandant should never allow any scandal to surface that could taint his reputation and should also know how to withstand the gales of discontent that frequently blew from literati grumblers. His survival depended largely upon his experience, his character, his judgment, and above all, his execution of routine assignments, one of which was sending tributes from Nanjing to Beijing safely and uninterruptedly almost year round. By the mid-sixteenth century, nearly 100 yellow boats of various sizes were used to transport all sorts of palace goods and materials from southern and central China to the north.[32]

The successful operation of these so-called imperial boats was so contingent on the navigability of the various lakes, canals, and waterways that it was the responsibility of the Nanjing grand commandants to maintain a sound infrastructure that would allow the cargo boats to navigate without any danger. And since punctuality and meeting datelines were also important considerations, the eunuch grand commandants, through the Nanjing Bureau of Transportation and Equipment, worked out a complex and convoluted schedule for their marine teamsters. A sixteenth-century freight document shows that these boats actually crisscrossed the Yangtze and the Grand Canal waterways within a 500 mile radius of Nanjing and generally ran a well-designed schedule. For example, from Nanjing to Wuhu and back required fifteen days, a round trip from Nanjing to Suzhou would take thirty days, and one from Nanjing to Huaian and Zhejiang, each forty days. But an imperial boat needed fifty days to make a round trip to either Fengyang or Xuzhou, and eighty days to the canal port of Linqing in Shandong province. Other port cities that the Nanjing imperial boats frequently visited included Jiujiang (fifty days), Nanchang (sixty days), Ganzhou (ninety days), Wuhan (sixty days), Changsha (ninety days), and Xiangyang in Huguang province (120 days).[33]

Clearly, money counted in the immensities of Nanjing, where handling tributes was the big business. But it was also here that the charges of corruption against the Nanjing Grand Commandant became commonplace. In 1517, two eunuch staffs from Nanjing, who were assigned to escort tributes up through the Grand Canal to Tianjin, were charged with blackmailing and receiving kickbacks. A circuit censor impeached the Nanjing grand commandant Huang Wei, alleging Huang with aiding and abetting his staffs in looting 230 silver taels from the Tianjin office. The case was investigated by the Censorate in Beijing, which found that Huang Wei was deceived by his subordinates and not in any way personally involved nor had he any prior knowledge of his staffs' wrongdoing.[34] In this particular case, the emperor gave the Nanjing grand commandant a coat of armor that protected him against the censor's charges. However, in the ensuing years, sleuths from the censorate would keep impeaching, and the grand eunuchs kept dithering.

It is possible that a tightly knit, powerful Inner Court elite had from time to time allowed eunuch commanders to shrug off allegations of corruption, nepotism, and abuses of their positions. But the main cause of so many conflicts among the various Ming agencies seemed to stem from its dualistic bureaucratic structure and the lack of clearcut administrative assignments. As a consequence, there were constant disputes over the duties as well as responsibilities between the civil departments and the eunuch agencies. And the issues that seemed to have the most political resonance in Nanjing were the management of military personnel and the tributary fleet. In early 1524, for instance, Nanjing was hit by a severe earthquake that resulted in a serious famine. Its grand commandant Wang Tang then requested the removal of 3,000 troops from the Hongwu Filial Tomb so that he could effect a curfew to safeguard houses and property and foil possible looting. But as this act violated a Ming tradition that the tomb of the dynasty founder was sacrosanct, and since no one had previously had the audacity to do what Wang did, a supervising secretary from the Ministry of War immediately filed an impeachment against Wang Tang. In the wake of what appeared to be a winnable case, several censors from Nanjing also added their voice against the grand commandant and joined the fray.[35]

The real festering issue in Nanjing concerned the tributary fleet, however, with the grand commandants constantly asking for more boats and marines, while military officials wanted to keep the number as low as possible. The Ministry of War time again pointed out that when Emperor Yongle moved the capital to Beijing, he only used two or three boats to transport imperial tributes, and that both Emperors Hongzhi and Zhengde saw a need to reduce the size of the fleet when it was growing out of control. The grand commandants countered with the argument that they were required to transport some 3,600 pieces of furniture and utensils annually to Beijing, and that other miscellaneous missions, numbering in the thousands, made it absolutely necessary to have a large fleet under their command. The ascension to power of Emperor Jiajing in 1522 saw a renewed dispute over the size of the fleet, as the court decreed a freeze to keep the number of yellow boats under the century mark. The functioning of the tributary fleet was, of course, intimately tied to the eunuchs' economic activities and will be discussed further in the following chapter. Interestingly enough, however, whenever the Nanjing Ministry of War was asked to trim its budget, it always used the tributary fleet as a shield to protect its own turf.[36] This type of officialism shows why the Ming government had gradually become a cumbersome bureaucracy, a massive glacier freezing the machinery of government so solid that it could no longer function by the late sixteenth century.

EUNUCH COMMANDERS AND MING BUREAUCRACY

The Nanjing grand commandant was a microcosm of the Ming's overlapping governmental structure and also typical of the powers and status of the eunuch commanders throughout the empire. Take, for example, another eunuch grand commandant in Fengyang, where this second most important eunuch post outside of Beijing evolved from a purely military garrison into an all-purpose bureaucratic establishment. At the beginning of the dynasty, the government deployed eight guards (wei) and one battalion (suo) for the protection of the ancestral tombs of the dynasty founder and for guarding the city of Fengyang and its special penitentiary, built to imprison convicted imperial clansmen. All these troops, at the outset, were under the command of the Jizhou regional commander. But, beginning in 1504, the eunuch grand commandant of Fengyang was not only empowered to drill the tomb guards, but also to use his troops to arrest bandits and maintain peace in the region. In fact, Emperor Zhengde even authorized his grand commandants in Fengyang—Qiu De and Wang De—to manage the general governmental affairs of its six neighboring subprefectures (zhou) and prefectures (fu), among them Xuzhou, Yangzhou, and Huaian. Other grand commandants in Fengyang, such as Zhang Yang, were frequently involved in collecting the fabled red tea and sending it to the emperor as tribute. Under the circumstances, the Ministry of War and other civil officials became alarmed and, indeed, many a censor attempted to melt down the eunuch portions of the huge Ming bureaucratic glacier, but they were never able to break it up.[37]

As the eunuchs began to solidify their stand in the Ming military establishment, a smog of recrimination and bad history also rolled into the Ming court. In the autumn of 1503, Liang Ji, the grand defender of Liaodong, and Han Zhong, a Liaodong circuit censor, filed incriminating charges against one another. Both were arrested for interrogation, and while Han was later transferred to Huguang province, Liang was demoted three degrees and reassigned to burn incense in an imperial tomb. Four years later, the ceremonial director Li Rong, with the permission of Emperor Zhengde, created twelve additional grand defender posts in the country. This move left many civil officials and regular military people baffled, as they rightly or wrongly believed that such was the nature of eunuch bureaucracy, and that the most insidious of ills would consequently afflict their society. As usual, several supervising secretaries and censors kept a lookout for those grand defenders who were ripe for plucking. In 1522, Zhao Qin, the grand defender of a Sichuan frontier post, Jianchang, was charged with corruption and misconduct. The minister of war Peng Ze took the opportunity to lobby for abolishing this branch office but was unsuccessful. Nevertheless, the eunuch grand defender was dismissed and sent to work in Nanjing as an obscure castrato.[38]

In 1517, after successfully running out a band of bandits and highwaymen from the Wuhan area, the Huguang grand defender Du Fu was riding high. But when he requested special permission to conduct a general inspection of the province, he faced immediate opposition, because the "touring, pacifying, and soothing" fell normally under the jurisdiction of the governor and high-ranking capital officials on temporary commission. In 1523, another Huguang grand defender, Li Jingru, found himself in hot water when he was impeached for sending excessive tributary fish and timber to the Inner Court. The newly installed Emperor Jiajing ordered Li to stop such practices, as they might constrain the ability of the Huguang people to stimulate their sluggish economy.[39] In 1549, the grand commandant Liu Yuan requested to have his powers broadened and banners changed so that he could move his tomb troops beyond the restricted Heavenly Longevity Hill in the suburbs of Beijing, but the request was also denied. Then in 1567, in the wake of the death of Emperor Jiajing, the Ministry of War and the Directorate of Ceremonials got into a "turf fight" when the post of the Mt. Taihe grand commandant was brought out for review. The former listed several valid reasons to close down this office, while the latter insisted that a grand eunuch ought to be stationed in this sacred mountain permanently. To unsnarl the sticky situation, the new emperor Longqing made a compromise by decreeing to keep the post, but restricting its grand commandant's assignments so as not to interfere with the operation of local officials.[40]

Personal ambitions and boundless craving for power were generally at the root of the literati's irreconcilable dislike of and hostility toward the castrati. Nevertheless, their ceaseless fights and recriminations were often interrupted by short spells of ostensible reconciliation, in which plausible stories about the eunuch commanders were recorded. For example, in 1509, Liao Tang, the grand defender of Shaanxi, exhibited courage and grace under pressure when he foiled a violent revolt by capturing and killing 134 Moslems in his province. Then Wang Tang, the grand defender of Zhejiang, 1516–1518, assembled a panel of cartographers and geographers and made new maps for all the subprefectures under his control.[41] Another homely example of a eunuch grand defender was Li Neng of Jizhou. Li Neng demonstrated that he could win a battle against the Mongols, as he did in 1524 when his troops slaughtered countless enemies and protected the northeastern wing of Beijing. One year later, this same grand defender imposed a surcharge on merchandise that went in and out of the Shanhaiguan Pass, so that he could raise necessary funds to repair and strengthen the various forts and barriers along the northeastern section of the Great Wall.[42]

The innovative measure that the Grand Eunuch Li Neng took in 1525 to raise funds signaled a deterioration of the Ming military settlements, as it had become more and more difficult every year for the local commanders to support their soldiers and meet the expenses of the army. In the early Ming period, when the military settlements were functioning as designed, the soldiers in general produced sufficient amounts from their farms to not only supply their own needs and support their officers, but also to save some surplus for emergency use. But, because the military profession had become hereditary, the officers inevitably tended to occupy such lands as private property. As time went on, the wei-suo soldiers had declined considerably in number and quality, and thus they were first augmented and finally almost superseded by mercenaries who were lured or coerced into service for pay. Moreover, many of the lands of military settlements were occupied by nobles, landlords, eunuchs, and Buddhist monks. Even wealthy merchants managed, by chicanery and bribery, to get military commissions and took part in grabbing state lands. As a consequence, grain production from state lands declined, and the military establishment gradually ceased to be self-supporting. By the first quarter of the sixteenth century, soldiers were paid with money instead of farm produce, and around 1600 an infantryman's basic pay was fixed at eighteen taels of silver per year. But the ever-increasing annual military allocations had to be made from all sorts of resources.[43]

The Ming military expenditures could be classified into the following categories: provisioning, repair of frontier forts, military awards, and horse purchases. The payment of provisions was under the charge of the Ministry of Revenues and was made by either the delivery in cash or delivery in kind from the state's main depository, Taichang. The payroll for such provisions registered 400,000 to 500,000 silver taels during the third quarter of the fifteenth century and 600,000 annually in the first quarter of the sixteenth century, but gradually shot up to more than 2 million taels in 1550. And in 1642, the basic pay of the troops alone had exceeded 20 million taels of silver. Money appropriated for repairing border walls, though originally to be born by frontier garrisons, later had to be supplemented by both the Ministry of War and the Ministry of Revenues. As for the military awards, there were essentially two kinds: one was given in recognition of one's service in the army, and the other was given to reward the soldier's meritorious deeds, such as killing or capturing enemies and bandits. Finally, a huge sum of funds was appropriated for the purchase of horses. For example, the Ming government yearly spent 48,700 silver taels on horses during Chenghua's reign (1464–1487), increased to 503,300 taels under the reign of Zhengde (1506–1522), and escalated to approximately the 1.4 million mark during Jiajing and Wanli's reigns (1522–1567, 1573–1620).[44]

As the numbers of steadily increasing expenditures added up to create serious deficits at the state's main depository and the sorry state of the military budget worsened by the year, the priority of a eunuch grand defender was no longer to wage war, about which he probably knew very little, but to use instinct and improvisation to find enough money to pay his troops. And because his real portfolio was his proximity to power, he ironically became a suitable person to handle the situation, which was coming apart at the seams. In 1522, Geng Zhong, the grand defender of the Zijingguang Pass, a strategically important Hebei barrier from which troops could be quickly dispatched to Datong, reported to the central government that there was no money left in his depository to feed his soldiers. The Ministry of Revenues then authorized him to sell the grain taxes in advance, at a price of 0.45 silver tael per picul, to raise necessary allocations for the next six months. During the same year, Datong and Xuanfu were beset by famine and inflation and reports indicated widespread dissatisfaction among the garrison troops. The grand defender of Xuanfu, at his wit's end, employed a risky but effective survival trick by coaching his soldiers to stage a make-believe mutiny so that he could force the central government to allocate an emergency sum of 200,000 silver taels to Datong and Xuanfu.[45]

From time to time, the central government would fecklessly try to reclaim the state lands illegally occupied by military leaders, mostly in the frontier regions of Liaodong and Shaanxi. It even took measures to trim the size of its army. In 1522, for instance, Gansu was experiencing a budgetary crunch, and the emperor agreed to close down a grand defender post at Liangzhou. Of its 3,000 auxiliary troops, one third were discharged, and the remainder were amalgamated with another unit. And whenever the Ministry of Revenues could not find enough money to meet the military payroll, officials who drew salaries under fictitious names could always be found and made to cough up some of the money they had obdurately cheated out of the taxpayers. But when the situation had become truly hapless, the ministry would even borrow money from the Court of the Imperial Stud, or Taipusi, which usually kept a few million silver taels as a horse-purchase reserve. Unfortunately, near the end of the dynasty, when the court was no longer able to support the army from the imperial treasury, the emperor was forced to dispatch his ministers to every corner of the empire to look for the money and grain. And as the problems became absolutely insoluble, the grand defenders either chose not to pay their troops in full or allowed their soldiers to obtain what the Ming military parlance called *maixian*, meaning "the selling of leisure." A soldier who paid about 200 coins monthly would be exempted from drill and other military obligations and was thereby free to work a second job. As a result, the discipline was ruined, and the military service became a sort of commodity market where businessmen could buy military commissions and the soldiers could purchase free time to pursue what they pleased.[46] The reported irregularities practiced by some of the eunuch grand commandants and grand defenders should, therefore, be considered the symptoms rather than the causes of the financially ailing Ming military system.

EUNUCHS AND TEA-HORSE TRADE

One of the most important facets of the Ming military establishment was the maintenance of a strong cavalry with sufficient horses for combat readiness, peacetime defense, and logistic transportation. Ming military leaders frequently revealed their penchant for service horses, saying that it was easy to recruit good soldiers but it was much more difficult to find good horses. Generally speaking, the Ming court obtained its horses from three sources—tributary gifts from its vassals, tea-horse trade in the western and northern frontiers, and from its own stock farm breeding. As early as 1374, Emperor Hongwu received 990 horses from the king of the Ryukyu Islands, 3,040 service horses from the king of Korea in 1387, and 670 high-quality Central Asian stallions from the ruler of Samarkand in 1390. In 1403, when Yongle assumed the Ming emperorship, the ruler of Hami presented him with 190 riding horses and, six years later, he dispatched his grand eunuch Huang Yan to Korea and received in 1410 some 10,000 horses of various kinds.[47] Because horses were critically instrumental in his victory over his Mongol foes, Yongle even demanded that the Mongol chieftains, who having been defeated were now becoming Ming vassals, send him the best steeds they could produce. In 1420, for example, both the Tartar chief Aruytai and the Oirat chief Esen each sent 900 horses to Emperor Yongle, their temporary overlord.[48] But the tributary exchange was a two-way street and, after receiving the gifts from its vassals, the Ming court always had to reciprocate. The people who were chosen to conduct such missions were once again mostly court eunuchs.

Supply of tributary horses was, however, not always reliable, but the Ming court did have a better and steadier source of networks to obtain its needed horses. At the onset of the dynasty, it established a number of the so-called Tea-Horse Trade Bureaus, or chamasi, to barter tea, salt, textiles, and silver coins for horses bred by aboriginal tribes in Tibet, Sichuan, Yunnan, Guangxi, Huguang, Liaodong, and so on. The most notable chamasi were set up at Diaomen, Naxi, and Baidu in Sichuan province, where tea and salt abounded, and also at Hezhou, Taozhou, and Xining in Shaanxi province, where the tea-horse trade covered such a broad area as Gansu, Ningxia, Mongolia, and Central Asia. After the Ming moved its capital to Beijing, the significance of the Sichuan bureaus diminished, and they were inactivated by the third part of the fifteenth century. Nevertheless, its tea, called *pacha*, continued to be collected and delivered by the porters to the Shaanxi tea-horse trade bureaus in exchange for Tibetan horses, which were renowned for their spiritedness. Mitsutaka Tani, an authority on the Ming horse administration, notes that half a million catties (about 666,666 English pounds) of Sichuan tea could be exchanged for more than 13,500 Tibetan horses.[49] The trade was generally based on the supply and demand of the commodities available and conducted with goodwill from both parties. Ming official documents indicate that the tribes provided fine horses for high-quality tea and jaded horses for inferior tea, and that the exchange rate fluctuated from time to time. For example, in 1382 forty catties of tea were given in exchange for a steed of rare breed, thirty for a mediocre horse, and twenty for an inferior horse. Eight years later, it would require more tea to barter for a really good horse. One document shows that it would take 120 catties of tea to exchange for a high-quality stallion, 70 for a common service horse, and as much as 50 catties for an ordinary horse.[50]

The first documented tea-horse trade with Shaanxi took place in 1375, when the grand eunuch Zhao Cheng brought a large quantity of tea and textile fabrics to Hezhou and bartered for a substantial number of service horses. Seventeen years later, Emperor Hongwu again commissioned his grand eunuch Er Nei, then director of palace foods, to the same place for an even larger scale of tea-horse trade. Accompanied by another grand eunuch from the Ceremonial Directorate, Er Nei led a squad of military and civilian porters, who carried some 30,000 catties of tea, which were exchanged for 10,340 horses. Stallions and geldings were then distributed to garrisons in Henan, Shanxi, and Shaanxi, while mares were sent to governmental stock farms for breeding. The emperor was unquestionably pleased with the outcome and had decided to make this business into a regular and governmentally controlled event. In 1393, soon after Er Nei's return, the Ming court issued a golden tablet certificate to each of the licensed tribesmen, who kept the lower half of the certificate, which was to be collated at the time of transaction with the upper half of the certificate that the eunuch trade commissioner brought with him from the imperial court.[51]

The Ming court also regulated that such trade could take place only once every three years; however, due primarily to increasing tea production, there were excessive tea and horses to be bartered freely beyond the governmental controls. Tea smuggling, illegal trading, and other irregularities ensued.[52] But the tea-horse trade in the northwest continued to thrive. In 1433, Emperor Xuande dispatched a grand eunuch by the name of Li Xin to Shaanxi for the same business. By this time, however, private tea had already begun to inundate the market, and it was sometimes alleged that the court eunuchs, who held the golden tablet certificates, were also involved in the illegal trade for their personal gain. A trade mission in 1445, headed by a court eunuch with a cargo of 420,000 catties of tea, was singled out as an example for the rampant abuses of power.[53] As the illegal tea and irregular trade continued unabated, the Ming court decided in 1449 to suspend the issuance of the golden certificate. However, half a century later, it made a radical policy change as it allowed merchants to share in the tea transportation and tea-horse trade in 1490. By 1506, the shares of the government and of the merchants were running at a 50/50 ratio; hence, the government reactivated the old system of the golden certificate while effectively managing to control the tea smuggling. Tea-for-horse transactions would continue until the downfall of the dynasty; the number of the bartered horses, however, varied from decade to decade. It ranged from a low figure of 1,000 in 1505 to 6,500 in 1571, but reached a high mark of a 12,000 annual average during the reign of Emperor Tianqi (1621–1627).[54]

The tea-horse trade suffered from occasional interruptions whenever the Mongols became active and aggressive in the western and northern frontiers and when they plundered the tribesmen who produced the horses. Consequently, the most reliable means of securing horse for the military lay in the Ming's stock farm breeding. Under the supervision of the Court of the Imperial Stud, four pasturage offices known as Yuanmasi were created in Northern Beijing, Liaodong, Shaanxi, and Gansu in 1406. The total number of pastures and ranches attended by expert breeders fluctuated from time to time, but in general the Liaodong office counted roughly 2,000 horses per year, while the Shaanxi ranches could produce up in 13,000–14,000 range. In addition, private breeders contracted with the Imperial Stud Court and bred the horses in stables instead of pastures. In 1507, the so-called nongovernmental stock farms delivered as many as 25,000 colts to the garrisons as service horses.[55]

But parallel to the Imperial Stud Court was the eunuch agency of the Directorate of Imperial Stables, which not only kept tabs on the general conditions of the military horses and stock farms, but also developed its own breeding program and trained its own cavalry. Often to the chagrin of the Ministry of War, which supervised the Imperial Stud, the Imperial Stables personnel constantly requested the best bred colts and rare stallions and mares. Influential directors of this agency, such as the grand eunuch Mai Fu during the early reign of Emperor Jiajing (1522–1566), often attempted to dictate the policy of the horse administration, resulting in numerous disputes with horse administrators. By the early sixteenth century this eunuch agency had grown into a gigantic operation, as it ran twenty stables and directly supervised fifty-six horse ranches, covering an area of more than 24,000 ching (or 360,000 acres) of pasture land.[56]

The Ming horse administration indeed represents yet another example of the Ming's characteristic dualism, which allowed both career officers and eunuch horse experts to share the responsibility of obtaining horses for the army. It is safe to say that trading and breeding horses in Ming China, like everything else in the government, could not have functioned according to His Majesty's wishes without the participation of the eunuchs. They, by design, had a foot in every camp simply because the emperor needed them to keep him apprised of what was transpiring among the various factions and different agencies in the empire. But even though the eunuchs had effectively burrowed into the Ming military machinery, the worth and achievements, as well as the shame and evil conduct of so many military figures, with the exception of those of Admiral Zheng He, have yet to be thoroughly and critically evaluated by either Chinese or Occidental historians.

Figure 1.
Grand eunuch Admiral Zheng He, c. 1371–1435
(courtesy of National Palace Museum of Taiwan)

Figure 2.
A typical ship of Admiral Zheng He's fleet
(courtesy of National Palace Museum of Taiwan)

Figure 3.
The Grand Canal

Figure 4.
The Jinshui River near the Imperial Palace once flowed into the Grand Canal

Figure 5.
The Imperial Palace

Figure 6.
The first emperor, Hongwu, 1368–1398 ,
(courtesy of National Palace Museum of Taiwan)

Figure 7.
The third emperor, Yongle, 1403–1424
(courtesy of National Palace Museum of Taiwan)

Figure 8.
The eighth emperor, Chenghua, 1465–1487
(courtesy of National Palace Museum of Taiwan)

Figure 9.
The eleventh emperor, Jiajing, 1522–1566
(courtesy of National Palace Museum of Taiwan)

Figure 10.
The thirteenth emperor, Wanli, 1573–1620
(courtesy of National Palace Museum of Taiwan)

Figure 11.
Empress Xiaoyizhuang, died 1588
(courtesy of National Palace Museum of Taiwan)

Figure 12.
A eunuch holding a baton (on the left), supervising food boxes carried by
palace cooks (courtesy of National Palace Museum of Taiwan)

Figure 13.
Eunuchs leading horses in front of the emperor, mid-sixteenth century
(courtesy of National Palace Museum of Taiwan)

Figure 14.
Eunuchs lighting firecrackers on an imperial barge
(courtesy of National Palace Museum of Taiwan)

Figure 15.
A eunuch holding tight the emperor's horse, mid-sixteenth century
(courtesy of National Palace Museum of Taiwan)

Figure 16.
Emperor Jiajing attended by his eunuchs during an imperial procession
(courtesy of National Palace Museum of Taiwan)

V

✠

Eunuchs and the
Ming Intelligence-Gathering
Apparatuses

THE EASTERN DEPOT

Ming emperors relied on eunuchs principally for the same reasons European kings and queens of the Middle Ages relied on celibate clerics to manage sensitive agencies, such as the chancery, exchequer, and inquisition bureaus. Critics who blame the eunuchs for causing the worst kind of problems and for besetting the Ming polity almost always cite their involvement in the Ming espionage and secret police handiwork. On a closer look, however, one can find that the number of Ming eunuchs who were assigned to spy for the emperor was indeed minuscule. Moreover, they were nothing but the appendages of the Ming dualistic security system and political control. What form of reckoning must then take place between the Ming despotism and the reckless conduct of individual eunuchs? And when confronted with such unpleasant records, how should contemporary historians evaluate them against other forms of institutional inhumanity, such as the KGB of the former Soviet Union, the Stasi of the former East Germany, the Gestapo of Nazi Germany, and even the CIA of the United States and the inquisitors of the Roman Catholic Church in the Middle Ages? Throughout human history, various forms of security apparatuses were used to maintain those in power, to purify political ideology, and to perpetuate one's religious creed. Intimidation, torture, banishment, and murder ultimately became the means for weeding out heretics and silencing dissidents and politically undesirable elements. The Ming's secret police establishment falls into these categories; the only difference is that the people who conducted the dirty work were castrated eunuchs instead of cardinals or communist cadres, or highly educated civil servants.

The most notorious eunuch security apparatus in the Ming dynasty was the Dongchang, or Eastern Depot, which rightly or wrongly has since the seventeenth century become the lightning rod of all criticisms against Ming eunuchism. The Eastern Depot was first established by Emperor Yongle in 1420, with the sole purpose of preventing subversive activities in the newly founded capital city of Beijing. Prior to this time, a small group of officers from the Jinyiwei, or the embroidered-uniform guard, who were the emperor's bodyguards, were also in charge of intelligence gathering and general surveillance work. These officers were not attached to the five chief military commissioners or to the regular imperial guards, as they were specially assigned to spy for His Majesty, to silence political opponents of the emperor, and to stop vicious rumors. As time went on, however, Emperor Yongle was said to have doubts about the professionalism and efficacy of his bodyguards in handling intelligence work. He thereby turned to his most reliable and generally more vigilant castrated servants to supervise the Eastern Depot, which in time grew into a monstrous secret police apparatus and, in fact, survived until the end of the dynasty.[1]

According to Liu Ruoyu, a learned eunuch and a witness to the operation of the system, the Eastern Depot was located north of the Dongan Gate in the present-day Dongchang Hutong area and had a grotesque, intimidating physical layout. Its main buildings, in addition to a well, included an Outside Depot, an Inside Depot, and two detention centers, commonly called *Zhenfusi*, or torture chambers. The Inside Depot was used to detain the most serious and dangerous suspects, whereas the Outside Depot served to temporarily incarcerate those charged with lesser crimes. At the entrance of the Eastern Depot's main hall hung a plaque with four big Chinese characters, "Chao Ting Xin Fu," or "Heart and Bowel of the Court." Inside the main hall, one could easily see a portrait of Yue Fei (1104–1142), the legendary general of the Song dynasty, one who was noted for his martyrdom and loyalty to his state. There was also a sculptured fresco highlighting all kinds of fierce-looking animals. By custom, all the names of the eunuchs who had directed this agency were inscribed on a stele inside a shrine, located just west of the main hall.[2]

In the Ming autocracy, the Eastern Depot was theoretically under the direct control of the emperor, but like everything else in the Ming court, the emperor once again chose his trusted castrati to supervise the agency. Initially, the Eastern Depot was charged to investigate only treasonable offenses and carry out espionage on behalf of the emperor. However, throughout the years, its power grew like a giant octopus, extending to every corner of the empire and becoming the diabolical force behind the throne. Even though the director of the depot was always chosen from among the most senior members of the grand eunuchs, most of the investigating work was carried out by the officers from the embroidered-uniform guard. And in many cases, the eunuch participation generally amounted to little more than passive supervision. But by making guard officers and the eunuchs scratch each other's backs in the depot, the Ming autocracy also applied political dualism to its intelligence operation.

Under the eunuch director, there were a battalion commander, ranking 5a or 5b, and a company commander, 6a or 6b, both from the embroidered-uniform guard. Immediately below these two commanders were a number of foremen, section heads, and lesser officers, about forty people in all. The military officers in the depot wore special outfits and long boots, easily becoming the most feared secret police in Ming China as they tortured, maimed, and murdered countless innocent people. In fact, when it came to unmitigated evil and unrelenting ferocity, the Ming eunuchs did not always win the contest over their colleagues from the guard. In addition to these top officers, about 100 agents, known as service captains, were routinely sent out to obtain information and seek out conspirators. These captains were divided into twelve sections, and each of them in turn hired a large number of "inquisitors," similar to the FBI's informants, to do the dirty work. It is estimated that, by the end of the sixteenth century, His Majesty's ubiquitous secret police numbered over 1,000 persons.[3]

While his depot agents watched over troublesome imperial clansmen, ambitious military commanders, fastidious literati-bureaucrats, mysterious religious leaders, and greedy landlords, the eunuch director was in constant contact with the emperor. He kept the emperor informed of any unusual traffic observed at the city gates, fires and other incidents in Beijing and Nanjing, and overheard conversations that were regarded as treasonable offenses with a potential of instigating public sentiment against the throne. Whenever there was a worthy piece of intelligence, the director prepared a report and, before sending it to the emperor, sealed it by affixing the one and only Eastern Depot Secret Seal, which was made out of a big chunk of ivory. Regardless of the time of the day, such a report had to be delivered directly and immediately. Clearly, the intelligence gathering was not limited to military and political affairs, but covered a wide scope of activities. The depot agents checked out periodically the market prices of various foodstuffs, such as rice, beans, oil, and flour. They also reported agricultural and business conditions to the court. They went around Beijing almost daily, in disguise, canvassing the streets for suspects, visiting government offices, particularly the Ministry of War, and listening to and taking notes at the trials. In short, they provided His Majesty with all of the intelligence about the state of the empire.

As the secret police demonstrated their love for the emperor by flaunting their disdain for the rest of the populace, the Chinese people, both inside and outside the government, feared and detested their crudity and arrogance. Their revulsion at the Eastern Depot and its agents stemmed from the depot's unaccountable power and corruption, since its investigating activities often enabled its agents to operate outside of the regular bureaucratic channels. Sometimes the depot agents hired idlers to prowl around the country and report what they believed to be misdeeds to their eunuch superiors. A slight rumor was often sufficient for the depot to launch an investigation, even if the investigation had to take place inside the palace. Once an alleged misdeed was believed to have been committed, officers from the guard would be immediately dispatched to arrest the suspect and bring that person to the prison attached to the depot. More often than not, the guard officers would demand payment and bribes. If refused, the suspect always suffered torture and severe beatings.[4] The function of the depot prison was only to elicit confession, without which no one could be convicted. Given the Chinese notion that torture was a legitimate means of extracting a confession, the suspect would either confess or die under severe physical abuse. Once a written confession was signed by the arrested party, the Ministry of Punishment would then pass an appropriate sentence. Needless to say, there was no such thing as due process or civil rights protection under the system; and the guard officers, in collusion with their eunuch boss, repeatedly made a travesty out of Ming judiciary principles. Scholars who are critical of Ming despotism often conclude that because of the brutal and terrorist handiwork provided by the depot, the Ming emperor and his family could live in a soft cocoon of extravagant luxury and the regime founded by the Zhu family in 1368 was able to last until 1644.

Even though the eunuchs and the guard officers worked hand in glove to maintain the security of the emperor and his family, they were frequently at odds over the operation of the Eastern Depot. It was never clear whether the emperor's bodyguards were also castrati or exclusively normal military personnel. What was obvious was that a certain degree of distrust always existed between the eunuchs and the emperor's bodyguards. And if one group appeared to be intruding on the turf of the other group, a power struggle would take place in the Eastern Depot in the form of personality conflicts, creating a sort of gerrymandering madness. For instance, a forceful and domineering guard commissioner often demanded that suspects arrested by the depot be sent to the guard for retrial before the Ministry of Punishment could pronounce sentence. On the other hand, if the Eastern Depot was managed by a powerful, astute eunuch, the castrati would gain the upper hand in controlling the surveillance apparatus, likewise, artfully maneuvering the guard to play the second fiddle in Ming security affairs.

During its first fifty years of existence, the Eastern Depot was actually dominated by two embroidered-uniform guard commissioners, Ji Gang and Men Da. Not until 1477 was the grand eunuch Shang Ming, who was concurrently the director of ceremonials, appointed to manage the depot.[5] Even then, the emperor's bodyguards continued to carry more weight in the operation of Ming espionage and spy activities. This was evidenced by the appointment, in 1479, of a guard officer, Zhao Jing, to run the Zhenfusi, the prison attached to the Eastern Depot. Shang Ming, the depot chief, and Zhao Jing, the manager of the depot prison, clashed over the investigation of the misconduct of a court eunuch by the name of Jiang Cong. The eunuch Jiang was assigned to oversee an agricultural farm but, without proper authorization, clandestinely slipped back to the Imperial City. Jiang was caught by the secret police, but after a brief interrogation, the manager of the depot prison set him free. Shang Ming was aghast to learn about such a hasty decision but could only submit the case to Emperor Chenghua for final judgment.[6]

This incident suggests that the eunuch director of the Eastern Depot did not always enjoy complete authority in matters of prosecution and indictment. And the growing distrust between the eunuchs and the emperor's bodyguards should not be dismissed as an accidental blip in an otherwise serene relationship. From time to time, the eunuch director had to comb the ranks of the emperor's bodyguards, providing them with all kinds of sinecures. In 1482, for example, after the guard officer Li Yu had broken up a plot and apprehended its conspirators, the eunuch director Shang Ming immediately recommended to His Majesty that Li Yu be rewarded and given a promotion. Unfortunately, like thousands of other Ming officials, Shang succumbed to corruption and the practice of nepotism as he sold offices and got his brother appointed a hereditary guard officer.[7] He nevertheless managed to stay in his post until early 1484, when he was ignominiously dumped by his emperor. Shang was thrown in jail for allegedly committing many serious crimes, including mismanagement of the Eastern Depot, sending reports with fictitious details to the throne, and repeatedly seeking out the wealthiest of his victims for purposes of extortion. By customary practice, an official who was charged with these kinds of crimes normally would be out on his tin ear. Luckily for Shang Ming, however, his sentence was banishment to Nanjing. There, Shang Ming received 100 beatings with a bamboo stick at the hands of the Nanjing grand commandant before he was sent to attend to a vegetable garden in Emperor Hongwu's Filial Tomb.[8] Such was the fate of the first eunuch director of the infamous Eastern Depot.

SUCCESSIVE DIRECTORS OF THE EASTERN DEPOT

But if the story of the first depot director ended in farce, the story of the second eunuch director certainly ended in tragedy. After the fall of Shang Ming, Emperor Chenghua chose Chen Zhun, a native of Shunde, to direct the Eastern Depot. *Ming shi*, the official Ming history, which is known for giving the reader Confucian moral platitudes, has a brief but implicitly favorable comment on Chen's lifestyle and dedication to public service. As soon as he took over the depot, Chen instructed his agents to report every seditious act directly to him, and more important, to stop engaging in frivolous, heresay investigation and harassment. During his tenure at the depot, the inhabitants in Beijing were said to feel more relaxed and less frightened. Chen, however, was a close friend of another tragic eunuch, Huai En, who, because of his uncle's political problems, was castrated when still a child. Huai En, nevertheless, served his emperor heart and soul and managed to work his way up to become the director of ceremonials. But as the Chinese love to say, "serving an emperor is like serving a tiger"—one slip-up by Huai En was sufficient to incur the wrath of the ill-tempered Emperor Chenghua. Huai En was later tortured to death by the guard officers in the depot's detention center. Huai En's friend, the depot director Chen Zhun, was devastated by this event and indeed was caught in a quandary. While trying to please the unpredictable Emperor Chenghua and continuing to work with the guard officers, he also attempted to do a credible job of protecting innocent people from being victimized by the secret police. Unfortunately, in the final analysis, he could not reconcile with the wiles of the brute mongers and ended his life by suicide.[9]

By 1488 when the new sovereign Hongzhi ascended the throne, there were voices within the literati circle suggesting the abolishment of the Eastern Depot, but to no avail. Nevertheless, Hongzhi's court, which lasted until 1505, was less tainted with scandal, owing mainly to the new emperor's humane rule and magnanimous personality. Hongzhi indeed was a "model Confucian ruler," unaggressive, benevolent, and trusting of his civil officials.[10] The Hongzhi Veritable Record, which was completed in 1509, only mentions Yang Peng as the eunuch director of the Eastern Depot. One entry reports that, during Hongzhi's reign, everything in the government had to follow the established regulations and all sensitive issues were also processed through regular bureaucratic channels, with important decisions handled by civil agencies. Another entry in the Hongzhi Veritable Record reveals that the Eastern Depot often involved itself in tax payment and money matters. Yang Peng, to eliminate tax evasion, worked out a plan by which the circulated paper monies were classified into five categories, some to be retired while others were kept to trace counterfeit issues.[11]

Up to this point, the eunuch directors of the Eastern Depot did not appear to have enjoyed excessive power, nor did any secret police chief roil the calm waters of court politics. However, because of the outlandish personality of the next emperor, the intelligence agency would soon witness several scathing scenes. When his father died, Emperor Zhengde (1505–1521), who was not yet fourteen years old, became the occupant of the dragon throne. Full of energy, intelligence, and curiosity, the young emperor nevertheless preferred hunting, fishing, and martial arts to court audiences and state business. He also loved to drink and play games with his sycophants, enjoyed companionship with women of questionable reputation, and made extensive tours in the provinces. Worst of all, he frequently spewed insults on his subordinates. In the end, he died childless in his well-publicized pleasure chamber, called the Leopard House, at the age of barely thirty. With such a person on the throne, his secret police went rampaging around the country, and their abuses increased in brazenness as well as in number. Indeed, under Zhengde's reign, the notorious eunuch Liu Jin rose to eminence and virtually dominated the Ming court for five years. A native of Xingping county, Shaanxi province, and originally surnamed Tan, Liu Jin chose to have a "self-castration" when he was a small child and was adopted by a court eunuch named Liu. He was known for his quick mind and eloquence. During his early career, he was not pleased with his numerous assignments, including that of beating the night drums. He later was selected to serve Zhengde when Zhengde was a crown prince and his association with other "seven tiger eunuchs" began to form a power bloc. After he was promoted to work in the Directorate of Ceremonials, Liu started to gain more access to His Majesty. With the enormous power he wielded, many a Western scholar actually called him a *eunuch dictator*.[12]

During the autumn of 1506, the minister of rites Xie Qian and the Imperial tutor Li Dongyang plotted to remove Liu Jin and his cohorts, nicknamed "the Eight Tigers," from their positions. Xie and Li sought and received the cooperation of the depot director Wang Yue, who also believed that the Eight Tigers had bedeviled the young monarch. Unexpectedly, the minister of personnel Jiao Fang leaked the news to Liu Jin and his cronies, and the plot was aborted. Liu Jin knew that he was in a fight for his life; therefore, he used every trick he knew to win the young Zhengde to his side. Liu was soon appointed the powerful director of ceremonials, and one of his tigers was made director of the Eastern Depot, replacing Wang Yue. Then a horrific purge followed as several dozens of influential civil officials and eunuchs were either sent into exile or their names placed on the death roll. Wang Yue was driven out of Beijing and later hunted down by Liu Jin's hired assassins at the Grand Canal port of Linqing.[13]

During the next five years, Liu Jin used fear to gain wealth and consolidate his power. He, for instance, promoted over 1,560 guard officers and assigned them to important government posts. His record of grisly crimes against his political opponents and imagined enemies indelibly undergirds the legacy of eunuchism as a divisive strand of Ming history and political life. But, although his repulsive exploitation of the episode should serve as a sober reminder of the danger of the government of men, one should not bristle at the idea that the Eight Tigers were truly the entire eunuch population writ small. The salience of the issue was not the vast majority of the castrati, many of whom actually fell victims to Liu Jin's dictatorship. The real issue lies in China's deep-rooted dynastic traditions and despotic system.

Once Liu Jin became the director of ceremonials (1505–1510), he made Qiu Ju manager of the Eastern Depot, but also requested and received permission to add two new spy agencies in the Inner Court: Xichang, or the Western Depot, and Neixingchang, or the Inner Branch Depot.[14] This may sound ludicrous, but the Inner Branch Depot was actually established to watch over the embroidered-uniform guard, the Eastern Depot, and the Western Depot. This situation threaded Ming governmental agencies, intimidating and importuning as Liu's secret police indicted, convicted, and eliminated hundreds of civil officials, military personnel, court eunuchs, and common people. In the Zhengde Veritable Record, which was completed in 1526, there are two entries regarding the devious operations at the Eastern Depot. One deals with cloth tributes from the Yangtze River delta, which covered the rich city of Suzhou. According to a tax scale of the Ministry of Revenues, Suzhou and its vicinity had to pay at least 300,000 bolts of cloth annually. During the year of 1505, however, the imperial warehouses in the area were reported to have collected only 25,000 bolts, far short of the required amount. The Eastern Depot soon launched an investigation and demanded that the Ministry of Revenues collect 50,000 bolts of cloth every ten days and that any officials who had failed to meet the quota be arrested and prosecuted.[15] The second entry reveals a pattern of frequent promotions for Liu's secret police. For example, in 1507, Emperor Zhengde promoted eighteen Eastern Depot agents and added twelve piculs of rice to Director Qiu Ju's annual salary.[16]

Liu Jin was executed in the fall of 1510; Qiu Ju, the secret police chief, lost his job but survived the purge until 1521 when he was sent to burn incense at Emperor Hongwu's Filial Tomb in Nanjing. An entry in Zhengde's Veritable Record shows that by the spring of 1511 the eunuch Gong Hong was supervising the depot. However, one year later the grand eunuch Zhang Xiong had replaced Gong Hong as the secret police chief.[17] It should be noted that by this time both the Western Depot and the Inner Branch Depot had been suspended, making the Eastern Depot the only espionage and intelligence gathering agency in the Ming court. It should also be pointed that, during the unsettling period of 1510–1512, there were frequent changes at the top eunuch echelon, and it became clear that Zhang Xiong, who was later promoted to become director of ceremonials, was only a caretaker at the depot. For the next nine years, from 1512 to 1521, the eunuch Zhang Rui, previously manager of the Imperial Stables, would be running the Eastern Depot.[18] But like almost all of their predecessors, neither Zhang Xiong nor Zhange Rui would survive the death of their imperial patron, the Emperor Zhengde.

Before becoming the secret police chief, Zhang Rui had been in charge of firearms, supervised the imperial guards, and took care of the emperor's steeds and exotic animals. The first thing he did as the depot director was to request the Ministry of Public Works to renovate and refurbish the depot buildings and facilities, and the entire project was completed by the autumn of 1514. In the late summer of 1518, just a few months after the arrival of the first ever Portuguese envoy in Beijing, Zhang Rui escorted the coffin of an empress to a specially selected burial site. For his job well done, Zhang was rewarded accordingly.[19] However, soon after Emperor Zhengde died, in the early spring of 1521, both the secret police chief and the director of ceremonials Zhang Xiong were arrested and later indicted. The new emperor Jiajing took advice from a group of censors and sent the two Zhangs and at least three dozen other prominent court eunuchs either to jail or into exile, usually after severe floggings.[20]

Emperor Jiajing was of a violent disposition and, as discussed in previous chapters, became deeply engrossed in Daoist ideology and alchemy. While trying to curtail the power of his eunuchs, Jiajing most of the time withdrew himself to search for immortality, allowing his grand secretaries to run the government. His first depot director was the eunuch Bao Zhong, who asked for twenty new officers from the Ministry of War, instead of the emperor's bodyguards, to bolster his staff. But Bao's tenure was brief, and by the fall of 1523, the chief of the Eastern Depot was Rui Jingxian.[21] And perhaps because Emperor Jiajing had earned a reputation for severity in dealing with the eunuchs, the Eastern Depot did not run riot. In fact, the depot's sentences and even investigation activities were often challenged by other branches of the Ming judiciary.

The tripod of the Ming judiciary included the Censorate, the Ministry of Punishment, and the Court of Judicial Review, or Dalisi. Generally, cases from local magistrates had to be ratified by successive reviews up the administrative hierarchy to the Ministry of Punishment. Cases from regional inspectors and Provisional Surveillance Offices were reviewed by the Censorate, while cases originated from military units were sent through the five Chief Military Commissions at the capital. But all sentence records approved by the Ministry of Punishment, the Censorate, and the Chief Military Commissions had to be submitted to the Court of Judicial Review for final scrutiny. The Court of Judicial Review, functioning like the Supreme Court of the United States, would check the propriety of judicial findings and sentences. It could let stand the original sentence or return a case for retrial, but if the case involved the death penalty, it always requested a decision by the emperor.[22] However, since the eunuchs at the depot and the guard officers, who took confessions from the alleged suspects, worked so closely with the emperor, they often obtained information from the palace about the sen-

tences of a trial. If they opposed the sentences, the depot would send its officers to spy or arrest their opponents and then asked for a retrial. Sometimes
they even fabricated incriminating evidence in their own favor and transmitted this to the public court. Clearly, the operation of the Eastern Depot had
undermined the functionings of the Ming judiciary within its constitutional
ambiguity. As a consequence, there were numerous confrontations between
the censorial branch of the government and the depot.[23] During the reign of
Jiajing, the eunuchs did not always prevail, as the influence of civil officials
was on the rise and the depot's powers were substantially restrained. For once
its agents did not always make one squirm.[24]

Neither the Ming Veritable Records nor *Ming shi* records any activities
associated with the Eastern Depot during the period 1524–1548. By the
summer of 1548 we know the court eunuch Mai Fu was already directing
the spy agency. Mai appeared to have the full support of the guard commissioner Lu Bing and the good will of the grand secretary Yan Song. But there
was once again hue and cry from other ministries when Mai secured promotions for his brother and several guard officers. A supervising secretary from
the Ministry of Punishment, for example, gave his full spiel on why these
secret police personnel did not deserve promotions and honors. He pointed
out that Mai had already piled up plenty of privileges and honors and that
serving the throne was his duty and responsibility. Therefore, Mai should not
use his position to add more privileges and power to his family and cronies.
However, one imperial rescript, whoever had a hand behind it, did not
accept this line of demur and approved all the promotion recommendations
from the depot director. Mai Fu, who seemed to have mastered the art of
power politics, also promoted the sons and nephews of several of his collaborators, among them guard officers and civil officials.[25] Contrary to what is
often said, the three elements of the Ming government—the eunuchs, the
guard officers, and the scholar-bureaucrats—colluded more often than they
collided when it came to the sharing of political spoils.

Mai Fu managed to stay in his post for quite a long time, and there is
no record to indicate his disgrace or downfall as his predecessors all had to
suffer. By 1588 the new director of the Eastern Depot was Huang Jin, who
also resorted to nepotism and freely brought his own relatives to fill the ranks
in both the depot and the embroidered-uniform guard.[26] Huang Jin also represented the last eunuch director of the depot who served under the inordi-
nately long reign of Emperor Jiajing. The accession in 1567 of Jiajing's son
to the throne also witnessed the rise of a highly cultured eunuch by the name
of Feng Bao. The new emperor, known to his posterity as Longqing,
admired Feng Bao, a native of Shenzhou in present-day Hebei province,
who loved books, frequently played the flute, and was also a noted calligra-

pher. And if there was such a title as *model Confucian eunuch*, Feng Bao certainly would deserve it.

Feng Bao's distinguished career began as a student at the Neishutang, where he learned the Four Books and the Classic of Filial Piety from a number of Hanlin scholars. In 1538, he got his first job, working as a scribe at the Directorate of Ceremonials where he would spend the next fifteen years of his life, copying hundreds of thousands of official documents. Feng was widely regarded as a warm, diligent, and compassionate person. For his accomplishments, he was promoted in 1553 to the seals office where he was responsible for supervising the affixing of heavy volume of correspondence every day. The opportunity to gain real powerful position came in 1560 when the Emperor Jiajing made him a managing grand guardian, or Sili bingbi taijian, of the Ceremonial Directorate. Together with three or five colleagues, Feng was now directly in charge of the drafting and transmitting of imperial decrees and palace papers. For his job well done, Jiajing gave him a woven silk garment embroidered with python and a jade belt, plus an annual imperial rice stipend. Moreover, he was allowed to ride a horse on the palace grounds and to sit on a chair, given to him by the emperor, during his private audience with His Majesty. After the death of Jiajing, the new emperor Longqing asked Feng Bao to be his personal secretary and in 1567 made Feng director of the Eastern Depot while concurrently serving as director of the Imperial Stables.[27] Longqing became mortally ill during the late spring of 1572, but at his deathbed, Longqing handed to Feng, in the presence of several senior officials, two copies of the "imperial will." And before Longqing passed away, he also made Feng Bao the Sili zhangyin taijian or the grand guardian of the Seal of the Ceremonial Directorate, the highest position any eunuch could hope to attain. Moreover, Feng continued to supervise the secret police apparatus.

At this juncture, the new Emperor Wanli was only ten years old and the teen monarch really respected and listened to only three persons—his mother, the empress dowager Cisheng; the grand secretary and imperial tutor Zhang Juzheng (1525–1582); and Feng Bao. It is reported that when Wanli was still a child, he used to ride on Feng Bao's shoulders and even after he became the emperor he affectionately called Feng Bao his "Big Companion." Wanli's wedding in 1578, thanks to Feng Bao's meticulous arrangement, went without a hitch. Under these circumstances, Wanli generally wrote *Approved* or *Acknowledged* in vermillion ink on the rescript drafts prepared for him by Zhang Juzheng, leaving complicated phraseology and details to Feng Bao's staff.[28] Throughout his career, Feng Bao maintained an intimate relationship with the empress dowager Cisheng and worked closely with the famed statesman Zhang Juzheng. Also, unlike the feisty and brusque

Liu Jin, Feng Bao was discreet and unassuming and learned how to comb the ranks of not only the civil officials but also the guard officers.

Of all the eunuch directors at the Eastern Depot, Feng Bao was unquestionably the most effective and the most powerful, obviously due to his competence, access to the Empress Dowager, his command of Emperor Wanli's awe and affection, and the collaboration of Zheng Juzheng in the Outer Court. As the top dog of the Inner Court, Feng put all his political skills to work—skills acquired over a lifetime. Under Feng's management, the Eastern Depot added a new facility and enlarged its field of operation, but inevitably aroused the jealousy and suspicion of many officials as well as eunuchs. Sometime after Emperor Wanli got married, Feng Bao offered to resign, citing his skin diseases and back problems. Indeed, once he broke his right foot, and both his lung and heart required constant care by palace doctors. It would take a heart of stone not to be moved by the stories Feng cited in his resignation memorial. His request was denied. But soon after the death of Zhang Juzheng, an ineluctable power struggle began, and Feng Bao became one of its victims.

It happened near the end of 1582 when Feng's enemies, including several eunuch turncoats, started to sway Emperor Wanli, who was then barely nineteen years old, to dismiss his "Big Companion." A censor from Jiangxi province presented to the young sovereign a list of twelve crimes against Feng Bao, accusing him of "deceiving the emperor and preying upon the nation." The censor also charged that Feng Bao had become extremely rich by taking graft, but when the arresting officers took over Feng's household, they found nothing as fabulous or priceless as the informants had claimed. They did, however, confiscate some musical instruments and artwork of historical importance, the kind of collection a Renaissance courtier in Italy would have wanted to possess. Incidentally, they also took over grand secretary Zhang Juzheng's household and found his property to have exceeded that of the eunuch Feng Bao by several times in value. At any rate, Feng Bao was banished to Nanjing, and his brother and an adopted son, both of whom served as high-ranking military commissioners, were also arrested and thrown to jail. Feng died in Nanjing a broken man, while his brother and adopted son starved to death in the state penitentiary. Eight of his former assistants were also demoted to burn incense in imperial mausolea or do other odd jobs.[29]

The rise and fall of Feng Bao is a well-written script that testifies, without a shred of doubt, to the fundamental weakness of the despotic Ming system. Here was a man who loved history and had learned about all the pitfalls of wretched excess and who, during his sixteen years in power, tried not to repeat the same mistakes of his predecessors. But, in the end, even his own eunuch colleagues repeatedly grumbled in Emperor Wanli's presence that he wielded too much power. As had happened so many times before, when different factions failed to resolve the fight over how to devolve power, a velvet coup ultimately toppled the eunuch "dictator," sweeping yet another eunuch to the dictatorship of the Eastern Depot. His name was Zhang Jing and he was hungering to replace Feng Bao. The *Ming shi* strongly implies that Zhang Jing was instrumental in bringing down Feng Bao, but when Zhang was running the depot he was time and again impeached for accepting bribes from official circles and committing other serious transgressions. But the politically wily Zhang Jing was really acting as a fiduciary of Wanli, who had come across as out of touch and even flaky. When a supervising secretary accused Wanli of accepting gems and bullion from Zhang Jing, the poor junior official was whipped sixty strokes in front of the Meridian Gate of the palace. However, rumors of Zhang's corruption persisted, and even the high-ranking officials from Nanjing remonstrated to Wanli to dismiss Zhang. Finally, after staying as the secret police chief for nearly seven years, Zhang Jing lost favor with the now grossly obese Wanli in 1590.[30]

The eunuch appointed to succeed Zhang Jing was Zhang Cheng, who also served concurrently as director of ceremonials, a position Feng Bao used to occupy. By this time, Emperor Wanli had become tired of his morning audience and study sessions and had decided to suspend them permanently. During the next quarter of a century, from 1590 to 1615, Wanli refused to see his civil officials as a group and, worse still, left many offices vacant, thus by all accounts, paralyzing government operation. In the meantime, Zhang Cheng dominated the Inner Court and acted like a de facto ruler. But, even though Zhang Cheng tried to stay the course by not allowing his policies to stray too far away from those of his predecessors, he could not, in the long run, escape the same predestined fate of former eunuch "dictators," such as Feng Bao and Qiu Ju. By the spring of 1596, he had lost all his power and was to become another obscure servile eunuch at Hongwu's Filial Tomb in Nanjing. And as had been the pattern for a fallen secret police chief, his household property was confiscated, and all of his brothers and nephews were stripped of their titles and sent to prison.[31] After the downfall of Zhang Cheng, two other eunuchs, Sun Xian and Zhang Li, were appointed to direct the Eastern Depot, but not much information is available about their activities, except that the depot was growing quieter and the torture chamber not as busy as before.[32]

Near the end of the sixteenth century, the profligate and irresponsible Wanli had truly become an isolated, laissez-faire sovereign who lurched about in search of solutions to his mounting fiscal crises. Fortunately, the Ming Inner Court was managed by Chen Ju (1539–1607), generally regarded one of the noblest and the most admirable Ming castrati. Chen Ju was by nature a cautious, meticulous, duty-awed person, and when he had to make difficult decisions or deal with tricky personnel changes, he always followed a broad outlook and kept the big picture in mind. His magnanimous and humane management style stood starkly different from that of some of the brutal depot bosses who preceded him. A native of Ansu, in the Northern Metropolitan area, Chen Ju was castrated and brought to the court before he reached his ninth birthday. He studied Confucian classics and worked his way up the eunuch ladder and by 1583, one year after Feng Bao was banished, had climbed to the position of a recorder, holding a 6a rank in the court.

A glimpse of one particular event recorded by his subordinate Liu Ruoyu gives us a profile of a man who had a low-key demeanor and who understood the importance of humility when occupying an influential position. During the spring of 1591, Chen Ju received an order to deliver a convicted prince to the special imperial penitentiary in Fengyang, a prison constructed exclusively for confining royal clansmen. After discharging his duty, Chen returned home to pay respect to his ancestors but took pains to avoid the pomp and circumstance that local officials and townsfolk had offered him.[33]

Chen Ju was a voracious reader and a patron of arts and poetry, and because of such unique qualities, he was often charged with collecting rare and out-of-print books for the imperial library. He also loved to buy for himself old volumes, particularly those published during the Han, Tang, and Song dynasties and if they were unavailable, always attempted to hire specialists to print them. He had in his own collections the Thirteen Classics and the Twenty-One Histories and among his favorite readers included *Rites of Zhou Dynasty, The Great Learning,* and the *Book of Change.* It is very possible that through his influence and inspiration his own brother, Chen Wance, earned a doctorate in 1592. Almost every Ming document confirms that when Chen was directing the Eastern Depot, both the image and the real operation of the intelligence gathering had improved immeasurably. Chen generally dismissed heresay accusations and skirted seamy allegations brought to his office by anonymous informants. He also put in a new policy to minimize the use of torture and terror for extracting confessions from alleged suspects. As a consequence, the people of Beijing no longer feared Big Brother looking over their shoulders, and in fact the business at the depot had dwindled so much that "the court-yard in the torture chamber was overgrown with weeds."[34] For these and other laudable deeds, Chen Ju elicited universal praise from both the castrati and the literati in the Ming court.

But in the midst of this relatively clear sailing came the so-called Witch Book, a printed volume by an anonymous author. The book, among other things, dealt with the most sensitive imperial succession issue, as it suggested replacing the crown prince with the son of an imperial concubine named Zheng. When Emperor Wanli learned that numerous copies of the book were made available to most of his powerful officials, he was disturbed and immediately ordered his secret police chief to find out who was the real author of such a "treasonable" book. The intent of the "Witch Book" was simple: it attempted to stir up a political storm during Wanli's waning years. During the investigation, Chen diligently followed his well-kept motto: "Obey the dynasty's established laws and study the teachings from the sage and the wise."[35] And thanks to his wisdom and sheer force of personality, Chen Ju helped to restore calm to the court and avert a potentially bloody and even fatal power struggle. Emperor Wanli seemed to be satisfied with the way Chen handled the "Witch Book" case because two years later, in 1605, Chen Ju was made the concurrent director of ceremonials and, for all practical purposes, became the de facto ruler of the Inner Court.[36]

At the turn of the seventeenth century, the Ming civil officials in the Outer Court had degenerated into at least five fistic factions, creating an endless power struggle among the literati. The Inner Court, thanks to the leadership of the grand eunuch Chen Ju, had become quiescent and was generally free from scandal or dispute. It is difficult to assess to what extent Chen Ju brought his civility to influence the cynical Wanli, but a few stories recorded in *Ming shi* might serve as clues to their relationship. Once an administration vice commissioner offended Wanli and was about to receive humiliating open-court floggings when Chen admonished His Majesty to let the official go. On a different occasion, folks in Yunnan province, possibly outraged by heavy tax burdens, killed a eunuch tax collector. This type of news instantly incurred the wrath of Wanli, who wanted to arrest every person involved in the rioting. As soon as Chen learned that some 8,000 people would have to be jailed in Yunnan, he talked the emperor out of his rash decision. Chen's advice might possibly have prevented a riot from becoming a rebellion.

Chen Ju was also a patriotic and humane administrator. Several entries in the Wanli Veritable Record indicate that Chen's principal concerns had always been the livelihood of the people and the defense of the empire. He often worried about how to feed the hundreds of thousands of refugees created by natural disasters and how best to strengthen the city of Liaoyang so that Manchuria could withstand the attacks of enemies. Even by the highest Confucian moralist standard, Chen Ju was a rare shining spot in the tarnished pile of Ming eunuchs. He passed away in 1607 at the age of sixty-eight, one of the very few eunuch "dictators" who died of natural causes. Realizing that there were absolutely no political clouds hanging over Chen's head, Wanli conferred upon Chen a title of *Pure and Loyal* soon after his death.[37]

Chen Ju had been familiar with brush, ink, and paper since childhood and was a contemporary of Dong Qichang (1555–1636), China's most important painter, calligrapher, and art theorist of the past 500 years. Dong was considered the finest calligrapher of his time and one who established the so-called Southern School of amateur Chinese painting. Even though there are no records connecting Chen's interests in history and the arts with Dong's political career, a few bits of coincidence are important to observe. Dong passed his doctorate examinations in 1592, exactly the same year Chen Ju's brother, Chen Wance, got his doctoral degree. Dong was then appointed to the Hanlin Academy and later served as the tutor to the crown prince when Chen Ju was running the Inner Court. Moreover, Dong Qichang had become an avid art collector and a prominent historian, the kind of career the grand eunuch Chen greatly admired and always wanted to pursue himself.[38] It is impossible to ascertain to what extent did Chen's patronage of Dong help to bring about the genius of the master in his early career. It nevertheless should be noted that there were many well-cultured, talented, and civilized eunuchs who served their emperor loyally, wisely, and effectively. And a few castrati, like Feng Bao and Chen Ju, actually promoted arts and appreciated the importance of historical works.

The next prominent eunuch to head the Eastern Depot was Li Jun, who was deeply involved in a gold mine scandal and, by 1610, was expelled from his post. For the next eight years, we do not know who was the depot director, since neither *Ming shi* nor the Wanli Veritable Record provides any names or information. By the summer of 1618, however, we learn that Lu Shou was made the director of ceremonials and concurrently was in charge of matters in the Eastern Depot. Lu Shou had been Wanli's trusted servant for many years, but as soon as Wanli passed away in 1620, a host of censors, from both the provinces and the Chief Surveillance Office, began to attack Lu and demand his removal. But before Wanli's son, Taichang (also known as Emperor Guangzong) could make any decision on this matter, he promptly fell ill and died, leaving Wanli's fifteen-year-old grandson Tianqi to deal with the Inner Court personnel.

Upon his enthronement, the young Tianqi (also known as Emperor Xizong) was confronted with several threatening problems, including increasing military challenges from both within and without, a worsening economy, ceaselessly cannibalistic bureaucratic factionalism, and a hopelessly excessive number of castrati in his court. Nevertheless, by dismissing Lu Shou from the two most powerful eunuch posts, Tianqi seemed to desire a clean slate for his government. Lu Shou was later confined to the Fengyang penitentiary on account of numerous political transgressions, which had now become standard crimes for ex-eunuch "dictators."[39] Unfortunately, the person Tianqi chose to replace Lu was to become the crankiest of all the depot directors. He was Wei Zhongxian, and for the next four years, from the twelfth moon of 1623 to the end of 1627, a pall hung over the gateway of the Eastern Depot. The once indolent torture chamber was revived to become the most dreaded place for every Ming official, while the great Ming sank to its lowest point in morale and efficiency.

The humility and wisdom of the scholar-castrato Chen Ju was the obverse of Wei Zhongxian's folly and abuse of power. There were men who had known power and had used it with restraint, but power was Wei's ultimate aphrodisiac and he used it ruthlessly and relentlessly to promote himself and his cronies. As soon as he took over the secret police apparatus, Wei threw down the gauntlet to anyone standing in his way. He turned loose his agents, who brutalized their victims with impunity. Under Wei, the Eastern Depot once again became a place of terror, where countless civil officials and even eunuchs were cruelly tortured and an untold number of innocent people were slaughtered. Hundreds of Wei's henchmen prowled around Beijing and other cities like famished hyenas, constantly looking for prey. They in turn hired undesirable idlers as assistants to spy on people.[40]

The influence of Wei Zhongxian spread like a dye. There was widespread corruption and abuse at different levels inside and outside the court, among civil as well as eunuch and military personnel. His henchmen, now occupying important and lucrative positions, openly practiced extortion. But Wei's rise and fall parallelled that of Liu Jin almost 100 years earlier, with both of them irreparably sullying the image of Ming eunuchism. In the end, however, both Wei and Liu had to pay dearly once their patrons passed away. By the autumn of 1627, Emperor Tianqi suddenly died; his seventeen-year-old brother, Chongzhen (known also as Emperor Sizong and Zhuang Lei Di) took the throne, and soon retribution against Wei had begun. After three months of tense waiting, an imperial rescript came to remove Wei from his depot post and further ordered him to be confined in the Fengyang penitentiary.[41] As stated in the first chapter, Wei had already committed suicide before the order of dismissal could be delivered. By launching a large-scale purge against Wei and his associates and by restoring the rights to those who had been wronged at the hands of Wei's cronies, Emperor Chongzhen hoped to remove the fear that had hovered around Beijing for several years. However, it was too little and too late, because the Ming state system had deteriorated to an incurable condition. In particular, partisan bickering continued while domestic rebellions and Manchu threats intensified. In the meantime, the Ming economy was in a total shambles and its society filled with moral squalor.

During the reign of this last Ming monarch, at least nine eunuchs were appointed to direct the Eastern Depot, with an average tenure of less than two years for each. One possible explanation might be that Emperor Chongzhen, who was one of the better Ming rulers, was wary about another eunuch dictatorship. But, although he was willing to frequently rotate his top eunuchs from post to post, he was adamant in maintaining the existence of the depot. In 1642, less than two years before Chongzhen hanged himself on the Coal Hill behind his palace, a censor repeatedly urged the emperor to abolish the spy agency, citing all of the evils that had been associated with the Eastern Depot. But even as conscientious a monarch as Chongzhen was, he continued to rely upon the service of the depot for intelligence until the last days of his reign.[42] In particular, Chongzhen was extremely concerned about the revolts and conspiracies that had now become regular events. Notwithstanding the intelligence provided by the depot eunuchs, Chongzhen could not stop the inevitable. And after an existence of 276 years, the Ming dynasty finally came to an end in 1644.

But long after the demise of the Ming, the legacy of the 244-year-old Eastern Depot lingers on, leaving a trail of horror, cruelty, and controversy. When slogging through the debris of the depot records, one cannot help but be equally awed by the enigma of Ming China. Undoubtedly, eunuchs and their agents in the Eastern Depot had sent tens of thousands of people to hell and seriously undermined the integrity of Ming political and judicial functionings. Moreover, a number of eunuchs at the depot did exercise quasi-dictatorial authority to advance their wealth and power. On the other hand, all of the eunuch directors had to live in perpetual state of apprehension, verging on insecurity and uncertainty. We have seen how tyrannical emperors capriciously sent one eunuch director after another—some honest and some rotten—into disgrace, exile, or death. In the final analysis, the emperors controlled the organs of government terror, and many of them callously abused the organs. Nevertheless, the Ming survived, and at times even prospered, for more than two-and-a-half centuries—longer than the majority of dynasties in human history. To solve this enigma, one may need to look closer into the remarkable resiliency of the Ming dualistic system that required the indispensable service of the eunuchs.

THE WESTERN DEPOT

In addition to the much maligned Eastern Depot, Chinese historians also view the relatively short-lived Western Depot (Xichang) with chagrin and repulsion. The *Ming shi* states that Emperor Chenghua first established the Western Depot in the first moon of 1477. An entry in the Chenghua Veritable Record, which was completed in 1491, details how Wang Zhi, the director of the Western Depot, used terror to extort confessions from alleged suspects before handing them over to the judicial officials for sentencing.[43] This particular emperor stuttered so miserably that he was ashamed to receive the audience of his officials and avoided contact with them whenever possible. Perhaps because of his handicapped physical condition, Chenghua was well-known for his oppression and cruelty. The purpose of establishing the

Western Depot was originally to deal with a transvestite named Li Zilong, who was said to have practiced witchcraft and possessed magical powers. With the cooperation of a court eunuch, Li somehow managed to get inside the palace during nighttime, where he mingled with many a superstitious woman in the imperial harem. The paranoid Chenghua decided to set up the Western Depot in a dilapidated old lime factory and appointed the Grand Eunuch Wang Zhi to search for any witches or weird people capable of spreading malicious rumors.[44]

Wang Zhi was a Yao aborigine from Southwest China. After serving an imperial concubine for several years, Wang was promoted to head the Imperial Stables of the Inner Court. As director of the Western Depot, Wang proved to be a monster, but also, in his twisted way, a genius. He practiced the worst aspects of terror during his tenure. From time to time, he would disguise himself as a civilian and, together with a dozen or so imperial guards who were also disguised, went out to search for suspects. During his first five months in office, Wang had started several trails, apprehending the transvestite, breaking up a salt smuggling ring, and restoring calm in the palace. However, his peculiar way of surveillance also stepped on the toes of a few powerful officials. For example, when the minister of war Xiang Zhong refused to stay out of his way, the minister was insulted. Other officials and ordinary folks were so frightened by Wang's entourage that everyone hid as soon as they heard the depot agents coming to their vicinity. But as terrifying as the world of Wang Zhi in 1477–1478 was, he also proved to be an effective spy chief in that he had a meticulous system of collecting random bits of intelligence. He was like a vacuum cleaner, and his agents sucked every morsel of information they could find on the subjects of Emperor Chenghua's encompassing curiosity.[45]

But as Wang Zhi was digging through every scrap of information, true as well as false, and investigating any person whose words or deeds he disliked, fear and distrust also spread through the ranks of the elite preeners. Several high-ranking officials were appalled by Wang's highhanded tactics and began to bring impeachment charges against him and his agency. Among them was the grand secretary Shang Lu, who time and again admonished the emperor to abolish the Western Depot altogether. A distinguished scholar in his own right, Shang was the only Ming official of his time to have placed first at every level of the civil service examinations. He was also known for his simple lifestyle, tolerance, and decisiveness. In one of his memorials to Chenghua, Shang stated that the agents who worked under Wang Zhi had become ever more arrogant and reckless. Even though they claimed to be executing the emperor's secret orders, they frequently tortured and killed innocent people. It went on to say that ever since Wang Zhi took charge of the Western Depot, scholar-officials felt uneasy at their posts, traders and merchants felt unsafe attending to their businesses, and even the common people could not devote all their efforts to their jobs. The memorial concluded that if Wang was not let go, no one could be sure if the world would be at peace or in peril.

Emperor Chenghua was annoyed by such criticism and was said to have responded, "I merely use a castrato—how would that endanger the world?"[46] Nevertheless, many other influential ministers, including the minister of war Xiang Zhong, also repeatedly impeached Wang Zhi, enumerating Wang's misconduct and the harm brought about by the Western Depot. Facing so much relentless criticism, Emperor Chenghua agreed to temporarily suspend the operation of the depot. But shortly afterward, Chenghua had Wang Zhi reinstated as the director of a revamped Western Depot. This was during the summer of 1477, and scarcely had the grand secretary Shang Lu heard the news than he requested an early retirement.[47] Shang's request was granted, but fear and terror would once again spread to many parts of the Ming domain, as the personnel of the Western Depot now was double that of the Eastern Depot in its intelligence gathering endeavors.

Even since he was a young child, Wang loved martial arts and military science. During the autumn of 1479, an opportunity finally allowed him to engage in defense affairs. A special imperial order commissioned Wang Zhi to inspect the empire's garrison strongholds and frontier fortifications. Every day, accompanied by a large group of retainers, Wang rode several hundred li, gathering intelligence and sending detailed reports to the emperor in Beijing. Everywhere he went, local officials generally ingratiated themselves before him and lavishly entertained his party. During the autumn of 1481, the now-roving director of the Western Depot was concurrently commissioned as an imperial military supervisor with a mission of checking a Mongol advance on Ming's northern frontier. Wang Zhi scored a victory at Xuanfu and was handsomely rewarded. He was later ordered to go to Datong and continue his military assignments. But after a long sojourn in Datong, Wang gradually lost favor with the emperor. He was reassigned to head the Imperial Stables in Nanjing, a clear demotion and a disappointment for such a power-hungry person. And after another round of political quibbling, the Western Depot was once again shut down. Wang was further demoted to be an ordinary eunuch without office, and several of his former associates were also stripped of their ranks. Miraculously, however, Wang Zhi was able to escape any further punishment and died of natural causes, a rare ending for the once most feared spy chief.[48]

From the third moon of 1482 to the tenth moon of 1506, most of which time parallelled the reign of the benevolent Emperor Hongzhi, the Western Depot remained inoperative. Hongzhi obviously did not feel threatened by the alleged witchcraft, but most likely this righteous sovereign had decided that his court should not let the secret police tail wag the dog. Unfortunately, his successor, Emperor Zhengde, was too mired in his own selfish interests and pleasure pursuits to take into consideration the welfare of his people. As Zhengde delegated his powers to his chief eunuch Liu Jin, more and more security personnel were hired to sustain Zhengde's luxurious lifestyle. As a consequence, the Western Depot was reopened, and under the directorship of Gu Dayong, Liu's confidant, its power was in general equal to that of the Eastern Depot. Even though the hierarchy of investigative functions between the two depots was never clearly defined, both depots sent agents to the four corners of the Ming empire. But as the Ming intelligence-gathering apparatuses grew into a gigantic octopus, the Chinese people at large suffered. For instance, in 1508 three families in Jiangxi province who constructed several dragon boats for festival purposes were construed, by the depot agents, to be raising a rebellious navy, and the heads of the families were put to death. Even those who lived in remote towns and isolated communities were scared to death as soon as they saw uniformed strangers speaking the Beijing dialect and lingering in their counties. Often the village heads had to use bribery to buy peace and tranquility for their communities.

As Liu Jin and his associates used every trick in the book to maintain their power by pandering to Emperor Zhengde's whims, they recommended that a third security apparatus be established to counterbalance the increasing influence of the two depots and the embroidered-uniform guard. The upshot was the creation of the Neixingchang or the Inner Branch Depot, located in the Fire and Water Department (Xixinsi) of the Inner Court. With Liu Jin personally directing this agency, the reign of terror had begun.[49] Alleged suspects routinely received heavy beatings and, if found guilty, were either exiled to the frontier or put to death. Some "guilty" inmates were required to wear the humiliating cangu; many succumbed to the pressure of its weight and died a few days later. Among the victims of this insidious punishment were an imperial seal minister and his deputy, a vice minister of Public Works and a censor. Two other censors who were found committing only minor crimes were nevertheless strangled to death by the secret police. One source reveals that the number of both civilians and soldiers who died at the hands of the Inner Branch Depot agents alone amounted to several thousands.[50]

Liu Jin had made too many enemies. His dictatorship had provoked not only an outraged chorus among the street people, but also a united front among the civil officials. In 1510, Prince Zhen Fan of Anhua raised a rebellion in Gansu province, specifically using Liu Jin's usurpation of power as raison d'être. A eunuch commander, Zhang Yong, put down the rebellion and brought the prince and his top eighteen accomplices to Beijing for punishment. At this juncture, Zhang Yong suggested to Emperor Zhengde that Liu Jin must go. Since Liu Jin could not and did not reduce Emperor Zhengde to tutelage, the dandy emperor finally seized the political initiative in 1510, ordering the execution of Liu Jin and closing down both the Inner Branch Depot and the Western Depot. Fifty-seven agents from the Inner Branch Depot were also arrested, and five ranking guard officers were indicted.[51] However, the director of the Western Depot, Gu Dayong, had his life spared. In fact, two years later, Zhengde was tempted to ask Gu to refurbish the Western Depot for another comeback. This idea, however, received an immediate, strong opposition from the grand secretary Li Dongyang. Since then, the Western Depot disappeared from all Ming Veritable Records. The Inner Branch Depot was briefly reestablished during the reign of Emperor Wanli, but it amounted to nothing significant. The Eastern Depot reclaimed its investigative monopoly, and its agents executed what the Ming dualistic system required of them until the very last days of the dynasty.

VI

꙾

Eunuchs and Ming Diplomacy

MING TRIBUTARY SYSTEM

Eunuchs as envoys were unique Ming phenomena, but the extent to which they influenced Ming diplomacy was both unprecedented and unfathomable. At least 140 diplomatic missions headed by eunuchs were recorded in Ming documents. Emperor Hongwu was the trendsetter as he commissioned a eunuch-envoy to Korea in 1369, two to Mongolia respectively in 1374 and 1378, one such mission to the Ryukyu Islands in 1383, and four similar appointments to Southeast Asia during the last two decades of the fourteenth century. At the beginning of the fifteenth century as Emperor Yongle got the itch to explore Southeast Asia and the Indian Ocean, he churned overseas navigation into a frenzy and caused horrendous diplomatic activities in the region. The agents whom he entrusted to bring some two dozen "barbarian" states to the Ming orbit were exclusively castrated courtiers. Between 1402 and 1424, a total of seventy-five eunuchs were appointed to execute Ming foreign policy. Eunuch-envoys continued to play significant diplomatic roles throughout the first half of the fifteenth century, but after the 1460s, their activities were generally limited to bearing missions to Korea, which was required from time to time to reaffirm its allegiance to the Ming emperor.

The duties of the Ming eunuch-envoys ranged from rewarding rulers of the lesser states and investing in office new kings and crown princes to escorting statues of Buddha, attending royal weddings and funerals of the vassal states, and commanding punitive expeditions. Vassal states frequently visited by Ming eunuch-envoys included Annam, Champa, Hami, Korea, Mongolia, the Ryukyu Islands, Tibet, and Turfan. Other states that did not have the same degree of acculturation and geographic proximity to China were visited by Ming eunuch-envoys less frequently, some only once in ten years. Borneo, Burma, Cambodia, Java, Japan, Nepal, and Siam belonged to this category. Ming documents indicate that Chinese eunuch-envoys had also conducted state businesses in Aden, Bengal, Brawa, Isfahan, Khorasan,

Malacca, the Maldives, Mogadiscio, Palembang, the Philippines, Samarkand, and Sri Lanka.

The tributary system is the Chinese version of imperialism, not by territorial conquest or economic exploitation but by the control of ideas and cultural domination. The Confucian concept of diplomacy differed from its European counterpart, which stressed legal equality of nations and the sanctity of state sovereignty. In international relations Confucian family morality was applied as a guide for the preservation of harmony. As such, China, the superior "middle kingdom," was not equal to her peripheral states, who were considered younger brothers or children in the family of nations. China produced the dominant civilization from which the peripheral states derived much of their culture. States around China were civilized only to the extent that they accepted Chinese ideas, customs, and institutions and agreed to use the Chinese lunar calendar to date their official documents. Such an ideology also engendered a chauvinistic concept that China was a world in itself, not a nation among nations and that no other human authority was equal to the Son of Heaven in China. As a consequence, there was no need for treaties or agreements of any kind at the foundation of the tributary system. The core of the system was the periodic exchange of visits of state envoys and the requirement of the lesser states to recognize China's cultural superiority and political suzerainty.

This system called for the "half devil and half child" sullen peoples of the surrounding states to voluntarily submit themselves to the Ming overlordship so that they could gain cultural advantage, political prestige, military protection, and above all, economic benefits. Once a tributary relationship was established, China would abstain from any interference in the internal affairs of the vassal states. And in the event the vassal state was experiencing disorder among its people or being invaded, the Chinese would take up the yellow man's burden and "send forth the best yet bred" to serve and defend their neighboring vassals. However, in many cases when the lesser peoples had strayed from the proper rules of conduct or refused to send tributary missions to the Son of Heaven, force was the ultimate sanction. They were often treated sternly and even callously. This too was justified on moral grounds because a child or younger brother, when he or she misbehaved, required punishment for rectification.

But the tributary system was also a mechanism of trade and foreign aid in that imperial presents sent to vassal states in return for tributary demands were always far greater in value than those received in China. The Chinese did not regard foreign trade as a means of enrichment; therefore they rarely sponsored it. The lesser states, however, did seek trade, and they were quite willing to pay a token tribute, such as horses, ginseng root, ramie cloth, furs, and straw hats, in return for lucrative trade privileges. Such indeed was a strong economic incentive that had drawn many peripheral states to the Chinese orbit. A case in point was the regular imperial presents sent to the rulers of Korea and the Ryukyu Islands. They often included such precious things as gold, platinum, books, medicines, porcelain ware with handsome patterns, and the highly prized woven silk garments, embroidered with sacred birds and animals. On special occasions, Ming emperors even gave magnificently embroidered five-clawed dragon robes, which gave immense prestige to the recipients, including the Sultan of Malacca, rulers of Tibet and Java, the Sheriff of Mecca and rulers of other smaller states in Southeast Asia and Central Asia. Moreover, the Ming government permitted the tribute missions to bring products for exchange and to purchase goods through Chinese officials. In this sense, the tributary system should be regarded as a subsidy by the Ming government. So far as the Chinese were concerned, it was uneconomical. However, this was a small price to pay so long as the Chinese, in the fullness of their strength, could set their mark upon "barbarian" lands and so long as the system secured for China peace and security! And the people who helped make this system work were mostly eunuchs.

The Ming tributary system had an auspicious start. It was established at the right time, when there was a power vacuum in East Asia. Korea and the Ryukyu Islands first recognized Ming as their overlords in 1368, and they were soon followed by Nepal and Burma respectively in 1384 and 1385. In the ensuing years, the tributary system also embraced both China's land frontiers and her maritime borders. At the height of the development of the system, some thirty-eight states regularly sent tributary missions to the Ming capital. In 1564, a Ming cartographer, Shi Huoji, drew two large maps, one describing countries of the "barbarians" of the eastern and southern seas and the other identifying countries of the "barbarians" of the southern and western seas. The compiler of these maps seems to have a good grip on accurate information regarding a vast number of names of places, and generally confirms what the Ming chroniclers had to say about the Ming tributary states. Since its inception, the Ministry of Rites was in charge of tributary operation. Carefully regulating all communication between the tributary states and China, the Ministry meticulously mapped out tributary routes either by land across Central Asia via Hami or through such designated sea ports as Guangzhou (Canton) and Ningbo. The ministry, in cooperation with interpreters provided by the Ministry of War, was also in charge of the reception and entertainment of tributary missions at the capital where they were received in restricted quarters and entertained and briefed according to status. Tributary envoys, of course, were given ritual feasting and were coached on the terrifying kowtow ceremony, which was considered nothing more than polite behavior in the circumstances. After all, Chinese ministers were also required to perform this ritual when they presented themselves to the Son of Heaven.

THE MONGOLS AND THE TIBETANS

During the early years of the Ming dynasty, the decline of Mongol power was followed by the inevitable exodus of able people toward greener pastures. The Mongols' best administrative brains left for other tribes of the steppe. They had for a long while lost the expansionist drive of their ancestors, and the once fearful Mongol cavalry was limping like a severely wounded bull. This allowed the Ming armies time and again to penetrate into the homeland of the Mongols and to take their enemies prisoners of war by the hundreds of thousands. Some of the POWs, including a Mongol prince, were exiled to the Ryukyu Islands in the same fashion as Oliver Cromwell treated prominent Irishmen when he shipped them to Barbados in 1649.[1] But even though the Ming's archenemies had split up into the Tartars (Eastern Mongols) and the Oirats (Western Mongols), the Mongols remained a formidable threat, since there was no restricted territory on which they could not trample. They often appeared in Liaodong, Datong, Gansu, Yanan, and Ningxia and utilized hit-and-run tactics against the Chinese. Chinese officials and priests, who were commissioned to the desert to perform funeral rituals so that the souls of fallen Ming soldiers could rest, were often captured and detained by the Mongols. In the meantime, skirmishes and petty wars of reprisal continued, and there was no end to the obscene killings and appalling savagery.

The Ming leadership did not want to fight the Mongols every inch of the way, as it had proven to be too costly. Instead, it sought a way to harness the exhausted but unyielding enemy by a divide-and-rule policy, and even by appeasement and bribery. Over a period of twenty years, the invidious Emperor Hongwu tried to reach an accord with the Mongols and to break barriers to restore tranquility north of the border. In 1374, Hongwu appointed two eunuch-envoys, one Chinese and the other Mongol, to achieve some kind of detente with the Mongols. A theme of conciliation ran through the whole mission as Emperor Hongwu sent to the Mongol chief silk robes with raised patterns in gold and silver. As a gesture of good will, he also returned an expatriated Mongol prince. In the winter of 1378, Emperor Hongwu once again appointed a eunuch-envoy for a peace mission.[2]

During Yongle's reign, a total of thirty-five eunuch missions were launched beyond the Ordos, nine led by Hai Tong to negotiate with the Oirats, five by Li Da to encourage states in Central Asia to look toward the Ming instead of the steppe overlord. Other missions, two led by Lu An, one each by Guo Jing and Yun Xiang, and even the more celebrated missions by

Hou Xian to Tibet, were all aimed at dealing with the Mongol problems because of their repeated attacks on Western Inner Asia, the southern oases of the Taklamakan desert, and Tibet. Emperor Yongle, whose mother, ironically, was believed to be of Mongol stock, personally led five expeditions into the steppe. In 1410, for example, he led over 100,000 troops and used cannons to defeat the Mongols. Again in 1422, Yongle commanded a punitive army of 235,000 strong and pushed the nomads out of their desert strongholds. But though Yongle's campaigns had blunted the military power of his steppe enemies enough to remove the immediate danger of a renewed Mongol invasion of China proper, they did not result in subjecting them to the Ming rule. The game of war, therefore, was followed by the game of diplomacy, and the eunuchs became the peacemakers. Entrusted by their emperor, most of these people had the inner toughness of men who came up the hard way but also had the social graces that made for easy conversation and negotiation.

The most important mediator between the Chinese and the Oirats was the eunuch Hai Tong, of whom the Ming chroniclers provide no background. In 1412, one of three Oirat chieftains by the name of Mahmud detained a number of Ming envoys and announced his intention of repatriating the Mongols in Gansu and Ningxia. Upon hearing this news, Emperor Yongle was outraged and, on February 26, 1413, dispatched Hai Tong to not only rebuke Mahmud but also to secure the release of all Ming detainees.[3] As Hai Tong was unable to accomplish his mission, Emperor Yongle, in the summer of 1414, decided to teach Mahmud a lesson by force. His army broke the Oirat defense resistance, killing more than a dozen Oirat nobles and taking thousands of Mongols prisoners of war; however, Mahmud's escape dimmed the joy of the Chinese victory.[4]

In keeping his view of war as an acceptable extension of diplomacy but not as an end in itself, Yongle wanted his chief diplomat Hai Tong to carry out a divide-and-rule ploy. Throughout the conflict, Hai Tong remained in the steppe, attempting to achieve at least two goals. First, he cemented a strong bond with Mahmud's chief rival, a Tartar leader by the name of Aruytai whose relations with the Oirats had frayed. Hai Tong used the instant gratification of the profit motive, giving the Tartars rice, sheep, and donkeys to seal a marriage between Aruytai's Tartars and the Ming Chinese. Second, Hai Tong mobilized his other wherewithal to prevent other Oirat chieftains, in particular Taiping and Batuboluo, from joining Mahmud's coalition. Hai Tong's divide-and-rule ploy was soon to bear fruit as Mahmud, effectively cut off from other Mongols, agreed to a new rapprochement and stopped raiding Chinese settlements along the northern and western frontiers. In the end, Mahmud not only released all of the Ming detainees, but agreed to pay tribute to the Ming emperor.[5] By 1415, Hai Tong indeed had accomplished his goals, and his skilled diplomacy might also have caused Mahmud's son, Toyon, to kill Aruytai in the later Mongolian fratricidal feud.

During the early fifteenth century, the Tartars were constantly feuding with the Oirats. They, in fact, had Mahmud assassinated in 1416. But the Ming court did not give short shrift to the Mongol problem, and Hai Tong once again found himself wheeling and dealing—this time with Mahmud's son, Toyon. During the spring of 1418, Hai Tong accompanied a special Oirat embassy to China, requesting and receiving for Toyon, the title of Shunning Wang, or Obedient and Tranquil Prince. All told, Hai Tong made a total of nine missions to execute Ming policy in the steppe. During the spring and summer of 1417, Hai Tong made two trips to the loessial borders to win over the warlike and potentially troublesome Oirat chiefs, who were then eager to curry favor with Ming China in hope for future economic aid. Again between the spring and fall of 1421, Hai Tong traveled the dusty roads to effect a reconciliation between the Chinese and the Mongols.[6]

The year 1421 was significant not because Hai Tong disappeared from all Ming records, but because the Ming government moved its capital from Nanjing to Beijing. For the next few years, a truce prevailed in China's northern border and the Mongols exchanged wool, camel hair, and hides for Chinese silks, cotton fabric, salt, tea, and rice. The maintenance of the northern frontier was turned over to the Ming's vassal Mongols who, to preserve their trade privileges, refused to join the more hostile Mongols beyond the Gobi Desert. Such a truce was, however, extremely fragile, and whenever the Ming government could not satisfy their demands, the warlike Mongols would toss the olive branch to the winds and renew raiding Chinese territory. In 1439, Mahmud's son Toyon died and his grandson Esen took over the Oirat leadership and began to gather the Mongol remnants into a confederation. At the height of Esen's power, 1439–1455, the Oirats expanded from the Ili basin into the Turfan and Kucha region, threatening again Ming border security. The Oirat's boundary now stretched from Kale Balkhash to Lake Baikal, and from Baikal to the approaches of the Great Wall. Karakorum, the former Mongol capital, became their possession, and Hami, a Ming tributary state, was run over by their cavalry. Esen also occupied Shazhou, in present-day Dunhuang, married its princess, and in 1445 seized the Ming frontier region of Wuliangha, which corresponds to later Jehol. During the winter of 1446, Esen came to Datong, requesting food stuffs.[7]

During the Ming dynasty, Datong was one of the so-called nine priority frontier fortresses. Located along the great northern loop of the Yellow River, Datong's defense barriers included a brick wall with stone foundation, forty-four watch towers on the wall, 580 stands for bow and arrow attack, and a suspension bridge across a moat ten feet wide and five feet deep. Beyond the main city were three smaller walls, about three kilometers in length, facing north, east, and south. During the Ming period, Datong was indeed an impregnable fort and had earned a reputation of having a "gold city and soup pond."[8]

At the time Esen was threatening the Yellow River loop, the grand defender of Datong was another forgotten eunuch by the name of Guo Jing. Before Guo was promoted to his post in Datong, he had served in various positions in government security affairs. It was obvious that Guo enjoyed the emperor's confidence and was therefore dispatched in July 1420 to Herat, in present-day Afghanistan, and Samarkand. Assisted by a scholar-diplomat named Chen Cheng, Guo Jing also journeyed to Badakhshan and Khotan and presented imperial messages and gifts to several rulers in Central Asia.[9] As the grand defender of Datong, Guo Jing was often involved in the tribute trade and the Mongol affairs, since Datong had become the border town through which the Mongol tribute missions had to pass before they could continue their journey to Beijing. Guo Jing had to see that no troublemakers, no merchants disguised as envoys bearing tribute, and no hostile tribal representatives were allowed to enter China proper. At the same time, he had to do everything possible to befriend the Mongols, to soothe them, and not infrequently to quarter and entertain his Mongol "guests."

Guo's refusal of Esen's request in the winter of 1446, however, had apparently wounded the Oirats' pride, as Esen returned to raid Datong in the summer of 1449. The Emperor Zhengtong went to Datong to battle Esen and suffered a disastrous defeat, losing more than 100,000 soldiers. In fact, Esen took the emperor prisoner at Tumu fort in northwest Hebei province. Three months later, Esen took his troops all the way to the northwestern outskirts of Beijing, but was repulsed by the Ming defenders. Soon afterward he released Emperor Zhengtong (1450) and three years later made peace with the Ming court. As the Chinese granted more privileges of holding fairs for trade with the Mongols, Esen agreed—until his assassination in 1455—to be a vassal of the Ming. But from about 1530 until 1583, a new Mongol chieftain, Altan Khan, again harried the central part of Shanxi and even burned the suburbs of Beijing. A distinguished warrior, Altan Khan plundered Datong and devastated Ningxia during 1529–1530. But while constantly ravaging the Chinese border towns and repeatedly demanding more barter of Mongol livestock for Chinese merchandise, Altan Khan also found spiritual solace in Tibetan Buddhism. Through the bonds of Buddhism, the Mongols and the Tibetans had for centuries shared a feeling of affinity. The Chinese were aware of such bonds and thereby tried to use the good office of the Tibetan lamas, who had great influence on the Mongols, to calm the Mongol marauders and remove the threat that had bedeviled several Ming emperors. The celebrated missions by the eunuch Hou Xian to Tibet, from

1403 to 1427, and other eunuch-led missions should be examined in such a historical context.

The history of Tibet is also a history of Buddhism. When the Tibetan ruler Song-tsen-Campo founded the sacred city of Lhasa in 639, he also built 180 Buddhist temples. Despite the high mountain barriers, Tibetans developed contact and established relations with the northern pastoral population of Mongolia and the agricultural communities of China and India. By the eighth century, Tibetan Buddhism had already developed its own Mahayana characteristics, mixed with miracle, magic, and mysticism. Since the late thirteenth century, the princes and abbots of Tibet had always depended on the Mongol emperors, who were then the rulers of China. Toward the end of the fourteenth century, an eminent religious reformer, Tsong-kha-Pa, established a new sect called the *Yellow Hats,* to distinguish it from the old sect called the *Red Hats.* The priests of the Yellow Hats followed a much stricter moral code and practiced celibacy. Tsong-kha-Pa's third successor, Sonam Gyatso, spread the new faith in Mongolia and converted the Ordos Mongols and their chief. In 1576, Sonam Gyatso, who was supposedly reincarnated from Tsong-kha-Pa, went to the Ordos, and Altan Khan conferred on him the title Dalai Lama Vajradhara. Dalai means ocean in Mongolian, thus implying one whose wisdom and knowledge is as deep as the ocean.[10]

Ming shi says that the purpose of Hou Xian's embassies to Tibet was to invite the Buddhist hierarch Halima, who was said to have possessed magic power, to Nanjing. But on further investigation, this might not have been the only purpose. By the early fifteenth century, the Tibetan lamas were known to command the obedience of the converted Mongols on spiritual matters. Emperor Yongle's chief motive was probably to cultivate good relations with the Tibetan lamas so that the Mongols could be tamed. At any rate, in the spring of 1403, when Hou Xian received the order to Tibet, he bore the title of deputy grand eunuch of the Directorate of Ceremonials and was accompanied by a prominent Buddhist monk named Zhi Guang. They went by land, possibly via Sichuan, or else following the Silk Road to Khotan and from there crossing the mountains to Lhasa. Even though no travel journal was available, we know that they traveled tens of thousand of li and did not return until 1407. It should be noted that at this time there were several abbots residing in different Tibetan monasteries and Halima was not the only one Hou Xian and his associates visited. But it was Halima who came to Nanjing with Hou Xian. The Emperor Yongle was obviously pleased with the occasion, as he promoted Hou to grand eunuch and gave a state banquet in honor of Halima at Fengtiandian, or the Respect Heaven Hall, the tallest palace building. Several members of the imperial family, including the empress, received blessings and spiritual guidance from Halima, who spent almost half a year in China. In the meantime, Hou Xian was ordered to accompany Admiral Zheng He on Zheng's second and third grand maritime expeditions.[11]

While Hou Xian was sailing through the Malacca Straits and exploring the Indian Ocean, other court eunuchs were being ordered to Tibet and Nepal for diplomacy, trade, and exchanging Buddhist scripts. Of all the Ming eunuch-envoys who were sent to the Himalayas, Yang Sanbao ranked next only to Hou Xian. Yang's three missions established good roots there, and as the years rolled by, relations between Tibet and the Ming grew stronger and stronger. Yang's first mission took place either before or during 1413, his second mission in 1414, and his last embassy in the late autumn of 1419. He visited several monasteries and won over many princes who subsequently pledged their allegiance to the Ming. It was very likely that Yang's first mission also took him to Nepal, whose king was later invested by Hou Xian. As a practice of tributary mission Hou Xian awarded the king of Nepal a seal of gilded silver and a patent. It was, however, not clear whether Hou Xian was joined by Yang Sanbao at the investiture ceremony.[12]

In 1415, Hou Xian was once again ordered to the region. This time he went by sea, first to Bengal, then to other South Asian states. As usual, Hou awarded their rulers with rich imperial presents he brought from China. In 1418, another court eunuch by the name of Deng Cheng brought a load of brightly hued brocade and satin to the King of Nepal. But not all eunuch missions were sent only for ceremonial or religious purposes. Hou Xian's 1420 mission was actually to defuse a conflict between Bengal and its neighboring state Jaunpur. Hou not only successfully prevented a war in South Asia, but also amended a rupture between Saifu-d-Din, ruler of Bengal, and Ibrahim, his adversary and king of Jaunpur. Hou Xian's last mission to the Himalayas took place in 1427, three years after the death of his patron, the Emperor Yongle. Hou Xian clearly was a man who had greatness thrust upon him, and his mission of good will was once again marked with flying colors. In fact, more than 460 people who were directly or indirectly involved with this mission received promotions and rewards. There is no question that Hou Xian was a man of courage, great ability, and high intelligence. The Ming chroniclers, in a rare show of fairness to the castrati, lauded Hou Xian's career and ranked him only next to Admiral Zheng He among the eunuchs of this period.[13]

Other court eunuchs who were dispatched to Tibet and Nepal included Qiao Laixi in 1424, Song Cheng in 1434, and Nguyen Zhi in 1437. Ming official history provides very little information on these missions, except to list the abbots and princes who received Ming imperial gifts, ranging from silks and platinum to images of Buddha, utensils for Buddhist temples and religious rituals, and gowns and clothes for monks.[14] *Ming shi*, nevertheless, gives us a fairly detailed account of the scale and travel route of one particular eunuch mission to Tibet. In 1515, Emperor Zhengde learned that a certain Tibetan lama could tell one's previous lives and was eager to bring him to Beijing. Zhengde was barely fifteen years old when he ascended the throne in 1506, but after almost ten years of reign he still had no sons and was anxious to meet with this holy man who could tell him about his past and his future, including the question of imperial succession, and appointed the court eunuch Liu Yun to head such a mission to Tibet.

Marching under colored banners decorated with pearls and jewelry, Liu's party left Beijing and followed a tribute route to Linqing, of Shandong province, a port city connecting the Grand Canal. It was said that Liu's party was so large that it caused the traffic in the Grand Canal to come to a halt. After reaching Nanjing, the mission sailed westward along the Yangtze River. Liu's boats formed a 200 li long line and some of his bigger ships could barely pass through the three Yangtze gorges. When they arrived at Chengdu, the capital city of Sichuan, his party had consumed 100 piculs of rice a day and spent 100 taels of silver on vegetables alone. And for bartering for Tibetan wool, furs, and medicinal herbs, Liu first requested 200,000 silver taels worth of goods, but after the protest of Sichuan officials, agreed to take some 130,000 taels worth of tea, salt, barley, brocade, and so on with him. After nearly one year's preparation, Liu Yun's party crossed the high mountains into Tibet.

Liu Yun's party, among several Buddhist monks and interpreters, also consisted of 10 military officers and 1,000 soldiers. After the two month journey, the embassy reached the targeted monastery. But the holy lama, clearly terrified by the heavily armed Ming mission, went into hiding and refused to see Liu Yun. Growing increasingly impatient, the angry Chinese threatened to chasten the Tibetans with force. The originally well-intentioned mission ultimately turned into an ugly sight when one night, the Tibetans attacked the Chinese, looting their weapons and treasure goods. Two of the Ming officers and several hundred more Chinese soldiers were killed or wounded. Liu Yun managed to escape to Chengdu unharmed, but this sordid episode would ricochet far beyond the Sichuan-Tibetan border. By the time Liu Yun returned to Beijing, Emperor Zhengde, Liu's master and protector, had passed away without issue. For the first time in Ming history, a prince from a lateral branch of the imperial family was chosen to be the Son of Heaven, as historians usually do not count the succession from Emperor Jianwen to his uncle Yongle. He was Emperor Jiajing, and literati who supported his succession took advantage of the occasion to terminate the influence of the castrati. Jiajing immediately ordered the punishment of Liu Yun and his associates. Liu Yun's extravagant and wasteful mission thus provided the necessary ammunition for the scholar-courtiers to fasten their moorings. The battle cry, "eunuchs should not meddle in government affairs, including diplomacy," was heard all over again. As a consequence, Ming chroniclers gave Hou Xian only two brief epigrammatic paragraphs while they presented a lengthy, acerbic criticism of Liu Yun's failed mission.[15]

While Hai Tong and Hou Xian were busy courting the Mongols and Tibetans, a Ming eunuch of Manchurian stock, Yishiha, also quietly carried the guidon in the exploration of Northern Manchuria and Eastern Siberia. In 1375, the Ming dynasty established the Liaodong Regional Military Commission at Liaoyang, using twenty-five guards (each guard consisted of roughly 5,600 soldiers) to control Southern Manchuria. In 1409, six years after Yongle ascended the throne, he launched three campaigns to shore up Ming influence in the lower Amur River valley. The upshot was the establishment of the Nuerkan Regional Military Commission with several battalions (1,120 soldiers theoretically made up a battalion) deployed along the Songari, Ussuri, Khor, Urmi, Muling and Nen Rivers. The Nuerkan Commission, which parallelled that of the Liaodong Commission, was a special frontier administration; therefore the Ming government permitted its commanding officers to transmit their offices to their sons and grandsons without any diminution in rank. In the meantime, the Ming court periodically sent special envoys and inspectors to the region, making sure that the chiefs of various tribes remained loyal to the Ming emperor. But the one envoy who was most active and played the most significant role in the region was the eunuch Yishiha.

Yishiha belonged to the Haixi tribe of the Jurchen race. The *Ming shi* provides no background information on this Manchurian castrato except that Yishiha worked under two powerful early Ming eunuchs, Wang Zhen and Cao Jixiang.[16] It is also likely that Yishiha gained prominence by enduring the hard knocks of court politics and serving imperial concubines of Manchurian origin, as Emperor Yongle kept Jurchen women in his harem. At any rate, in the spring of 1411, Yongle commissioned Yishiha to vie for the heart and soul of the peoples in Northern Manchuria and Eastern Siberia. Yishiha led a party of more than 1,000 officers and soldiers who boarded twenty-five ships and sailed along the Amur River for several days before reaching the Nuerkan Command Post. Nuerkan was located on the east bank of the Amur River, approximately 300 li from the river's entrance and 250 li from the present-day Russian town of Nikolayevka. Yishiha's immediate assignment was to confer titles on tribal chiefs, giving them seals and uniforms. He also actively sought new recruits to fill out the official ranks for the Regional Commission.[17]

Two years later, in 1413, Yishiha undertook a second mission to the area, bringing with him large quantities of foods, clothes, and agricultural tools. That mission did a great deal to mollify some of the tribes who continued to make contact with the Mongols. Yishiha stayed there for nearly a year, during which time he artfully maneuvered his trusted Jurchen friends to leadership positions. And by constructing a Buddhist temple called *Yunning*, or Forever Tranquil, Yishiha also attempted to convert the Oroqens and other ethnic groups of the region into Buddhism. In 1414, he ordered the erection of a stone monument near the Yunning Temple on which he scribed his major activities in four different languages—Chinese, Mongolian, Jurchen, and Tibetan. During this mission, Yishiha also visited Sakhalin Island and was said to have conferred a Ming title on a tribal chieftain there. And according to a stone monument found in an old shipyard of Jilin City, Yishiha probably undertook another mission around 1420, as he used many of the Jilin ships to transport grain and utensils to the Nuerkan region.

By 1420, Yishiha's experience, character, record, and judgment had certainly made him not only an expert on the frontier defense of the region, but also might have well provided him a coat of armor that protected him against jealous and wily court rivals. His next mission to the Nuerkan Command Post ended in 1425 as he and his party were awarded by Yongle's successor, the Emperor Hongxi. During the reign of the fifth Ming sovereign, Emperor Xuande, Yishiha was dispatched at least three more times to the lower Amur River, inspecting, spreading imperial will and Ming policies, and reporting on the frontier defense and general conditions of the region. In 1432, when the commissioner in chief Kang Wang retired, Yishiha escorted Kang's son Kang Fu, who resided in Beijing at the time, to assume his inherited position. A party of 2,000 soldiers and an armada of fifty big ships arrived at the Siberian frontier fortress during the summer season. Almost immediately, Yishiha ordered the refurbishing of the Yunning Temple and the erection of yet another stone stele to commemorate the occasion. All told, Yishiha had made a total of nine missions to this desolate but strategically important region, pacifying the minority groups and serving as Ming's expansionist agent.[18] Yishiha was later promoted to grand defender, or zhenshou, of Liaodong and received an annual salary of forty piculs of rice in 1444. Three years later, he was awarded an annual increment of thirty-six piculs of rice as a consequence of a memorable military campaign.[19]

It is clear that Ming's missions to Tibet and Siberia had both religious and political motives; namely, to enhance Buddhism and to isolate the warlike Mongols. This policy continued into the late sixteenth century when Emperor Wanli, grandson of Jiajing, and his chief minister Zhang Juzheng openly discussed how to use the good office of the Tibetan lamas and the influence of Buddhism to harness the marauding Mongol warriors.[20] However, it was quite apparent that Buddhism alone could not deter the Mongol raids, which continued to cause instability on China's northern and western borders. This led the Ming policy makers to search for a further flank that could provide support to withstand the attacks of the nomads. Ming's diplo-

matic activities to the Taklamakan desert and Central Asia were also designed
to contain the marauding Mongols, but the eunuch-envoys who were commissioned to execute this policy were less publicized than those sent to Tibet
and Nepal.

EUNUCH MISSIONS TO CENTRAL ASIA

However, winning the states in Central Asia to the orbit of the Ming empire
proved to be both difficult and expensive. For one thing, the area was ruled
by the Moghuls, a mixture of Turks and Mongols whose overlord Tamerlane
claimed to descend from Genghis Khan. For another, the long desert crossing
and the small patches of physically isolated oasis states made it extremely difficult for the Ming court to maintain a long-term, reliable relationship with
them. Nevertheless, if their Han and Tang ancestors could do so well, then
the Ming Chinese certainly could do so also, not necessarily to penetrate and
dominate its inhabitants by armed force, nor to follow the humiliating "silk
and women" policy practiced by early Han rulers, nor even to purchase
peace with gold and silver as Song emperors often did, but to formulate a
unique system that would benefit both parties.[21] After all, it was economically profitable to the states in Central Asia if they became Chinese trade part-
ners and political allies. They needed silks, tea, and porcelain from the Chinese, while they could sell the Chinese such items as metalware, jade, gold,
horses, delicacies like raisins, and slaves. The Ming policy makers also found
that control and protection of trade often brought handsome revenue to the
rulers of the region and that Chinese luxuries were the most valuable gifts in
negotiating alliance terms.

Against the backdrop of such a political strategy, Emperor Hongwu, as
early as 1385, sent Fu An and Liu Wei to obtain the homage of the rulers in
Hami, Kara-khoja (Turfan), and Ilibaligh. At this juncture, Tamerlane more
than once sent embassies to Nanjing bearing tribute gifts, in 1387, 1392, and
1394. In return, Hongwu despatched Fu An to Samarkand with a letter of
thanks addressed to Tamerlane. After the deaths of Hongwu and Tamerlane,
their sons and successors, Emperor Yongle and Shahrukh, kept the relations
going. The agents who were employed to do the job were once again primarily court eunuchs. In the spring of 1407, Emperor Yongle selected two
eunuchs, Ba Tai and Li Da, to follow the paths of Zhang Qian, the great
explorer and diplomat of the Han dynasty. The Ming official history mentions that Li Da was sent five times to Central Asia, but provides very little
information on Li Da's social and political background. Fortunately, during
Li Da's third mission, he was accompanied by two civilian officials, Chen
Cheng (d.1457) and Li Xian (1376–1445), who kept a rare travel journal and
submitted a written report to the court after their return. These documents

described what they saw, heard and did during the trip and outlined the topography, local products, and unique customs of the places they visited. Students of Ming history call these reports "the most important source for the situation in Central Asia during the early Ming period."[22] Naturally, Chen Cheng, a vice director of the Bureau of Honors in the Ministry of Personnel, and Li Xian, a bureau secretary in the Ministry of Revenues, deserved all the credit the Ming chroniclers had given them. But once again nothing was said about the chief envoy Li Da, who displayed the kind of integrity, courage, and endurance that was the hallmark of Ming eunuch-envoys.

Li Da's first diplomatic mission, taking place in the spring of 1407, was to deliver Emperor Yongle's message and gifts to the prince of Bish-baliq, a powerful nomadic tribe dominating an area west of Hami, east of Samarkand, south of Oirats, and north of Khotan.[23] During the summer of 1408, Li Da was once again ordered to return to the region, venturing further west to a state in modern Afghanistan, Badakhshan. Badakhshan, located northeast of present-day Endekhud, was at that time a thriving commercial center, where merchants from the Pamirs region came to trade goods regularly in its fairs. Li Da's first two missions, obviously fruitful for everyone concerned, served to spread the news that the Ming court was eager to establish contact, commercial as well as political, with Central Asian states. Consequently, more and more states from the region, such as Herat, Andekan (Endekhud), Lukchak, Kara-khojo, and Kashgar, sent their envoys, bearing tributes and official credentials, to Nanjing. Some of them brought horses, lions, and rare animals to the Ming court.[24]

By the 1410s, all kinds of foreign delegations were doing business in the Ming capital. Whether it was the diplomatic norm of the time or was simply Emperor Yongle's personal diplomacy, he chose Li Da and two civilian officials, Chen Cheng and Li Xian, to escort the return trip of several Central Asian envoys. Not much was known about Li Xian's experience, but Chen Cheng was a seasoned diplomat, having been Ming's representative to Annam and having also served as assistant commissioner of foreign affairs in Guangdong. This mission, Li Da's third to the Western region, was to be documented, thanks to Chen Cheng's travel journal. All told, it took the mission 269 days, from February 3 to October 27, 1414, to reach its final destination, during which time the Ming envoys visited nineteen states and places.[25]

There are no records as to how many people took part in this journey, but judging from the distance they had to cover, the gifts they had to carry, and the degree of difficulty of logistics, the mission must have included substantial numbers of soldiers, interpreters, medical and religious personnel, and experts—all of whom were needed to lead a huge caravan across thousands of miles of desert and treacherous mountains. Horses, carts, food, and other necessities were also required for survival during the risky trip. The mission, conducted under brilliantly colored silk banners, started from Suzhou in Shaanxi province, took four days to cross the westernmost pass of the Great Wall, then began the difficult desert journey westward. On the twenty-fifth day, they arrived at Hami and the party spent five days camping at a nearby orchard. Braving the relentless desert wind for ten days, Li Da's caravan arrived at the historical city of Gaochang, a nearby fortress of Kara-khojo and a staging post along the Silk Route. They rested for four days before continuing their journey toward Kara-khojo or Turfan.

By the time they arrived at Turfan, the Chinese envoys had spent fifty days and nights on the dusty and barren desert, but the reward was to enjoy Turfan's delicious grapes and melons. Passing through the world's second lowest depression, 505 meters below sea level, was not an easy task and, for the next two weeks, Li Da and his associates struggled amidst the rocky cliffs and hostile terrain. Occasionally, they saw desert rivers with shifting channels banked by elm, poplar, and palm trees. For the most part, however, it was plain desolation and lifeless salt marsh. For almost a month during the spring of 1414, they skirted the northern rim of Tian Shan, the Heavenly Mountains, which range 19,500 feet high and 1,850 miles long all the way from China's Turkestan to Russia's Central Asia. By the late spring, their journey was slowed down by heavy snow which blocked most of the mountain passes.

On the 125th day of their journey, the Ming mission reached Almalik (Almaligh), which means in Turkish "a place producing fruit." It was, however, barely half of the distance of the entire journey even though Li Da and Chen Cheng had already traversed over 3,000 miles. On the 139th day, they made their way to the Issyk-Kul Lake, in present-day Kirghiztan. They camped near the lake and later continued westward along the lake for two more days. On the 161st day, Li Da's party entered Yanghi, in the present-day Kazakhstan Republic of the former Soviet Union. For the next several days, they were to dust their feet in the valley between the Amu River and the Syr River, but they realized that in only twenty more days they would reach Samarkand, Central Asia's most important political and cultural center. As a matter of fact, the authorities of Samarkand sent officials to receive the Ming envoys, who felt relieved that they had gone through the most difficult part of their journey. In their 171st day, they arrived at Tashkent and had the chance to relax for two days.

On the 175th day of their journey, the Chinese came to the shore of the Syr River, and since they had only five or six boats to ferry personnel and baggage, they decided to have their horses swim across the river; many of them unfortunately died by drowning. Two days later, they made their way to the state of Shahrukhia and presented to its governor valuable gifts they had carried with them all the way from China. They were now in Uzbek territory, and after sleeping in tents for 185 nights, they finally arrived at Samarkand. It was a rich and exotic city. The Ming envoys saw a magnificent mosque and several buildings covered with thousands of blue-glazed tiles. It was late summer and Li Da's party, after taking care of all official business, elected to spend ten days in Tamerlane's capital city.

By the time the Ming envoys arrived at Samarkand, Tamerlane had been dead for nine years and his fourth son, Shahrukh (ruled 1405–1447), was then the most powerful ruler in Transoxiana and Iran. He, however, established his capital at Herat, which had replaced Samarkand as the center of Islamic piety (Sunni orthodoxy). Naturally, the Chinese had to go to Herat to seek an audience with Shahrukh. As such, they now traveled toward the southwest and on their 200th day, they arrived at Kez, the birthplace of Tamerlane. Kez means "blue city," but Tamerlane actually built a white palace to enhance the luster of this green and beautiful city. From Kez, the Chinese travelers turned straight southward and, within ten days, made their way to the Amu River. They camped for two days on the shore and, on their 125th day, arrived at Badakhshan. After safely escorting home several foreign envoys, the Chinese returned to Kez and within a week came to Endekhud. While the Ming envoys had no difficulty mapping their route, they could not easily find the whereabouts of the most important person they wanted to see; namely, Shahrukh. At one point, Li Da and his associates had to wait in a mountain village for half a month, but missed him entirely. Finally, on their 269th day of the journey, they came to Herat. Chen Cheng's travel journal did not mention whether or not they were received by Shahrukh; however, we know that the Chinese embassy did not return to China until November of 1415. We also know that, in 1417, Shahrukh sent Ardashir Togachi to the Ming court and that in the ensuing years he and Emperor Yongle exchanged several embassies.[26]

The mission to Transoxiana was indeed an exhaustive and expensive diplomatic endeavor in money, time, and wear and tear on the body and spirits of Li Da and his associates. No record indicates how many of Li Da's staff perished along the harsh steppe or how many yards of silks were munificently bestowed on the Moghul leaders. It would appear that both Li Da and Chen Cheng, the principal officers, had fared well enough to warrant reappointments for future missions. In fact, before Li Da could warm his seat at home, he had to scurry back to Samarkand and Herat in 1416. While Chen Cheng could take a longer rest, he too was ordered to escort yet another group of tribute envoys on their return trip to Central Asia. Chen's mission, as usual, was directed by a court eunuch. This time it was Lu An, and they spent the months of April and May 1417 in Herat. Approximately one-and-a-half years later, during the winter of 1418, Li Da was preparing for his fifth and final journey to the same seventeen states he had visited earlier. It is safe to say that, during the decade of the 1410s, one eunuch-led mission was always going to or coming from Herat every year.

The twenty year period between 1405 and 1425 represented the heyday of eunuchs' diplomatic activities, thanks to Emperor Yongle's bold expansionist foreign policy. But Yongle died in the summer of 1424, and within the next decade Central Asia gradually declined in importance, at least in the eyes of the Ming policy makers. During this decade, Ming records show only ten such missions, half of them sent to Hami for relatively short and easy journeys. Also during this decade, Yongle's successors tossed a wet blanket on a plan to build large ships for Admiral Zheng He's maritime expeditions. They also closed down several tea-horse exchange markets, such as the one along the Yunnan-Annam border. In the same vein of strategic consideration, fewer and fewer envoys were sent to frequent the Silk Route states.

Historians can only surmise the reasons behind such a drastic shift in Ming's foreign policy towards the steppe states. Certainly, there was a change in the Ming leadership, and perhaps these missions were too costly. It was also possible that the Ming policy makers by the 1430s believed that the nomads of the steppes, though superb horsemen and warriors, were no match for the Chinese armies equipped with the latest firearms and cannons and that Central Asia no longer could play the role of intermediary vital to the Chinese-Mongol rivalry. It was also likely that the scholar-officials decried the ballyhooed eunuch successes in diplomacy and persuaded Yongle's successors to stop these missions. But, whatever the reasons behind the discontinuance of the Silk Route embassy, the Ming eunuch-envoys had proven to be effective mediators and skilled goodwill messengers. They were most suitable for their unique and astonishing assignments.

MING EUNUCHS AND CHINESE-KOREAN RELATIONS

Since the turn of the twentieth century, Zheng He and Hou Xian have become two of China's most honored historical persons, and their expeditions certainly are the most publicized diplomatic activities of the Ming eunuchs. But while Hou Xian and Zheng He's stories had human faces, the several dozen Ming eunuchs who were commissioned to Korea received neither effusive accolades nor were their names mentioned in the *Ming shi* under the rubric of court eunuchs. When searching through the various Ming Veritable Records, however, one can easily discover that the Ming court, in an artful and unobtrusive manner, heavily relied upon eunuchs in conducting diplomacy with Korea. They show that the Ming court, from 1369 to 1634, sent more than forty eunuchs to Korea in at least thirty-one separate missions. As a consequence of these missions, the relationship between the two East Asian nations was one of uniqueness, intricacy, and typically Confucian values. And although Ming's relations with the Mongols were always precarious, those with Annam often tenuous, and those with Southeast Asian states short lived, her ties with Korea were strong, stable, and long lasting.

Even before the Ming rose to power, Korea often used the term *sadae*, or serving the great, to confer legitimacy on the authority of a new regime and its ruler. And before General Yi Songgye installed himself on the throne of Korea in 1392, the Ming emperor had already used eunuchs as diplomatic agents in dealing with Korea. In the summer of 1369, for instance, Emperor Hongwu delegated a Korean-born eunuch, Jin (Kim in Korean) Liyuan, to escort home some 160 displaced Korean nationals. During the mission, Jin carried with him Hongwu's message and gifts to the king of the Koryo dynasty.[27] In fact, cultural exchange between the two countries became more frequent, and the Koreans continued to learn from the Ming Chinese in how to improve their cotton cultivation, medical knowledge, and the manufacture of firearms and gunpowder for their various kinds of cannon. One prominent eunuch who was often dispatched to Korea was Huang Yan who went to Korea first in 1373 and again in 1409 and 1419.[28] It would not be difficult to compare Huang Yan's shrewdness with Hai Tong's astute diplomatic skills in dealing with the Mongols, Li Da's endurance in Central Asia, or with Hou Xian's courage demonstrated in his missions to Tibet. All of these eunuch-envoys seemed to be extremely ingenious in serving their emperors. Thanks to the unflagging efforts by people like Huang Yan, the most crucial issue between the two countries—Ming's insistence on establishing a garrison in the Hamhung plains north of the Iron Pass in 1388—did not lead to wars along the Yalu River. Instead, with good intelligence from Huang Yan and others, Ming was able to defuse a potentially disastrous conflict.

Scarcely had Yi Songgye established the Yi dynasty (1392–1910) before he sent a huge tribute mission to Nanjing, asking to be a Ming vassal. Yi delivered the seals of the Koryo (Wang) kings to Nanjing and requested new seals with Choson or "Morning Freshness" for the name of his new dynasty. And to ease any suspicions concerning his loyalty, the general was fain to dispatch his eldest son to Nanjing where he explained the whole "usurpation" situation to the satisfaction of Emperor Hongwu. Hongwu was well aware that, during the Hamhung crisis of 1388, General Yi opposed the policy to invade the Liaodong region of Manchuria, and that he marched his army back from Wihwa Island in the mouth of the Yalu River. Throughout the next two-and-a-half centuries, the Yi dynasty of Korea displayed unwavering loyalty to its Ming overlord, while China stood by Korea through weal and woe. And as the kings of Yi dynasty ingratiated themselves to Ming eunuch-envoys, Sino-Korean borders had become market places instead of war zones.

At first, Korean tribute missions were sent to the Ming court once every three years, but they gradually increased in frequency, often to three times a year. Such missions served to offer felicitations on the occasion of the lunar New Year, to congratulate the Ming emperor on his birthday, and to honor the birthday of the imperial crown prince. Other missions were dispatched to mark the passing of the winter solstice, to mourn the death of the emperor, or to attend the investiture ceremony of a new empress. Since the tributary relationship was a two-way street, the Ming court had to reciprocate by sending envoys for various purposes, in particular, the enthronement of a new Korean king. For example, in 1419, Ming emperor Yongle dispatched court eunuch Huang Yan to invest General Yi's twenty-two-year-old grandson, Sejong (1418–1450), as the new king of Korea. In 1423, King Sejong wished to install his eldest son as the crown prince and requested Yongle's blessings and official sanction. A Ming eunuch by the name of Hai Shou was delegated to Korea to officiate the ceremony.[29]

After the Ming capital was moved to Beijing, Korean missions to China and Ming missions to Seoul could now travel by land, from Manchuria to Beijing, instead of by the more precarious sea route. Like other foreign guests, Korean envoys were quartered in the Huitong guan, or International Inn, in Beijing while the Ming envoys were housed at the Inn of Great Peace, just outside the South Gate of Seoul. Consequently, more Korean tribute horses were remitted to China and, by the same token, increasingly larger volumes of Chinese publications and calendars were brought to Korea.[30]

But Korean cultural accomplishments should not be read as a metaphor for her dependence on China. The Koreans had indeed demonstrated their indigenous creativity. Take metal printing for instance—even though the Chinese had the use of movable type since the eleventh century—the Koreans were the first in human history to have extensively used this technology. "Chuja," or cast type as it was called, was known to Korea as early as 1232, but the general use of movable type began in the year 1403, nearly fifty-two years before Johann Gutenberg brought forth the first Latin Bible printed with movable type. Between 1403 and 1484, the Korean royal family sponsored eight gigantic printing projects by movable type. In fact, one may speculate that it was the Koreans who had made available this technology to Ming eunuch-envoys and their Emperor Yongle, who was then compelled to outspend his vassal in printing books.[31]

During the second quarter of the fifteenth century, Ming eunuchs Yin Feng and Chang Sheng not only served to bring the two Confucian states politically closer, but also helped to open up the treasures of Chinese and

Korean literature to one another. Korea and China exchanged remarkable ideas and books on religion, philosophy, history, morals, science, and technology. Yin Feng's missions, in 1424 and 1425, brought to Korea samples of China's best literature. His two other missions were to install new Korean kings, Munjong in 1450 and Sejo in 1456.[32] In his latter missions, Yin was accompanied by Korean-born eunuchs who were also serving the Ming court. Several Ming eunuchs with the surnames of Jin (Kim in Korean), Zheng (Chong), and Cui (Ch'oe) were often assigned to escort aging Korean women who were brought to the Ming palace at a young age, but who now wished to retire to their native home. Jin Xin, Zheng Tong, and Cui An were among the most prominent Korean-born eunuchs who won the confidence of their Ming masters and were entrusted with important missions to Korea, their native land. Jin Xin was either the chief envoy or associate envoy in five separate missions, in 1452, 1456, 1465, 1483, and 1485; the last mission was to install Yonsangun (r.1494–1506) as the crown prince of Korea. Zheng Tong's name appeared in at least five embassies to Korea, including the 1468 mission to invest the new Korean king Yejong (1468–1469). Other Korean-born eunuchs who rose to powerful positions included Jin Fu, Li Zhen, and Jin Yi during the first quarter of the sixteenth century. They often served as liaison officials between Seoul and Beijing.[33]

Throughout the fifteenth and sixteenth centuries, relations between Ming China and Yi Korea indeed went on smoothly, despite the unsettled boundary question in the Yalu and Tumen regions. However, one nagging problem constantly irritated the Korean court. This problem had to do with General Yi Songgye's paternal identification. According to the *Da Ming huidian*, or the Great Ming Administrative Code, published in 1511, Yi In-im, a notorious anti-Ming rascal, instead of Yi Cha-chun as claimed by the Korean government, was the true father of General Yi Songgye. The Korean government time and again requested that such a "misunderstanding" be corrected and that the Yi royal lineage be clarified in official Ming documents, but the Ming authorities turned a deaf ear to such repeated appeals. In fact, it was to become a thorny diplomatic issue between the two states, and not until 1587—nearly two centuries of protest—did the Ming government agree to insert a footnote into a new edition of the *Da Ming huidian*.[34] Eunuch-envoys who had intimate relationships with Korean leaders, such as Jin Yi and Chen Hao, were more sympathetic to the Yi royal family on this problem, but their pleas were generally rebuffed by the neo-Confucian literati who compiled the official Ming documents.

Soon after the sore spot over General Yi's genealogy was removed, the Yi dynasty faced its most formidable challenge from without. In 1587, the Year of the Pig, Toyotomi Hideyoshi, the ruler of Japan, sent an embassy to Korea, calling for an alliance in his attack against Ming China.[35] Through a eunuch intelligence network from the Ryukyu Islands, Emperor Wanli of China had learned of the rumor of a Korean-Japanese alliance and immediately inquired about it as the Korean policy makers stalled and delayed the Japanese request. The Korean bureaucratic elite at this time was splintering into irreconcilable factions, and King Sonjo (1567–1608) was a weak and wavering leader. Nevertheless, Sonjo replied to Emperor Wanli, telling the facts of his choice which were also his answer to Hideyoshi's letter.[36] "What talk is this of our joining you against China? From the earliest times we have followed law and right. From within and from without all lands are subject to China. . . . When we have been fortunate China has rejoiced and when we have been unfortunate she has helped us. The relations which subsist between us are those of parent and child. This you well know. Can we desert both emperor and parent and join with you? You doubtless will be angry at this and it is because you have not been admitted to the court of the emperor instead of harboring such hostile intents against him? This truly passes our comprehension."

It is impossible to ascertain to what extent the Korean-born eunuchs influenced King Sonjo's decision to turn down the Japanese request. But the refusal inevitably brought about disaster for Korea. The years 1592 and 1597 witnessed massive Japanese invasions of the Korean Peninsula. No eunuch heroes were mentioned in either Chinese or Korean documents, but the Korean admiral Yi Sunsin and the Ming general Li Rusong (1549–1598) were forever immortalized by their nations. Yi's famed turtle ships, the world's first ironclads, repeatedly defeated the Japanese naval forces. Li, a descendant of a Korean family that had lived in Liaodong for six generations, garnered enough firepower and personnel to expel the Japanese from both Pyongyang and Seoul. It cost the Ming government more than 7 million silver taels to defend Korea, and as the Ming government was broke, its empire was being broken up by the bandits from within and the Manchus from without. In 1628, the last Ming emperor Chongzhen ascended the throne, but the dynasty was about to run its course.

During the waning years of the Ming dynasty, the Ming court continued to dispatch eunuch-envoys to Korea for routine ceremonial purposes and also for dealing with yet another threat from the rising Manchus. But in 1610, when the Ming eunuch-envoy Ran Deng was dispatched to Seoul to invest a crown prince, he learned that outside the walls of each principal Korean city on the prescribed routes to Seoul, there were specially maintained lodges for Manchu officials. When Ran Deng arrived in Seoul, he and his entourage were, as usual, quartered at the Inn of Great Peace, just outside the South Gate of the city. But he soon learned that a Manchu embassy was lodged at the so-called Jurchen Inn of Northern Peace, inside the East Gate of the city. The Ming envoy realized that the Korean government had done all it could to physically separate the Ming embassy from that of the Manchus.[37]

Clearly, the Yi dynasty had begun to vacillate between the old but weakening Ming overlord and the new rising power of the Manchus. In 1625, Ming eunuch-envoys Wang Min and Hu Liangfu came to Korea to ask for a large sum of silver and ginseng roots, only to experience a lukewarm reception. Ming was now too weak and too poor to help the Koreans resist their northern enemy. A few months after Wang Min and Hu Liangfu returned to Beijing, the Manchus launched their first invasion of Korea. And in 1636, the second Manchu invasion took the royal family prisoner and forced King Injo (1623–1649) to capitulate. By the terms of the surrender, Korea vowed, among other things, to sever its ties with Ming and dispatch troops to assist the Manchus in their campaign against Ming. Actually, two years before the Manchu conquest of Korea, the Ming court sent its last eunuch mission to warn the Korean king not to stray from the policies of his predecessors. This eunuch was Ling Jining who, after traveling through northern Korea, instinctively knew that nothing except a miracle could save the relationship that began nearly two and a half centuries earlier.[38] Nobody knows what Ling Jining reported to his emperor, but we all know that Ling's master, Emperor Chongzhen, committed suicide on the approach of the rebels, exactly ten years after Ling Jining's mission to Korea.

In this chapter we have discussed several dozen diplomatic missions conducted by eunuchs during the Ming dynasty. Unfortunately, during the past 350 years, with the exception of Zheng He and Hou Xian, almost no Chinese historian deemed it important or worthy to study them critically or give them a fair shake. Of all the reasons why eunuchs rarely elicited the praise of Chinese historians, the most important and the most exasperating was the tendency of literati to promote other literati in Chinese annals. Since the scholar-officials monopolized the writing and publishing of history, they felt comfortable dealing with versions of themselves. Often they did not feel comfortable with sharp-edged and allegedly self-indulgent, fat castrati. So it came as no surprise when the Ming chroniclers diminished the importance of eunuchs like Hai Tong, Li Da, Huang Yan, and so many others who bumped their heads against a glass ceiling of literati myopia. As a consequence, eunuchs' brusque competence, which abounded during the Ming period, never projected exemplary images of them as the focus of historical discourse. Good images and meritorious deeds were always reserved among a cozy coterie of scholar-officials who simply cut eunuchs out of the loop.

VII

❊

Eunuchs and Ming Maritime Activities

EUNUCHS AND THE MING MARITIME TRADE

Ming's policy toward Central Asia and Korea represented only one aspect of its grand design to incorporate all the neighboring states into its tributary system. In addition to the overland missions, numerous maritime missions—again directed mostly by court eunuchs—came from and went to Ming vassal states during the late fourteenth and fifteenth centuries. To facilitate its operations, the Ming government established three maritime trade superintendencies in Quanzhou, Ningbo, and Guangzhou for its vassal states to send cargoes for exchange with Chinese goods. It also specified the frequency, number of ships, goods, and personnel of tribute mission allotted to each vassal state. For operational control, the Ming government prepared a series of numbered paper passport tallies, usually 200 for each vassal state. They were torn from four stub books and sent to each vassal state ruler while the eunuch superintendent in the port of entry retained the stub books and the provincial administration office kept a duplicate copy. Such passport tallies and stub books were always replaced with new issues whenever a new emperor was enthroned. When a tribute mission arrived at the designated port, its envoy and staff members were quartered in the government hostel. Guangzhou, for instance, had a facility with 120 rooms, Quanzhou had 63 rooms, and Ningbo had 36 rooms. The envoy first presented his king's official message, often inscribed in gold leaf, and the eunuch superintendent meticulously recorded the numbered tallies against the stub books in his office. After a satisfactory verification, the eunuch superintendent would entertain his "guests" while immediately reporting the arrival of the tribute mission to the Ming court.

Tribute goods generally consisted of both "official tribute" and "private cargo," the former to be sent to the emperor while a portion of the latter, after paying a 6 percent commission, could be sold or bartered at the port of entry. The eunuch superintendent always bartered the best 60 percent of the cargo on behalf of the Ming government and let the foreigners sell the rest to licensed Chinese merchants.[1] The tribute mission, not to exceed 150 people, then was required to send part of its mission and portion of its cargo to the Ming capital. The Ming government would pay all their travel expenses and also provide horses, boats, or other means of transportation. However, its travel itinerary, including routes, dates, and stop stations, had to be reported and approved by the Ming authorities. After their arrival in the capital, officials from the Ministry of War would check their identification documents and quarter them in the Huitong guan, or International Inn. Actually, there were two inns, one in Nanjing (Southern Inn) and the other in Beijing (Northern Inn), the latter located just outside the East Gate of the Forbidden City. The Southern Inn had three facilities with a kitchen staff of 100, while the Northern Inn had six facilities and three times as many cooks and kitchen aids. Both inns were also staffed with physicians who obtained drugs directly from the Imperial Hospital. Once every five days, the intendant of the inn presented a list of wine, meat, tea, pasta, and the like to the Bureau of Food Stuffs. It was estimated that the Ming government annually purchased at least 100 piculs (approximately 13,330 pounds) of rice to feed tribute envoys. Sometimes, thousands of foreign "guests" and tribute envoys from all over Central Asia, Tibet, East Asia, and Southeast Asia inundated the capital city. In addition, the Ministry of War had to appropriate large quantities of hay, beans, and grain for feeding tribute elephants, horses, and other kinds of animals.[2]

After going through all the ceremonial protocol, including kowtowing to the emperor, the tribute envoys could then barter the remaining "private cargo" with Ming officials, or else sell in the private sector while at the same time purchasing Chinese goods. The International Inns were usually open to trade for five days; afterward, the tribute mission returned home by following the same route. The Ming government stored both the official tribute goods and the private merchandise it had purchased in the imperial granaries, always under the watchful eyes of court eunuchs. It then set an artificially high price and sold for several times higher than the exchanged value. Pepper, for example, was often used for compensating service rendered the government. In 1403, Emperor Yongle rewarded four catties of pepper and thirty taels of silver to his minor official for getting the imperial seal completed. An estimated quarter of a million servicemen received pepper in 1420 as a substitute for winter clothing.[3] It was indeed a unique practice that the Ming government got cheap foreign tribute goods under monopoly and used them as payment to its officials and military personnel.

TRADE WITH JAPAN AND THE RYUKYU ISLANDS

Against the backdrop of such a strict and complex system the Japanese came to trade with Ming China. According to the Ming stipulations, Japan could send only one tribute mission every ten years, each mission limited to two ships and 200 persons with no one allowed to bear arms while visiting China. But since trading with China was exceedingly profitable at the time, many Japanese warlords competed for the prized market; as a consequence, the Ming court later agreed to increase its frequency, allowing three ships and 300 persons for each Japanese tribute mission.[4]

Japan sent its first tribute mission to the Ming court in 1401. Seven years later the shogun Ashikaga Yoshimitsu died. By custom Emperor Yongle dispatched a eunuch-envoy, Zhou Quan, to express His Majesty's condolence and, according to the Ming official account, also to invest Yoshimitsu's son as "king of Japan."[5] But because the shogun was totally occupied with Japan's domestic problems, the Ming court had not heard from the Ashikaga shogun for nearly a quarter of a century. In 1432, Emperor Xuande decided to find out the conditions of his "vassal" in Japan. He commissioned eunuch Chai Shan to the Ryukyu Islands, and through the king of Ryukyu, the Ming emperor urged the shogun of Japan to renew his relationship with China. Within only a few months, there were two missions bearing tributes from Japan, one in the summer of 1433 and the other in the fall of the same year. In fact, between 1433 and 1549, a total of eleven Japanese tribute missions visited Ningbo. As they did with Central Asian states, Ming authorities often dispatched Chinese officials to escort the return of Japanese tribute envoys. In the Ming records, we learn that in the late summer of 1433, the eunuch Lei Qing was chosen to do the job. Lei presented to the Ashikaga shogun platinum, gold, and silver.[6] In general, the cargo the Japanese brought to China included sulphur, copper ore, lacquerware, swords, and fans, while they purchased Chinese silk and fabrics, silverware, and books, particularly Buddhist texts. It is interesting to note that during the imperial audience, the Korean envoy was assigned to the seventh row of the eastern side of the palace hall, while the Japanese envoy was asked to stand on the seventh row of the western side of the palace hall.

The Ming court did not send as many eunuch-envoys to Japan as it did to Central Asia or Korea, possibly because Japan was the only "vassal" state of the Ming empire that did not practice eunuchism. Nevertheless, the relationship between the two countries was greatly altered by a court eunuch named Lai En. In 1523, when Lai was in charge of the tribute affairs at the port of Ningbo, he had to deal with a wrangling feud between two rival Japanese tribute delegations. It was alleged that Lai took bribes from one delegation, certifying them as bona fide envoys; likewise, he denied the trade privilege to the other delegation. Frustrated and angered by Lai En's decision, the group—who had no means of redress—burned and looted Chinese towns and cities along the east coast. So serious and disturbing was the incident that the Emperor Jiajing decided to close down the Ningbo trading port to the Japanese "now and forever." Some of the Japanese traders, barred from official and profitable business, reportedly joined the already menacing pirates and raided and ravaged coastal China for the next century. The eunuch Lai En has been blamed ever since for poisoning the Sino-Japanese relations.[7]

While the Japanese resorted to smuggling and piracy, the people from the Ryukyu Islands maintained a cordial and stable relationship with China throughout the entire Ming period. Since the accession of the Emperor Hongwu, the Ryukyuans had repeatedly beseeched the Ming court to allow their tribute missions to visit Nanjing. In 1372 and again in 1374, the king of Ryukyu sent his brother to pay tribute to the Ming emperor. With some horses and other native Ryukyuan products, particularly sulphur, they obtained 70,000 pieces of Chinese porcelain ware and several thousand of iron tools in return. During the spring of 1382, Emperor Hongwu commissioned a eunuch-envoy named Lu Qian to escort the return trip of the Ryukyuan tribute mission. One year later, three factions in the archipelago were engaged in an acrimonious feud, and Emperor Hongwu dispatched his high-ranking eunuch-official, Liang Min, who was director of palace servants at the time, to mediate the disputes; in fact, he worked out a peaceful settlement. Since then, the kingdom of Ryukyu had truly been a loyal vassal state of the Ming and had dutifully observed all the required obligations of a tributary state. For instance, several Ryukyu princes came to study in China; periodically, the king of Ryukyu would send young girls and castrated boys to the Ming court. By custom, the Ming court would commission trusted court eunuchs to invest new Ryukyuan kings, and so on. One eunuch who had become an expert on Ryukyuan affairs was Chai Shan, who was dispatched to the island kingdom on four separate missions in 1425, 1426, 1428, and again in 1432. Chai Shan's contributions to Sino-Ryukyuan relations was in the same vein as Hai Tong's diplomacy with the Mongols and Li Da's missions to Central Asia. But once again, Ming chroniclers provide almost nothing on Chai Shan's background or the details of his missions.[8]

It was obvious that trading with Ming China was vitally important to the economy of the Ryukyu Islands. But it was interesting to note that most of the Ryukyuan traders were ethnic Chinese who sojourned in and rendered their service to the kingdom of Ryukyu. Even before the establishment of the Ming dynasty, Chinese traders, coming and going in trading junks, would stay at the ports of call for several months or even years. The official writings of the Ryukyu kingdom reveal that, since the early fifteenth century, a substantial number of Chinese had settled in or near Naha port. They were employed by the Ryukyuan authorities to engage in maritime activities and to help build a prosperous economy for the island kingdom.[9] It should also be noted that the market network of maritime trade in the East

Asian waters was dominated at the time by the Chinese and that the Chinese shipping technology had been the most advanced. Chinese junks were well known to be the best cargo and passenger carriers, and Chinese sailors commanded a good knowledge of navigation surpassed by none in East Asia.

Against this background, in the early fifteenth century, the king of Ryukyu asked for and received thirty-six families from Fujian province to manage his maritime affairs. These people, and very possibly their descendants, became the task force to carry out Ryukyuan maritime trade, including, of course, tribute missions to China. In 1411, a Ryukyuan official by the name of Cheng Fu petitioned the Ming emperor, during a tribute mission, to allow him to stay in China. Cheng had left China to serve the Ryukyuan kingdom for more than forty years, and now, at age eighty-one, wished to retire to his native home in Jiangxi province. His request was granted. In 1469, another Ryukyuan official named Cai Jing, whose grandfather was born in Fujian, requested that the Ming emperor posthumously give official titles to his deceased parents. Cai Jing's request, however, was denied.[10] Granting or denying requests of this sort depended heavily upon recommendations from eunuchs who had expert knowledge on Ryukyu affairs.

TRADE WITH SOUTHEAST ASIA

China's trade with the Ryukyu Islands was infinitesimal when compared to her commercial transactions with Southeast Asia. The Chinese had engaged in sea trade widely with Southeast Asia long before the intrusion of Europeans in the early sixteenth century. Throughout most of its history, Southeast Asia has been oriented toward China and India, and its vacant rice-growing lands and highly lucrative spice trade had acted as a magnet, attracting hundreds of thousands of Chinese settlers. As early as 987 A.D., a Song emperor sent eight eunuchs to Southeast Asia to purchase spice, rhinoceros horns, pearls, and other exotic commodities such as ambergris. The varieties of imported spices from Southeast Asia numbered more than 330 and at one time Song's trade with the region accounted for one-twentieth of its state revenues.[11]

Of all the different spices, pepper was highly valued for medicinal and seasoning purposes. Marco Polo observed that for one shipload of pepper that went to Alexandria or elsewhere in the West, there came a hundred to Quanzhou harbor along the Fujian coast.[12] In the 1340s, the Arabian traveler Ibn Battuta described in detail the Chinese junks plying between the Indian Ocean and the South China Sea. The other item that the Ming court constantly demanded was ambergris, which was so rare that sometimes it took more than a decade to find in the Southeast Asian region. It was obvious that long before the establishment of the Ming dynasty, Chinese court eunuchs, traders, sojourners, and adventurers of all kinds had frequented such South-eastern states as Champa, Cambodia, Siam, Malacca, Java, Sumatra, Palem-bang, Patani, Brunei, Sulu, and so on.[13] Ming China's active trade and diplo-macy with Southeast Asia, therefore, should not be viewed as a novel practice, but a continued Chinese tradition. Furthermore, Ming's employ-ment of the court eunuchs for conducting both maritime trade and diplo-macy was nothing nefarious, nor did it represent any ominous precedent. It was simply an imperial Chinese legacy.

Of all the Southeast Asian states, Annam was the most sinicized buffer, and for nearly a thousand years, China had placed her around the sharper edges of imperialism. It was annexed by Ming as a Chinese province from 1407 until 1427, when the Ming emperor ordered the withdrawal of some 80,000 Chinese troops from her territory. But the Annamese struggled to avoid the snare of dependence on her northern neighbor; therefore, they adopted a policy of "march southward" so that the people of the more crowded Red River delta could move down the coastline in search of rice paddies. This southern expansion resulted in a series of bloody wars against its seafaring southern neighbor, Champa, who had to rely upon Ming's pro-tection. Consequently, Champa sought an intimate relationship with China and dispatched the greatest number of tribute missions to the Ming court, sometimes twice a year. As early as 1369, a tribute mission sent by the King of Champa, Adaazhe, presented elephants and tigers to the Ming emperor Hongwu, who rewarded the Chams with 3,000 copies of the Chinese calen-dar. In 1371, an envoy from Champa brought with him a sheet of gold leaf, which was one foot long and five inches wide and inscribed the following message for Hongwu's perusal:[14] "The enthronement of the Great Ming emperor has pacified the four seas. It is like the heaven and the earth sustain-ing the ten thousand things, and like the sun and the moon shining over the whole world. Adaazhe was but a blade of grass or a tree, but appreciate greatly your giving me a gold seal and investing me as the king of Champa. Because of Annam's aggression against my territory and slaughtering my peo-ple and officials, I beg your pity and kindness to bestow us weapons, musical instruments and musicians so that the Annamese would know that we are civilized people and that we are your vassals. It is hoped that they will then stop bullying us."

Emperor Hongwu was delighted to comply with Champa's requests and also took a personal interest in bringing his two vassal states to peace. In 1383, the Champan king again presented to His Majesty 200 elephant tusks and other Champan rare products, and in return, the emperor gave the Chams 19,000 pieces of porcelain plus numerous Chinese books. Three years later, the crown prince of Champa came to Nanjing and presented fifty-four elephants to the Ming emperor. On this occasion, Emperor Hongwu chose a court eunuch to escort the prince of Champa in his return trip. The chief eunuch who was in charge of tribute trade in Guangzhou also regaled the Champan delegation with the best lodging and even gave it travel expenses.[15]

The acrimonious war between Champa and Annam resumed soon after the death of Emperor Hongwu. However, in 1406 the Ming forces, with full cooperation of Champan troops, invaded and captured Hanoi. The persons who seemed to have coordinated the joint military and diplomatic alliance were two court eunuchs, Ma Bin and Wang Guitong. Ma was previously dispatched to Java and was a veteran on Southeast Asian affairs, while Wang's mission was to allot the victory spoils to Champa. By the fall of 1410, during Ma Bin's mission to Hue, Champa had aggrandized her northern territory at the expense of Annam.[16] In 1418, a grandson of the Champan king came to pay tribute to the Ming Emperor Yongle, who selected a court eunuch by the name of Lin Gui to escort the prince home and to perform all the required tributary functionings. Partly thanks to the eunuch diplomacy, the relations between Champa and the Ming remained cordial for the next sixty years.

However, the resilient Annamese once again regained their independence from the Chinese and, under the Later Le dynasty (1428–1789), resumed its traditional southward expansion. In 1470, the Annamese invaded and captured the city of Hue and took the Champan king and his family prisoner. Almost immediately, the Annamese King Le Thanh-tong dispatched an envoy to the Ming court to explain his raison d'être and also to reiterate his willingness to pay tributes to the Ming emperor. There was great consternation in Beijing; no plans were forthcoming. In fact, the Ming government at this time simply did not have the wherewithal to mobilize an offensive army to save Champa. In the midst of this quagmire, the Ming emperor could do nothing to defuse the regional problem in present-day Vietnam.

Beginning in the 1470s, the Annamese not only seized the immensely rich Mekong delta from Champa, but also grabbed territory from the Khmer people of Cambodia. The Khmer people were believed to have originated from south China and had, since the late sixth century, sent tributes to the Sui, Tang, and Song dynasties. They had built the world's largest religious edifice at Angkor Wat and, at the height of their power in the thirteenth century, established the Angkor empire and ruled not only Cambodia, but also part of Vietnam, Laos, the Malay peninsula, and southwestern Siam. However, by the early Ming dynasty, Cambodia had been on the decline for more than a century and saw its territory being dismembered by both Annam and Siam. Consequently, its rulers also sought protection from the Ming Chinese and were more than willing to pay the required tributes; in fact, sometimes as frequently as thrice a year. Moreover, they even circumscribed their laws to attract the Chinese settlers. One source reveals that Cambodians who murdered Chinese would receive the death penalty, whereas Chinese who slew Cambodians would be only fined a sum of money.[17]

The Ming court received the first Cambodian tribute envoy as early as 1370, but the items of trade between the two countries were similar to those between China and Champa; that is, Cambodia presented to the Chinese elephants and spices (at one time 60,000 catties of incense was recorded in one mission) while the Chinese gave them chinaware, calendars, silver and gold seals, and coins. The first Ming eunuch sent to Cambodia, no name given, was dispatched in 1386. The eunuch-envoy brought a thousand pieces of chinaware as gifts to the Cambodians. In 1404, Emperor Yongle dispatched an investiture mission, also led by a court eunuch, but three members of the mission disappeared after their arrival in Cambodia. To make up for the loss, the king of Cambodia ordered three Cambodian natives to join the Chinese delegation when it returned to China. This incident certainly incurred the wrath of Emperor Yongle who insisted that the recalcitrant Chinese be found and that the three impecunious Cambodians be returned to their native land.[18]

After the death of Emperor Yongle, tribute bearing from Cambodia gradually dwindled, and ceased entirely after 1460. But its neighbor Siam, whose law, politics, and religion were more India-oriented, began to gravitate toward the Ming orbit. The Thai people, under their king Phra Rama Thiboda, founded a kingdom, with Ayutthaya as capital, almost eighteen years before the Ming came into existence. During the next four centuries, the Thais or Siamese prospered and conquered territories from Cambodia and its neighboring states. Like the Chams and Cambodians, the Siamese sought both political and commercial ties with powerful Ming China. During the Ming period, the superior technology applied by the Chinese sailors had made maritime journeys relatively safe and reliable. Sailing with the wind, a Chinese junk took only ten days to sail from Fuzhou to Champa, three days and three nights to sail from Champa to Cambodia, and ten days and ten nights to sail from Champa to Siam.

The Siamese tribute mission first arrived in Nanjing in 1371 and ever since had followed a regular frequency. Items of tribute trade included, among other local specialties, elephants, turtles, black bears, white monkeys, incense, and the highly prized pepper and sappanwood. Sappanwood and pepper, like other tribute goods, were an imperial monopoly during the Ming times. Ming records show that the kingdom of Siam, which received an official investiture gold seal from the Ming emperor in 1377, shipped to China 10,000 catties of pepper and 10,000 catties of sappanwood in 1387 and again 170,000 catties of combined pepper, sappanwood, and incense in 1389. It is to be noted that pepper, sappanwood, silk, fabrics, silver, and paper money were interexchangeable as currency during the Ming dynasty.[19]

In 1395, the king of Siam died and the Emperor Hongwu dispatched court eunuchs Zhao Da and Zhu Fu to attend the royal funeral and at the same time to invest the new king. Soon after Yongle ascended the throne, he sent court eunuch Li Xing to express His Majesty's pleasure concerning China's relations with Siam and to reassert Ming's suzerainty over her vassal state.[20] As in the case with Ryukyu and Korea, court eunuchs were frequently commissioned to attend royal funerals and to renew Ming's commitment as the overlord and protector of her vassals. Eunuch-envoys Guo Wen in 1409 and Yang Min in 1419 certainly had carried out their prescribed duties when they visited Siam. In addition to such routine missions, special eunuch assignments were found in the Ming records from time to time.[21]

In the fifteenth century, a great number of Chinese had gone to Siam searching for better economic opportunities or rendering service to the Siamese maritime trade. As in the case of the Ryukyu kingdom, the king of Siam from time to time appointed Chinese to conduct the tribute trade with the Ming court. For example, a Siamese tribute envoy of Chinese origin, Ma Yongliang, requested of the Ming court in 1447 that he be allowed to return to his consanguineous family in Fujian province. Another Chinese to serve the king of Siam was Xue Wenbin, also of Fujian native and originally a salt merchant. After a shipwreck, he drifted to Siam and later earned the trust of the Siamese royal family. Xue too was commissioned as a Siamese tribute envoy to the Ming court.[22] There was no question that Sino-Siamese trade and diplomacy needed people like Ma Yongliang and Xue Wenbin, because they knew both the Chinese and the Siamese languages. Without these people, the tribute operation often encountered difficulties. This was because, in the Siyi guan or College of Translators, established in 1407 and enduring throughout the dynasty, there might not always be specialists for every vassal state. A case in point happened in 1491, when a Siamese tribute mission arrived in Beijing, but nobody in the College of Translators could read or speak the Siamese language. The Ming government had to go to Guangdong province to find experts for emergency help. Again in 1515, the king of Siam presented a gold leaf to the Ming emperor, but no one could read the message that was inscribed on the leaf. As a result, the Ming court secured two members of the Siamese mission to work at Beijing's College of Translators so that they could teach their native tongue to the Chinese.[23]

Some eunuchs who were responsible for the tribute operation were more pyrite than gold, and their misconduct did not escape the scrutiny of Ming chroniclers. In 1509, a Siamese ship was wrecked and anchored in Guangdong, but the eunuch trade superintendent Xiong Xuan taxed its goods and weapons, which was in violation of the tribute policy under the circumstance. Emperor Zhengde was said to have been outraged by Xiong's act and wasted no time in reprimanding him. Xiong was later removed from his generally lucrative office in Guangdong and reassigned to a lesser job in Nanjing. Another case that tarnished the image of the Ming eunuchs took place in 1522, when Niu Rong, the eunuch trade superintendent of Guangdong, got his office mired in a slough of fiscal mismanagement. Niu also permitted his relatives to engage in selling and buying tribute goods without authorization. For practicing nepotism and other abuses, Niu was sentenced to die.[24] There is very little background information regarding this particular case of graft, but numerous Ming records reveal that, by the first quarter of the sixteenth century, the Ming government was flaccid, its officials were on the take, soldiers were loafers, and it was almost every man for himself. Court eunuchs were no exceptions.

At the height of Siamese power, its territory extended all the way to the southern tip of the Malay peninsula, including Malacca, an entrepôt for East Asia and West Asia. Traditionally, the chieftain of Malacca paid a sum of forty ounces of gold to the king of Siam annually so that he could maintain his autonomy. In 1403, Emperor Yongle dispatched eunuch-envoy Yin Qing to Malacca, and a new chapter of history of this seafaring Malayan state had begun. After making contact with the Ming court, the chieftain requested that Yongle invest him as "king of Malacca," which was granted in 1405. In the ensuing years, Admiral Zheng He visited Malacca on several occasions; further strengthening Ming's ties with this small seaport state. Monuments commemorating Zheng He's extraordinary deeds can still be found in Malacca today.

Of all the Ming maritime vassals, the kings of Malacca made the most personal trips to the Ming court. In 1411, the king and queen of Malacca visited China with an entourage of some 540 people. Emperor Yongle appointed court eunuch Hai Shou to accommodate the huge tribute mission, housing and entertaining them according to the protocol. Yongle also gave the Malaccans 2 dragon robes, 100 gold coins, 500 platinum coins, thousands of various metals, and a large quantity of silk fabric.[25] It was indeed a profligate spending on such a small vassal. No wonder Malaccan kings, princes, and members of the royal family, time and again, came to China to pay personal tributes to the Ming emperor. To please their Chinese overlord, they brought such tribute items as agate, coral trees, turtle shells, golden cranes, Malayan cloth, rhinoceros horns, elephant tusks, black bears, black monkeys, parrots, incense, rose perfumes, and so on.

In addition to the handsome rewards the Malaccans always received from the Ming court, there were other reasons for such frequent tribute missions. In the network of the Ming trade and diplomacy, Champa and Malacca played the most vital roles. While Xinzhou, the chief port of Champa frequented by the Chinese junks, became the point of departure for trips to Cambodia, Siam, Borneo, Sulu and the Philippines, Malacca served as the staging post for voyages to Sumatra, Java, Sri Lanka, and the states in the Indian Ocean. Moreover, Malacca had large, specially built Chinese warehouses and became a supply base for Chinese trade missions to the Indian Ocean and the Arab world. As mentioned earlier, advanced technology and sophisticated means of transportation as well as carefully mapped sea routes had made tribute missions reasonably safe and convenient. Two years before Zheng He's virgin voyage, the Ming government had built thirty-seven ships in Fujian and fifty more in Nanjing.[26] The Ming government not only monopolized the trade, but also provided the trade junks, as it had repeatedly granted Chinese sailors and ships to its vassal states, in particular Siam, Java, and Malacca. Chinese ships, manned by Chinese sailors and protected by a network of security forces in the East Asian waters, were among the most important reasons that such vassals as the Malaccan king and others made frequent trips to the Ming court. For example, in 1407 a Chinese pirate chief by the name of Chen Zuyi was arrested by Admiral Zheng He at Palembang in east Sumatra and brought back to Nanjing for execution. During the first quarter of the fifteenth century, Chinese trade junks and armed patrol ships were all over the maritime world of Southeast Asia. When the Portuguese occupied Malacca in 1511, they still found five Chinese junks there.[27] In the light of these well-developed maritime activities, the eunuch Ma Bin's mission to Java in 1403 and Yin Qing's mission to Malacca, also in 1403, should be seen as harbingers of Admiral Zheng He's spectacular seven expeditions. Even the less publicized eunuch-led mission by Gan Quan to Malacca in 1421 should also be viewed in the same context.

Until Zheng He's grand expeditions, the Chinese trade junks, despite crisscrossing the Southeast Asian waters, seldom went beyond the Malacca Straits, leaving in general the Indian Ocean to the West Asians. Malacca and Sumatra (Achen) thus became the terminal ports for Chinese maritime traders. In 1403, Emperor Yongle dispatched eunuch-envoy Ma Bin to Java and, on his way, Ma also visited Sumatra, hence making the first official contact on behalf of the Ming court. Two years later, Admiral Zheng He went there to invest its chief as "king of Sumatra," and Sumatra was officially brought into the orbit of the Ming tributary system. In 1434, the king of Sumatra sent his brother Halizhihan to head a tribute mission to China, but Halizhihan later died in Beijing. During the next year, eunuch-envoy Wang Jinghong went to Sumatra to tender His Majesty's sympathy, but on his way, Wang Jinghong reportedly died in a shipwreck off the cost of Java. The Sumatran king subsequently dispatched his other brother to escort the return of the surviving Ming delegates. In 1439, a Chinese native by the name of Song Yong was sent by the Sumatran king to be deputy of a tribute mission to the Ming court. Sumatran special tribute items included, among other goods, various kinds of pepper, precious stones, aloe, crystals, sappanwood, sulphur, knives, and arrows.[28]

Ming eunuchs were also vital in maintaining China's relations with Borneo, whose commercial contacts with China began during the Song dynasty. The first Borneo tribute mission arrived in Nanjing in 1371, and soon after its chief was invested as "king of Borneo," he decided to pay a personal tribute to the Ming emperor in 1405. The king brought along his wife, brothers, and sisters and, upon arriving in Fujian, his party was met by a high ranking court eunuch. On their way to Nanjing, every county and prefecture showed hospitality and welcome to the royal party. In the early fall of 1408, Emperor Yongle received the audience of the Borneo king. Unexpectedly, however, the king died two months later in Nanjing. The Ming court gave him a state funeral and today his monument still remains in Nanjing. Tribute specialties from Borneo included such items as peacocks and stalactites, the latter among the most valuable drugs in early modern China.[29] After the king was properly buried, Emperor Yongle selected eunuch Zhang Qian to escort the remainder of the royal family in their return trip. This same eunuch Zhang Qian made at least one more mission to Borneo near the end of 1410.[30]

The other major Southeast Asian state that was frequently visited by court eunuchs was Java. Partially because of the diplomatic skills and efforts of the eunuchs, Javan tribute missions were very frequently dispatched throughout the fifteenth century, the numbering next to Siam and Champa. In the late thirteenth century, Kublai Khan once sent an envoy to Java, but the natives, for whatever reasons, had the Mongol envoy's face tattooed. This certainly incurred the wrath of the great Mongol Khan, who launched a punitive expedition against the Javans. Soon after the establishment of the Ming dynasty, a tribute-bearing mission from Java arrived in Nanjing, and as usual, Emperor Hongwu gave the Javans hundreds of copies of the Chinese calendar. The king of Java later submitted a gold leaf inscribed with the usual flattering message to please his Ming overlord. In 1381, a Javan tribute mission presented to the Ming court 300 "black slaves" and one year later, 100 more slaves, both young boys and young girls, plus 75,000 catties of spices.[31] In addition to Admiral Zheng He's repeated visits to Java, at least four other eunuch missions were dispatched to the spice island kingdom. Ma Bin in 1403 gave an official investiture gold seal to the Javan king, Zhang Yuan was sent in 1410 for special awards, and Wu Bin went there twice during 1412–1413 for more routine tributary exchanges.[32] After 1466, in part because the Ming had changed its foreign policy, fewer and fewer Javan missions frequented Chinese ports. As in the case of Siam, Malacca, and others, Java sometimes appointed Chinese natives to conduct its tribute trade with the

Ming government. This was also true in the relatively limited trade relations between China and the Philippines.

Early Ming maritime pursuits were as colossal as they were logical and comprehensible. Before the founding of the Ming dynasty, hundreds of thousands of Chinese, primarily from Fujian and Guangdong, had been engaging in trade and commerce of all sorts in Southeast Asia.[33] Chinese communities were known to have existed in just about every major Southeast Asian port city when the last Yuan emperor lost his mandate of heaven. By the end of the fourteenth century, Chinese maritime technology had developed to a level unsurpassed in the world. The Chinese had replaced Indians and Arabs in dominating the maritime trade of Southeast Asia in the fifteenth century. Since trade was so lucrative and beneficial to both China and the Southeast Asian states, a commercial entrepreneurship had developed and a market of supply and demand of goods had also been identified and secured long before the Ming came to power.

The Ming emperor soon realized that trade with the region was one of the best means to enrich his nation. He also believed that the best way to maintain a policy of untrammeled economic growth, notwithstanding the viability of the policy, was to have the government monopolize the trade. This is why he used primarily his own servants, the castrati, to supervise the tributary trade. Consequently, he prohibited Chinese civilians from sailing overseas or participating in maritime pursuit, nor would he allow foreigners to come to China except for tribute missions. The fact that Admiral Zheng He's fleet were all heavily armed indicates that no smugglers or pirates would be tolerated to interrupt Ming's trade monopoly. It was against the background of the Ming trade monopoly, Chinese advanced maritime technology, and the Chinese diaspora in the region that several Ming eunuch missions were dispatched to Southeast Asia before Zheng He commanded his first expedition in 1405. Political motives, such as searching for the whereabouts of Yongle's nephew, the deposed Emperor Jianwen, may have been contributing factors. Nevertheless, Zheng He's seven navigations should be viewed from a broader historical perspective and examined in the same light as were numerous other eunuch-led missions before, during, and after Zheng He's voyages.

ZHENG HE'S SEVEN NAVIGATIONS

Between 1405 and 1433, the Ming government undertook seven maritime expeditions that visited some thirty states in Southeast Asia and along the Indian Ocean coast, reaching as far as Hormus and Somaliland in Africa. Each voyage involved tens of thousands of government troops and employed more than a hundred ocean-going vessels that traveled several thousand miles. The Chinese fleet was 90 times bigger than that of the Portuguese under Vasco de Gama and capable of transporting 150 times the number of marines. As a result of these expeditions, more than sixteen states between Java and the Persian Gulf sent tributes to the Ming court, and numerous envoys from foreign countries journeyed to China to pay their homage to the Ming emperor. The commander of the fleet, Zheng He, was ever since fondly called the *Eunuch of the Three Gems.*

But as fascinating as these voyages were, Ming chroniclers only used some 700 words in the 330 chapters of Ming official history to describe such epic events. And perhaps because Zheng He was considered one of these "rapacious eunuchs" by his literati rivals, official Ming historians cared to spare only thirty words to identify Zheng He, the half man. In fact, we might not even know about Zheng He and his most significant contributions to maritime explorations had it not been for the three little books written by Zheng He's subordinates. One is called *Yingyai shenglan* or *The Overall Survey of the Ocean's Shores*, dated 1433, written by Ma Huan; the second one was entitled, *Xingcha shenglan* or *The Overall Survey of the Starry Raft*, dated 1436 and authored by Fei Xin; and the third one, written by Gong Zhen, was called *Xiyang fanguo zhi* or *Description of the Barbarian Countries of the West.* Based on these three books, plus many newly discovered monuments, artifacts, and other related sources, recent scholars, many of whom are Europeans and Japanese, have been able to reconstruct a clearer picture of these most extraordinary but least known—so far as the Occidental world is concerned—maritime activities of the fifteenth century.[34]

One immediate question is, Who was Zheng He and why was he chosen to command these large-scale voyages no human being had ever done before his time? From scanty sources, we know that Zheng He was born in 1371 in the Kunyang county of China's Yunnan province, a southwestern frontier region adjacent to Burma and Laos. His hometown neighbors the Moon Mountain to the south and is only a short distance to one of the loveliest lakes in China, the Dianchi Lake. His father's surname was Ma and, since he had made a pilgrimage to Mecca, he was respectably called a Haji by his people. Growing up with an older brother and four sisters, Zheng He's boyhood was one that could be commonly found in a typical prominent Muslim family. In fact, the family was apparently quite affluent, because Zheng He's grandfather was also a Haji and held high office in Yunnan. Based on what the Chinese records can tell us, his ancestors came originally from present-day Xinjiang, even possibly from Central Asia. In China's vast western region, there were a variety of ethnic groups, ranging from the more numerous Mongols, Uygurs, and Kazaks to the minority groups of Kirghizes, Uzbeks, and Tajiks, most of whom spoke the Turkic language and used Arab script for centuries. Long before Genghis Khan's rise to power, one after another had adhered themselves to the Islamic faith. It is generally believed that Zheng He's forebears belonged to either one of these stocks or a mixture of several elements over time. They were not only multilingual and hard-working, but also brave and adventurous, the remarkable traits that Zheng He inherited.

In the early thirteenth century, when the Mongol forces swept across Central Asia, Zheng He's ancestors were active in helping Genghis Khan's empire building. According to a Mongol document, Kublai Khan, Genghis Khan's grandson, appointed Saiyid Ajall, Zheng He's great-great-great-grandfather, the governor of Yunnan in 1274.[35] During his six year tenure in Yunnan, Saiyid pacified the aboriginal tribes, brought prosperity to the region, and established cordial relationships with both Annam and Burma. Clearly, Saiyid won Kublai's confidence and had also established a good reputation among his people. For the next century, the Saiyid family served their Mongol rulers with loyalty and dexterity and were rewarded accordingly.

However, by the time Zheng He's father Ma Haji and mother Wen survived to adulthood, Yunnan was no longer blessed with its traditional aura of enchanting dances and songs, because the Mongol rulers were by then corrupted and softened by the wealth of the nation they conquered. When Zheng He was still in knee pants and surrounded by lofty uncles, buxom aunts, and gangling cousins, his father's Mongol patrons had lost the valor and vitality that were the hallmarks of the nomadic Mongols. Chinese nationalism revived and emerged, which took the form of active Buddhism, organized banditry, and mass revolts. In only a few years, the popular uprisings ravaged all of China and by the summer of 1368 the fun-seeking last Mongol emperor had fled Beijing. The Mongol's dominance in Yunnan was over, and Zheng He's family was down on its luck. In 1382, when Zheng He was eleven years old, Yunnan fell to the Ming forces. A Mongol prince and his family, together with some 380 Mongol officials, were captured and sent to Nanjing, then the capital of the new dynasty. Zheng He's father, then only thirty-nine years of age, died in the war of retribution, and the young Zheng He was taken into the camp of General Fu Youde as a prisoner of war.

Historians who are interested in Zheng He and the illustrious Ming maritime explorations have been beset by a big problem; that is, what had happened to Zheng He between the time he was captured by Ming forces in 1382 and the time Emperor Yongle appointed him commander of the navigation fleet in 1404. During the latter date, Yongle not only solemnly changed his surname from Ma to Zheng, but also promoted him to be eunuch of the Inner Court. Bestowing an imperial name to a favorite official was nothing new in imperial China, and in fact, five other eunuchs, all from China's frontier regions, all having served in the military, also received new surnames in 1404. But Zheng He was someone special because he was also chosen to command an historical naval reconnaissance, and he was only thirty-three years of age.[36] How could this Muslim prisoner of war from Yunnan rise to such an important position in such a short period of time? What did he do to gain the trust and confidence of the emperor? Why did Yongle change his name from Ma to Zheng? These and other questions must be answered before the story of his voyages can be told in proper historical perspective.

Zheng He's rise to power began with the most unbearable punishment of castration. We know that during the early days of the Ming dynasty, there was an increasing population of castrati in Nanjing and that victorious Ming generals often had their captives' penes and scrotums cut off before taking them as slaves. Not all the castrated war prisoners were brought to the capital; many, in fact, were given to local officials and members of the imperial family.[37] By a stroke of fate, Zheng He, then Ma He, was given to Emperor Hongwu's fourth son, Zhu Di. In 1381, Zhu Di was installed in the Beijing area as the prince of Yan and began building a power base in Northern China.

Available records indicate that Zheng He had a tremendous personality, and that he developed disproportionately long arms and legs that made him stand out among other courtiers. His voice was fresh and his black eyes tender and modest, traits that often won favor with his master. As Zheng He matured, he proved to be a skilled military strategist. He easily established a strong bond with his fellow castrati and displayed an unflinching loyalty to Zhu Di. During the last quarter of the fourteenth century, the Ming and the Mongols waged a rancorous war along China's northern border, and Zheng He was involved at least twice in the campaign. He had journeyed across the barren, brown wasteland of North China, learned how to look for hoofprints and horse dung, and recorded every water well and dead animal he could find along a northbound overland trek. He was, by the time the civil war broke out, a seasoned warrior, a confidant of the prince of Yan, and was generally considered one of the best commanders in the prince's camp.

In October 1399, when the civil war was reaching its crucial stage, the prince of Yan led an offensive attack by personally commanding the siege of Da Ning garrison. His enemies, led by a loyalist general, Li Chinglong, countered with nine battalions of fresh troops and besieged Beijing. At this critical juncture, Zheng He dug in around a Beijing water reservoir, the Zheng Village Dike. He was able to stall the enemies' advance and bought enough time for the prince to dispatch relief troops. As a result, the prince successfully broke up General Li's forces, inflicting frightening casualties on Li's battalions and turning the tide of war to his favor. Historians in general believe that this may be the most decisive battle of the Ming civil war and the prince, best known for his harsh punishment for failure in duty and swift reward for valor, immediately promoted Zheng He to director of palace servants after he assumed the emperorship as Yongle. Zheng He, was, for a brief tenure, in charge of all palace construction, such as repairing royal mansions and mausolea; procuring fireworks, copper, tin, wood, iron utensils and implements; and supervising civil engineering. On the lunar New Year Day of 1404, Emperor Yongle bestowed on him a new surname, Zheng, in memory of the victory at the Zheng Village Dike.[38] This was a rare honor, and Ma He has ever since been known to posterity as Zheng He.

It was probably in his capacity as supervisor of court civil engineering and procurer of metals and fireworks that Zheng He became very knowledgeable about weapons and ship construction. Only a few weeks after he got his new name, Zheng He received an imperial order to build a navy 100,000 strong to stop the menace of the Japanese pirates, who had repeatedly marauded the China coast. Several Chinese and Japanese documents record that Zheng He actually went to Japan to enlist the cooperation of the Japanese authorities in suppressing the increasingly threatening raiders. One source says that Ashikaga Shogun turned over some twenty leading marauders to Zheng He while another states that Zheng He invested Ashikaga as "the king of Japan," rewarding Ashikaga's efforts in the campaign against piracy.[39] Such sources appear to be credible because his credentials as a competent shipyard supervisor, a successful navy commander, and a skilled envoy made him the most qualified person for undertaking the historical navigation in 1405. Even though he was only thirty-four years of age, Zheng He was trading on a thick portfolio of achievements, having fully demonstrated great competence in planning, commanding, and organization.

Zheng He's voyages followed the charts illustrated in a book of dubious origin, the *Wubei bishu* or *Secret Book of the Military Affairs*, which most scholars believe was a plagiarized copy of the *Wubei zhi* or *Treatise on Military Preparation*, written by Mao Yuanyi of the Ming dynasty. These charts were used by the Chinese captains who navigated the vessels of Zheng He and his suite and took them to various foreign countries. In 1886, George Phillips, the British consul at Swatow, identified seventy-six places from Quanzhou to Sumatra and eighty-eight places from Sumatra to the East Coast of Africa, hence completing the maps from China to the Malacca Straits and the Indian Ocean.[40] Again in 1909, Charles Otto Blagden was able to identify sixteen additional places named in the charts.[41] And in the 1930s, the French Sinologist Paul Pelliot, the Dutch scholar J. J. L. Duyvendak, and later the British writer J. V. G. Mills continued to investigate and identify the place names given by Zheng He's subordinates, such as Ma Huan and Fei Xin.[42]

Ma Huan was a Muslim and, possibly in the capacity as an interpreter, took part in three of Zheng He's expeditions. His *The Overall Survey of the*

Ocean's Shores, translated by Mills into English in 1970, is divided into eighteen chapters; nineteen states and localities in the book have been identified. Each chapter gives a description of the boundaries, the distances, the customs, the products of the state and also highlights on political events. Generally speaking, Ma Huan's work is in close agreement with the account in official Ming history.[43]

Fei Xin, on the other hand, made at least four voyages either as a secretary or clerk interpreter, but his *The Overall Survey of the Starry Raft* recorded only Zheng He's third expedition (1409–1411). Much of the information in Fei Xin's book probably came from Wang Dayuan's *Daoyi zhilue* or *Description of the Barbarians of the Isles*, dated as early as 1349. It was generally believed that Fei Xin wrote his work in 1436, some twenty-five years after the expedition had taken place; thus, he had to rely upon Wang's work for reference.[44] In terms of accuracy and importance, Fei Xin's book is far inferior to Ma Huan's work, but Fei's book identifies forty states and localities and provides some invaluable information on Java, Nicobar, and East African localities that Zhang He and his eunuch associates visited.

Aside from the navigation routes and divergence of the places, the second most difficult issue surrounding Zheng He's voyages is the true date of each expedition. Certainly, *Ming shi* and Ming Veritable Records have given some authentic sources, but they are incomplete and sometimes confusing, as for example the return dates of the second and third voyages. Such confusion was further compounded when in the 1930s two of Zheng He's inscriptions were discovered, which immediately prompted sinologists like L. Carrington Goodrich and J. J. L. Duyvendak into the reexamination of the whole issue. The first inscription came originally from a tablet erected in the Celestial Spouse Palace at Liujiagang in the present Suzhou region on March 14, 1431. The second inscription was originally from a stone erected by Zheng He and his associates near the temple of the Three Peak Pagoda by the Southern Mountain of Changle county in Fujian province. This inscription was believed to have been written between December 5, 1431, and January 3, 1432. Professor Goodrich of Columbia University had secured a rubbing of this inscription. In 1939 when visiting Columbia University, Duyvendak reported facsimiles of these two inscriptions and translated them into English.[45] He also wrote a lengthy article verifying the true dates of the seven expeditions. Table VII.1 is a synthesis of these scholars' findings.

Next to the dates of the expeditions is the question of the number and the size of the ships and their equipage. The biography of Zheng He in the *Ming shi* records only that, for the needs of an embassy to the countries of the Western ocean, the court ordered Zheng He and his colleagues to build sixty-two large ships, each of which was 440 feet long and 180 feet wide. Other documents furnish somewhat different, more detailed records than

Table VII.1.
Documents Recording the Dates of Zheng He's Expeditions

	Ming Shi	Ming Veritable Records	Liujiagang Inscription	Changle Inscription
1. Initial Order	July 11, 1405	July 11, 1405		
Departure			1405	1405
Return	Oct. 2, 1407	Oct. 2, 1407	1407	1407
2. Initial Order	Oct. 7, 1408	Oct. 17, 1408		
Departure			1407	1407
Return	July 6, 1411	July 6, 1411	1409	1409
3. Initial Order	No record	No record		
Departure			1409	1409
Return	July 6, 1411	July 6, 1411	1411	1411
4. Initial Order	December 1412 with an error in the cyclical date of the day.	Dec. 18, 1412		
Departure			1413	1413
Return	Aug. 12, 1415	Aug. 12, 1415	1415	1415
5. Initial Order	Dec. 28, 1416	Dec. 28, 1416		
Departure			1417	1417
Return	Aug. 8, 1419	Aug. 8, 1419	No date	No date
6. Initial Order	March 3, 1421	March 3, 1421		
Departure			1421	1421
Return	Sept. 3, 1422	Sept. 3, 1422	No date	No date
7. Initial Order	No exact date given	June 29, 1430		
Departure			1430	1431
Return	No record	No record	No date	No date

Note: It is apparent that the chroniclers who compiled *Ming shi* and Ming Veritable Records got the dates of the second and third expeditions all mixed up. Note also the fact that the two inscriptions, with the exception of the seventh expedition, almost entirely agree on the dates.

that of the *Ming shi*. For instance, *Family Biography of Zheng He* lists the total number of ships put to sea in the first expedition as sixty-three, of which the largest ones were 444 feet long and 180 feet wide and the middle-sized ships were 370 feet long and 150 feet wide.[46] The number and the size of the ships recorded in *Family Biography of Zheng He* is thereby in agreement with those given in Ma Huan's *Survey of the Ocean's Shores*.

These expeditionary ships were built not only to transport personnel and merchandise, but were also for combat. It is inconceivable—as recorded in the *Ming shi*—that Zheng He's fleet did not include a great number of more mobile and faster small-sized vessels suitable for amphibious landings and fighting enemy ships in the open sea. In his *Survey of the Ocean's Shores*, Ma Huan often refers to the fleet as *dazong baochuan*, or great treasure fleet. Well, the term *zong* has since puzzled the sinologists. Some speculate that the term derives from the Javan language *zong*, which means large vessel. Others maintain that it is the same as *junk*, a name used widely by the medieval Europeans when they referred to the Chinese ship. The key to this problem is whether all the sixty-two ships were 440 feet long and 180 feet wide, or if only a smaller number were of much stouter construction while the majority of the ships belonged to the middle-sized and small-sized categories. The fact that the total number of ships involved in different expeditions varied from 48 to 249 while the total persons involved in different expeditions remained about 27,000 led Paul Pelliot to conclude that *zong* meant a fleet rather than an individual large vessel. A *zong* therefore consisted of smaller numbers of nine-masted ships and larger numbers of middle-sized and small-sized vessels, numbering between 50 and 100.[47] Zheng He's common maneuver was to split up the zong from which small flotillas were dispatched to places far off the main route. For example, in one of his voyages, Zheng He dispatched eunuch-envoy Hong Bao to carry out a mission from Calicut to Mecca, and during his last voyage (1430–1431), his associate Wang Jinghong led one or more vessels to Southern Taiwan, where Wang encountered Taiwanese aborigines.[48]

It is clear that Zheng He's mission had commercial as well as political and military purposes. Therefore, his fleet had to be equipped for an all-round capacity. A nine-masted or eight-masted ship carried, in addition to a large crew, huge amounts of merchandise; it also provided stores necessary to feed large numbers of men for a long voyage. For this reason, the nine-masted and eight-masted vessels were probably the most reliable and most efficient vessels afloat in the fifteenth century Asian waters. But Zheng He's fleet also had to have fighting capacity. *Ming shi* as well as other documents mention that Zheng He intended and utilized his navy to fulfill his multifaceted missions. For example, during the first expedition, his fleet was engaged in a sea battle against a notorious pirate chieftain in Palembang; in his second and fourth expeditions, he used his naval superiority to defeat and capture the kings of Sri Lanka and Sumatra.

In the light of these military records, one has to wonder about the importance of smaller vessels in case of necessary naval operation in foreign lands. Small-sized ships, because of their weight and mobility, could proceed under oars when entering and leaving harbor or in an emergency. This attribute made them faster and more dependable than the large-sized vessels. They were fitted out for offensive war and capable of vigorous self-defense. Indeed, large vessels and small vessels both were needed for Zheng He's expeditions because they complemented each other and served different purposes. The following five different sizes of ships were very likely commanded by Zheng He.[49]

Name of Ship	No. of Masts	Length	Width	Total No.
Treasury ship	9	444 ft.	180 ft.	36
Horse ship	8	370 ft.	150 ft.	700
Grain ship	7	280 ft.	120 ft.	240
Billet ship	6	240 ft.	94 ft.	300
Combat ship	5	180 ft.	68 ft.	180

This information may provide the answer to the question of why the same number of people employed different numbers of ships on practically the same mission. From the scattered records, we know that the first expedition employed 62 ships, the second expedition required 249 ships, the third 48 ships, the fourth 63 ships, but the seventh expedition launched more than 100 ships. (There is no record for the numbers of ships involved in the fifth and sixth expeditions.) Two other valuable documents may also shed some light into this question of total ship involvement: *Wubei zhi*, or *Treatise on Military Preparation*, and a book on Ming shipbuilding written by Li Zhaoxiang, who in 1551 became the director of the Longjiang Naval Arsenal near Nanjing where most of Zheng He's ships were constructed. Based on the information from these two documents and other sources, Zheng He and his fellow navigators might have deployed several different sizes of ships, ranging from the nine-masted, 444 foot long vessels to the three-masted, 130 foot long vessels.[50]

Although no precise description exists of the ships that made up Zheng He's fleet, we have relatively detailed information about the men. Zheng He's people, as their achievements had proven, were a competent and professional company. They seemed to have been recruited formally through government agencies. The fleet's principal officers were all court eunuchs bearing the civil service ranks from 6b to 4a. But once again, discrepancies are found in different sources as to the numbers and names of the eunuch-envoys who accompanied Zheng He on his seven voyages. Figures actually range from six, as recorded in Liujiagang inscription, to more than seventy, as recorded in *Family Biography of Zheng He*. In *The Dictionary of Ming Biography*, L. Carrington Goodrich lists the following eunuchs as principal officers: Wang Jinghong, Hou Xian, Li Xin, Zhu Liang, Zhou Man, Hong Bao, Yang Zhen, Zhang Da, and Wu Zhong.[51]

In a big fleet, especially a fleet armed for war and employed on many special services, there would certainly be several groups of professional people. At the top of these professionals were, of course, the military personnel. High-ranking regional military commissioners such as Zhu Zhen (3a) and Wang Heng (4a) were assigned to accompany Zheng He on his seventh expedition.[52] Other military officers were also assigned to participate in the expeditions. Several dozen battalion commanders, ranking from 5b to 5a with the surnames of Ma, Liu, Zhang, and Xu were found in the documents. Most of these battalion commanders appeared to have come from the frontier region. Their sinicized names were usually given by the court after serving the emperor with distinction. Yongle Veritable Record gives evidence of their accomplishments during the expeditions; hence, promotions were given to several of them. Other subaltern officers such as company commanders and flag-army commanders numbered in the hundreds.

Zheng He's fleet also carried professional groups ranging from religious leaders to physicians who were responsible for the spiritual and physical well-being of the entire crew. Other specially trained people, such as purveyors, were responsible for the provisions—food, water, wine, and firewood—and the stowage of cargo and ballast. The large crew of Zheng He's ship was needed not only to fight the ship in case of trouble but also to handle running gear that, by modern standards, was coarse and clumsy. In his *Qianwen ji* or *Stories from the Past*, Zhu Yunming (1460–1526) had one passage describing the personnel of the seventh expedition: "The sixth year of Xuande (1431)—people employed to go to the Western Ocean included subaltern officers, soldiers of the flag-army, purveyors, pilots, leadsmen, interpreters, accountants, physicians, boatswains, caulkers, scaffold builders, carpenters, civilian landsmen and others amounted to 27,550."[53] Based on *Ming shi* and other sources, we know that more than 27,800 people were deployed during the first expedition, between 27,000 and 30,000 took part in the third expedition, approximately 28,560 were involved in the fourth expedition, and about 27,550 were used for the seventh expedition. There were no records on the numbers of people employed for the second, the fifth, and the sixth expeditions.

It is abundantly clear that Zheng He's fleet was uniformly larger than those of the Portuguese and the Spanish. The Portuguese laboriously rounded Cape Bojador on the Saharan coast in 1434, and not until sixty-four years later did Vasco da Gama make it to the Malabar coast of India. Da Gama, with his three ships—probably less than 100 feet long—and 170 men, is renowned for entering Calicut harbor in May 1498. The Ming expeditions, relying upon centuries of Chinese commercial contacts with the Indian Ocean, ranged from Nanjing to Borneo to Zanzibar, receiving embassies and distributing imperial rewards in Sumatra, Malacca, Sri Lanka, and the Arabian coast and Mecca. Having only items such as washbasins and beads to trade, the Portuguese quickly turned to force and terror to extract from India the riches they sought. The Chinese, with a complacency founded upon economic self-sufficiency, came with gifts. For example, the three religious communities of Sri Lanka—Buddhist, Hindu and Islamic—received imperial rewards, including some 3,000 pieces of gold, 15,000 of silver, and 300 rolls of silk, as well as perfumed oils and lacquered ecclesiastical ornaments.

In numbers, wealth, skill, technology, and sophistication, then, the Ming Chinese surpassed the Portuguese. The last major Chinese expedition, however, was in 1433; hence, when the Portuguese entered the Indian Ocean two generations later, they encountered no Asian power that could contest European domination of the sea. The history of the world and the relationship of East and West would have been vastly different had the Ming court not discontinued such maritime activities. Historians thus face several questions regarding these pre-Columbian naval expeditions. For all their competence, why did the Chinese lack any incentive to reach Europe via Africa or to sail across the Pacific and discover America? Of course, the biggest puzzle was, Why was there no more maritime reconnaissance after the mid-fifteenth century?

Even before the death of Emperor Yongle on August 12, 1424, there was trouble in the Ming's vaunted maritime expeditions. The literati bemoaned the rising power of the eunuchs and did everything possible to scuttle the project, overtly and covertly. A prominent scholar-official, Xia Yuanji, led a blistering attack against Zheng He's expeditions, charging that they betokened fiscal madness. Xia was thrown to jail for advocating their abolition, but a few days before the fourth Ming emperor Hongxi acceded to the throne (September 7, 1424), Xia was set free and the court ordered the cessation of all maritime missions. Thus, between his sixth and seventh voyages, Zheng He was stationed in Nanjing and in charge of the beautification of the southern capital. While his ships lay idle and gathered rust, as it were, there was an outbreak of conniving, feuding, and finagling between the literati and the castrati. The winners were usually those who could garner the strongest backing of the emperor. In the summer of 1430, the fifth Ming emperor, Xuande, decided that he wanted to revivify the Ming imperial prowess and ordered the seventh and final expedition. This was Zheng He's last adventure, but he was growing old. Soon after his return from Africa and the Arabian states, he died at the age of sixty-five. In the ensuing years, a renewal of the maritime expeditions was propounded several times, but there was no patron like Emperor Yongle anymore. During the reign of the eighth Ming emperor, Chenghua (1464–1487), a court eunuch suggested that Zheng He's navigation routes and records be reviewed, but after a thorough search and probing, none of Zheng He's files could be found. It was later determined that Liu Daxia, a director of the Transportation Bureau, had burned all of Zheng He's documents. Liu was quoted to have said that Zheng He's expeditions had cost hundreds of thousands of silver taels and lives and were not worth trying again.[54] The fire that destroyed the documents of Zheng He's epic events is a glaring testimony to a long-held suspicion that *Ming shi* does not tell the whole story about the Ming eunuchs.

VIII

⌖

Eunuchs' Involvement
in the Ming Economy

MANAGING THE IMPERIAL PLANTATIONS

In the Chinese dynastic system, the emperor theoretically was the sole owner of all the lands of his realm and could do whatever he wished with any unclaimed and uncultivated lands. Rulers of the Han dynasty (202 B.C.–220 A.D.) often established imperial estates and built stonewalls of privilege within their domain. The Five Dynasties (907–960) witnessed the rise of a collection of grand duchies of various sizes, each with its own royalty. This tradition continued throughout the Song dynasty (960–1279) and culminated in the Qing dynasty (1644–1912) when the latter created 868 imperial plantations, which covered a total acreage of more than 13,200 ching, or approximately 200,000 acres of land.[1] The formalized structure of the Ming royal plantations therefore was not unique, and the fact that the eunuchs were assigned to manage all these plantations raised eyebrows among their nemeses and a simmering dispute over who—the eunuchs or the officials from the Ministry of Revenues—should exercise control over these lands magnified the problems of the Ming's dualistic bureaucracy.

The Ming fiscal system made no clearcut distinction between imperial income and state income, theoretically all tax revenues from the land were imperial income. The lands under its system were divided into two categories—guantian, or the state land, and mintian, or the people's land. According to a record of 1393, the entire country had 8,507,623 ching, or 12.76 million acres, of cultivated land, of which one seventh belonged in the state land category.[2] The state lands included plots reserved for educational and religious purposes; confiscated real estate from impeached and convicted officials; various plantations awarded to imperial relatives, meritorious ministers, generals, and eunuchs; and farms assigned to military garrisons and special artisan and civilian groups. Of these state lands, the plantations—which usually were created by special imperial decrees—remained the most arcane

165

and controversial. The plantation system began in 1425, when Emperor Hongxi bestowed half of a former military settlement in the suburb of Beijing to a Daoist group and used the other half to build an imperial villa called *Renshou gongzhuang*, or the Humanity and Longevity Plantation.[3]

Soon after this first imperial villa became operational two more imperial estates were established, and in 1459 Emperor Tianshun, to find supplementary income to defray the expenditures of his children, decreed the establishment of three more imperial plantations, one for the crown prince, one for Prince De, and a third one for Prince Xiu. Six years later, when Chenghua ascended the throne, he converted a 1,000 ching landholding—confiscated from the grand eunuch Cao Jixiang—into an elaborate estate and called it a *huangzhuang*, or imperial village. In the ensuing years, more and more huangzhuang were seen in other parts of the country; and by 1489, as a Ming document shows, there were five huangzhuang in the vicinity of the capital, covering a total acreage of 12,800 ching. In addition, 332 different sized and shaped imperial plantations were scattered around the country, constituting a total acreage of 33,000 ching.[4] Almost all of these estates were owned by the emperor and his relatives and managed by court eunuchs.

The proliferation of the imperial plantations drew the attention of the officials responsible for both tax collection and fund disbursement. Among them was the minister of revenues Li Min who, within his limited authority as the chief fiscal administrator, could not do anything about these boondoggles to effect a cessation of the insidious drain on state revenues. Minister Li complained to the emperor, declaring that the plantation managers did not operate these estates efficiently and that they and their subordinates often hired hoodlums and ruffians to do their bidding. Worse still, they forcibly took over people's land, extorted their money and other valuables, and debauched their wives and daughters. He went on to say that if people dared to make the slightest protest, they found themselves being sued on fabricated charges. When the sheriff came to arrest them, whole families trembled with fear. Li averred that this was the reason that people hated the plantation managers to the marrow of their bones. Similar complaints against the allegedly malfeasant eunuch managers came from an investigating censor; ultimately, the generally frugal and responsive Emperor Hongzhi decided to disestablish the Humanity and Longevity Plantation and also ordered the return of any unlawfully seized lands to the people.[5]

The Humanity and Longevity Plantation's first brush with closure came during the reign of a benevolent emperor, but as soon as Zhengde was seated on the dragon throne, he reversed his father's policy on imperial villages. In fact, within one month of his accession—the summer of 1505—Zhengde decreed the establishment of seven new imperial plantations and later increased the number to more than thirty. After Zhengde, every Ming monarch was eager to lavishly endow large plots of land to his relatives and favorite ministers and eunuchs, often disregarding an array of formidable fiscal problems he had to face. There are conflicting reports as to the exact number and total acreage of imperial estates, but the statistics taken as a whole are mind-boggling. Most of the estates were located in northern China; in particular, they were concentrated in the four fu, or prefectures, of Shuntian, Baoding, Hejian, and Zhending. The ratio between the total acreage of the imperial plantations (12,800 ching) in these four areas and that of the people's lands (165,565 ching) was 1:12.9 during the reign of Emperor Hongzhi, but it increased substantially to 1:4.4 during Zhengde's reign.[6] And this trend, possibly the largest and worst example of land concentration in history, continued until the collapse of the dynasty. For example, Emperor Wanli (1573–1620) created three royal plantations, totaling 21,666 ching, with their incomes exclusively reserved for three empresses. He then proposed to carve out 40,000 ching of the best lands from the Henan, Shandong, and Huguang provinces so that he could give them as a special gift to his favorite son, the prince of Fu. Only after vehement opposition from several of his top officials did Wanli agreed to halve the size of this land endowment. In 1589, the prince of Lu took over an estate, totaling just over 36,328 ching with an annual income of nearly 50,000 silver taels. This plantation extended from the arid Hebei, north of the Yellow River, to the alluvial wet lands in Henan, rivalling six other royal estates in the area. In addition to the revenues from the land, the plantation made levies on houses, salt, lakes, river ports, forest products, mines, and other resources.[7]

Once a prince received an outright grant of land, he and his offspring were entitled to hold it for several generations and sometimes in perpetuity. Moreover, the imperial estates always grew in size and number by a snowballing process. A Ming royal estate differed in several respects from the European manor. Ming estate's fields were not all in one place, and the estate was not centered around a castle or seigneurial residence. Furthermore, it had no seigneurial demesne farmed by serfs: instead, the lands were either rented to or farmed by tenant farmers, hired laborers, or bond servants of various kinds.[8] In essence, an imperial estate was a group of plots, often scattered around a number of counties, but bound together under a common proprietor who inherited the privileges and income created by the establishment of the estate. The Anlu huangzhuang in present-day Hubei province was typical and aptly serves as a microcosm of the Ming plantation system and of the roles eunuchs played in managing these unique properties.

The Anlu royal estate was created in 1486 when Emperor Chenghua invested his second son as the prince of Xingxian. Xingxian died in 1519, and his twelve-year-old son inherited both his estate and title. Then two years later the young prince of Xingxian was chosen to become Emperor Jiajing when his cousin, the Emperor Zhengde, died without issue. As a consequence, the princely estate was upgraded to an imperial estate. As of 1542, it included fourteen plots of land, ranging from a small tomb garden for a deceased princess that covered 15 ching to a cluster of villages that occupied an area of more than 1,500 ching of land. Within this gigantic estate, which was scattered around four counties of the Chengtian fu, there were thirty-six villages and two big lakes, with a total acreage just over 8,404 ching, which later increased to 10,611 ching of land. Based on the tax records of 1532, the ratio between the total acreage of the Anlu plantation and that of the people's lands (19,400 ching) in the Chengtian fu would be roughly 1:1.8. It was indeed a very peculiar land ownership phenomenon.[9]

The owner of this gigantic plantation was, of course, Emperor Jiajing, but the people who managed this real estate were also the grand eunuchs whom he appointed to guard his father's burial site, called *Xianling*, or the Prominent Tomb. The eunuch's official title was grand defender of Xianling, which had its headquarters in Zhongxiang county of the Chengtian fu. As mentioned earlier, the eunuch grand defender took orders directly from the Ceremonial Directorate; accordingly, local authorities were prohibited from entering the land of the imperial estate. Strangely enough, the location of the tomb was to become the nucleus of an extensive system of Ming garrisons and agricultural production in central China. There were times when audacious local officials, such as censors and governors, would attempt to stop the gradual encroachment on people's lands by the plantation managers, but these efforts were generally to no avail. In 1541, for instance, a governor of Huguang by the name of Lu Jie criticized the grand defender Fu Lin for maladministration and requested His Majesty to reduce the land taxes and rentals and also to have investigating censors reform the plantation operation. Emperor Jiajing, however, trusted the eunuch Fu Lin's confessional and reprimanded the governor's shortcomings. He then ordered the erection of more stone markers to revalidate the boundaries of the tomb estate.[10]

It is obvious that Ming emperors, as a rule, permitted their eunuchs to exercise more personal control over not only the properties but also the people who worked within the estate domains. Generally speaking, a typical imperial plantation was managed by a grand eunuch who was assisted by military officers, ranging in number from ten to forty. His staff also included several scribes and accountants, plus hundreds of coolies and soldiers. In actual operation, the estates were left in the hands of military officers who had built a reputation as callous bullies among the peasant populace. Charges of extortion and larceny against them and their eunuch bosses were frequently reported. For example, in 1480, the eunuch manager and his staff drew the ire of the local people when they attempted to expand a royal estate owned by the crown prince in Jingzhou. In 1506, the eunuch Zhang Zhong was accused of directing his staff to make profits for his own personal gain while he was managing an imperial estate near Tianjin. In a related vein, the grand eunuch Liu Xiangfeng, manager of a huge plantation in the Beijing area, was impeached for extortion in 1512. Occasionally, the estate managers chose to use force to settle the disputes over the land boundary. In the winter of 1504, for example, the eunuch manager in a Baoding plantation sent his troops to arrest more than 200 peasants who protested against the encroachment of the imperial estate upon their lands.[11]

Even though the imperial estates had become one of the principal sources of royal wealth, the Ming court did not seem to have a coherent and systematic approach to the collection of their taxes and rentals. In the Anlu huangzhuang, which occupied most of the choice lands, tenant farmers usually paid three times as much taxes as their neighbors who worked on the people's lands. In addition to the land taxes, most imperial estates also drew their income from commercial properties, timber, fish, and iron ore production. It was estimated that the annual income of the Anlu estate from all these sources, including some 2,299 shops and stores, was about 30,000 silver taels. It indeed had become one of the biggest employers in the Hubei region, and the evidence shows that it could and did, from time to time, contribute to the vagaries of the economy of central China.[12] As a rule, all the tax revenues, either in cash or in kind, were handled by the eunuchs, who maintained separate incomes and accounting from the Ministry of Revenue officers— another example of dualistic bureaucracy. Local officials, however, were required to provide horses, coolies, and other necessary means of transportation to deliver consignments of grain to strategic points designated by the court. If there was a surplus of grain, temporary vaults were constructed for storage, and additional porters were recruited to deal with the situation.[13]

As the plantations became bigger and more numerous, peasants were required to pay more taxes to offset the revenues that had disappeared from the private land registration. The exorbitant rates that contemporary writers complained about were mostly surcharges and unscheduled, irregular, and sometimes unauthorized impositions of the peasants. For example, all ditches and roads that ran through the peasants' lands were considered taxable areas. Peasants who could not produce enough to meet tax payments often found it wise to hand over their holdings voluntarily to the big landlord or sell their holdings at lower than market prices to the adjacent plantation owner. The snowballing of the plantation certainly had serious economic and social consequences, as it created an army of desolate proletarians.[14] But however strong it was, eunuch power was basically transitory and unstable. Eunuch bosses like Cao Jixiang and Liu Jin could hold on to their plantations just as long as they enjoyed their emperor's favor. The withdrawal of favor meant not only their political oblivion, but also execution.[15] In the case of Wei

Zhongxian, after the death of Emperor Tianqi, the new emperor found it politically correct to punish Wei severely for real or imaginary crimes that Wei had allegedly committed. In the end, all these lands invariably reverted to the emperor.[16]

EUNUCHS AS TAX COLLECTORS

In addition to land taxes, Ming revenues also came from a variety of other sources, and the eunuchs, to a great extent, contributed to the morass of the Ming tax system. Levies on the transaction of real and personal properties yielded a substantial amount of tax dollars, while license fees on games, fishing, vehicles, and boats also counted a small portion of the state revenues. Permits to produce wine, vinegar, textile goods, firewood, and agricultural tools usually generated a sizable state income. And sale tax on all sorts of commodities and daily necessities, including foods and vegetables, plus wedding and funeral ritual utensils, all added up in the accounting of the public coffers.[17] However, because the Ministry of Revenues never prepared an annual budget in the manner of a modern state in the West and because it was always understaffed, the emperor had to delegate, from time to time, officials from different ministries to help collect the taxes. And oddly enough, these officials were generally authorized to disburse the funds they had collected. Under the circumstances, graft, embezzlement, and corruption became unavoidable, and the eunuchs were no exception to this rule.

The system of tax collection quickly broke out of its rut only ten years after the dynasty was established when the Ministry of Revenues reported that of the more than 400 tax offices in the empire, 178 of them did not have tax collectors or revenue inspectors. To supplant the regular official channels, Emperor Hongwu dispatched court eunuchs, National University students, and officials from several other agencies and commissions to help enforce the revenue code and collect the taxes. By the time Emperor Xuande (1426–1435) was occupying the dragon throne, it had become commonplace to see Imperial Guard officers, censors, army commanders, and the like working side by side with the revenue officials in collecting the revenues at the nine capital gates.[18] And as years went by, more and more eunuchs were sent to do likewise, and by 1466 they had become an integral part of the Ming revenue collection machinery.

In the Ming period, one thirtieth of all forest products and construction materials, including lumber, bamboo, hemp, limestone, iron, tong oil, water reeds, and bricks, had to be deposited in state warehouses before they could be used by the individuals or sold in the market. This custom was what the Ming fiscal parlance called *choufen*, or "extract and divide." Since woods were vitally important materials for palace construction and royal furniture as well as other premium uses, the Ming autocrats saw to it that they had direct and free access to such high-quality wood as walnut, redwood, cedar, teak, and mahogany. The eunuchs were therefore frequently assigned to brand the young plants for exclusive imperial use in the future and were also charged to extract and divide the government shares of forest products.

Emperor Hongzhi was believed to have been the first Ming sovereign to dispatch court eunuchs to take on this type of duty near the end of the fifteenth century. And sometime around 1517–1518, Emperor Zhengde appointed eunuchs Li Wen and Ma Jun to institutionalize the extraction practice, respectively, in Huguang and Zhejiang provinces. Before long eunuchs were extracting and dividing construction materials in Fujian, Jiangxi, and several other provinces. But of all the eunuch tax collectors, the grand eunuch Xia Shou was to become the most feared official in Zhending prefecture, as he supervised the revenue extraction of water reeds and other local products.[19] By the early 1520s, it was estimated that the Directorate of Palace Carpentry alone requested more than 200,000 silver taels worth of wood to meet its annual needs. And Wuhu, the city that was located at the confluence of the Yangtze River and the Qingyi River in southern Anhui, was to become a major supplier of palace wood and construction materials. During the Ming period, it usually took three or four days to sail from Wuhu to Nanjing, and with its excellent accessibility by water, Wuhu became an important clearinghouse of rice and farm produce and was able to provide no less than 10 percent of all the wood and bamboo demanded by the Inner Court.[20]

Other construction materials and minerals that were extracted in kind as taxes included 2,000 leaves of gold annually from Zhejiang province, 2,500 catties of water latex and 500 catties of black lead from Henan, and 5,875 feet of the most durable lumber as well as 20 sandalwood logs from Shandong. Every year eunuchs from the Directorate of Palace Carpentry were also responsible for securing 3,000 big pots and pans from Shanxi province, 5,000 catties of white round rattan from Guangdong, and 200 catties of rams' horns and 500 catties of wool from the northwestern province of Shaanxi. An itemized revenue account (around 1500) also shows that the Directorate of Palace Carpentry received yearly 300 pieces of "white cat" bamboo, which were noted for their long knots, from Suzhou prefecture and 300 catties of small copper threads as well as 500 catties of red alum from Daming prefecture. It also obtained as taxes 3,000 catties of sand from Hejian prefecture, 400 catties of nitrate from Gongping prefecture, and 3,000 sheets of paper plus 10,000 catties of zinc from Luanzhou in present-day Hebei. In addition, this eunuch agency collected annually 500 catties of blue sweet clay and 300,000 catties of hydrocarbonated coal from Beijing, and on top of these, some 50,000 catties of lime from the Ministry of Public Works.[21] In addition, the eunuchs routinely processed hundreds of thousands of catties of fuel wood and supervised the branding and harvesting of highly prized rare woods.

In addition to extracting taxes from forest products and minerals, Ming eunuchs also became involved in collecting religious tithes. It is almost universal that people can find ways to evade paying taxes to their governments, but are generally very enthusiastic in making offers to their devotional statues and giving donations to temples and churches. In 1516 Emperor Zhengde first authorized his eunuch grand defender in the sacred Mountain Tai in Shandong province to levy the so-called incense taxes on pilgrims who climbed up the rugged 5,000 foot mountain. Operating the mountain like a modern national park, the eunuchs set up fee stations at the entrance to the fabled Bixia Si (Azure Cloud Temple), where the faithful prayed to their gods and hoped to catch a spectacular sunrise from the summit. No one knows the exact amount of such religious tithes that were collected there every year, but an early seventeenth century writer named Yu Yan noted that toward the end of the dynasty the Ming government itself had become dependent upon the income of the temple for funds. He even maintained that the revenues generated from the temple of Mountain Tai alone served to pay the salaries of the government officials of Shandong province. In light of such a relatively convenient source of state income, the Ming court naturally set up similar "incense fees" collection stations at Mt. Taihe in Hubei as well as at other sacred mountains throughout the nation.[22]

From time to time, the Ming eunuchs were also engaged in extracting taxes on fisheries, tea production, and fruit, as well as collecting tolls on roads and bridges. Reports on these types of activities are, however, exiguous and their data insufficient to draw a clear picture. But the one area of fiscal activity that was well documented was the unique "gate taxes," which required all persons—merchants, tourists, civilians, and officials without passes—to pay fees before they were allowed to enter or exit the nine capital city gates. As it turned out, the Ming court was able to garner a substantial amount of revenue from this source, and the monies were used to pay for its sacrificial foods and the expenses of the Imperial Kitchen. By the early sixteenth century, all the fee collectors at the gates were eunuchs, each gate being staffed with at least ten castrati and usually supervised by a deputy from the Palace Servants Directorate. Merchants who brought merchandise to sell inside the capital city were required to pay 30 percent in copper coins and the rest in paper money. A highly reliable document reveals the extent to which the nine capital city gates could generate tax dollars. At the beginning of the Hongzhi reign (1488–1506), the nine gates yielded 665,080 guan in paper money and 2,885,130 copper coins. Twenty years later, the total amount was 715,820 guan of paper money and 2,054,300 coins; and between 1512 and

1523, the average annual figures were 2,558,920 guan in paper money plus 3,190,360 copper coins.[23] However, constant inflation often made paper money drastically depreciate in value. In 1390 a note of 1 guan of paper money was worth about 250 coins, but three years later its value dropped to only 160 coins. By the 1430s, the value of paper money had fallen to a thousandth of its original value, and by the second quarter of the sixteenth century very few people cared to use paper money, as silver had become the most popular medium for business transaction.[24]

Ming eunuchs also learned how to make money for their masters and mistresses by running a number of "imperial stores." A grand eunuch, Yu Jing, was believed to have first started this line of business both inside and outside the capital city and was reported to have earned a net profit of 80,000 silver taels every year.[25] According to Liu Ruoyu, a eunuch who lived toward the end of the dynasty, there were six imperial stores that sold general goods to the public and reaped an annual profit of tens of thousands of silver taels. Liu said that the operation of these stores began during the reign of Jiajing (1521–1567), and the sale revenues all went to an old empress dowager. Liu also revealed that when the eunuch boss Wei Zhongxian was at the zenith of his power in the 1620s, he took over the management of the stores and hired his own clerks to run them.[26]

It is difficult to account for all the revenues collected and the profit earned by the eunuchs, but reliable data estimated that in the 1590s and 1600s, the eunuchs remitted to the imperial treasury nearly a million silver taels every year, plus an uncounted number of jewels and precious articles. All these incomes from irregular and unscheduled sources, as they did not appear on the tax ledgers, helped to make up the shortfall of revenues that could be generated from Ming's institutionalized sources. One may even argue that the emperor needed to use his unscrupulous eunuch tax agents to find enough revenues so that he could provide an efficient and honest administration. On the other hand, the Confucian moralists usually regarded any increase in the tax quota as evil and incompatible with their traditional ideal of good government and found it necessary to condemn the conduct of the eunuchs.

EUNUCHS' ROLE IN THE MING SALT MONOPOLY

Next to the land taxes and the revenues extracted in kind from every conceivable commodity, the salt monopoly became the most reliable source of state income during the Ming regime. From 1570 to 1600, for instance, the Ministry of Revenues received a total of 2.6 million silver taels per year, of which 1.08 million taels came from the salt revenues. The salt revenues were generally used to maintain the troops on the border or for relief in time of drought or famine. It was frequently used in exchange for horses, metal, cloth, and for paper in printing paper money. Occasionally, the emperor would use salt to subsidize the stipends of imperial relatives, award his meritorious officials, and cultivate goodwill with foreign rulers. From time to time, salt was used as a collateral for the government to borrow funds for emergency purposes. During the Ming period, salt was produced from seawater along the coast and from lakes and wells in the interior. The government hired salt rakers, known as *yanding*, to work in the pits. Each was required to deliver to the government a fixed quota of salt annually. After paying salaries to the salt rakers, the government then sold the salt to the licensed merchants, who paid a tax of one twentieth of the price at which they bought the salt and who later sold the merchandise on the market. However, the salt rakers often produced more than they were required and "illegally" sold the surplus to whomever could pay them a higher price. This type of commodity was branded private salt and resulted in rampant smuggling throughout the dynasty.

Because it was a monopoly, the Ming government reaped huge profits from the salt operation. It established six Salt Distribution Commissions, or *Du zhuanyunyan shisi*, to administer the sale and distribution of the salt. They included the Lianghuai region in modern Jiangsu, the Liangzhe region in Zhejiang, Changlu in the Northern Metropolitan area, the Hedong region in Shanxi, the Shandong region, and the Fujian region, with a total of fourteen branch offices throughout the nation. Each salt commission, headed by a rank 3b official, in turn supervised various numbers of salt farms. Consider for example, the Liangzhe Distribution Commission, which covered an area extending from the Chongming Island at the mouth of the Yangtze River all the way to the southern Zhejiang coast and had thirty-five salt farms under its supervision. In his *Miscellany from the Bean Garden*, Lu Rong (1436–1494), a 1466 doctorate, remarks that this region alone produced about 222,300 yin (1 yin equals 400 catties) of salt every year. Half the salt was delivered, in cash, to the capital and the other half was sold to the merchants who found their own networks to sell the salt to the public. Depending upon the quality of the salt, the price ranged from 0.35 silver tael per yin to 0.6 tael per yin.[27] In addition, the Ming established seven Salt Distribution Superintendencies, or *Yanke tijusi*, each headed by a rank 5b official, to make the salt levies. They were located in Haibei of Guangdong province, Sichuan, Wujing (Five Wells) of Yunnan, Heiyanjing (Black Salt Well), Anning, Baiyanjing (White Salt Well), and at the Inner Mongolian town of Chahannaoer.[28]

Like the Ministry of Revenues, the special salt agency was understaffed and the emperor, from time to time, had to use censors, eunuchs, and even military personnel to pinch hit for the salt administrators. It is believed that as early as 1407 Emperor Yongle had already appointed his eunuchs to help manage the sale and distribution of salt. By the reign of Emperor Chenghua (1464–1487), the appointment of eunuchs to supervise the salt operation had become commonplace. In 1466, the grand eunuch Li Tang requested and received an imperial permission to open up a salt farm in Liaodong. In 1503, the grand eunuch Long Shou of the Palace Servants Directorate needed more cloth and textile materials for the Inner Court. He was authorized by the court to sell the salt in the Lianghuai region to raise 30,000 silver taels to pay for the fabric. Four years later, another grand eunuch from the same directorate, Yang Zhen, also received special permission to sell 8,000 yin of Changlu salt so that he could purchase the necessary textile materials for the Inner Court.[29]

In 1464, the grand eunuch of the Palace Foods Directorate, Pan Hong, reported that there were 59,000 yin of surplus salt from the Lianghuai region and begged Emperor Chenghua to allow his nephew Pan Gui to buy his salt from the government. The Ministry of Revenues opposed such a violation of the salt laws, but the emperor ignored the protest and affirmed the award to Pan Gui so that he could buy and sell the government monopoly with a license. In 1507, the grand eunuch Cui Lei applied this same scheme to defraud the government. And another grand eunuch from the Imperial Treasury, Wang Zan, when trying to apply the trick to enrich himself, was confronted by the impeccable grand secretary Li Dongyang.[30]

It is interesting to note that, in the 1990s, purchase agents can use a piece of plastic in the form of a credit card to make business transactions, and a Ming imperial agent could also use a "sale permit of salt" to purchase goods worth hundreds of thousands of dollars. In 1485, the court eunuch Liang Fang sold the hundreds of thousands of yin of surplus salt from the Lianghuai Distribution Commission to purchase pearls and precious stones for Emperor Chenghua. Two years earlier, another eunuch, Wang Jing, also used a sale permit of salt to purchase rare books and medicinal herbs for the Inner Court. Wang Jing came to the south in 1483 to collect antiques, rare paintings, and calligraphy. He got hold of 15,500 yin of salt, persuaded the princely establishment of Ning to buy 32,500 silver taels worth of his salt before hiring several hundred boats to carry the leftovers to Jiangxi and Nanchang, and finally sold them at a high price. But Wang Jing and his entourage behaved rather truculently and created a serious public relations problem for the court. He was soon impeached and brought to trial. After being found guilty of corruption, Wang Jing was exiled to an army camp in the frontier. And soon after the death of Emperor Chenghua in 1487, Liang Fang, the other eunuch salt broker and imperial purchase agent, was demoted and sent to Nanjing and all his properties were confiscated.[31]

Once the eunuch received an imperial permit to sell or deliver salt, he normally would hire carts and boats to transport the commodity. And right in front of the caravan he would raise high a yellow flag emblazoned with two big words—"Imperial Award"—so that local officials would not give him and his team any problems. Insolent eunuchs were reported to have coerced local merchants to buy their salt at higher prices. In 1485, the eunuch Xiong Bao went to Henan on a state ceremonial mission. He carried a large quantity of salt and forced the Henan retailers to buy his salt. In 1509, the grand eunuch Yang Zhen hired 600 boats to carry some 8,000 yin of the Changlu salt to Nanjing. Along the way, Yang found a way to sell all his salt for 16,200 silver taels. In 1515, the grand eunuch Liu Yun from the Ceremonial Directorate received a special permit to sell 10,000 yin of the Changlu salt plus 60,000 yin of the Lianghuai salt so that he could purchase necessary goods for his mission to Tibet.[32]

Because of low salaries and the lack of paper money, the Ming government often used salt and cloth to subsidize the stipends of its officials. This is why the Inner Court always kept a plentiful inventory of salt for all kinds of awards and subsidies. Before 1500, the inventory of the top grade white salt was fixed at 175,000 catties, but soon after Zhengde became the emperor the figure increased to 351,844 catties.[33] The Inner Court did not always use up all the salt in its store houses; hence, the emperor was permitted lots of leeway in disposing of the surplus salt. In 1466, for example, Emperor Chenghua gave a large quantity of salt to two of his favorite grand eunuchs, Chen Xuan and Pan Wu. During the early 1500s, the grand eunuch Gao Feng became the court's designated salt broker, empowered to sell all the excess white salt. Eunuch bosses, such as Li Rong, Liu Jin, and Wei Zhongxian, often received their largess from this source. For instance, in 1508, after learning that there was a surplus of salt totaling 1.6 million yin in the Lianghuai region, Liu Jin ordered to have it sold to the merchants of his choice, with the money to be remitted to the Inner Court within three days.[34] Liu Jin, in particular, realized that salt was the second most important source of state income, after the land taxes; therefore, he took emphatic measures to arrest salt smugglers when he was running the Ming secret police apparatuses.[35]

The Ming salt administration really began to break out of its rut when the eunuch grand defenders in various stations were given carte blanche in the salt management. Some used the salt revenues to construct office buildings; others relied upon salt to salary their troops. The means the eunuchs applied to get their hands on such a revenue pie varied, but the issue became a frequent source of criticism against them. In 1518, for example, when the grand defender of Wuchangfu, Du Fu, began to "borrow" money from the salt merchants so that he could complete a new office building, he was attacked by a group of antipathetic, angry officials from the Ministry of Revenues. Du Fu had the support of the emperor and in fact continued to raise this type of "soft money" for nearly three years. In 1525, Wang De, the eunuch grand defender of Fengyang, took a special interest in the collection of the salt revenues. He ordered the inspection of the validity of all the salt licenses and the legality of their registration. He was said to have stoked fear and resentment in the prosperous towns in the central Grand Canal region. Once again, the Ministry of Revenues protested, but Emperor Jiajing ignored this routine stab at his grand defenders. For all practical purposes, then, the Ming eunuchs had truly become ex-officio salt superintendents.[36]

EUNUCHS AND MING MINING

The Chinese had been mining gold, silver, copper, iron, lead, mercury, and various kinds of minerals long before the Ming dynasty was established. In fact, in 1279 an official abrasive depot was established in Datong. Also, collection of water-worn jade nuggets by women and girls in Khotan inspired the Ming miners to search for more precious stones within China proper. The Ming Chinese also learned how to use shijinshi (gold testing stone), a pure black and delicately smooth stone produced in Sichuan, for testing alloys of silver as well as gold. They had also developed a roller mill to crush garnets and mastered the technique of sifting the crushed materials.[37]

Emperor Hongwu, the founder of the dynasty, was said to have rejected a proposal to explore some reportedly rich silver deposits in Shandong and Shaanxi provinces, as he was at that time still busy consolidating his rule over China. But a 1386 account shows that there were forty-two silver smelters in Fujian province, and that seven counties in Zhejiang province were mining silver, with each producing 2,000 taels per year. Hongwu's son, the Emperor Yongle, began to show more interest in mining when he approved the opening of eight silver mines in Shaanxi and three in Fujian and also established mining agencies in Guizhou, Yunnan, and even in northern Annam, then under Chinese military occupation. Yongle further dispatched his eunuchs and censors to supervise the mining operations in Huguang and Guizhou. As a consequence of the series of new programs and activities, the annual silver production in Fujian increased to more than 30,000 taels, and that of Zhejian to over 80,000 taels.[38] But when Yongle commissioned the eunuch Wang Yan to prospect gold mines in southern Manchuria, the assay turned out to be a dismal disappointment. Relying primarily upon traditional lore, Wang hired some 6,000 miners to gather gold dust at Heishan (the Black Hill) in Liaodong, but after three months of travail, could produce only eight taels of gold. With the cost overrun and criticism aimed at Wang Yan mounting, the project was scrapped.[39]

Between 1425 and 1450, the total output of minerals in Ming China remained stable, even though several old mines had been shut down. However, illegal mining activities were reported in the sealed-off mines, usually perpetrated by daring private prospectors. In responding to such reports, the emperor generally dispatched officials, including his eunuchs, to the scene, and if the mines were determined profitable, he would reopen them. Emperor Jingtai (1450–1457), for instance, sent the eunuch Dai Xibao to Fujian to reclaim the mines being pirated. In the ensuing years, more and more eunuchs were commissioned to the provinces to do likewise. In fact, in 1460 alone, four eunuchs—Luo Yong to Zhejiang, Luo Gui to Yunnan, Feng Rang to Fujian, and He Neng to Sichuan—were charged to bring every promising mining project in the empire under strict government control. As a result of this renewed effort, the annual revenues from the mines increased substantially, totaling 183,000 taels of silver. They included 50,000 taels from Zhejiang, more than 20,000 taels from Fujian, 100,000 taels from Yunnan, and 13,000 taels from Sichuan. When Chenghua assumed the emperorship in 1465, he continued to follow the advice of court eunuchs and opened up twenty-four gold mines in the twelve counties along the Sichuan-Hubei mountainous region. These new enterprises hired some 55,000 miners, but many of them later died from the hardships they had to endure.[40]

It is rather interesting to note that during the Ming times, castrated courtiers, rather than high-brow scholars and bureaucrats, stood in the forefront of China's mining and metallurgical renovation. Somehow the literati officials managed to create an image that the eunuchs were universally prodigal, while the literati promoted frugality and always tried to lessen the burden of the taxpayers. But as the historian Ray Huang points out the Ming court actually had too little taxing power, and the people at large were not overtaxed.[41] Insisting that the people in his province had paid more than their tax dues, a circuit censor from Zhejiang charged, in early 1488, that the grand eunuch Zhang Qing was chewing up hundreds of thousands of silver taels from his taxpayers, many of whom, according to the censor, had to sell their children and mortgage their property to meet tax obligations. The censor also reported that the two silver mines, which used to be able to yield over 22,000 silver taels per year, had been exhausted and their production had decreased to less than one tenth their previous capacity. He complained to the emperor that Grand Eunuch Zhang utterly disregarded the situation and continued to levy a yearly royalty fee of 3,000 silver taels on these two mines. Since the censor's charges were serious enough, the court instructed both the Ministry of Revenues and the Ministry of Personnel to investigate the conduct of the grand eunuch and also review his mining policy in Zhejiang. Ultimately, the investigation threw a wrench into the mining enterprises, as hundreds of thousands of miners were laid off and their supervisors lost their jobs.[42]

After more than half a century of mining, several usually productive mines in Zhejiang, Fujian, and Yunnan had begun to show signs of exhaustion.[43] This is why Emperor Jiajing (1522–1567), who was known for his superstitious conduct, ordered a large scale search for new mines. Jiajing seemed to believe that the discovery of minerals meant that the heaven was bestowing favors upon him, the Son of Heaven. Consequently, from 1546 to 1557, Jiajing commissioned more than 40 eunuch superintendents and 1,180 soldiers to prospect new mines. The cost was said to have reached over 30,000 taels, while the silver ore extracted was worth only about 28,500 taels. It was clearly a net loss, but the emperor did not want to call off the mining enterprises.[44] During this decade, the eunuchs who were involved in the mining activities enjoyed access to His Majesty and, along with it, various degrees of political clout. And for a while, even the civil officials and the populace at large became really enthusiastic about searching for auspicious minerals, such as borax, jade, and various kinds of abrasive.[45]

After the death of Jiajing, the mining craze gradually subsided as his son, Emperor Longqing, generally downsized mining enterprises, including suspending stone quarry operations. But Jiajing's grandson, Wanli, who was not quite ten years old when he assumed the emperorship in 1572, later turned out to become perhaps the most enthusiastic promoter in the history of Chinese mining. As early as 1584, Wanli had shown keen interest in pursuing mining affairs, but because he was still very young he was easily dissuaded by his grand secretaries from investing in any new mines. However, a dozen years later, when Wanli became more astute and fell upon hard times in terms of his treasury reserves, he decided to launch a large-scale mining project to reduce the deficit in his treasury and return a nubbin of fiscal normalcy to the court's finances. Ample data support this line of policy, as Wanli had been forced to careen from fiscal crisis to crisis. For instance, in 1592, the Ming court spent 2 million taels on a military expedition to its northwest Ningxia border region. During the winter of the same year and for the next eight long years, the Ming military expenditures in Korea topped 7 million taels. Furthermore, during the 1596–1597 period, Wanli spent a huge sum of cash to reconstruct five of his palace buildings.[46]

Wanli's mining activities began in earnest in 1596 when petitions to dig mines came from all over the empire, with one province petitioning to open thirty-one mines. A host of trusted eunuchs were then dispatched to various locations to manage all the affairs relating to the prospecting of minerals.[47] For example, Wang Zhong was sent to Changping in the suburb of Beijing, Wang Hu to several prefectures in present-day Hebei, Lu Kun to Henan, Cao Jin to Zhejiang, Li Jin to Guangdong, Shen Yongshou to Guangxi, Pan Xiang to Jiangxi, and Yang Rong to Yunnan. All of these eunuch mining superintendents received official seals and were given broad authority to execute the mining policy of the emperor in their respective regions. Some of them were later accused of being arrogant, as well as insensitive to the local environment and economic conditions. Others were said to be downright mean to boot and, because of the exorbitant mine taxes they imposed on the people, they frequently aroused the anger and hatred of the population.[48] Among the most controversial eunuch mining managers were Chen Zeng in Shandong, Chen Feng in Hubei, and Gao Huai in southern Manchuria.

Chen Zeng's association with mining began in 1584, when the Ming court responded to a petition for opening up a new mine in the mountainous Fangshan county, located in present-day Hebei. Chen took several mining experts with him, but after conducting an initial investigation, he concluded that the potential was not very good and suggested that Emperor Wanli table the petition. Four years later, Chen made another extensive investigation tour to Mt. Wutai in Shanxi province and reported rich ores of silver in the area. Wanli was very excited about the prospect of starting a new mining project; however, because of the opposition of an influential grand secretary, Shen Shixing (fl. 1583–1591), it was aborted. In 1590, the eunuch Chen Zeng again detected some very promising jade mine in northern China, but once again, due to Shen's objection, Chen Zeng could go nowhere. Chen undoubtedly continued to receive encouragement from His Majesty and finally got his chance to prospect his long cherished mining enterprise when he was commissioned to Shandong in 1596. For the next decade, until his death in 1605, Chen stayed in Shandong, surveying six prefectures and twenty-nine counties and looking for every mountain, hill, and valley to mine. In the end, however, Chen became one of the most hated men, so reported by his contemporary writers, as he frequently clashed with local officials who time and again demanded his removal from Shandong. Emperor Wanli naturally turned a deaf ear to such requests and dismissed the charges against his eunuch as malicious nonsense. Under the circumstances, Chen Zeng was said to have grown even more arrogant, as he publicly boasted that the memorial of the governor of Shandong would never reach His Majesty's desk, but the report submitted by him would be speedily conveyed to the emperor. It was well known that Wanli detested the morning audience and refused to receive his literati-bureaucrats, however, if there were memorials concerning the mining projects or revenue matters, he reportedly would be anxious to receive them day or night.[49]

The second most controversial eunuch mining superintendent was Chen Feng, whose two-year stint in Huguang reportedly terrorized every provincial official and merchant in central China. After working for several years in the Directorate of Imperial Stables, Cheng Feng received a commission to prospect mines and collect minerals and metal for the state mint and for promoting the general metallurgical industry. Chen Feng's broad credentials allowed him to break a funding logjam for the court's so-called wootz steel project, which produced steel by the mixing of a specified amount of carbon with iron. By this time, the Chinese smelters had mastered a method by which a small amount of "black earth" was added to the ore to promote full fusion of the metal and its perfect running in thin molds. Chen Feng apparently was an aggressive and eager manager, consequently stepping on the toes of many people and at times behaving recklessly. For instance, on a tip from an informer, he ordered the excavation of the tomb of the wife of a Tang dynasty prime minister and obtained a huge sum of gold for his master, the Emperor Wanli. When the local officials refused to cooperate or hid mining information from him, he would have them thrown into jail. Such forceful measures inevitably aroused the resentment of the populace, and one would expect that the censors and other bureaucrats would do everything in their power to torpedo Chen Feng's mining and metallurgical enterprises. After only two years of service, the eunuch Chen Feng was recalled, leaving many of his dream projects unattended.[50]

The third notorious eunuch mining superintendent was Gao Huai, who rose to prominence after serving with distinction in the Directorate of Palace Foods. Gao Huai made his mark in Liaodong and Korea and was reported to have gathered hundreds of thousands of taels of silver for Emperor Wanli. Whenever Gao surveyed prospective mines, he brought along a huge entourage. His henchmen sought every piece of gold and silver up and down the Shanhaiguang Pass. And on several occasions, they even traversed all the way to Korea to get their hands on Korean pearls and steeds, which they sent to Wanli as tribute. One frontier garrison commander despised Gao so much that he swore he wanted to flay Gao's skin and eat Gao's body. But in spite of repeated cavalier attempts on the part of local officials, Emperor Wanli kept Gao on the job for more than a decade.[51]

During the course of surveying, prospecting, and processing of minerals and ores, problems were bound to occur, and there is no doubt that abuses and atrocities were committed by the eunuchs. Several eunuch superintendents probably forced out civilians after minerals were discovered on their properties. Farmers whose lands possessed precious ores were subjected to barefaced extortion. Excavations might also have damaged many a tomb and graveyard—heinous offenses in the eyes of the Chinese—and disturbed the tranquility of hundreds of rural and remote communities. This was, of course, the price that Ming society would have to pay if it understood the usefulness of developing some sort of industrial economy.

It should be noted that, from 1597 to 1605, the revenues from all of the mines totaled around 3 million taels of silver. Moreover, during the course of prospecting gold and silver and processing other metals, the Ming eunuchs led the way in improving iron-casting technology. At the beginning of the dynasty, there were only thirteen blast furnaces in the country, and the total output of iron was roughly 7.5 million catties. These figures increased substantially by the sixteenth century. In fact, the demand of charcoal for smelting iron had so depleted the resources of timber that several of the provinces were threatened with complete deforestation. However, it is believed that the Chinese had by the end of the sixteenth century developed rather advanced techniques in iron casting.[52]

It would be presumptuous to say that the eunuchs spearheaded Ming China's mining and steel industry; and that had they been given free reign to pursue their metallurgical activities, Ming China might have produced an Abraham Darby, or a Henry Cort, or even a Henry Bessemer before England did in the eighteenth and nineteenth centuries. There is no denying, however, that the literati-gentry as a class vehemently opposed this type of enterprise and indeed did everything possible to discredit eunuch mining entrepreneurs and obstruct any industrial projects that might have led to machinery innovations or even to a full-scale industrial revolution. They stood their conservative and traditionalist ground, and in collusion with the generally ignorant and superstitious populace, jeered, criticized, and slandered the eunuch mining superintendents. Many a eunuch mining personnel were attacked by mobs, and some of their assistants were killed and their offices burned. In Wuchang several thousand civilians threw stones at the grand eunuch Chen Feng. In Yunnan the eunuch superintendent Yang Rong had to call in soldiers to beat off several thousand rioters. In Jiangxi the eunuch superintendent Pan Xiang was forced to burn down his porcelain mills. In Suzhou and Hangzhou eunuch managers were frequently chased out of their lodges.[53] Case after case of antimining incidents abound in Ming documents. They suffice to lay bare the unfavorable social and political atmosphere within which the eunuch promoters of mining and metallurgy had to operate. But considering the tremendous odds against them and the generally inconsistent, on-again and off-again support of their emperors, it is really a wonder that the Ming eunuchs dared to espouse such unpopular enterprises and achieve a modicum of success, however limited it might have been, in early modern China. In the final analysis, however, what they had achieved was not enough to catapult China into an industrial age.

EUNUCHS AS PURCHASING AGENTS AND MANUFACTURING MANAGERS

As stated earlier, Ming palace supplies, such as wax, tea, fresh food, dyes, charcoal, lumber, dried fish, paper, medicine, and other commodities and daily necessities were extracted annually from the people. When the court needed more than it received from such sources, the emperor always sent his eunuchs to purchase more on his behalf, in particular to buy pearls from Guangdong, silk fabric from the lower Yangtze region, and porcelain from Jiangxi. Other eunuchs would be stationed permanently in the locale where special goods were produced or manufactured. Emperor Yongle was believed to be the first Ming monarch to commission court eunuchs as imperial purchasing agents, when, during the summer of 1406, he sent the eunuch Li Jin to Shanxi to buy its fabled medicinal herbs called *tianhua*, or the heavenly flowers. A decade later, Yongle sent another eunuch named Ma Qi to Annam to collect pearls and precious stones and, near the end of 1424, just about three months after the ascension of Yongle's son, the Emperor Hongxi, Ma Qi was once again sent to Annam to buy gold, silver, pearls, and perfume for the imperial court.[54] During the reign of Xuande (1426–1435), eunuchs were sent all over the empire and beyond to purchase flowers, trees, birds, animals, and all sorts of rare goods.[55]

When a eunuch purchasing envoy came to town, he almost inevitably would disturb the tranquility of the community by demanding that local officials provide lodging, food, and supplies for his entourage, which usually numbered from 100 to 200 persons. He would also hire many workers to carry out his mission. But when the eunuch left town, the books of the local government, which most of the time operated on a shoestring budget, could not be balanced, and the hundreds of temporary workers also lost their livelihood. Under the circumstances, a host of censors and supervising secretaries would impeach the eunuchs and would declaim all the faults and blunders that were supposedly committed by them. A case in point involved the eunuch Wang Jing, who was commissioned by the Emperor Chenghua in the early 1480s to find and buy medicinal herbs, rare books and manuscripts, and priceless antiques of all kinds. Wang's mission began in northern China, where he searched in every county for books of ancient print as well as for aphrodisiacs, among them the legendary golden scorpions and icy plums. His mission then swung to central China, then to Jiangxi, and finally came to Suzhou and Hangzhou of the southeastern region. Wang Jing often used the salt revenues, amounting in the hundreds of thousands of taels, to defray his expense, but he also coerced the local officials to pick up the tab of his mission. Consequently, he became a persona non grata in the eyes of the local magistrates and governors. In the end, however, Wang Jing, like hundreds of his eunuch colleagues, was prosecuted for abusing his power and was sentenced to serve in a frontier army.[56]

Other items that the eunuchs purchasing agents loved to obtain included wax, carpets, precious stones of all colors, diamonds and gems, strange-looking crystals, aloe, and above all, pearls. There is no doubt that most of the palace women, including the empresses and the princesses, had a great passion for pearls. In Ming China, the place that produced the highest quality pearls was the southern province of Guangdong. In the early fifteenth century, pearls were found at Dongwan near the Pearl River, at Lianzhou, and in the Leizhou Peninsula. Soon, a eunuch bureau for the cultivation and management of pearls was established in Guangdong. But since it took several years for the pearls to grow inside the oyster shells, harvesting this imperial monopoly was not frequent. During the reign of Emperor Xuande, an official suggested a eunuch mission to pick up pearls in Guangdong; he was thrown in jail. The first recorded harvesting of pearls took place during the reign of Emperor Tianshun (1457–1465), possibly because the eunuch superintendent of the pearl farms suspected that a local magistrate was stealing the pearls at Lianzhou. The second time the Ming court dispatched a eunuch commission to obtain pearls was in 1499, and this mission met with astounding success. The pearls, because they had been cultivated for nearly four decades, were large, mature, coruscating, and valued at about 28,000 taels of silver.[57]

Soon after this striking harvest, the eunuch superintendent was withdrawn from the Pearl Bureau, but when Zhengde ascended the throne, he had this office reinstated and ordered another big harvest in 1514. A dozen years later, Emperor Jiajing, who was anxious to obtain pearls for his relatives, ordered another harvest, but because the baby pearls had not had enough time to grow, the result was disappointing, as the pearls that were harvested were generally small and soft. During the course of the harvesting, some fifty divers lost their lives and mounting criticism was broached from many corners of the empire. The eunuchs in charge of the pearl production took the blame, and the Pearl Bureau was once again closed down. But whenever there were many royal weddings or many titles conferred upon the young princes and princesses, there would be a great demand for pearls, and consequently, eunuchs would be dispatched to Guangdong to do the job. In 1557, Emperor Jiajing actually demanded the shocking number of 800,000 pearls from the sea in Guangdong. And in 1572, Emperor Longqing ordered the acquisition of 20,000 gems from Yunnan and 8,000 pearls from Guangdong. Longqing's son, Emperor Wanli, at one time commissioned eunuchs Li Jing and Li Feng to Guangdong to obtain more than 5,100 taels worth of pearls.[58]

In the true sense of the word, pearl cultivation was an imperial monopoly, and so was the manufacture of the world renowned porcelain. Porcelain is called *china* because as early as the Han dynasty (206 B.C.–220 A.D.), the Chinese had already developed advanced ceramic techniques, used to make vessels of elegant form, ornamented with painting and reliefs. By the Ming era, the Chinese porcelain had become thinner, often exquisitely decorated with flowers and other patterns in blue and many other colors, including purple, red, yellow, green, and white. In 1436, the people from the Fuliang prefecture in Jiangxi province presented to the Ming court some 50,000 beads of beautiful, hard-paste china. Emperor Zhengtong was very pleased, but after rewarding the potters with lots of paper money, he decreed that from then on, no individual would be allowed to make porcelain, and those who violated the decree would be put to death; hence, the beginning of the state monopoly of the manufacture of porcelain in the Ming dynasty. To guarantee the porcelain's quality and enforce the imperial policy, the eunuch boss Wang Zhen sent several eunuchs to inspect the manufacture of the porcelain in Jiangxi; and by the reign of Emperor Chenghua, eunuchs were permanently stationed at the chief porcelain-producing town of Jingdezhen.

The eunuch-managed kilns at Jingdezhen used a pure, soft, white clay called gaolin and mixed it with another substance, usually crushed rocks, as raw material. A glassy glaze and the air-dried clay mixture were then baked together—only once—and when fired they did not change color. Among the most popular porcelain produced at Jingdezhen included the blue ware, white ware, the enameled ware, and the three color ware, but the most highly prized was the "blue dragon on white earth" vase painted with flowers. The Ming court used a large quantity of such wares for sacrificial ceremonies, for burial purposes so that the dead royal members would not need to worry about their livelihood in the other world, for decorating palaces, and for awarding the Ming's vassals in foreign lands. In 1537, Emperor Jiajing ordered thousands of beads of porcelain to be buried in the seven new royal tombs. In 1558, Jiajing's eunuchs delivered 30,000 beads of porcelain from Jiangxi. But the figures continued to rise, as the demand always far outstripped the supply for such beautiful and practical utensils. Jiajing's son, Emperor Longqing, for example, ordered his eunuchs at Jingdezhen to make him over 100,000 sets of chinaware, and Jiajing's grandson, Emperor Wanli, requested the manufacture of 159,000 plates of the exquisite ware. Wanli later ordered an additional 80,000 sets of porcelain from Jiangxi. The magnitude of this order was truly astronomical, and they were not filled until 1610.[59] To be sure, Ming eunuchs also supervised porcelain manufacture in other parts of China, but the porcelain produced at Jingdezhen remained the most sought after merchandise, not only by the Asians but also the Europeans. In fact, European craftsmen attempted constantly to produce imitation Jingdezhen chinaware, but always met with failure until 1700, when they discovered the secret of using gaolin.

In addition to supervising the cultivation of pearls and the manufacture of porcelain, the Ming eunuchs were also in charge of managing the production of various kinds and fashions of textile fabric for the court. Soon after the establishment of the dynasty, Emperor Hongwu began to restore an attitude that favored artisans, as they were grouped into two categories. The zhuzuo (resident) families were required to work in government-run workshops and were subject to the Ministry of Public Works; the lunban (rotary) families had to work only a certain number of days every year in those workshops.

The professions of artisan were thereby made hereditary within the family, passing from generation to generation. In Nanjing, Emperor Hongwu wasted no time in establishing loom workshops for splicing, spinning, and twisting bast fibres and silk filaments into fabric, and more than 1,000 highly specialized weavers were hired to do the job. During the ensuing years, textile factories with spinning and reeling devices as well as dyeing mills were set up in the areas where raw materials for textile fibers abounded. The more notable ones included those in Suzhou and Songjiang (nowadays Greater Shanghai), in Hangzhou and Shaoxing of Zhejiang province, in Quanzhou of Fujian province, and in Sichuan. By the late sixteenth century, Suzhou and Hangzhou alone could produce up to 150,000 bolts of fabric every year. Textile mills were also established in the northwestern provinces of Shanxi and Shaanxi, where the court took advantage of their plentiful wool from sheep, camels, and the like. By the mid-sixteenth century, these mills could manufacture some 74,000 bolts of woolen textiles annually and produced the best winter cloth and carpets for the imperial court. All these workshops and mills usually employed a large staff of artisans and were managed by eunuch superintendents who enjoyed high prestige and influence among their peers. In fact, textile superintendent was one of those "fat cat" positions that ambitious eunuchs generally coveted and would pursue by underhanded means to secure appointments from the Directorate of Ceremonials.[60]

It appears that these eunuch–managed mills manufactured various kinds of textiles for broad use. For instance, they used hemp for making ropes, sacks, and for coarse heavy fabrics often demanded by the military and manufacturing sectors. The Ming weavers also used ramie yarns in sewing cloth garments and leather shoes, for underwear, curtains, and mosquito nets. In addition, they selected the bast fibers from certain bean vines to produce fishing nets and supply a useful and economically profitable textile material for weaving cloth of various qualities. Fabrics woven of banana fibers always had an exotic touch during the Ming times; several regions were famous for this raw material, among them Fujian, Guangdong, and Guangxi. Ultimately, however, the production cost of cotton fibers became more competitive and reduced the importance of all other bast fibers used in the manufacture of textiles. However, the luxury silk fabrics, no matter how expensive the production costs might be, remained the most desirable of all by the imperial family. Silk fibers were reeled off from the cocoons in continuous lengths of several hundred meters. Moreover, they provided almost uniform tensile strength and elastic structure and, during the Ming times, both the private and government-run loom workshops could produce silk fabric of high quality and complex design in countless varieties, catering to all tastes and fashions.[61]

Each government-run textile mill was required to produce an annual quota of fabrics for the court, but beginning in 1460, eunuchs were sent to various regions, mostly in the five prefectures of the lower Yangtze River valley, to purchase additional fabric for the imperial family, the army, and the Inner Court personnel. When a deputy minister from the Ministry of Public Works opposed the manufacture of 7,000 additional bolts of silk fabric, the Emperor Tianshun had him thrown in jail; and after that, more and more eunuchs were stationed in southern China for purchasing cloth. They were usually authorized to use the salt revenues to pay for the fabrics they bought. In 1506, the Directorate of Royal Clothing reported that its inventory of colored fabric, satin, gold embroidery, sparkling shines, dragon, bull, flying fish, giraffe, lion, flying immortal, heavenly deer, and others were running short of supply. The court ordered the manufacture, on top of the annual quotas of over 17,000 bolts, of more of the most exquisite textiles. Soon after Jiajing assumed the emperorship, he appointed more eunuchs to supervise textile manufacturing in Nanjing, Suzhou, Hangzhou, and Shanxi. In fact, Jiajing listened to the Grand Secretary Xia Yan (1482–1548), who suggested to the emperor that the empress should perform the ceremony of cultivating silkworms—a ritual by which women might learn feminine virtues and also assure a good crop. In 1530, he ordered the reanimation of the sericultural ceremony after 400 years of neglect. But it was not long before the ceremony was abolished, because Beijing was too far removed from centers of sericultural practice, where people earned their living from cultivating mulberry trees and raising silkworms and cocoons.[62]

The annual expenditure for textile manufacturing continued to soar until it reached 400,000 silver taels during the mid-sixteenth century. Some of the mills were periodically shut down, due primarily to natural disaster and political pressure. But the incessant disruption of the workshop operation actually cost the government more money. Moreover, the eunuch superintendents were not allowed to develop a long-term manufacturing strategy, let alone to promote the general economic growth of the country. Considering all the favorable conditions that existed in sixteenth-century China, one wonders why neither Suzhou nor Hangzhou could lead the world in the textile revolution and become either Birmingham or Manchester. The Ming eunuchs' other major economic involvement was in the area of foreign trade, which is discussed in Chapter VII. But again, their promotion of trade with foreign countries was frequently interrupted by a group of literati officials whose cultural inertia and inward-looking mentality prevented them from appreciating the importance of cross-cultural contact with the peoples inhabiting distant shores. Nevertheless, in spite of all the interferences, never-ending impeachments, and worst of all, the real threat of capital punishment, the Ming eunuchs, as a group, had remarkably assumed an unprecedented role in the stewardship of the Ming economy.

IX

Miscellaneous Duties
of the Ming Eunuchs

EUNUCHS AND IMPERIAL SEALS

In the Chinese dynastic tradition, imperial seals were generally equated with power and whoever won the mandate of heaven also became the custodian of a set of sacred imperial seals. Chinese imperial seals were more like the Roman consular fasces that symbolized imperium. They were in fact the source of all power as the following saying succinctly reflects the Chinese political culture: "The state existed when the seals existed, and when the state was overrun by an enemy, the seals became antique." Likewise in every dynasty officials in charge of seals were selected with the utmost care, and the Ming founding monarchs naturally paid very close attention to the seals they inherited or later created. At the time the dynasty was established, Emperor Hongwu also set up a special seal office, the Shangbaosi, to safeguard and utilize imperial seals. To make sure that his seal officials would never abuse their positions or misuse the seals, the Ming emperor also appointed a number of eunuchs to keep an eye on his civil seal officials. Such a dualistic system was certainly consistent with the Ming dynasty's ruthless despotism and its practice of political surveillance.

So long as the reigning monarch ruled with an iron fist, as during the first five emperors, he usually could keep his seal officials, civil as well as eunuch, in check. Emperor Hongwu used to get out of bed at cockcrow and appeared at court to receive all his subordinates before sunrise. He repeatedly threatened death to any eunuchs who became involved in politics. His son and third emperor Yongle was quoted as saying, "I'll follow my father's instructions so that without sealed documents, eunuchs could not change anyone's job, military or civilian."[1] However, as time went on, Ming emperors became dissipated and lazy, and the imperial leadership began to show signs of anemia. On the accession of the Emperor Zhengtong in 1436, for example, the afternoon court meeting was discontinued. Worse still, during the latter half of the Ming period, several emperors seldom received their officials. Emperor Wanli (1573–1620), in fact, refused to grant any interview to his ministers for over twenty years. But when the emperors became uninterested in government and lived in seclusion in their harems, even the carefully designed dualistic system began to malfunction. And as power always corrupts, the imperial seals, symbol of all power, easily became the tools of corrupt seal officials.

The special agency in charge of royal seals began as early as the Shang dynasty (1766–1122 B.C.). Although the number of seal officials varied from dynasty to dynasty, the appointees to such an office unquestionably enjoyed the confidence of the reigning monarch. During both the Tang and Song dynasties, eunuchs were known to have been assigned to this unique office, but the Ming ruling family had decided to have civil and eunuch seal officials work together when it came to protecting and utilizing imperial seals. Liu Shaoguang became the first civil bureaucrat appointed to prepare, maintain, and affix the various imperial seals. Liu, rank 5a, was called the *director* of the newly established Shangbaosi in 1367 and was assisted by a deputy, rank 5b, and a small staff. At the beginning of the dynasty, most of the officials in the Seal Office, together with the Central Drafting Office, were sons, nephews, and relatives of influential ministers, Hanlin scholars, and military commanders. Nevertheless, such a practice should not be characterized as outrageous nepotism or an evidence of sinecurism, because loyalty was the most important criterion for this type of job. Obviously, it was an extremely sensitive agency, as the Ming founder's instructions had indicated:[2] "The seal is the symbol of the heaven. In ancient times, the sages who gained control of the seal also ruled the world. Therefore, seals are sacred tools and can be entrusted only to men of loyalty, diligence, and integrity. You are now seal officials and should approach your duty with dexterity and extreme caution day and night. You should keep everything secret and deep, safeguard every intelligence, and behave properly around your colleagues and peers."

Throughout the Ming period, the seal officials numbered from three to twenty, but their duties, in addition to taking care of the imperial seals, included maintaining and issuing a host of tallies, stamps, tablets, and passes. There were twenty-four imperial seals, seven of which were made in and around 1539 when Jiajing was the reigning emperor. Each one of these seals had its own unique and specifically stated functionings. The first and foremost seal was called *Huangdi fengtian zhi bao*, or the "Treasure of Emperor's Respecting Heaven," which the Ming inherited from the Tang and Song dynasties. The Respecting Heaven Seal was used exclusively for imperial sacrifices to the heaven and earth. The second most sacred seal was called *Huangdi zhi bao*, or the "Emperor's Treasure," which would be used only for imperial decrees and amnesties. When the emperor conferred new noble titles or gave awards, certificates, and accolades, he used the third seal called *Huangdi xing bao*, or the "Emperor's Branch Treasure." And when the Ming emperor sent messages to his clansmen and ministers or moved his troops from station to station, he used the fourth seal called *Huangdi xin bao*, or the "Emperor's Trust Treasure." If, on the other hand, the emperor needed to confer titles or give honors to his deceased ancestors and relatives he always relied upon his fifth seal, called *Huangdi zunqin zhi bao*, or the "Treasure of Emperor's Respect for Relatives." All personal instructions from the emperor to the imperial princes had to be sealed with *Huangdi qinqin zhi bao*, or the "Treasure of Emperor's Loving Relatives." There were two seals of this type: larger one utilized for the highest grade of princes, and a smaller one for the rest of them. The seventh seal, called *Tianzi zhi bao*, or the "Treasure of the Son of Heaven," was used for making state sacrifices to mountains, rivers, ghosts, and spirits. When conferring titles on and giving awards to his vassals in foreign countries, the Ming emperor relied upon the eighth seal, *Tianzi xing bao,* or the "Branch Treasure of the Son of Heaven." On the other hand, if the emperor requested services and demanded tributes from his tributary vassals, he utilized the ninth seal, *Tianzi xin bao,* or the "Trust Treasure of the Son of Heaven," for correspondence.

These nine seals constituted the most important sources of powers, covering all the political, military, cosmic, diplomatic, and imperial clan affairs. The tenth and eleventh seals were used for the promotion or demotion of his civil bureaucrats and service officials. If, when receiving the regular audience of his officials, the emperor wished to give impromptu instructions, his words would be written and affixed with the thirteenth seal. The fourteenth seal, called *Yuqian zhi bao*, or the "Treasure in Front of His Majesty," was utilized for making marks on imperial documents, manuscripts, and books of all subjects in the Imperial Library. The fifteenth and the sixteenth seals were also applied to the same purpose. The twenty-fourth and last imperial seal was the Treasure of the Heir Apparent, used exclusively for attending to the business of the crown prince. This seal was routinely brought to the Literary Flora Hall where the crown prince exercised his symbol of power.[3]

What caused the Emperor Jiajing to make seven new seals—seventeenth to twenty-third—remains a puzzle. These seals were added to satisfy a variety of imperial functions and affix the ever-increasing palace documents. They ranged from announcing the dates of the emperor's hunting trips, giving accolade certificates to meritorious people, and officiating religious ceremonies to declaring the existence of a rebellion and issuing proclamations to calm the populace. However, two reasons might possibly be cited for creating more seals in the Ming palace: one is Jiajing's superstition in Daoist religion and the other is his trust of a scholar-official named Yan

Song (1480–1568). Ming documents provide ample stories about Jiajing's crotchety personality, including his desire to become an immortal. Only a few years after he was enthroned, he became dissipated and uninterested in state affairs, consequently allowing his sycophant Yan Song to run the country. It is possible that Yan Song needed new tools to consolidate his power base and thus persuaded Emperor Jiajing to make several new imperial seals. But whatever the reasons, Jiajing's reign provides some interesting insight into the importance of the Seal Office.

As Yan Song frequently wrote beautiful essays and poems for Jiajing in praise of his zeal and commitment to Daoist practice, he was soon promoted to the high position of grand secretary, and his son Yan Shifan was made a vice minister in the Ministry of Public Works. To counter the influence of the eunuchs, Yan Song decided that he had to place his son in charge of the Seal Office.[4] Father and son remained in power for over twenty years. During this period, the power of the eunuchs was substantially weakened while the Yans acquired riches and great influence. Having access to the imperial seals and working in collusion with his grand secretary father, Yan Shifan, himself a very astute politician, became even more corrupt and abusive than his father. In the political circle of Beijing, the young Yan earned the nickname "little premier."[5]

It is not difficult to understand the potential power of the Seal Office officials, because, in addition to the twenty-four imperial seals, they were also in charge of giving out and taking in all kinds of government authorization seals. For example, newly appointed grand commanders, governors, various ranks of commissioners, inspectors, and the envoys to be accredited to foreign countries all had to obtain their seals before leaving the capital. The reverse was equally important. Every retiring military commander and governor, as well as every returning commissioner and envoy who had discharged his duties, had to return the seals to the Seal Office. Under the system, every imperial authorization, assignment and decision would require the use of imperial and other seals. Accordingly, custodians of the seals were among the first to learn the timing of an important appointment as well as secret information about state affairs. For this reason, the Ming founding monarchs designed a multifaceted and seemingly secure system to safeguard state secrecy and the source of all power. No wonder the grand secretary Yan Song would fight so hard to get his son appointed director of the Seal Office.

However, the Seal Office was an agency with no building or physical identity. All the twenty-four imperial seals plus the utmost important state authorization vehicles were stored in the palace women's office. Whenever a seal official from the Outer Court requested the use of a particular seal, he first sent a note to the Shangbaojian, the eunuch's seal office in the Inner Court, located just outside of the Xihua Gate nearby the Taiyi Lake.

Through the Shangbaojian, the civil seal official obtained the emperor's permission to use the particular seal in question. The civil seal official, always accompanied by a eunuch seal official, then went to the Palace Women's Clothing Bureau to get the seal. And during the application of the seal on written documents, the civil official would do all the stamping and affixation while the eunuch watched. And when the seal was returned to storage, the same routine was followed; that is, the civil official carried the seal while the eunuch kept an eye on both the seal official and the seal. Such was the typical dualistic Ming security system.[6] In fact, it was the same practice that the Ming emperor applied to conduct his diplomacy—having a chief eunuch envoy supervise civil diplomats on a mission to a tributary state—and to guard his granaries—the civil official was responsible for the inventory and bookkeeping while the eunuch kept the keys.

Despite the seal officials' access to power, their job was not exactly a bed of roses. They might need a certain amount of luck and also a modicum of skill to survive in the despotic Ming system. During the regular imperial audience, two seal officials, again accompanied by eunuchs, carried the imperial seals and walked immediately in front of His Majesty. After the emperor was seated, they placed the seals on a table and stood motionless close by. When the ceremony was over, they returned the seals to storage and left the palace. In the event His Majesty left the palace or the capital city, the seal officials had to carry the seals and follow the emperor wherever he went. Whenever there was an important state ceremony, the seal officials, both civil and eunuch, became busier. For instance, if His Majesty decided to make an imperial proclamation, the grand secretary or whoever was involved first made a draft and had the Central Drafting Office copy the draft before submitting it to the emperor for final approval. It was difficult to ascertain how many copies of such proclamations had to be affixed with one particular seal. But it should be reminded that the Ming empire had 15 provinces, 159 prefectures, 234 subprefectures, and 1171 counties, plus many trade routes, canal stations, army camps, and so on.

Near the end of every year, all of the imperial seals had to be brought to the Directorate of Astronomy (located between the Court of State Ceremonials and the Imperial Academy of Medicine), whose functions included conducting heavenly observations, forecasting weather conditions, fixing the calendar, and interpreting natural phenomena. But the director of astronomy was also charged to select an auspicious day for cleaning and washing the imperial seals. Once a date was chosen, the seal officials, once again civil as well as eunuch, washed all the seals with perfumed water at the Huangjimen, or the Polar Gate, in the Forbidden City. At this time of the year, the Seal Office also had to submit a report itemizing the total number of seal affixations and stampings during the previous twelve months.[7] It was estimated that, on the average, the imperial seals were used over 30,000 times every year and that the annual budget allotted to buy vermillion pigment for inking the seals amounted to sixty silver taels.[8] But behind all this fascinating trivia was the fact that the civil and eunuch seal officials might not claim credit for the good things that happened during their tenure, but they always bore the blame for the ills that befell the seals.

The eunuchs who were assigned to double up the safety of imperial seals generally worked under the Shangbaojian or the Directorate of Imperial Seals, established since 1367. By 1395 this directorate was upgraded to include a 4a eunuch director who was assisted by two deputies with 4b rank, a recorder with 6a rank, an intendant, also 6a, and numerous staff members. As well as looking over the shoulders of civil seal officials, these eunuchs were responsible for affixing seals on every container, envelope, and utensil in the palace. In particular, they had to make sure that the bottles and jars containing wines, herbs, dried food, sweets, and pills that His Majesty regularly used were absolutely safe from poison or contamination. They carefully inspected each one of them and covered the tops with special yellow envelopes before sealing them with stamps and storing them for future use. The eunuchs in this directorate worked on a twelve hour shift, changing guard every afternoon. Those on duty always had the keys to the seal storage tightly secured around their waists and were on constant alert for any emergency order from His Majesty or the crown prince.

The eunuch agency Yinshoujian, or the Directorate of Document Filing, on the other hand, was in charge of a variety of passes, tablets, and tallies that were used as credentials by palace personnel and government officials to gain access to palace buildings and move in and out and around the Forbidden City. The first category of such credentials was the gold tablets, which had five classifications—humanity, righteousness, decorum, wisdom, and trust—and were issued to the elite military personnel on morning patrol and night watch. The Chinese character of the word *humanity* was written in the shape of a dragon on a gold tablet and could be worn only by the personnel from the commissioners in chief, vice commissioners in chief, assistant commissioners in chief and the senior consorts (husbands of imperial princesses). The word *righteousness* was made into the shape of a tiger, and this credential was issued only to the "guard" commanders who had hereditary privileges. *Decorum,* on the other hand, was made like a giraffe and was issued to battalion commanders, while the word *wisdom,* written like a lion, was given to company commanders for passing through palace gates. Finally, the character of *trust* was made like a wisp of auspicious cloud and was worn by generals as identification badges.

The second category of authorized credentials under the custody of the seal officials was called the *half-a-word copper tally*, which had four classifications—rotation, east, west, and north. A word, such as *east* or *west*, was chiseled on a piece of copper; the left half of the copper word was issued to the garrison guards who patroled the wall, and the right half of the word was issued to the guards who were stationed at the gate. It was quite obvious that a collective responsibility system was installed to prevent any individual misconduct or carelessness. From time to time the eunuchs from the Inner Court would stop a guard and ask to verify his pass word tally. The third category, called the *order tablets*, were issued to night watch guards in the Imperial City and those who were charged with issuing fire alarms and managing nighttime emergencies. These identification tablets had six classifications— afternoon, wood, metal, earth, fire, and water—generally following the Daoist cosmic elements. The fourth category that provided credentials for government personnel, called the *copper tablets*, dealt primarily with the security check of ordinary garrison guards. Ordinary garrison guards who were assigned to sensitive posts had to wear the Chinese word *valor* chiseled on a piece of copper.

It is clear that the seal officials in the Ming dynasty had very broad powers indeed and extensive responsibilities beyond just safeguarding the seals. In addition to the afore mentioned authorized passes, they were also in charge of the so-called ivory tablets, which were issued to ministers and officials, who had to wear them during the regular imperial audience. The ivory tablet credentials in turn had five classifications. The dukes, marquises, and earls wore the ivory tablet of *merit*, imperial relatives wore the ivory tablet of *relative*; civil bureaucrats wore the *literary* ivory tablet; military people wore *military*; and teachers, musicians, and instructors of all sorts wore the ivory tablet with the word *music* on it. By the Emperor Jiajing's reign, every ivory tablet had an assigned number and functioned like a contemporary ID card. They were not transferable, and anyone who lost the tablet had to immediately report to the Directorate of Document Filing. If the holder of the ivory tablet died or no longer needed the tablet, it had to be returned to the Directorate of Document Filing.

Other credentials that were closely scrutinized by the eunuchs were authorized passes to attend a royal funeral service. During the funeral proceedings or memorial services for the deceased, all participants had to wear the so-called Inner Court funeral tablets, which had three classifications— companion officials, sacrifice officials, and execution officials. The last category of authorization and identification documents that were jealously guarded by the seal officials was passports for official travel. Ming officials, civil as well as military, who needed to attend to state business in the empire or beyond the border had to first receive the notice of appointment and then obtain a passport from the seal officials. Several classifications were used to identify the nature and means of travel. A copper tablet made into a double-fish shape with the word *discipline* on it was issued to military personnel, whereas the same type of tablet with the word *goodness* on it was issued to imperial chefs, revenue officials, and other civil servants. In addition, five other classes of passport tallies—horse, water, double-horse, double-boat, and communication—specifically spelled out the means of transportation the officials on business had to take.[9]

The Ming seal officials, both the civil bureaucrats and the eunuchs, were undoubtedly among the most important imperial appointees. They had custody of the most sensitive imperial documents, seals, and credentials and were among the first to learn about top state secrets, including military and political appointments. They would be the first to know which official was to be sent where, for what purpose, traveling by what means, and so on. They were indeed in a unique and extremely powerful position if they dared or knew how to play the ruthless political game. Precisely for this reason the Ming founding fathers set up the dualistic security system, having both the civil seal officials and the eunuch seal managers look over each other's shoulder. They were trained to perform with a high degree of perfection within the parameters of the team concept. It is incredible that this system would work for more than two-and-a-half centuries with no major scandal or serious conflict.

This does not mean that there were no problems in the management and operation of so many seals, credentials, and authorization papers. For one thing, the civil seal officials did not have their own offices. They came every morning, rain or shine, to the seal storage office in the palace and then did what they were charged to do. After they had discharged their duties, they had no place to go. And with no commodious office or any building attached to them, they had no power base. In fact, sometime they wandered around the palace court like "vagabonds," as one seal official described his predicament.[10] But who were these men who had to carry and affix imperial seals day in and day out? Well, of the ninety-nine civil Seal Office directors between 1368 and 1589, twenty-five (25.25 percent) were appointed because of hereditary privileges and fifty-six (56.57 percent) were holders of doctoral degrees (jinshi). Of the ninety-two deputy directors of the Seal Office from 1368 to 1590, seven (7.61 percent) were appointed because of the merit of their fathers or grandfathers, and sixty-seven (72.83 percent) came through the channel of civil service examinations.[11]

The civil seal officials spent most of their time doing routine work, but occasionally found themselves in scuffles, including verbal exchanges and fistfights, with their eunuch counterparts. Some might treat the eunuchs with contempt, others felt compelled to comb the ranks of the castrati. Punishment for negligence, misconduct and irresponsibility was in general quite severe. For eunuchs, it was often exile to the frontiers, and for civil seal officials, it was corporal punishment. In 1485, for instance, Xu Han, then the director of the Seal Office, was beaten thirty times with a bamboo stick, and in 1507, the Seal Office Director Gu Xuan and his deputy Yao Xiang were both beaten nearly to death before they were banished.[12] Consequently, the more timid or opportunistic seal officials, who seemed made of malleable stuffs, had to ally themselves with eunuch bosses. When the chief eunuch Liu Jin was in power in the early sixteenth century, virtually all of the seal officials ingratiated themselves to him and became his lackies. When the notorious eunuch Wei Zhongxian took over the Ming political apparatus in the early 1600s, he made his nephew Wei Fumin director of the Seal Office. Civil seal officials and their eunuch counterparts all had to work for the same despotic Ming emperor. As such, their political fortunes or misfortunes, and even lives, depended on imperial whim. The trick was to learn how to master the rules of the power game and maintain a check and balance between the Inner Court and the Outer Court.

EUNUCHS AND MING FLOOD–CONTROL PROJECTS

Throughout most of China's dynastic history the taxes essential for unified state power were collected in kind, and most of these were grain, salt, silk, and porcelain. Other tributes levied upon the population also included bricks, tiles, and nanmu logs needed for the construction of the imperial palaces. Most of these commodities, which were the fundamental sources of supply for the royal family, the central bureaucracy, and the imperial guards, were produced in the southern region of China. Consequently, an artificial canal running north and south, as against China's principal rivers, which all run from west to east, had to be created to transport these commodities. Because the artificial canal cut through five extremely turbulent rivers, recurrent flooding became the major concern of every ruling family. He who could harness the rivers and keep the canal traffic constantly flowing, would secure his "Mandate of Heaven" and bring peace and prosperity to the realm. A theory known as "hydraulic despotism" has been applied to this kind of political phenomenon. And the way the Ming emperors unbridledly utilized their eunuchs to control floodings along the Grand Canal has lent support to the soundness of this theory.

The first digging of a section of the canal, about fifty-three miles, began in 495 B.C., from Suzhou to Wuxi. Within a decade, because of its economic and military importance, it was extended further north, and the canal linked up the mighty Yangtze River and the Huai River (see map C). During the Sui dynasty (589–618 A.D.), Emperor Yang Di (r. 605–618) conscripted more than 1 million workers to dig more canals and ultimately connected Luoyang via Kaifeng with the Huai River and Huaian so that he could exploit the riches of southern China and ride his legendary dragon boat all the way down to Yangzhou. When the Mongols came to power they built a new waterway linking Beijing, their capital, to the south. By 1327, the Grand Canal had attained definitive form and become the first and longest canal in the world. From Beijing to Hangzhou, its southern terminus, the canal covered a distance of 1,112 miles, comparable to an interstate freeway from New York to Florida. It flowed past Tianjin, Hebei, Shandong, Jiangsu, and Zhejiang. It crossed and touched the Yellow River or Huanghe, the Haihe, the Huai River, the Yangtze or Changjiang, and the Qiantang River.

After the Ming moved its capital from Nanjing to Beijing, the Grand Canal had truly become the main artery of the empire and a vital link between southern China and northern China. Likewise, success or failure of the canal operation always had great economic and political consequences. Troops and military equipment were often moved by the canal. Officials, businessmen, and tourists frequently traveled on the waterway. Moreover, the canal and its network of rivers brought to the emperor brocade, mirrors, and seafood from Yangzhou; satin from Zhenjiang; damask silk from Changzhou; glutinous rice from Suzhou; and gauze from Zhejiang. It was also through this transport system that the capital city received porcelain, wine, and tea sets from Jiangxi; and paper and brushes from Anhui. However, the repair and unceasing maintenance of the canal and its adjoining rivers proved extremely costly and indeed became a nightmare for every reigning monarch. The major culprit was the recurrent flooding of the Yellow River.

Originating from the eastern fringe of the Tibetan plateau, the 2,800-mile-long Yellow River flows through mountain passes, marshes, deserts, steppes, and the plateaus of northern China. Its riches and waters provided the vital means to sustain the Chinese civilization throughout its history. Unfortunately, the same river has also brought numerous disasters to the Chinese people; thus, it was called the *Sorrow of China*. When it cut through the loess region of northern China, it annually carried some 35 billion cubic feet of dusty, windborn silt into the plain. More than half of such silt would deposit in the riverbed before the river reached the sea. As years went by, the riverbed rose and dikes had to be built higher and higher to confine the water within its channel. In some areas the riverbed was actually higher than the adjacent land. And because the eastern section of the North China plain is for the most part only a few feet above sea level, whenever there was a heavy rain the Yellow River often changed its course. This caused the easily eroded loess sediment to choke the river course, creating a serious overflow. When the waters broke through the dikes, they spread in immense lakes over the farmland. Millions of people would then die of drowning and the ensuing famine. Worse still, the Grand Canal traffic would come to a halt, and the

Map C. The Grand Canal of China

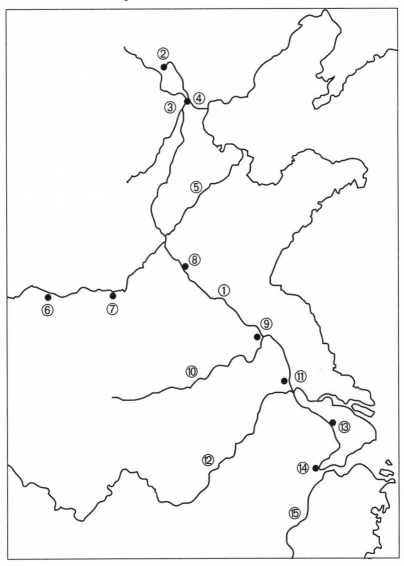

MAP KEY
1. Grand Canal
2. Beijing
3. Tianjin
4. Haihe River
5. Huanghe River
6. Luoyang
7. Kaifeng

8. Jining
9. Huaiyin
10. Huaihe River
11. Yangzhou
12. Changjiang River
13. Suzhou
14. Hangzhou
15. Qiantang River

grain and other tributes that the palace could not do without could not be delivered. There was then a panic, a crisis, and a cry of havoc at the court.

To avert such dangers, different dynastic governments had constructed numerous smaller canals to drain the tributaries and lakes of the East China lowlands. But beginning in the Song dynasty (960–1278), the once well-maintained flood controls and irrigation projects began to deteriorate, primarily because of war and human neglect. During the Ming period, the Yellow River broke through its northern bank fourteen times and its southern bank five times.[13] Kaifeng, a city located in Henan province and only a few miles south of the river, was victimized time and time again during the first century of the Ming power. It was inundated by the Yellow River waters in 1375, 1384, 1390, 1410, 1416, and in many other sorrowful years. The flooding of 1410, for example, damaged thousands of acres of land and destroyed more than 14,000 families. The flood of 1416 caused the waters to spill into fourteen counties and seriously choked up the Huai River.[14] Such disastrous floods would continue throughout the Ming period, and when they happened, the emperor would name a commissioner, giving him only a token appropriation, to arrest the problem. The commissioner, who generally got a grant in aid to do the initial planning and organization, would request more support from both the central and local authorities. Under such circumstances His Majesty always dispatched his trusted castrati to the scene and to muster all the necessary personnel, materials, equipment, government funds, food stuffs, boats of all sizes, and medical supplies to finish the job. The Ming hydraulic projects, like Ming diplomacy, foreign trade, or safeguarding the imperial seals, could not be completed without the involvement of His Majesty's personal servants.

The first Ming eunuch known to have been commissioned to deal with flood control was Mu Jing, whose rise to prominence was a graphic testament to the precarious conditions of Ming eunuchs. Mu was originally Emperor Jianwen's eunuch, but was confiscated by Emperor Yongle after the civil war. Known for his straightforward personality, Mu Jing more than once offended his master and barely escaped execution. According to a seventeenth century writer, Cha Jizuo (1601–1677), Mu Jing accompanied Yongle in one of his campaigns against Chieftain Aruytai of the Mongols. After witnessing a seemingly endless hide-and-seek war of retribution beyond the Great Wall, Mu Jing repeatedly suggested to Emperor Yongle that he abandon the futile pursuit and return home. Emperor Yongle disagreed and at a moody moment called Mu Jing a "rebellious barbarian." Mu looked at His Majesty and replied: "I'm not certain who is the real barbarian!" This sharp exchange definitely incurred His Majesty's wrath, and the emperor ordered Mu Jing's execution on the spot. Mu Jing, surprisingly, remained calm and collected and was ready to die, whereupon Emperor

Yongle was reported to have slowly murmured: "Of all the people brought up by my family, how many of them are worth more than this slave?" Mu Jing was immediately set free and in fact became closer to the emperor.[15]

In 1424, several dikes at a port town, Hexiwu, southeast of Beijing, broke apart and created a crisis. Officials from the Ministry of Public Works rushed to repair the dikes, but mainly because of the swift current, the initial botched work quickly proved ineffective. At this time, Emperor Yongle had already passed away, but the court continued to rely upon Mu Jing, who was dispatched to take over the repair project. Mu was to work with Marquis Zhang Xin, who had valuable technical and organizational knowledge from fighting floods at Kaifeng in 1410. Grand Eunuch Mu and Marquis Zhang commanded an army of 5,000 burly workers and were able to seal the breaks, repair the damaged dikes, and more important, restore the irrigation system of the area.[16]

In an agrarian economy like that of Ming China, grain tributes, flood control, and irrigation were intimately related. They were more than just a question of peasant welfare, but of vital interest to the ruling family. During the summer of 1436, both the Nanjing and Beijing metropolises received unusually heavy rainfall, causing the waters to swell in both the Yellow River in the North and the Yangtze tributaries in the South. By early autumn of that year, the dike at Yaoerdu of the Grand Canal had broken, resulting in great loss of life and property. More serious, the floods essentially blocked the canal traffic. At the outset, the court dispatched a regional vice commander and an assistant commissioner in chief, both military officers, to grapple with the calamity. They mobilized local troops, canal Special Army Corps, and boat trackers to harness the rivers, but could not make a dent in the problem. Emperor Zhengtong again turned to the grand eunuch Mu Jing, now qualified as a veteran troubleshooter, to handle the emergency. Mu was assisted by another marquis and a minister from Public Works. He was authorized to improvise whatever was required to restore the canal transport system. *Ming shi* does not record this event, but the Zhengtong Veritable Record unmistakably gives the grand eunuch Mu Jing laudatory remarks.[17]

To keep the traffic between the capital and the grain belt in the south flowing uninterruptedly, another main artery of the Ming empire, the Yangtze River, also had to be maintained from time to time. Zhenjiang, the confluence point of the southern section of the canal and the Yangtze, was only forty some miles east of Nanjing and a few miles south of the vitally important canal port Yangzhou, which was the center of the salt trade for centuries. About 5,000 or 6,000 years ago, the Yangtze entered the sea at a point between Zhenjiang and Yangzhou; then about 2,000 years ago, the river swung east again to enter the East China Sea. The arbitrary conditions set by Mother Nature often dictated human behavior. Accordingly, whenever there was an overflow of the Yangtze in Nanjing, the entire southern section of the Grand Canal would feel the impact and the grain ships would be grounded. This happened in the late autumn of 1441 when the Yangtze repeatedly broke its banks in Nanjing and the Ming flood-control operation was taken to the task.

Emperor Zhengtong first appointed Wu Zheng, a vice minister of Public Works, to lead a team of hydraulic specialists to repair the damaged banks. Wu assembled a flotilla of boats filled with stones, tree branches and twigs, ready to scuttle the riverbanks. Because the water was too deep, this scheme failed, and the team had to abandon the project. Wu, in his memorial to the emperor, suggested that they wait until the water receded and the harvest season ended so that he could recruit more available peasants to deal with the situation. The emperor was in the meantime soliciting other experts, and apparently, he derided Wu's ideas. As a result, he named two new project directors to take charge of harnessing the Yangtze. They were Li Xian, then the grand commandant of Nanjing, and Liu Ning, a grand eunuch. In his instructions, the emperor told Li and Liu to always take the interests of the soldiers and peasants into consideration and, while attempting to combat the disaster, to never abuse their power or take liberty with the populace. Li Xian and Liu Ning together collected sufficient personnel to reroute all branch streams into the main course and made good use of the silted island to slow the current. With this accomplished, the Grand Canal was reopened.[18]

It is quite obvious that the Ming dualistic security system was also applied to flood-control and hydraulic projects. Time and again we witness a civil bureaucrat or a noble jointly commissioned with a court eunuch dealing with flood calamities and repair of the Grand Canal. Several of these eunuchs had multiple talents and rich organizational experience. One such eunuch was Nguyen An, who was involved in at least three hydraulic projects and left an impeccable record behind him. In the late summer of 1444, a torrential rain hit the Nanjing area and a gargantuan volume of water from the lower Yangtze spilled over to more than ten prefectures in the most productive Yangtze delta. Almost immediately, the court ordered a vice minister of Public Works, Wang You, to go with the grand eunuch Nguyen An to inspect all the lock gates and dikes along the Grand Canal. They checked more than twenty stations, added new levees, and rebuilt stone abutments to safeguard the canal system. But the station at Anerdu was so severely damaged that they had to bring in countless workers and heavier tools to make radical repairs.[19]

The story of the eunuch Nguyen An is like a Hans Christian Andersen fairy tale. A native of Annam, Nguyen An, like several foreign-born Ming eunuchs, was assigned to important positions during and after the civil war, when talented Chinese generally stayed away from government service.

Brought to China as a tribute, Nguyen An quickly earned Emperor Yongle's trust, mainly because of his remarkable loyalty, frugality, and above all, his well-known incorruptibility. But Nguyen An was also a talented artist, ingenious architect, and an expert civil engineer with a calibre comparable to the Renaissance da Vinci or Michelangelo. Emperor Yongle first commissioned Nguyen An to design and construct the fabulous palace in Beijing, and soon after the completion of the magnificent Forbidden City and a number of office buildings, Nguyen An was promoted to grand eunuch. As a matter of fact, Nguyen was literally running the Ministry of Public Works during the first quarter of the fifteenth century. In the early spring of 1438, an earthquake shook Beijing and caused terrible damage to the palace. Nguyen An was once again charged to repair the damaged structure and also to build three new pavilions in the Forbidden City. He recruited some 6,000 carpenters and masons to help him do the job. Many of these artisans apparently could not endure the working conditions and attempted to escape. It was said that some of them had to wear the notorious cangu while working in the palace. His other assignments generally involved civil engineering, construction, procurement of materials, and the like. Several times he was awarded large sums of money, but when he died, while fighting yet another Yellow River flood at Zhangqiu, he was a penniless man. Nguyen An's story can indeed refute a long-held myth that the Ming eunuchs all enjoyed opulent salaries, worked short hours, and took bribes.[20]

Nguyen An's other notable mission was a detailed and thorough inspection tour of the Grand Canal in early 1449. Accompanied by another court eunuch, Chen Kun, Nguyen An and his repair team began their journey by traveling some fifty-one miles of the Tonghuihe (Channel of Communication Grace), which was the northernmost part of the canal. Their first stop was Tongzhou, and after checking out the capstan slipways and the trees planted alongside the Baihe (White River), they proceeded southward to Tianjin. From Tianjin, Nguyen and Chen followed the Yuhe (Imperial River) and then came to the major canal port of Linqing. They later sailed on the Huitonghe (Union Link Channel) to cross the northern course of the Yellow River, and before they could reach the summit section of the canal in western Shandong, they had to inspect the locks of the eighty-mile Chahe (Lock-gate River) section. Since the summit section was critical to the navigability of the canal, they carefully inspected the famed "water box" reservoirs, which stored the water supply, and the sluice gates that controlled the water level of the canal. Ming records show that, in 1411, the government mobilized 165,000 men and used 200 working days to build these projects in the summit section. Nguyen's team then came to Jining and Huaian and completed their inspection tour in Nanjing.[21]

The inspection tour undertaken by Nguyen An was probably a routine assignment for the Ming eunuchs. It was, to a certain extent, called for by the market conditions and commodity prices of northern China; that is, if the Grand Canal was well maintained, rice, cotton, wheat, rape, jute, legumes, bast fibers, edible oils, and other daily necessities could make their way to Beijing and other northern Chinese cities without interruption. But as stated earlier, the Yellow River frequently created problems to frustrate this economic lifeline. In 1452, for instance, the bank at Shawan (Sandy Bay), in Shandong province broke, and its waters carried a huge volume of silt into the Grand Canal and effectively choked up the north-south artery.

Actually, the Yellow River at Shawan had become a real nuisance and threat to the livelihood of the Chinese many years before. Its troubles began in 1391 when the river changed its course, overflowing all the way from Kaifeng to Fengyang of Anhui province, the birthplace of the Ming founder, and entered the Huai River. This route was then called the *Large Yellow River*, and a deviation to the river course that flowed through Xuzhou and discharged its water to the Grand Canal was called the *Small Yellow River*. Both rivers were protected by very high levees, and their riverbeds were actually higher than the adjacent farmlands. As vulnerable as these rivers were, a horrendous flood in 1448 inundated more than 2,000 li (about 700 miles), ultimately threatening the canal port of Linqing. Most of the hydraulic experts maintained that a dam or large-scale project should be constructed at Shawan so that the Large Yellow River could discharge its waters to the sea.[22] The government did so but could count for only temporary relief because, four years later, the river—swollen by days of pounding rains— crested well above flood stage at Shawan and overnight created hundred of thousands of refugees in Shandong, Henan, and the Huai River valley.

Emperor Jingtai, who had ascended the throne for only two years, received various proposals as how to deal with the disaster. Some officials pointed out that the Grand Canal, which crossed the Huai River at right angles, was the major source of all problems because the canal interfered with the rational conservation of Huai waters and that a new canal should be dug to restore the topographical equilibrium. Others, who were more passive and even superstitious, regarded the action of the rivers as a reflection of the way in which the cosmic powers sent warnings to the Son of Heaven. They said that the current at Shawan was too swift and even if rocks and metals were thrown into the river, they would be washed away like feathers. This group of officials thereby recommended that the emperor hire high Daoist priests and perform rituals to ask the river gods for mercy. Emperor Jingtai was said to have been extremely worried, and accordingly wasted no time in naming the best qualified team to harness the Yellow River at Shawan.[23] The team was headed by the minister of public works, Shi Pu, as well as two court eunuchs, Li Xian and Nguyen Luo, and a censor.

Ming records provide no background information on Li Xian and Nguyen Luo, nor can we relate Nguyen Luo to the great Nguyen An or two other contemporary eunuchs, Nguyen Hong and Nguyen Lang, both of whom were very influential during the early Ming period. For example, were they brothers or cousins, all ethnic Annamese and tributes from the king of Annam, or were they prisoners of war? At any rate, the team of Shi Pu, Li Xian, and Nguyen Luo quickly constructed a stonewall embankment at Shawan and also dug two new channels to divert excessive waters into the Grand Canal. These efforts temporarily slowed the river's rise and earned them a respite from the danger of more flooding. By the early spring of 1452, they had successfully repaired the damaged banks at Shawan. Believing that his flood-control team had staunched the flow and averted the danger, the emperor kept his vow and offered an imperial sacrifice to the river gods. He also ordered the construction of two votive temples, one at Heiyangshan (Black Ocean Mountain) and the other at Shawan, and twice a year, during the spring and fall, the emperor personally appealed to the river gods for flood relief.[24]

But the foundation of the new projects at Shawan was mostly sandy or clay soil, and the busy water could easily undermine them. Moreover, it was difficult to find materials to build really strong barricades on the flat plain of Shandong and Henan. Consequently, another torrential rain in the sixth moon of 1452 (lunar calendar) easily caused the new embankment to go astray. The northern bank at Shawan broke again, and the waters swept in turgid rage down through the plain. Within hours, the Grand Canal was filled with silt and all the grain ships were stranded. Emperor Jingtai dispatched his vice minister of Public works and two eunuchs, Li Xian and Wu Gen, to deal with the flooding. In the meantime, the emperor conferred a new and highly respectable title to another river deity, requesting eternal benevolence. All the efforts gave only a short reprieve as the Shawan banks broke twice during the fourth moon and the fifth moon of 1453.[25] Such was the repeated story of the eunuch involvement in Ming's hydraulic operation and flood control. A common scene was a eunuch, standing side by side with a minister of public works or a nobleman, commanding thousands of undernourished workers who rolled willow, bamboo, and tree branches into long coils around rocks and metal and sunk them at the base of an embankment. Silt would quickly settle and cover them with a layer of sediment, providing a second layer of reinforcement. No one actually knows how many eunuchs were commissioned to coordinate the gigantic earthworks of dike repair. Even those who were successful rarely elicit praise from Ming biographers. The majority of the eunuch flood fighters simply faded into obscurity without a trace.

In general, the southern section of the Grand Canal was less trouble-some than the northern section, but the Ming emperor was keenly aware of the periodic hydraulic problems in Hangzhou. Situated on the Qiantang River, Hangzhou was not only famous for its beautiful scenery, but also for its silk industry, green Longjing (Dragon Well) tea, delicious fish, crabs, and prawns. Hangzhou was devastated by the Mongol invasion in the late thirteenth century, but recovered by the early Ming time. Once again, Hangzhou had become an important commercial and agricultural center of Southeast China. Occasional hydraulic maintenance was called for because the southernmost part of the Grand Canal, centered around the famed West Lake, often caused floodings and suffered storm attacks from the Qiantang River bay. The West Lake was originally a shallow bay adjoining the Qiantang but, over the years, was transformed into an inland lake by an embankment of its outlet. Beginning in the tenth century, the Chinese constructed a fifty-mile long seawall, called the *Qiantang estuary,* to not only protect the city from the attack of the notorious sea tides, but also facilitate the irrigation of the region. Bai Juyi (772–846), a Tang poet and skilled administrator, was the first to build a dike and a channel in the western side of Hangzhou, linking the West Lake with the Grand Canal. During the Song dynasty, another famed poet and statesman, Su Dongpo (1037–1101), not only dredged the bottom of the lake, but also built an irrigation network with nine channels taking water from the lake to its neighboring farmlands.[26]

All these projects began to crumble and the irrigation channels were silted and settled by squatters by Ming times. During the autumn of 1475, Emperor Chenghua received a report from the Ministry of Public Works that detailed a drastic hydraulic repair project for Hangzhou. The emperor authorized his grand defender of Zhejiang province, the grand eunuch Li Yi, to undertake the project. Li Yi, unlike the jack-of-all-trades Nguyen An, was not an engineer, but with his position and influence, he was able to assemble experts and workers and collect the necessary materials for overhauling the entire West Lake irrigation system. In addition, he also built a stone bridge, a new lock, and a dike for controlling the water level of the lake. All told, everything went well and the project greatly benefited the people for many years to come.[27]

Four years after the eunuch Li Yi had completed the hydraulic project in Hangzhou, another court eunuch was assigned to engage in a different kind of water conservation: the target was the Lugouqiao (Reedy Moat Bridge), located only a few miles southwest of Beijing. When the Venetian Marco Polo visited there in 1290, he thought the bridge was unequalled by any in the world, and he described it in effusive terms. For this reason, the bridge has been called the *Marco Polo Bridge* by Westerners who could not pronounce its difficult Chinese name. Near this bridge on July 7, 1937, the

Japanese provoked its Chinese defenders to start the Second World War in East Asia. Since the bridge crossed the Yongding River, both the bridge and the river served main routes carrying considerable cart and boat traffic to and from the capital city. Because it was so strategically situated, the Ming government always considered the maintenance of the bridge a top priority public work.[28] As the safety of the Marco Polo Bridge was a vitally important project, the Ming emperor would make sure that one of his trusted castrati was involved in the bridge's repairs. This is why during the last quarter of the fifteenth century two influential eunuchs were charged with such a hydraulic work.

Early in 1479, the eunuch Zhang Zhijing, then a deputy director of the Palace Servants Directorate, received an order to reinforce the bridge, which had been standing since 1280. Zhang collected some 30,000 soldiers to grade and pave several miles of road nearby the bridge, added new levees along the riverbanks, and checked every section of the 700-foot long structure. His engineers tested all the eleven segmental arches, which spanned an average of sixty-two feet each, and selected ten stocky mounted men to ride abreast upon the deck. They also repaired the carved marble railings, which sustained the edge of the bridge, and refurbished the 283 stone lions that were supposed to guard both the bridge and the river. Ten years later, the support system adjoining the bridge appeared to be weakening, and the new emperor Hongzhi, who was barely enthroned, commissioned an earl, a vice minister of public works, and a powerful eunuch, Li Xing, to do the repairs. Li Xing's team supervised an army of 20,000 workers, dredged the bottom of the Yongding River, and had the piers up and down the stream all buttressed with new masonry structures.[29] It should be noted that there would be more maintenance and repairs throughout the dynasty, but the original Marco Polo Bridge survived, amazingly, until 1689, when it was finally washed away by a horrendous flood.

Readers may recall that there was also a eunuch named Li Xing who was accredited as a chief Ming envoy to Siam in 1403. But that was almost four generations before this Li Xing rose to prominence. Regrettably, but not surprising, *Ming shi* gives us no information about either one of them. But judging from his deeds recorded in Hongzhi Veritable Record, which was completed in 1509, the latter Li Xing appeared to be a mix of hubris and humility, often emitting signals of both confidence and modesty. At the time he was assigned to direct the Marco Polo Bridge repair project, Li was the director of the Palace Servants Directorate of the Inner Court, a position once held by the distinguished Admiral Zheng He. Likewise, Li was in charge of all palace construction and civil engineering, the maintenance of royal mansions and mausolea, and the like. No wonder, when another devastating flood hit the lower stretch of the Yellow River in 1494, Emperor

Hongzhi again chose him to coordinate an extremely complex and difficult hydraulic project.

By 1489, the "Sorrow of China" was becoming even more troublesome as its lower course had divided into several branches, directly threatening the Huai River and the Grand Canal. First, a dike broke near Jinglongkou in the summer of 1492, causing a number of grain ships to capsize in the northern section of the Grand Canal. Then the dike at Zhangqiu near the confluence of the Grand Canal and the Yellow River also broke. Emperor Hongzhi first dispatched his vice minister of public works, Chen Zheng, to close the dikes, but Chen died on the job. There was an atmosphere of panic when the court chose Liu Daxia to take over the emergency work. Liu was probably one of the most introspective and outspoken officials in the Ming court and had had a long love-hate relationship with the castrati. He was briefly imprisoned in 1483 and suffered thirty strokes of bamboo in 1493, presumably at the hands of court eunuchs.[30] Liu was also believed to have burned all of Admiral Zheng He's navigation documents and have generally downplayed the importance of Ming naval expeditions.

At the time of his appointment, Liu Daxia was a second vice censor in chief. His first priority was to save lives and forestall any potential dangers. As a competent organizer, Liu accomplished both goals with flying colors. However, his authority over the river repair was by no means complete. In fact, he lacked the necessary political clout and financial appropriation to tackle the mammoth problem head-on. And as the waters continued to wash off the river crest and linger in the flat lowland, Emperor Hongzhi decided to send additional officials to fight the floods and reopen the grain traffic. He made the grand eunuch Li Xing the first in command, and an earl Chen Rui the second in command to work with Liu Daxia, who had actually become the third in command of the new team.[31]

After Li Xing and Chen Rui joined the team, more resources, both personnel and materials, were made available to the flood fighters. For example, Li Xing took 20,000 silver taels from his inner court office to bolster the financing of the repair work. Other government funds and food stuffs stored in Henan and Shandong granaries were also distributed to the 120,000 workers brought to chart a new course for the Yellow River. In his instruction, the emperor even authorized Li Xing and his colleagues to tap into the government treasures in the Zhejiang and Wuhu areas. Moreover, all the local authorities had to chip in whatever they could and many of the artisans in the lower Yellow River valley and Nanjing metropolis were drafted for corvée service. Furthermore, the imperial decree also asked boats and ships of all sizes, whether privately owned or government property, to get into action. With such a well-coordinated endeavor the team was able to close the major dike breaks by the winter of 1494–95. Li Xing then recommended that the name of Zhangqiu be changed to a safer and more peaceful one, hence, Anping (safe and peace) Town. He also suggested that a votive temple be erected to express His Majesty's gratitude for a river that had chronically made the Chinese lives anxious and miserable. Emperor Hongzhi approved all of these recommendations and for a while the grand eunuch Li Xing, Earl Chen Rui, and Liu Daxia had won plaudits from both the court and the public.[32]

But the deluge would not recede fast enough for them to finish the massive project. Furthermore, they were concerned that the soil and clay used to seal the dike breaks might turn soft and slacken when the spring brought in warmer weather, so that any sizeable rain could rapidly undermine their fragile accomplishment. Li Xing thereby suggested that they be allowed to stay on for a much longer time so that they could continue to dredge the bottom of the river and, most important, build a new dike at Huanglinggan (Yellow Hill Bluff) at the upper stream of the river. Li also requested and received permission to erect another shrine at Huanglinggan to house the presumed "God of the Yellow River," who was since repeatedly asked to look after the welfare of the Chinese. The emperor giddily celebrated this shining outcome and personally engraved an inscription on a plaque to be hung at the entrance of the shrine.[33]

By the summer of 1495, Li Xing's team had finally harnessed the river by directing the full volume of its water through a seventy-li-long (about twenty-three miles) southeast course from Henan to Jiangsu so that it flowed via Xuzhou and Huaian. The section between Henan and Xuzhou was buttressed by a new 360-li (roughly 120 miles) bank, and the Yellow River got a facelift. It now converged with the Huai River to empty its water into the sea. It should be reminded that the river would continue to overflow and indeed repeated its menacing destruction in the lower stretch of its course, as it did in 1526, 1534, 1558, and again in 1587. Consequently, unceasing drainage and periodic new embankment projects were required to keep the river following the new course. In 1605 for instance, 170 miles of the river were drained at a cost of 800,000 silver taels with a team of 500,000 workers. But the course charted by the grand eunuch Li Xing, Earl Chen Rui, and the vice censor Liu Daxia would remain intact until 1855, when the Yellow River found yet another outlet to the sea.[34]

The dreadful and recurrent pattern of flooding, misery, and reconstruction of the Yellow River followed a chain of reaction as inexorable as the equinoctial process. But life went on, and the Ming political dualism continued to function as it was designed by its founders. In consequence of the success in harnessing the river and keeping the grain traffic open, the project directors always received promotions and imperial awards. But the flood-control issue could also cause the fall of one's career and even banishment. Frequently, a project director was impeached or replaced even before his rehabilitation work had time to take effect.[35] Nevertheless, whenever there were diverse opinions and different theories awaiting imperial decision, His Majesty always loved to dispatch a grand eunuch to the spot. This allowed him to utilize his network of influence at every government level, mustering all the necessary technical, financial, and political resources to control the river and reopen the grain traffic. The stories of Ming water control and hydraulic management thereby offer a tantalizing glimpse of what a dualistic system and political despotism could achieve.

EUNUCHS AND MING JUDICIARY REVIEWS

Ming's characteristic dualism was also reflected in its judiciary operations, as the Ming emperor frequently exercised his authority to grant clemency and pardons and used court eunuchs to periodically attenuate the prison population. Such a unique practice actually reinforced a laudable Chinese tradition that recognizes human fallibility; specifically concerning those who have the power over those who do not. It also seemed to suggest that there was a link between cosmic forces and the conduct or misconduct of the ruler. Consequently, whenever there were strange and disturbing happenings in the empire, such as plagues and natural disasters, the emperor tended to believe that someone in his government was unjustly holding innocent people in prison or had done something immoral against his subjects. Therefore, to restore the yin-yang equilibrium and placate the heavens, His Majesty often granted clemencies and the like, either reducing prisoners' sentences or setting them free. Beginning in the second quarter of the fifteenth century, a major, nationally publicized judiciary review became well established, by which original charges and verdicts, trial records, the propriety of judicial findings, and sentences were routinely reexamined. And the chief review commissioner was always a grand eunuch who transcended the three regular Ming judiciary departments and held in his hands the life and death of hundreds or even thousands of people.

A prelude to such a judiciary tradition took place in 1438 when Wei Yuan, the minister of punishment, was impeached by a supervising secretary (who ranked only 7b but had great prestige and authority in the Ming system) for sentencing an innocent woman by the name of Han to be strangled. The woman was charged with committing adultery and murdering her husband, both of which allegations she vehemently denied. Because the death penalty required ratification by the emperor and the woman was able to provide credible corroboration of her testimony, Emperor Zhengtong granted the woman a pardon. Obdurate and furious, Minister Wei then requested a sort of blue-ribbon jury to retry the case. Among the jurors were a grand eunuch from the Inner Court and a chancellor from the Hanlin Academy; in the end, however, they could not find convincing and compelling support for the findings set forth by the Ministry of Punishment. Minister Wei was now in hot water; fortunately, though, the emperor was willing to let the book close on that case, but a precedent of involving grand eunuchs in judiciary review was thereby established.[36]

The first full-fledged judiciary review that required the presence of a prominent eunuch took place in 1441, when China was beset with deadly natural disasters. Emperor Zhengtong named the grand eunuch Xing An, who was assisted by He Wenyuan, deputy minister of punishment, and Wang Wen, the chief minister of the Court of Judicial Review, to look into the records of prisoners who might qualify for special imperial pardons. As it was a national affair, the emperor also commissioned two officials to Nanjing to undertake the same task. In his decree, Zhengtong gave the following reasons for such an important occasion:[37]

> Since I took over my ancestors' throne, I've been working diligently day and night, keeping forever in mind not to offend the heavens above while constantly worrying about the welfare of my subjects below. Time and again, I ordered a stop to unlawful surveillance and unreasonable demands from the people. I also dismissed many a cruel official and took measures to help the poor and the sick. Unfortunately, during the last two years, floods, drought, locusts, and insect pestilence have brought untold miseries and losses to our country, damaging particularly heavily in the Beijing areas. I've lately undergone a thorough introspection and wonder perhaps if our criminal justice was too harsh, consequently disharmonizing the forces of yin and yang. Within the confines of our state penitentiaries, some prisoners are serving between three and four years, or between eight and nine years, while others are sentenced to serve a decade or two of their lives therein. . . . My order to you is to go through all the severe and lengthy sentences and to right those who have been wronged. In particular, I want you to see if the heavier sentences could be reduced or if there were improprieties in judicial findings and procedures. Above all, you should determine if there are questionable verdicts or charges without solid bases. I want you to carefully review such cases and report them to me truthfully so that I can make appropriate and just decisions.

There is no record as to how many cases were reviewed by the Grand Eunuch Xing An or how many prisoners were set free upon his recommendation. Also, who was Xing An and what qualities did he possess to warrant such an important assignment? A brief profile of Xing An not only could shed some light on the powerful eunuchs in general, but also might give us a clue about the future review comissioners, who would be periodically appointed to undertake similar assignments. Xing An was not as well versed in literature as several other directors of the Ceremonial Directorate that have been discussed in the book. But perhaps because of his lack of quick wit and sharp mind, he always consulted with grand secretaries and ministers on matters of critical importance. *Ming shi* chroniclers portray Xing An as one of the most conscientious and truly incorruptible castrati. In 1449 when Emperor Zhengtong was detained by the Mongols at the Tumu fortress, a number of high-ranking officials urged Zhengtong's brother, later assumed in the temple of Jingtai, to move the capital back to Nanjing. Xing An, who strongly opposed the move, was said to have threatened to execute anyone who dared to ever voice such a "treasonous idea." Moreover, Xing An and Yu Qian (1398–1457), then minister of war, were instrumental in warding off the marauding Mongols at the suburbs of Beijing. Thanks to these achievements and his other meritorious services, when Zhengtong was later restored to the throne—and when so many of his brother's confidants, including Yu Qian, were put to death—Xing An's life was spared.[38] An extremely pious Buddhist, Xing An's story shatters many legendary eunuch stereotypes—corrupt, abusive, treacherous—that have been repeated in a hundred variations!

But Xing An's special commission to give parole and clemency to unjustly convicted prisoners was not meant to be a regular event. By 1499, however, extraordinary occasions once again called for an even larger and better publicized judiciary review. During the early summer of the year, Yu Shiyue, the chief minister of the Court of Judicial Review, petitioned the emperor that the prolonged drought might have been caused by the injustice of the criminal system, and that special commissioners be appointed to review dubious testimonies and grant pardons to innocent people so as to please the heavens. Other officials echoed Yu's concerns, and the upshot was the appointment of the grand eunuch Jin Ying as the judiciary review commissioner. Jin Ying constructed a platform in front of the Court of Judicial Review and covered it with a glittering yellow canopy. He sat at the center of the platform and handled the whole spectrum of the affair while the officials from the Ministry of Punishment and the Censorate obediently responded to everything he requested for corroboration. The imperial commission righted several prisoners who had been wronged, listening to many a detainee who was waiting to be tried. Others who had been sentenced to labor in chains were sent back to their original stations for lighter assignments, but those who committed perjury, fraud, or robbery were exiled to frontier military service. And finally, the inmates who were sentenced to wear the humiliating cangu were given a second chance for another imperial ratification.[39]

Jin Ying's career, unfortunately, was tainted by controversy and allegations of corruption. Two of his household servants were charged with taking bribes from salt merchants, and a third one was alleged to have helped an Imperial Guard commander obtain a promotion through Jin Ying's influence or complicity. Jin Ying himself was also accused of embezzling funds from Nanhaizi, a hunting resort for the imperial family located just south of the capital city. At any rate, Jin Ying was brought to the Censorate for interrogation and found guilty as charged. He was sentenced to die, but a special imperial grant of clemency saved his life, although two of his servants were speedily executed.[40]

Although Jin Ying shamed the eunuch rank and file and was marooned by his master, the positivie response from the general public made it necessary to hold such a special judiciary review once every five or six years. Officially, every imperial decree stated that the purpose of the review was to right any wrongs and please the heavens to alleviate the nation from natural disasters. On a closer look, however, one can see that the act was born out of practicality: its aim was to thin out the ever increasing prison population. It was generally believed that state penitentiaries in Beijing and Nanjing were not well equipped to handle and incarcerate convicts serving lengthy jail terms, and indeed it had become a real burden for the government just to feed and care for the inmates so confined. Consequently, periodic paroles and furloughs became necessary, and occasional imperial pardons had the effect of greasing the wheel of Ming criminal operations. Accordingly, in the summer of 1455, the emperor appointed the Grand Eunuch Wang Cheng to undertake such a review assignment. In his decree, Emperor Jingtai gave almost the same reasons as did his brother in 1449; namely, that he had been paying attention to possible abuses in justice and their relation to the incessant natural disasters that had devastated the nation. He therefore wanted his review commissioners to go to the jails in Beijing, Nanjing, Zhejiang, and other areas to listen to the complaints of the prisoners and see if the level of proof used to convict suspects was too low. Specifically, Wang Cheng and his associates were instructed to hear appeals from prisoners on death roll and decide if they could reduce the capital punishment to lighter jail terms. The commissioners did set free many convicts who were found guilty of lying, cheating, or street panhandling. They also reversed numerous cases, and the people in general slathered praise upon Emperor Jingtai.[41]

That the review commissioners routinely set free an incredibly large number of light offenders and reduced so many heavier sentences to misdemeanor offenses suggests that there were many loopholes and miscarriages in Ming justice. Another interesting fact coming out of the reviews is that Ming censors were not always the nemeses of the eunuchs, as has been often exaggerated. On the contrary, the two groups were often close colleagues and collaborators rather than enemies and adversaries. A case in point was the review session of the summer of 1468. A grand eunuch, Xu Hao, headed the review commission and, as usual, was assisted by ministers from the Censorate, the Ministry of Punishment, and the Court of Judicial Review, generally known as the *three pillars* of the Ming judiciary. The commission apparently struck a tone of collegiality, and Grand Eunuch Xu never drew the ire of the judiciary moguls. All told, they reduced several death penalty sentences to wearing the cumbersome cangu and disposed of numerous first-time offenders with token punishment. Many who had yet served their full terms were ordered to join the army in the frontier, while dozens of inmates received a whipping with a bamboo stick before being sent home.[42] And while Xu Hao and his associates were busy checking out loopholes and setting prisoners free, a separate panel—headed by the Grand Eunuch An Ning, who was also the commandant of Nanjing—was also trying to ease the prison congestion in the south.[43]

Some of the Ming monarchs probably had become convinced that criminal justice, if left unchecked, tended in time to lose its moorings and even float away from control. It was therefore imperative that routine reviews be installed so that no questions would be insinuated about the propriety of the criminal procedures. Against this backdrop, Emperor Chenghua, in the summer of 1472, named two separate panels to interview prisoners serving lengthy terms and take depositions from those waiting to be sentenced. Huang Gao, a grand eunuch from the Ceremonial Directorate, and Song Wenyi, a deputy grand eunuch, headed panels to deal with prison problems in Beijing and Nanjing, respectively. They were, of course, assisted by high-ranking officials from the three regular law enforcement agencies. Several death sentences were reversed and numerous small-time criminals were furloughed. At the same time, lesser eunuchs were sent to various provinces to do likewise.[44]

The interval between the grand judiciary reviews was not always five or six years; sometimes it lapsed for almost a decade or so. The next time a grand eunuch got his writ to review questionable prison sentences was the stifling summer of 1481. The chief commissioner was the saintly Huai En. In his appointment edict, Emperor Chenghua lashed out for the first time at his law enforcement personnel. He then requested his review commissioners have sympathy for the people and exercise restraint and ask for validation before pronouncing verdicts: "Don't overlook evidence, don't prolong the agony of the suspects and their family. And always try to give the suspects the benefit of the doubt and listen to their appeals. But most important, you must have compelling reasons before applying the 'nine tortures' for extracting confessions." Chenghua repeatedly reminded his commissioners that justice was to be based on established creed and anyone who abused his office or deviated from the creed would ultimately bear the responsibility.[45]

There is no record to substantiate if any judiciary officials were punished because of their deliberate doctoring of documents or because they made a mockery of the Ming justice system. However, in the Ming officialdom it was commonplace that today an individual was the judge, but tomorrow his power would vanish into thin air and he became a prisoner. Even the grand eunuch Huai En, who was highly regarded for his integrity and straightforward personality, could not escape this tragic path. Four years after he discharged his assignment as the chief review commissioner (1485), Huai En provoked the anger of Emperor Chenghua over a report about some unusual astronomical omens. It was reported that the emperor threw his ink slab at Huai En but missed him entirely. This made Chenghua even angrier, and the next object His Majesty could find was his tea set, which he smashed into pieces. At this point, Huai En removed his hat and robe and sobbed bitterly while crawling on the floor. Chenghua's anger finally abated, and he ordered Huai En to get out of his sight. Later, Huai En claimed that he had suffered from a stroke and could no longer serve His Majesty. Only after Chenghua sent for his personal physicians to heal Huai's injured body and soothe his hurt feelings did he consent to come out of his bed.

Huai En's handling of the emperor's rage was fraught with personal as well as political peril, but that was the chance every eunuch had to take. He often spoke what the emperor did not want to hear, and because of his closeness to the emperor, Huai En was probably worth a dozen censors whose prescribed duties including repeated admonitions to the monarch. Huai En was credited with persuading the emperor from committing monumental folly, but once again this was always at the risk of his own life. For example, he vigorously protested Emperor Chenghua's intent to replace his oldest son with a younger son as crown prince and was therefore confined in the Fengyang special penitentiary. It is interesting to note that Huai En was a contemporary of the notorious spy chief Wang Zhi. Certainly, because of his obstinacy and self-righteousness, even the most wicked eunuchs were afraid of him. Time and again he turned down priceless gifts from fortune climbers, and his reputation ultimately helped him regain his powerful position in the Ceremonial Directorate when Hongzhi ascended the throne in 1487. According to *Ming shi*, during Huai En's heyday of power, clean and efficient people were appointed to ministerial posts, and after his death, Emperor Hongzhi conferred upon him a title of *Prominent Loyalty*.[46]

At the time the benevolent Hongzhi became the Son of Heaven of China, the basic rituals of the grand judiciary review had well been established. Under Hongzhi, such reviews were held twice, once in the summer of 1491 and again in 1500. During the latter event, a three-foot high platform was constructed in front of the Court of Judicial Review where an imperial proclamation was posted. Under a brilliant yellow canopy sat a grand eunuch, who was flanked by three top law enforcement officials. Other bureau chiefs and censors were required to bring with them documents ready for scrutiny. The atmosphere was solemn and the bureau chiefs and censors were nervous, but the lucky prisoners, who were standing in front of the platform, could not wait to tell their version of the stories. From time to time, the review commissioners had to wrestle with difficult decisions, but in the final analysis, the views of the grand eunuch, who held a hand on the tiller throughout the entire process, always prevailed. A case in point illustrates this pattern very well. A young brother, assisting his older brother in a brawl, had caused the death of a member of the other party involved in the dispute. The grand eunuch Huang Ci believed that the death penalty given to the young brother was too harsh, but the minister of punishment Lu Yu insisted that the man deserved the capital punishment. Huang then asked: "If you watched a friend being beaten up, you'd rush to help him even though you did not have proper dress to cover your body. You definitely would go faster if the victim was your own brother." After this exchange, the minister withdrew his protest and acquiesced to the grand eunuch's decision to free the young man.[47]

Thus far, Ming documents have failed to provide such details as the number of prison detainees furloughed, how many death penalty cases were reversed, and so on. An entry in the Zhengde Veritable Record, dated 5th moon of 1506, does give us a good glimpse of what really went on during the review process. Before the review was to take place, the emperor first dispatched thirteen bureau chiefs and circuit censors to gather information and prepare review materials from Shandong, Guangdong, Yunnan, Henan, South Beijing Metropolis, Sichuan, Shaanxi, North Beijing Metropolis, Fujian, Huguang, and Shanxi. After the preliminary screening was completed, the Grand Eunuch Li Rong was appointed to proceed with the grand review. It so happened that, during the review proceeding, the weather in Beijing was unbearably hot and humid and that caused Emperor Zhengde to order more lenient and speedier decisions. As a consequence, ninety-seven death roll prisoners were set free. Seven people who were convicted on charges of filial piety violations were also sent home, while thirty-four convicts who were sentenced to wear the cangu got a reprieve until further imperial ratification. Also, ninety people who were waiting to be executed were now exiled to the frontier military service, five people received whippings and were let go, while another four prisoners were granted a retrial.[48] And while the grand review was taking place in Beijing, the grand eunuch Fu Rong, who was also the commandant of Nanjing, held a similar review with his three assistants from the Nanjing judiciary ministries. All told, they set free fifteen prisoners, removed the cangu from five persons, reduced sentences for fifteen inmates who were on death roll, and sent several others into exile.[49]

The five year span between the 1506 review and the 1511 review witnessed the rise of the eunuch dictator Liu Jin and a palpable fear that the ranks of the castrati would swell in the empire, posing in particular a serious political challenge to the literati. But Zhang Yong, a war hero who later helped to bring down the eunuch dictator Liu Jin, headed the 1511 grand judiciary review in Beijing. Once again, before the grand review took place, pertinent records from all the thirteen provincial administration offices had already been sent to the Ministry of Punishment and other top judiciary officials were summoned to assist Zhang Yong in reaching merciful decisions. At his review session, Zhang sent sixty prisoners on death roll to serve in the frontier army, most of whom having first received corporal beatings. He also ordered the removal of the cangu from five of the ten people whose sentences were reviewed. After receiving appropriate whippings with the bamboo, seven young prisoners charged with filial piety violations were sent home, as were eight diseased detainees who came forward and confessed their wrongdoings.[50] Five years later, another grand eunuch by the name of Huang Wei conducted a similar review in Nanjing. An entry in the 1516 Zhengde Veritable Record indicates that Huang Wei sent ten death roll prisoners to the frontier army, removed the cangu from thirty-three people, and most interesting, released two women prisoners after whipping them with bamboo.[51]

During the autumn and winter of 1522 and the spring of 1523, China saw excessive rain and snow. Also, wind and hail storms laid waste to thousands of acres of crop land. The generally superstitious Jiajing believed that there was definitely a link between the Ming justice and the horrendous disasters.[52] Consequently, in the early summer of 1523, he appointed Zhang Zuo, a grand eunuch from the Ceremonial Directorate, to carry out the traditional review. But Jiajing did not want this review to be only a perfunctionary session. He specifically ordered Zhang Zuo to carefully scrutinize questionable records of arrest, indictment, trials, and sentencing. Judiciary officials who intentionally suppressed evidence would be rebuked or punished while verdicts and heavy sentences based upon hearsay testimonies and circumstantial evidence would be declared null and void. All told, Zhang Zuo's commission concurred with forty-seventy cases of the death penalty, reversed twenty-four cases of capital punishment, and submitted two others to the emperor for further consideration. Twenty criminals were ordered to wear the cangu, but eight others were granted a retrial. Seventy-five thieves and street panhandlers who had returned stolen goods were immediately set free, but 136 people who committed larceny were required to return stolen goods before their sentences could be reduced. Also, twenty-six people retained in jail as hostages because their criminal relatives were still at large did not receive clemency, yet thirty other similar detainees were sent home. Finally, about 113 people who had committed misdemeanor violations were either fined or whipped before being sent home. In summary, Zhang Zuo reviewed approximately 500 cases in Beijing, while another grand eunuch was conducting the same clemency session in Nanjing during the summer of 1523.[53]

As stated earlier, the once-every-five-year review tradition was not always strictly observed, as the next grand review did not take place until 1531, a hiatus of exactly eight years. By this time the Grand Eunuch Zhang Zuo had a wrinkled face and stooped shoulders, but nevertheless he was appointed for the second time to head the review commission. He ordered the removal of the cangu from the necks of 19 convicts and had 723 prisoners whipped before granting them parole. Four prisoners on death roll were spared execution but exiled to join the frontier army. During this review, three military commanders who were originally sentenced to die also luckily received imperial pardon.[54] But the lapse between the review dates got longer and longer, as the Jiajing Veritable Record tells us that the next session took place in the summer of 1541 and the last review under the reign of Jiajing was held in 1556, a lapse of exactly fifteen years. The 1541 review comissioner was the grand eunuch Bao Zhong, whereas the commissioner of the latter event was the powerful director of the ceremonials Huang Jin. Both men had similar ups and downs in their eunuch careers. Bao had the honor of escorting a royal coffin in 1539, an extremely important assignment, while Huang worked his way up through the Directorate of Palace Carpentry (Yuyongjian), managing the manufacturing of palace furniture, including imperial beds. Both men gained favor with Emperor Jiajing, who time and again turned a deaf ear to various calls of impeachment against Bao and Huang. In fact, after the deaths of Bao in 1548 and Huang in 1567, several of their brothers and nephews received hereditary military positions.[55]

The next grand review commissioner earned his grand eunuch position in the Ceremonial Directorate by way of the Palace Dyeing Bureau (Neizhiranju). He was Chen Hong, and in the summer of 1571, together with Liu Zuchiang, minister of punishment, he reviewed over 300 cases. Thirty-six prisoners on death roll were exiled to the frontier army units, 1 was exonerated and pronounced innocent, and the jail terms of 277 prisoners were each reduced by one year. In addition, sixteen people received whippings before regaining their freedom and several others were ordered to have their cangus removed.[56] This might well be the only judiciary review undertaken by Emperor Longqing, but the tradition continued into the reign of his son, Emperor Wanli. In the summer of 1576, Wanli appointed the now rugose and hoary Feng Bao, director of the ceremonials, to perform the traditional ritual in Beijing and the grand eunuch Li Qing to do likewise in Nanjing. Assisted by the minister of punishment, Wang Chonggu, Feng Bao did more or less the same chores as his predecessors—granting pardons, reducing sentences, and having minor offenders whipped before sending them home. But interesting enough, Feng Bao also decided to release all the diseased female prisoners at this particular session.[57]

The grand judiciary reviews were clearly aimed at providing a respite between past agonies and future troubles, as well as to serve as a balm to temporarily soothe the pains of the overcrowded jail population. But such palliative measures did not in essence go to the root of the crime problem; namely, grinding poverty and antiquated laws. At the beginning of the seventeenth century, partly due to the floundering economy and the general moral malaise, crimes had been increasing in brazenness as well as in number, as the ranks of the homeless continued to swell. To underscore the problems, a deputy minister of punishment actually complained to Emperor Wanli in 1606 that there were simply too many criminals and too few law enforcement personnel to maintain law and order. Even though in the summer of 1637 the last Ming emperor Chongzhen customarily appointed the grand eunuch Cao Huachun to conduct the grand review, the Ming judiciary system, for all practical purposes, was largely paralyzed.[58]

Generally speaking, the eunuch commissioners felt greatly honored to discharge their fiduciary duties. Moreover, granting clemency to prisoners on death roll and releasing prisoners from the penitentiary were considered not only merciful acts but also virtuous deeds to be reckoned both by the heavens and by the eunuchs' fellow men. It is reported that many a eunuch review commissioner, prior to death, requested to have his tomb frescoed with the scene of the grand review. The most popular mural featured a seated grand eunuch commissioner facing the south, with a handful of judiciary officials flanking him. And in the background would be numerous minor bureaucrats ingratiating themselves before him, and hundreds of prisoners begging for his mercy.[59] Unfortunately, these eunuchs' worthy deeds and virtuous acts have been grossly ignored and indeed all but forgotten by posterity.

The roles and duties of the Ming eunuchs in safeguarding the imperial seals, fighting recurrent floods, and conducting regular judiciary reviews indicate that they were very active both inside and outside the palace and frequently functioned as the emperor's personal agents. And as the Ming emperor maintained the principle of "l'etat c'est moi," palace affairs, staffed by the eunuchs, and government affairs, handled by civil officials, virtually became intertwined. In fact, the emperor's personal spending and state expenditure were inseparable, and thus the line between palace and government functions ultimately grew awfully murky. Certainly, this arrangement had created a constant source of friction and tension between the civil officials and the eunuchs, but that was precisely what an absolutist monarchy intended to do. While eunuchs were to supplement, not to replace the scholar-officials, both groups worked for the same person and cringed at the same Son of Heaven. However, as power always corrupts, so would absolutist power bring about absolute corruption. Unavoidably, there were many notorious and putrid eunuch bosses, but the number was, by Ming standards, rather insignificant when considering the fact that hundreds of thousands of castrati did their damnedest to serve the emperor and his family and that never before in Chinese history had government real salaries been so low as under the Ming. The vast majority of the castrated men, indeed, had proven not to be miscreants.

X

※

Conclusion

This study confronts a vast topic at the heart of Ming imperial government and tries to explore it systematically and thoroughly. It deals with every aspect of eunuch functions within the labyrinthine complexity of Ming government over a span of nearly three centuries. Previous chapters attempt to make the case that eunuchs in imperial service were not, as they have generally been portrayed in the scholarly literature, a minor if bizarre adjunct to a government of civil servants and military officers, but a fully developed third branch of Ming administration that participated in all the most essential matters of the dynasty. It hopes to pull away the veil of condemnation and jealousy imposed on eunuchs by pious Confucian compilers of the *Ming shi* and other official sources to reveal a richly textured tapestry. Eunuchs, likewise, are portrayed in a balanced manner that gives due consideration to able and faithful service along with the inept, the lurid, and the iniquitous.

Eunuchism was by itself the worst form of human exploitation: it not only subjected its victims to servile status, but also robbed the castrati forever of their manhood. And it could thrive only under the worst kind of governmental system; namely, monarchic absolutism. Since the priority of a dynasty was to perpetuate itself, the emperor invariably found his castrated servants the most convenient and reliable agents to maintain and safeguard the two most primordial desires of men—power and women. And while the Son of Heaven, who held the ruling power through the Mandate of Heaven, could do no evil and was not to be held liable for any mistakes he made, his eunuchs were eminently culpable, becoming tailor-made scapegoats when and if something went wrong with the despotic institution. Worse still, they had, since ancient times, become the targets of ridicule and contempt; and Chinese writers used a host of derogatory and even ribald appellations to characterize this group of peculiar Mandarins. Their designations ranged from *yanren*, or castrated persons, and *huozhe* (literally meaning "persons of fire," but actually a demeaning transliteration of the non-Chinese name *qoja* or *khoja*), to *siren*, or those who serve (originated from *Zhouli*), and *jingshen*

221

nanzi, or young men whose bodies had been thoroughly cleaned. Those who worked in the imperial quarters were either called *shiyu* or *fengyu*, meaning the royal servants. Others were called *neishi*, or Inner Court messengers, and *neiguan*, or Inner Court officials. The highest rank of the castrati and also the most respectable designation was *taijian*, or grand eunuch. But as a group, the most common term was *huanguan*, which means commissioned castrati.

Even though the Chinese believed that something was inherently wrong with eunuchism, every royal family since antiquity had used eunuchs as court functionaries, specifically assigned to work in the seraglio-like palace compound. Growing up with his eunuchs, the crown prince, who ultimately became the ruler of the realm, naturally preferred to be surrounded by familiar faces in a cold-blooded world of politics and intrigue. The eunuch's relationship with the ruler, at first probably only one of obsequious retainer, gradually developed into one of valued confidant. And who could better help him maintain his absolute power and to manage his harem than his own childhood confidants? This intimate association with their ruler hence became the source of eunuch influence and alleged duplicity. In the hectic world of administration, eunuchs provided the ruler with a convenient device to bypass the civilian bureaucracy and avoid the endless obstructions and moral exhortations from the scholar-officials. In particular, when the ruler grew tired of the burdensome rituals of holding audience—thrice a day in the morning, afternoon, and evening during the Ming era—he appreciated the informality and directness of eunuch employment. His Majesty therefore frequently delegated his trusted castrati to run the state as well as the court.

The apogees of eunuch power occurred during the Later Han dynasty (25–219 A.D.) and the Tang dynasty (618–906) when the eunuchs virtually became king makers. One of the reasons for such political abnormalcy was that, near the end of both the Later Han and Tang, emperors tended to die young, whereas their eunuchs, who were entrenched in powerful positions, enjoyed longevity. The experienced senior eunuchs were then able to provide political continuity and stability, hence also gaining trust from the dowager empresses with whom the eunuchs also had established a long and intimate association. But the Ming eunuchs differed from those of previous dynasties both quantitatively and qualitatively, as they were more numerous and also had penetrated deeper into practically every governmental agency, in fact dominating the political, military, diplomatic, judiciary, ceremonial, security, and economic affairs of Ming China. And as Lenin once said, quantity has a certain quality of its own. That is why we have witnessed in this book the rise of so many skilled, intelligent, and capable grand eunuchs who served as commanders of the army, admirals, ambassadors, and superintendents of various agencies. Their achievements and reputations were, however, often overshadowed by many a wicked and cynical eunuch boss—or eunuch dictator, as preferred by the antieunuch historians. But the eunuch dictators usually were not allowed, under the Ming system, to stay in power for more than three to four years, and almost never exceeded more than six to seven years in power. In general, the Ming eunuchs, after years of strict training and obedient service, had learned the imperial system well enough to carefully walk the line between being the emperor's surrogates and being his servants. In fact, with the exception of Cao Jixiang in the late 1450s, no Ming eunuch dared to depose a crown prince or select his own imperial candidate as did the eunuchs in the Later Han and the Tang.

One of the immediate questions is, Why did the Ming employ so many eunuchs, from a few hundred at the beginning of the dynasty, to about 10,000 by the end of the fifteenth century, and reaching approximately 100,000 at the time the dynasty fell to the hands of the Manchus? One reason, among other factors as discussed in Chapter II, was the ever-increasing demand for eunuch service by the imperial family, which grew at an exponential rate throughout its 276 years history. When the dynasty was founded, the number of imperial family members was 58, but that figure would explode to more than 10,000 by 1549, and the explosion continued throughout the seventeenth century. Table X.1 is an estimate of the Ming royal scions.[1]

Table X.1
Size of the Ming Royal Family

Date	Members of the Royal Family
1368–1398	58
1403–1424	127
1506–1521	2,495
1553	19,611
1562	28,840
1569	28,492
1594	62,000
1604	Over 80,000

Under the circumstances, the employment of castrated servants became inevitable, and in fact, even the most outspoken critics of the eunuchs never suggested the elimination of the service of the eunuchs entirely. However, the eunuchs always took the blame when they had to help their emperor raise money east and west so that the royal family could spend it north and south.

Eunuchism in the Ming dynasty also possessed several other attributes not common during previous dynasties. First of all, the Ming eunuchs were, in general, better trained and more heavily indoctrinated with two of the Confucian virtues, loyalty and filial piety. Since childhood, the young castrati were instilled with a deep and abiding affection for the Son of Heaven, and they regarded their emperor in the categories of the cosmic and institutional, rather than the human. In this way, the imperial will was equated with divine will, and as the emperor possessed the celestial quality of the political system, the eunuchs were more willing to dedicate their lives to the service of their "sage," as they fondly called their emperor. Like their literati counterparts, the eunuchs studied the teachings of Confucius, Mencius, the Buddha, and Laozi. Many educated Ming castrati, driven by high ideals, became less concerned with "position" than with "moral reputation." They actually imitated the conduct of the Confucian scholars, many of whom had taught them when they were young, and strived to win respect and honors from their peers and court officials. And the records show that these "beardless courtiers" for the most part satisfactorily performed their assigned duties according to imperial wishes. They guided foreign envoys and Chinese officials to the throne; they presented to the emperor the sacred seals to be affixed on imperial edicts; they helped their masters and mistresses perform the highly intricate and time-consuming court rituals; they took part in endless and rigorous drills; they transformed a political complex into an enlivening and even fun place to live and play; and they transmitted hundreds of thousands of imperial edicts and decrees to all parts of the bureaucratic hierarchy every month. They were indeed the grease and cogs of the Ming despotic machinery.

Second, the Ming autocrats used frequent and severe punishment to curtail excessive eunuch power and prevent them from staying in office for too long or becoming political liabilities. Practically one out of every two prominent Ming eunuchs ended his career in execution or exile to do hard labor in the frontier. Moreover, untold thousands of them were periodically subjected to indiscriminate flogging, which was greatly feared by all eunuchs, high and low. It should be noted that most of the Ming monarchs were ruthless, cruel men. The founder of the dynasty Hongwu and his son Yongle were both known for conducting bloodbath purges against their own officials and associates, putting hundreds, even thousands, of innocent people to death as stern warnings against corruption, power abuse, and treason. They were tough, decisive, alert, and able rulers, and their eunuchs all learned how to behave accordingly. Later it became a Ming tradition for a new emperor to wipe the slate clean by launching a purge against all the powerful eunuchs of his predecessor. Consequently, whenever an emperor died, numerous eunuchs would unexpectedly be thrown into jail, or exiled to undesirable places, or even executed. But violent and bloody purges against loyal and capable grand eunuchs also took place whenever a reigning emperor needed scapegoats to cover up his own mistakes or silence the critics of his derailed policies. The execution of the grand eunuch Cao Jixiang by Emperor Tianshun in 1461, the demotion of the spy chief Shang Ming in 1484 by his "beloved" Emperor Chenghua, the strangulation of the notorious Liu Jin on order from Emperor Zhengde in 1510, and the exile in 1583 of the ceremonials director Feng Bao by his "boyhood companion" Emperor Wanli were but four of the countless ruthless purges waged by the Ming autocrats against their once-most-trusted eunuchs. It is to be concluded therefore that the power of the Ming eunuchs was in general transitory and unstable and that, no matter how high they climbed or how intimate their association with their masters might have been, the Ming absolute monarchs would never hesitate to throw them away—as if they were but a pair of worn out shoes—when and if they were considered either political liabilities or irritants to the throne. The world of the Ming eunuchs, indeed, had the firmness of a bubble, the stability of a spider's gossamer web: it was filled with uncertainty.

Third, the Ming eunuchs always had to work hand in glove with the best Confucian scholars, who were recruited to serve the state through the civil service examination system. Several of these academic talents also proved to be skilled administrators and even had the fortune to enjoy political longevity. After Hongwu abolished the institution of premiership in the 1390s, the emperor had in fact become the head of the court as well as the state and had the leeway of appointing virtuous and able persons, who "knew the people's sickness and sorrows," to be his grand secretaries. The grand secretaries were hired to help the emperor deal with the hundreds of petitions that came to the attention of His Majesty every day. Since 1402, Emperor Yongle began to invite a handful of the most profound scholars to the Literary Flora Pavilion to take part in the decision-making process and have meals there, earning the name *Neige*, or the Inner Cabinet. Among the truly conscientious and righteous grand secretaries were the three Yangs—Yang Shiqi (1365–1444), Yang Rong (1371–1440), and Yang Pu (1372–1446)—who together served under four different emperors and generally had firm control over state affairs. Yang Shiqi retained his post in the Grand Secretariat for forty-three years, Yang Rong for thirty-seven years, and Yang Pu for twenty-two years. The longevity of the three Yangs indicates the continuity of the state policy and the general political stability of the Ming empire in the early fifteenth century. During the sixteenth century, a number of grand secretaries also enjoyed the uninterrupted support and trust of their emperors and gave able assistance to their autocrats. For example, Zhang Juzheng

(1525–1582) was a grand secretary for eighteen years, Yan Song (1480–1568) served in the same capacity for twenty years, and Xu Jie (1503–1583) carried his portfolio for seventeen years. The Ming dynasty was indeed blessed with many of such talents, who also learned how to work closely with their eunuch counterparts and, in a sense, provided some sort of balance in the Ming polity—a characteristic of dualism.

The grand secretaries, to maintain their positions, almost all found it necessary to cooperate with the managing grand eunuchs in the Ceremonial Directorate, as the latter, since the mid-fifteenth century, gradually took control of the flow of all state documents and, in many cases, also functioned as the emperor's surrogate. From their office, Wenshufang, the grand eunuchs attached a piece of paper containing a recommendation to every document coming in the palace. Those emperors who preferred doing carpentry or chasing hare and foxes to handling boring paperwork obviously could not pay personal attention to state matters. As a result, the ceremonials grand eunuchs were asked to make decisions on their behalf. A typical instruction from His Majesty to the ceremonials director would run like this: "You proceed with diligence. I know already." The director then was authorized to give "the red ink," officially conveying imperial sanction to the documents. The director would communicate the imperial decisions to the grand secretaries, who would put them into regular imperial edicts and send them to the proper governmental agencies for implementation.[2]

Under the circumstances, the managing grand eunuchs in the Ceremonial Directorate functioned as the media between the emperor and the grand secretaries, since the latter rarely had personal contact with His Majesty on a daily basis. And as the grand secretariat and the Ceremonials Directorate had become the two pillars of the decision-making apparatus, the relationship between the ceremonials directors and the grand secretaries developed into one of symbiosis. Astute and forceful grand secretaries usually were able to find ways to check the power of the ceremonials director, especially when the emperor was a hands-on and conscientious ruler. And those who learned how to collaborate with the powerful ceremonials director also tended to retain their posts in the Grand Secretariat longer than those who loved to confront and challenge their eunuch counterparts. In actual political interaction, some grand secretaries could not help but ingratiate themselves in front of the ceremonials director by calling the latter *gong gong*, meaning "grandpa." On a few occasions, the grand secretaries even were forced to call the most powerful eunuch boss *qiansui*, meaning "one-thousand-year," compared to *wansui*, or "ten-thousand-year," which they called the emperor. When that happened, it always indicated that the Ceremonial Directorate had assumed the center of the power structure, while the Grand Secretariat was playing only a peripheral sideshow. Since its inception in 1402 and until the end of the dynasty in 1644—a period of 243 years—the number of grand secretaries totalled 163. Among them, at least twenty-three were brought to the Grand Secretariat on the recommendations of the Ceremonial Directorate, while some twenty-eight grand secretaries, who had shown independence and refused to kowtow to the ceremonials grand eunuchs, were actually driven out of office by the eunuch bosses. The Ming political equilibrium, to a great extent, depended upon the balance and smooth interaction between these two small yet all-inclusive groups.

Fourth, beneath the second layer of the Ming dualistic structure lay its well-established censorial system, with the practice of constant impeachment against high-ranking eunuchs effectively curbing eunuch power. This was truly a remarkable system, with the emperor functioning as the fulcrum on which the balance between his eunuch functionaries—his Inner Court servants—and the censors and supervising secretaries—his ears and eyes of the Outer Court—was maintained. To divide and weaken the power of his ministers and prevent any single agency or group from threatening his monarchic absolutism, the Ming autocrat established thirteen circuits of investigating censors, with one for each province. Ranging from 7 to 11 persons in each circuit, a group of 110 investigating censors were charged with keeping under surveillance all personnel, including the eunuchs, and operations of the entire empire. They were also given other broad responsibilities and powers in suggesting and initiating preventive, corrective, and punitive measures to safeguard the emperor and the imperial institution he represented. The censors had direct access to the emperor and were responsible primarily to him. In addition, the Ming also established six offices of scrutiny, which were paired with the six ministries, each office employing from four to ten supervising secretaries. The approximately sixty such supervising secretaries checked and screened all the documents passing through the ministries, exercised editorial powers in drafting government documents, submitted remonstrances against unwise policies and acts, and frequently were sent on special investigatory missions by the emperor. Throughout the Ming period, the supervising secretaries and investigating censors participated jointly in countless special impeachments against abusive eunuchs.

The censors in general were among the brightest talents recruited from the eight-legged system. The generally low-paid, low-ranking censors and supervising secretaries always fought to uphold Confucian principles, old traditions, and existing institutions, while at the same time condoning the practices of polygamy, foot binding, and slavery. On the other hand, they worked closely with the people, knew the system, and were willing and eager to provide the throne with an "outside" perspective. But they frequently felt frustrated, as they found themselves generally running a sideshow instead of directing the main event. Censors who talked about the evil of eunuchs sometimes made stabs at them, but often just trying to float such trial balloons redounded to their regret and even personal harm. The eunuchs, on the other hand, cut their political teeth in the Inner Court and entered politics from entirely different experiences. Once they had gained access to power and wealth, they were naturally the most vulnerable to the temptation of fraud, waste, abuse, and mismanagement. Consequently, we can detect the pattern of the censors and supervising secretaries grinding their axes and standing ever ready to discredit their eunuch nemeses. To be sure though, numerous censors chose to collaborate with the eunuchs so that they could share political spoils and riches, but the majority of them opted to follow their consciences. In the final analysis, however, the Ming autocrat was the sole beneficiary, as these two irreconcilable forces fought to check one another. The survival of the Ming dynasty for over two and a half centuries involves too many factors for one encompassing generalization, but the dynasty's "check and balance" system should nevertheless be considered one of the most important reasons.

Since the onset of the dynasty, eunuchism had been so well institution-alized that any personnel change amounted to only replacing new wine in an old bottle and did not in any significant way alter the nature of the system. Ming eunuchism, therefore, should better be studied from its institutional effects rather than from the impact brought about by individual castrati. The first emperor Hongwu somehow gave historians the impression that he did not permit his eunuchs to get involved in his administration, but he actually used his eunuchs to conduct tea-horse trading; to carry out diplomatic mis-sions to Mongolia, the Ryukyu Islands, and Korea; and even to supervise his expeditionary army, as in the case of the grand eunuch Wu Cheng in 1378. The power of the third emperor Yongle, one might even argue, was based substantially upon a group of extremely talented and fearless eunuchs, as he appointed several dozen of them to execute all sorts of assignments on his behalf. During the early years of the Xuande reign (1426–1435), several of the grand eunuchs who served Yongle were executed on charges of real or fabricated crimes, but the fifth Ming monarch soon learned that he could not practice his absolutism without the service of eunuchs. He therefore appointed the eunuch Jin Ying the grand commandant of Nanjing and, by so doing, actually added more weight to the importance of the eunuch office in the Ming's "auxiliary" capital. Moreover, Xuande favored one particular eunuch, Chen Wu, and promoted him to a position that drew envy even from the nobles. A native of Annam, Chen Wu was brought to the Ming court by Emperor Yongle at a tender age. It appeared that Xuande was very much impressed with this castrato, not only giving him his new name, Wang Jin, but also commissioning him to supervise a number of major military expeditions. Wang Jin in fact was to be the person who sealed off all of

Admiral Zheng He's treasure ships used for the seven historical navigations between 1405 and 1431. At the height of his influence, Wang Jin received all kinds of honors and awards, including rare books, jade belts, gold saddles, steeds, gold coins, and other treasures.[3]

In the colossal Ming despotic institution, however, the eunuchs were both indispensable and expendable, as the autocrats favored them for usually three to four years and then had them summarily hung out to dry.[4] In 1442, the teenaged Emperor Zhengtong had the veteran eunuch Guo Jing, who once was an envoy to Central Asia and the grand defender of Datong, executed and one year later also approved the capital punishment of two other prominent eunuchs, Zhang Huan and Gu Zhong. And in 1445, four more influential grand eunuchs from the Ceremonial Directorate were also imprisoned. But Zhengtong also enthusiastically promoted the controversial Wang Zhen until Wang became one of the most powerful eunuch "dictators" in Ming history. Zhengtong further allowed another eunuch, Xi Ning, to accumulate an immense sum of money. Unfortunately, when Zhengtong's brother assumed the imperial reign as Jingtai, Xi Ning, then the director of Imperial Carpentry, was eliminated. Jingtai then found his own indispensable eunuch in the person of Cao Jixiang who, like hundreds of other powerful eunuchs, could not escape the predestined eunuch tragedy, as he met his death in 1461. This pattern of the rise and fall of the eunuchs would continue to grow as the roots of Ming absolutism sank deeper into the soil. Only one month after Chenghua became the eighth emperor of the Ming dynasty, the summer of 1465, he needed an indispensable eunuch by the name of Niu Yu to help him out of his marital crisis. But Niu Yu soon discovered that the imperial favors he had been receiving were only like the morning dew, as the stuttering Chenghua grew increasingly paranoid and tyrannical. Historians generally give Chenghua's son, the Emperor Hongzhi, high marks for attempting to curtail the influence of the eunuchs. But once Hongzhi fell prey to superstition and the possibility of an everlasting life, he had to find his own indispensable eunuch. The eunuch was Li Guang, who was then the director of palace servants, but was especially known for his black magic. Claiming he could make magic water and immortal pills, Li Guang soon became Emperor Hongzhi's confidant and openly took bribes from the nobles as well as ministerial officials. Li would enjoy imperial patronage until 1498, when a large conflagration that engulfed several buildings in the palace convinced Li to take his own life.

Emperor Hongzhi died when he was only thirty-six sui. His son, the impulsive Emperor Zhengde, would bring Ming absolutism to a higher level. In so doing, Zhengde needed more wicked eunuchs, and the result was a lax and corrupt court run amok by the notorious "Eight Tigers." In 1522, when the eleventh Ming emperor assumed the reign as Jiajing, he first tried to reduce the number of castrated servants by launching a large-scale purge against Zhengde's eunuchs. However, after only a few months, Jiajing was forced to reverse his retrenchment policy, as he learned that he needed the blood of his eunuchs to keep his despotism, this Frankenstein's monster, alive. Such being the true nature of the Ming polity, it mattered little even if an individual monarch wished to pursue a different style of management or simply to make some cosmetic change in government because, in the final analysis, the Ming despotic system could not function without the service of its eunuchs. Longqing, the twelfth emperor, and Wanli, the thirteenth emperor, both discovered this secret, and the stories went on and on.

After putting to death the eunuch "dictator" Wei Zhongxian and dozens of Wei's cohorts, Chongzhen, the sixteenth and the last Ming emperor, for a while probably thought that he could start his regime with a clean slate and run his empire without the "evil" influence of the eunuchs. But he too quickly realized that he could not completely trust his own ministers or his frontier commanders. Within a year, Chongzhen began to appoint eunuchs to supervise his armies, command his Imperial guards, and safeguard all the nine imperial gates and every palace door. And by the winter of 1632, his eunuchs were taking over the defense assignments in Datong, Xuanfu, and other strategically important posts. They were also in charge of logistic supplies and ammunition manufacturing. Moreover, as seen in the past, his eunuchs were once again assuming the roles of tax collectors, tea-horse traders, judiciary reviewers, and even the superintendents of the state university. During the seventeen years that Chongzhen occupied the dragon throne, he used more than fifty scholars as his grand secretaries, seventeen persons as his ministers of punishment, fourteen as ministers of war, and executed seven supreme commanders or viceroys. This clearly suggests that Chongzhen had a deep suspicion of his literati-officials and generals. In the end, whenever he needed officials whose loyalty could be counted to maintain the great Ming absolutist institution, he had no choice but to turn to his eunuchs. The essence of the Ming monarchic absolutism indeed lies in its institutionalized eunuchism and, with it, the dualistic system. In that sense, the eunuchs themselves were only the pawns, as well as the victims, of this peculiar system.

APPENDIX 1
Eunuch Agencies and
Their Duties in Ming Dynasty

Silijian (Ceremonial Directorate)   In charge of palace entertainment, ceremonies, and punishment; supervised special royal missions and eunuch personnel; directed all eunuch services, transmitted and gave advice on petitions, recorded imperial documents, and kept the palace books.

Neiguanjian (Palace Servants)   Responsible for all palace construction and civil engineering; procured fireworks, copper, tin, wood, iron utensils, and implements; repaired royal mansions and mausolea.

Yuyongjian (Palace Carpentry)   Manufactured screens, beds, chairs, tables and furniture; provided games and toys; made artistic and decorative objects from sandalwood, lacquerware, ivory, and pearl.

Sishejian (Outfittings)   Made draperies, cushions, rattan blinds, raincoats, and umbrellas for emperor's outings.

Yumajian (Imperial Stables)   In charge of firearms, supervised Imperial Guards; took care of exotic animals and horses.

Shengongjian (Imperial Temples)   Cleaned imperial mausolea; burned incense and lit altar candles.

Shangshanjian (Palace Foods)   Prepared court meals and banquets; offered food three times a day to emperor's ancestors.

Shangbaojian (Imperial Seals)   Kept sacred seals, imperial decrees, proclamations, and seals to be authorized to grand commanders.

Yinshoujian (Document Filing)   Stored and safeguarded written appointments of peerage, official documents and checks.

Zhidianjian (Palace Custodians)   Cleaned palaces and other imperial structures.

Shangyijian (Royal Clothing)   Made ceremonial robes, everyday apparel, headgear, and footwear.

Duzhijian (Entourage Guards)   Served as front guards and swept roads during every imperial visit to the Outer Court.

FOUR DEPARTMENTS

Xixinsi (Fire and Water Department)   Handled firewood and charcoal for the palace use; dredged ditches and kept the tanks full of water for fire fighting.

Zhonggusi (Entertainments)   Played musical instruments, beat drums, staged theatricals and shadow-picture plays.

Baochaosi (Toilet Paper)   Produced expensive toilet paper and other paperware.

Huntangsi (Bathhouse)   In charge of bathhouses and bathing equipments.

EIGHT BUREAUS

Bingzhangju (Armament Bureau)   Manufactured and took charge of bows and arrows, swords, lances, suits of armor, and firearms.

Yinzuoju (Silverware)   Made gold and silver pieces for royal use and imperial gifts frequently granted meritorious officials.

Wanyiju (Nursing Home)	Took care of retired and aging palace personnel and confined court ladies expelled from the palace so that court secrets would not be revealed. The only eunuch office located outside the Imperial Palace.
Jinmaoju (Headgear)	Made headgear, footwear, and banners for princes and princesses.
Zhengongju (Garments)	Manufactured summer, winter, and special garments for palace personnel.
Neizhiranju (Dyeing)	Produced indigoes and dyed linen, silk fabric, and cloth.
Jiucumianju (Wine, Vinegar, and Noodle)	Supplied wine, vinegar, sugar, soy sauce, noodle, beans, and so on.
Siyuanju (Vegetables)	Supplied vegetables, fruits, nuts, and seasonal delicacies.

In addition, Ming eunuchs were assigned to ten major warehouses, eight palace anterooms, a dozen palace gates, plus numerous temporary offices in the capital and throughout the empire.

APPENDIX 2
Glossary of Chinese Characters

A-da-a-zhe　阿答阿者
Anding　安定
An Ning　安寧
Anletang　安樂堂
Anlu huangzhuang　安陸皇莊
Ansu　安肅
Aruytai (Mongol)　阿魯台
Ba Tai　把泰
Bai Juyi　白居易
Baidu　白渡
Bao Zhong　鮑忠
Baochaosi　寶鈔司
Baoding　保定
Bingzhangju　兵仗局
bingbi taijian　秉筆太監
Cai Lun　蔡倫
Cao Huachun　曹化淳
Cao Jin　曹金
Cao Jixiang　曹吉祥
Cha Jizuo　查繼佐
Chai shan　柴山
Chama　茶馬
Chamasi　茶馬司
Chang Sheng　昌盛
Changping　昌平
Changsha　長沙
Changle　長樂
Chen Cheng　陳誠
Chen Feng　陳奉
Chen Hao　陳浩
Chen Hao of Ning (prince)　寧王
　宸濠
Chen Hong　陳洪
Chen Ju　陳矩
Chen Kuan　陳寬

Chen Kun　陳昆
Chen Rui　陳銳
Chen Shan　陳山
Chen Wance　陳萬策
Chen Xuan　陳鉉
Chen Zeng　陳增
Chen Zhun　陳準
Chenghua (eighth emperor)　成化
Chengtianfu　承天府
Chongzhen (sixteenth
　emperor)　崇禎
Chun Ming mengyulu
　春明夢餘錄
Cisheng Taihou (dowager)　慈聖
　太后
Constantine (prince)　當定王
Cui An (Korean)　崔安
Cui Lei　崔累
choufen　抽分
Da Ming huidian　大明會典
Dai Xibao　戴細保
Dalisi　大理寺
Daoyi zhilue　島夷志略
Datong　大同
Deng Cheng　鄧成
Diaomen　碉門
Dong Ji　董基
Dong Qichang　董其昌
Dongchang　東廠
Dongwan　東莞
Du Fu　杜甫
Du Liang　度量
Du Tai　杜泰
Du zhuanyunyan shisi　都轉運鹽
　使司

Duzhijian　都知監
dazong baochuan　大䑸寶船
Er Nie　而聶
Esen (Mongol)　也先
Fanjingchang　番經廠
Fei Xin　費信
Feng Bao　馮保
Feng Guan　馮貫
Feng Rang　馮讓
Fengtiandian　奉天殿
Fengyang　鳳陽
Fu An　傅安
Fu Lin　傅霖
Fu Rong　傅容
Fu Wang (prince)　福王
Fu Youde　傅友德
fengtian zhibao　奉天之寶
fengyu　奉御
folangji chong　佛郎機銃
Gan Quan　甘泉
Gao Feng　高鳳
Gao Huai　高淮
Gao Xu of Han (prince)
　漢王高煦
Geng Zhong　耿忠
Genggufang　更鼓房
Gong Hong　龔洪
Gu Dayong　谷大用
Gu Xuan　顧璿
Gu Yanwu　顧炎武
Guanglusi　光祿寺
Gui Wang (prince)　桂王
Guo Jing　郭敬
Guo Shoujing　郭守敬
Guo Wen　郭文
geng　更
gong gong　公公
guan　貫
Hai Shou　海壽
Hai Tong　海童

Han Zhong　韓重
Hanfenlou biji　涵芬樓秘笈
Hangzhou　杭州
Hanjingchang　漢經廠
Hanlin　翰林
He Jin　何進
He Neng　何能
He Wenyuan　何文淵
Hejian　河間
Hexiwu　河西務
Hezhou　河州
Hong Bao　洪保
Hongwu (first emperor)　洪武
Hongxi (fourth emperor)　洪熙
Hongzhi (ninth emperor)　弘治
Hou Xian　侯顯
Hu Liangfu　胡良輔
Huai En　懷恩
Huaian　淮安
Huang Ci　黃賜
Huang Jin　黃錦
Huang Rang　黃讓
Huang Wei　黃偉
Huang Yan　黃儼
Huangjimen　皇極門
Huijimen　會極門
Huitongguan　會同館
Hunhe (river)　渾河
Huntangsi　混堂司
Huzhou　湖州
huangdi zhibao　皇帝之寶
huanguan　宦官
huangzhuang　皇莊
huayin　花銀
huozhe　火者
Ji Gang　紀綱
Ji Xiang　吉祥
Jia Lu　賈魯
Jiajing (eleventh emperor)　嘉靖
Jiao Fang　焦芳

Jianchang　建昌
Jiang Cong　蔣琮
Jiang Wan　姜綰
Jiangnan　江南
Jianwen (second emperor)　建文
Jiaotaidian　交泰殿
Jiaxing　嘉興
Jin Fu　金輔
Jin Wang (prince)　晉王
Jin Ying　金英
Jingdezhen　景德鎮
Jingletang　敬樂堂
Jinglongkou　荊隆口
Jingshifang　敬事房
Jingtai (seventh emperor)　景泰
Jingzhou　景州
Jinmaoju　巾帽局
Jinyiwei　錦衣衛
Jiucumianju　酒醋麵局
Jizhou　薊州
Juyongguan　居庸關
jingshen nanzi　淨身男子
Kang Fu　康福
Kang Wang　康旺
Ke Shi (mistress)　客氏
Kim Liyuan (Korean)　金麗淵
Kim Yi (Korean)　金義
Kuai Xiang　蒯祥
Kunninggong　坤寧宮
Lai En　賴恩
Lan Zhong　藍忠
Le Mi (Annamese)　黎秘
Le Xian (Annamese)　黎賢
Lei Qing　雷晴
Leizhou　雷州
Li An　李安
Li Da　李達
Li Dongyang　李東陽
Li Feng　李鳳
Li Guang　李廣

Li Gui　李貴
Li Jing　李敬
Li Jingru　李景儒
Li Jinzhong　李進忠
Li Jun　李竣
Li Min　李敏
Li Neng　李能
Li Qing　李慶
Li Quan　李全
Li Rong　李榮
Li Rusong　李如松
Li Tang　李棠
Li Xian　李賢
Li Xian　李暹
Li Xin　李信
Li Xing　李興
Li Yi　李儀
Li Yingshen　李應昇
Li Yu　李玉
Li Zhaoxiang　李昭祥
Li Zhen　李珍
Li Zilong　李子龍
Liang Fang　梁芳
Liang Ji　梁玘
Liang Min　梁民
Lianzhou　廉州
Liao Tang　廖堂
Ling Jining　靈繼寧
Lingqing　臨清
Lingtai　靈台
Liu Daxia　劉大夏
Liu Jian　劉健
Liu Jin　劉瑾
Liu Jing　劉靖
Liu Lang　劉瑯
Liu Ning　劉寧
Liu Ruoyu　劉若愚
Liu Shaoguang　劉紹光
Liu Xiangfeng　劉祥鳳
Liu Yongcheng　劉永誠

Liu Yuan　劉遠
Liu Yun　劉允
Liujiagang　劉家港
Liyifang　禮儀房
Long Shou　龍綬
Longjiang　龍江
Longqing (twelfth emperor)　隆慶
Lu An　魯安
Lu Bing　陸炳
Lu Jie　陸杰
Lu Kun　魯坤
Lu Qian　路謙
Lu Rong　陸容
Lu Shou　盧受
Lu Yu　陸瑜
Lü Bi　呂毖
Lugouqiao　蘆溝橋
Luo Gui　羅珪
Luo Yong　羅永
lunban　輪班
Ma Bin　馬彬
Ma Huan　馬歡
Ma Jing　馬靖
Ma Jun　馬俊
Ma Qi　馬騏
Ma Yongcheng　馬永成
Ma Yun　馬雲
Mahmud (Mongol)　馬哈木
Mai-de-li-ba-la (Mongol)　買的
　里八剌
Mai Fu　麥福
Mao Yuanyi　茅元儀
Men Da　門達
Mu Jing　沐敬
maixian　賣閒
Nanhaizi　南海子
Naxi　納溪
Neichengyun ku　內承運庫
Neifu gongyongku　內府供用庫
Neiguanjian　內官監

Neishutang　內書堂
Neixingchang　內行廠
Neizhiranju　內織染局
Ningxian Wang (prince)　寧獻王
Niu Rong　牛榮
Nguyen An (Annamese)　阮安
Nguyen Hong (Annamese)　阮弘
Nguyen Lang (Annamese)　阮浪
Nguyen Luo (Annamese)　阮洛
Nguyen Zhi (Annamese)　阮至
Nuerkan　奴几干
neicao　內操
neishi　內使
Pan Gui　潘貴
Pan Hong　潘洪
Pan Wu　潘午
Pan Xiang　潘相
Pang Tianshou (Achilles)　龐天壽
Peng Shao　彭韶
Peng Shu　彭恕
Peng Ze　彭澤
Piaoerying　票兒銀
pihong　批紅
Qianqinggong　乾清宮
Qiantang (river)　錢塘
Qianwen ji　前聞記
Qiao Laixi　喬來喜
Qin De　秦德
Qin Jin　秦金
Qin Wen　秦文
Qiu De　丘得
Qiu Ju　丘聚
Qu Shisi (Thomas)　瞿式耜
Quanzhou　泉州
qinqin zhibao　親親之寶
Ran Deng　冉登
sadae (Korean term)　事大
Sanbao tuotuo　三保脫脫
Sanqianying　三千營
Shang Lu　商輅

Shang Ming　尚銘
Shangbaojian　尚寶監
Shangbaosi　尚寶司
Shanglinyuanjian　上林苑監
Shangshanjian　尚膳監
Shangyijian　尚衣監
Shanhaiguan　山海關
Shaoxing　紹興
Shawan　沙灣
Shen Shixing　申時行
Shen Yongshou　沈永壽
Shengongjian　神宮監
Shenjiying　神機營
Shi Huoji　史霍冀
Shi Pu　石璞
Shin Guisheng (Korean)　申貴生
shiyu　侍御
shoubei　守備
Shuntianfu　順天府
Silijian　司禮監
Sishejian　司設監
Siyi guan　四夷館
Siyuanju　司苑局
Su Dongpo　蘇東坡
Sun Chengze　孫承澤
Sun Xian　孫暹
Sun Xu　孫敍
Suzhou　蘇州
siren　寺人
Taichang (fourteenth emperor)　泰昌
Taiyiyuan　太醫院
Taozhou　洮州
Tianjin　天津
Tianqi (fifteenth emperor)　天啓
Tianshifang　甜食房
Tianshoushan　天壽山
Tianshun (sixth emperor)　天順
Tong Guan　童貫
Tongzhensi　通政司

Tumu　土木
taijian　太監
tianzi zhibao　天子之寶
Wang An　王安
Wang Cheng　王誠
Wang Chonggu　王崇古
Wang Dayuan　汪大淵
Wang De　王德
Wang Guitong　王貴通
Wang Heng　王衡
Wang Hu　王虎
Wang Jiaqing　王家慶
Wang Jin　王瑾
Wang Jing　王敬
Wang Jinghong　王景弘
Wang Min　王敏
Wang Shizhen　王世貞
Wang Shouren　王守仁
Wang Tang　王堂
Wang Wen　王文
Wan Xiang　王相
Wan Yan　王彥
Wang Yanzhi　王彥之
Wang You　王佑
Wang Yue　王岳
Wang Zan　王瓚
Wang Zhen　王振
Wang Zhi　汪直
Wang Zhong　王忠
Wanli (thirteenth emperor)　萬曆
Wanyiju　浣衣局
Wei Bin　魏彬
Wei Dan　魏淡
Wei Fumin　魏撫民
Wei Liangdong　魏良棟
Wei Pengyi　魏鵬翼
Wei Zhongxian　魏忠賢
Wenhuadian　文華殿
Wu Bin　吳賓
Wu Cheng　吳誠

Wu Gen　武艮
Wu Hai　吳海
Wu Jingzi　吳敬梓
Wu Sangui　吳三桂
Wu Shizhong　吳世忠
Wu Zheng　吳政
Wu Zhong　吳忠
Wubei bishu　武備秘書
Wubei zhi　武備志
Wuchangfu　武昌府
Wuhu　蕪湖
Wujunying　五軍營
Wuliangha　兀良哈
Wuyingdian　武英殿
wei suo　衛所
wumingbai　無名白
Xi Ning　喜寧
Xia Shou　夏綬
Xia Yan　夏言
Xia Yuanji　夏元吉
Xiang Zhong　項忠
Xiao Jing　蕭敬
Xichang　西廠
Xie Qian　謝遷
Xing An　興安
Xingdu　興都
Xining　西寧
Xiong Xuan　熊宣
Xixinsi　惜薪司
Xizhifang　西直房
Xu Han　許瀚
Xu Hao　徐浩
Xu Jie　徐階
Xu Yong　許鏞
Xuande (fifth emperor)　宣德
Xuanfu　宣府
Xuzhou　徐州
xinbao　信寶
xingbao　行寶
Yan Shifan　嚴世蕃

Yan Song　嚴嵩
Yang Lian　楊漣
Yang Min　楊敏
Yang Peng　楊鵬
Yang Pu　楊溥
Yang Rong　楊榮
Yang Sanbao　楊三保
Yang Shiqi　楊士琦
Yang Xiong　楊雄
Yang Zhen　楊鎮
Yangzhou　揚州
Yansui　延綏
Yanke tijusi　鹽課提舉司
Yaoerdu　要兒渡
Ye Xianggao　葉向高
Yi Songgye (Korean)　李成桂
yin　引
Yin Feng　尹鳳
Yingtianfu　應天府
Yinshoujian　印綬監
Yinzuoju　銀作局
Yishiha　亦失哈
Yizhou　易州
Yongle (third emperor)　永樂
Yu Jian　于謙
Yu Jing　于經
Yu Shiyue　俞士悅
Yu Yan　余寅
Yue Fei　岳飛
Yujiufang　御酒房
Yumajian　御馬監
Yumuchuan　榆木川
Yun Xiang　雲祥
Yuqianzuo　御前作
Yuyaofang　御藥房
Yuyongjian　御用監
yanding　鹽丁
yanren　奄人
Zhang Cheng　張誠
Zhang Jing　張鯨

Zhang Juzheng　張居正
Zhang Li　張鯉
Zhang Qian　張謙
Zhang Qing　張慶
Zhang Rui　張銳
Zhang Tianshi　張天師
Zhang Xin　張信
Zhang Xiong　張雄
Zhang Xueyan　張學顏
Zhang Yang　張陽
Zhang Yong　張永
Zhang Yu　張瑜
Zhang Zhijing　張志景
Zhang Zhong　張忠
Zhang Zuo　張佐
Zhangqiu　張秋
Zhao Cheng　趙成
Zhao Da　趙達
Zhao Jing　趙璟
Zhao Qin　趙欽
Zhao Zhong　趙忠
Zhaoqing　肇慶
Zhaoyu　詔獄
Zhen Fan of Anhua (prince)
　安化王寘鐇
Zhendingfu　眞定府
Zhenfusi　鎮撫司
Zheng He　鄭和

Zheng Qiang　鄭強
Zheng Tong (Korean)　鄭同
Zheng Xiao　鄭曉
Zhengde (tenth emperor)　正德
Zhengongju　針工局
Zhengtong (sixth emperor)　正統
Zhenjian　鎮江
Zhenshou　鎮守
Zhi Guang　智光
Zhidianjian　直殿監
Zhongchangshi　中常侍
Zhonggusi　鐘鼓司
Zhongshutang　中書堂
Zhou Man　周滿
Zhou Quan　周全
Zhu Di　朱棣
Zhu Fu　朱福
Zhu Geng　朱賡
Zhu Quanzhong　朱全忠
Zhu Yuanzhang　朱元璋
Zhu Zhen　朱鎮
Zhuozhong zhi　酌中志
Zijingguan　紫荊關
Zu Yunming　祝允明
Zuiwei lu　罪惟錄
zhangyin taijian　掌印太監
zhuzuo　住作
zunqin zhibao　尊親之寶

NOTES

CHAPTER I. INTRODUCTION

1. Zhang Tingyu et al., eds., *Ming shi* [History of Ming Dynasty], (Taipei: Dingwen Publishing Co., 1979), 244, Biography 132, p. 6319; hereafter cited as *MS*. Also see W. Theodore de Bary, "Chinese Despotism and the Confucian Ideal: A Seventeenth Century View," in John K. Fairbank, ed., *Chinese Thought and Institutions* (Chicago, 1957), pp. 163–203.

2. Richard Millant, *Les Eunuques: A Travers Les Ages* (Paris, 1908), pp. 8–9, 235–243; Garter C. Stent, "Chinese Eunuchs," *Journal of North-China Branch of the Royal Asiatic Society*, n.s. 10 (1877): 166; and Jitsuzo Kuwabara, "Shina no kangan," *Toyo shi setsuen* 22 (1936): 344–358.

3. Taiji Shimizu, "Jigu kangan no kenkyu," *Shigaku zasshi* 43 (1932): 83–128.

4. For more, see Taisuke Mitamura, *Chinese Eunuchs: The Structure of Intimate Politics*, translated from *Kangan: Sokkin Seiji no kozo* (Tokyo, 1963), pp. 14–16. Shortly after Dr. Chen Cunren died, Taiwan's *Zhuanji wenxue* [Biographical Literature] reprinted six of his articles regarding the effects of castration on body and mind. See *Zhuanji wenxue* 57, nos. 3–6 (1990) and 58, nos. 1 and 2 (1991).

5. Liu Ruoyu, *Zhuozhong zhi* (Shanghai: Commercial Press, 1935), 14, pp. 71–73. Also see George A. Kennedy, "Wei Chung-hsien," in Arthur Hummel, *Eminent Chinese of the Ch'ing Period*, 2 vols. (Washington, D.C., 1943–1944), vol. 2, pp. 846–847; and *MS*, 305, Biography 193, Eunuchs 2, pp. 7816–17.

6. Charles O. Hucker, *The Censorial System of Ming China* (Stanford, Calif.: Stanford University Press, 1966), pp. 171, 200–204; John Ross, *The Manchus* (London, 1891), pp. 123–126. Yang Lian's entire Chinese memorial is collected in *Yang Dahong ji* in *Congshu jicheng* edition, printed in late Qing period.

7. For a more detailed analysis of the events between 1620 and 1628, see a study by Ulrich Mammitzsch, "Wei Chung-hsien (1528–1628): A Reappraisal of the Eunuch and the Factional Strife at the Late Ming Court" (Ph.D. dissertation, University of Hawaii, 1968), pp. 125–295.

8. See for example, Karl Wittfogel, *Oriental Despotism* (New Haven, Conn., 1957); Frederick Mote, "The Growth of Chinese Despotism, A Critique of Wittfogel's Theory of Despotism as Applied to China," *Oriens Extremus* 8 (1961): 1–41; Heinrich Busch, "The Tunglin Academy and Its Political and Philosophical Significance," *Monumenta Serica* 14 (1949): 1–163; and Wolfgang Franke, *Preliminary Notes on the Important Chinese Literary Sources for the History of the Ming Dynasty (1368–1644)* (Chengdu, 1948), Studia Serica Monographs Series A., no. 2. Also see Paul Pelliot, "Les Grands Voyages Maritimes Chinois Au Debut XVe Siecle," *T'oung Pao* 30 (1933): 252–265; Robert C. Crawford, "Eunuch Power in the Ming Dynasty," *T'oung Pao*, 49 (1961): 115–48; and Ulrike Jugel, *Politische Funktion und Soziale Stellung der Eunuchen zur Spateren-Hanzeit (25–220 n. Chr.)* (Weisbaden, Germany, 1976).

CHAPTER II.
THE DEMAND AND SUPPLY OF MING EUNUCHS

1. Enid R. Peschel and Richard E. Peschel, "Medical Insights into the Castrati in Opera," *American Scientist* (November–December, 1987): 580.

2. Ding Yi, *Mingdai tewu zhengzhi* [Politics of the Secret Police During the Ming Dynasty] (Beijing, 1951), pp. 23–24.

3. Zhang Tingyu et al., eds., *Ming shi* [History of the Ming Dynasty] 304, Biography 192, p. 7765. For more see Huang Zhangjian, "Lun Huang Ming zuxunlu suoji Mingchu huanguan zhidu," or "On the Early Ming Eunuch System as Recorded in the Ming Emperors' Instructions," *Academia Sinica History and Philology Institute Collections* (Taipei, 1960), *jikan* 32, pp. 77–98.

4. Gu Yingtai, *Mingshi jishi benmo* [Ming History Compiled According to Subjects], (Reprint Taipei, 1956) juan 8, Hongwu reign, 8/2/1; also Hongwu Veritable Record, 120, 10th moon of 11th year, Hongwu reign.

5. Hongwu Veritable Record, 93, 9th moon, 7th year of Hongwu reign; 133, 9th moon, 13th year of Hongwu reign; and 193, 8th moon, 21st year of Hongwu reign. Also see *Zheng He xia xiyang* [Zheng He's Expeditions to the Western Ocean], ed. China's Maritime History Society (Beijing, 1985), pp. 148–149.

6. Hongwu Veritable Record, 155, 6th moon of 16th year, Hongwu reign; 169, 12th moon of 17th year, Hongwu reign; 179, 12th moon of 19th year, Hongwu reign.

7. *MS*, 321, Biography 209, Foreign countries 2, Annam, p. 8323.

8. Ibid., 325, Biography 213, Foreign countries 6, Malacca, p. 8418.

9. Chenghua Veritable Record, 106, 7th moon of 8th year, Chenghua reign.

10. The twenty-eight eunuch-led missions to Korea are described in various veritable records of the sixteen Ming emperors. For example, the twenty-sixth mission can be found in Wanli Veritable Record, 434, 3rd moon of 38th year, Wanli reign while the twenty-eighth mission is recorded in Chongzhen Veritable Record, 7, 1st moon of 7th year, Chongzhen reign.

11. *MS*, 304, Biography 192, Eunuchs, p. 7728.

12. Tianshun Veritable Record, 313, 3rd moon of 4th year, Tianshun reign.

13. Xuande Veritable Record, 6, 6th moon of 10th year, Xuande reign.

14. Zhengtong Veritable Record, 185, 10th moon of 14th year, Zhengtong reign; Jingtai Supplementary Record, 25, 8th moon of 2nd year and 33, 4th moon of 3rd year, Jingtai reign.

15. *MS*, 305, Biography 193, Eunuchs, p. 7810.

16. Hongwu Veritable Record, 239, 6th moon of 28th year, Hongwu reign.

17. Hongxi Veritable Record, 8, 3rd moon of 1st year, Hongxi reign. A case in point was the story of Huai En whose cousin was a vice minister of war but was executed by Emperor Xuande on a charge of treason. Young Huai En was castrated for a crime he knew nothing about. See also *MS*, 304, Biography 192, Eunuchs, p. 7777.

18. Ibid., 307 Biography 195, Sycophants, P. 7876; also Yongle Veritable Record, 31, 9th moon of 2nd year, Yongle reign.

19. *MS*, 207, Biography 95, Yang Zuzhong, p. 5481.

20. Ibid., 2, Basic annals 2, Hongwu reign, p. 20.

21. Strictly speaking, the princes possessed no territory because, outside their palaces, civil officials were appointed directly by the emperor to manage all government affairs. The first emperor had a total of twenty-six sons and sixteen daughters, and the thirteenth emperor had eight sons and ten daughters born of eight wives.

22. Wu Han, *Zhu Yuanzhang zhuan* [Biography of the First Ming Emperor] (Shanghai, 1949), pp. 262–263.

23. For more see Charles O. Hucker, "Governmental Organization of the Ming Dynasty," *Harvard Journal of Asiatic Studies* 21, (1958): 8–11.

24. Hongxi Veritable Record, 2 and 3, 9th moon and 10th moon of 22nd year, Yongle reign.

25. Xuande Veritable Record, 3, 7th moon of 1st year and 29, 7th moon of 2nd year, Xuande reign.

26. Zhengtong Veritable Record, 22, 9th moon of 1st year and 166, 5th moon of 13th year, Zhengtong reign.

27. Xuande Veritable Record, 23, 12th moon of 1st year, Xuande reign.

28. Ibid., 93, 7th moon of 7th year, Xuande reign.

29. Yongle Veritable Record, 60, 11th moon of 6th year and 79, 11th moon of 9th year, Yongle reign.

30. Xuande Veritable Record, 22, 10th moon of 1st year and 37, 2nd moon of 2nd year, Xuande reign.

31. Zhengtong Veritable Record, 70, 8th moon of 5th year, Zhengtong reign; 94, 7th moon of 7th year, Zhengtong reign; and 151, 3rd moon of 12th year, Zhengtong reign. Prince Yi of Luoyang, for example, got 8 castrated men in 1443 for his son's wedding present.

32. Ibid., 153, 4th moon of 12th year, Zhengtong reign.

33. Chenghua Veritable Record, 136, 12th moon of 10th year, Chenghua reign.

34. Ibid., 153, 5th moon of 12th year and 164, 3rd moon of 13th year, Chenghua reign. Nanhaizi was an imperial hunting preserve located Southeast of the Forbidden City.

35. Ibid., 187, 2nd moon of 15th year, Chenghua reign.

36. Ibid., 204, 6th moon of 16th year and 291, 6th moon of 23rd year, Chenghua reign.

37. Ibid., 252, 5th moon of 20th year, Chenghua reign.

38. Hongzhi Veritable Record, 75, 5th moon of 6th year, Hongzhi reign.

39. Ibid.

40. Zhengde Veritable Record, 20, 9th moon of 2nd year, Zhengde reign.

41. Ibid., 146, 2nd moon of 12th year, Zhengde reign.

42. Jiajing Veritable Record, 5, 8th moon of 16th year, Jiajing reign. Emperor Jiajing accepted 3,455 castrated men in 1536, once distributed 2,990 eunuchs to various princes, and on a different occasion, sent a group of 2,001 new recruits to work in imperial estates.

43. Ibid., 188, 6th moon of 15th year, Jiajing reign.

44. Wanli Veritable Record, 11, 3rd moon of 1st year, Wanli reign; 77, 7th moon of 6th year, Wanli reign; and 205, 11th moon of 16th year, Wanli reign. For more about Emperor Wanli's reign, see an outstanding work by Ray Huang, *1587, A Year of No Significance* (New Haven, Conn.: Yale University Press, 1981).

45. Wanli Veritable Record, 358, 4th moon of 29th year, Wanli reign.

46. Tianqi Veritable Record, 1, 1st moon of 1st year, Tianqi reign.

47. Ibid., 26, 2nd moon of 3rd year and 30, 6th moon of 3rd year, Tianqi reign.

48. For more see Lloyd E. Eastman, *Family, Field, and Ancestors: Constancy and Change in China's Social and Economic History, 1550–1949* (London: Oxford University Press, 1988), pp. 71–79; also *MS*, Foreign country, 3, Japan.

49. There is much debate on the matter of an increased rootless, vagrant population and the use of bond servants during the late sixteenth and early seventeenth centuries. For more, see Gu Gongxie, "Xiaoxia xianji zechao" [Selected Notes During the Summer Break] in *Hanfenlou biji* (Shanghai, Commercial Press, 1916–21), vol. 1, p. 6ab.

50. Gu Yanwu, *Rizhi lu jishi* [Notes on the Recording of Daily Learning] (Reprint Hubei: Congwen Publishing Co. 1872), vol. 8, pp. 67–68.

CHAPTER III.
INSTITUTIONALIZATION OF THE EUNUCH AGENCIES

1. Hongwu Veritable Record, 44, 8th moon of 2nd year, Hongwu reign.

2. Ibid.

3. Ming "Treatise on Officialdom," is included in Zhang Tingyu et al., eds., *Ming shi*, juan 72–76. Eunuch officialdom is provided in juan 74, pp. 1819–26 in Dingwen publishing edition (Taipei, 1979).

4. Huang Zhangjian, "Lun Huang Ming zuxunlu suoji Ming chu huanguan zhidu," [On the Early Ming Eunuch System as Recorded in the Ming Emperor's Instructions], *Academia Sinica History and Philology Institute Collections* (Taipei, 1960), *jikan* 32, p. 94.

5. Qian Mu, *Guoshi daqang* [Outlines of Chinese History] (Chongqing, 1944), p. 467.

6. Hongwu Veritable Record, 161, 4th moon of 17th year; 241, 9th moon of the 28th year, Hongwu reign.

7. Liu Ruoyu, *Zhuozhong zhi*, (Shanghai, Commercial Press, 1935), pp. 100, 201–207.

8. *MS*, 181, Biography 69, p. 4813; 185, Biography 73, p. 4901.

9. Xu Fuyuan et al., *Huang Ming jingshi wenbian* (Reprint Taipei: Guofeng Publishing Co., 1964), 381: 10–11.

10. Wang Shizhen, "Zhongguankao" or "On Eunuchs," in *Yanshantang bieji* (Taiwan: Ming blockprint edition, reprint, 1964), vol. 10, p. 4383; hereafter cited as "On Eunuchs."

11. Ibid., p. 4414. Also see Ding Yi, *Mingdai tewu zhengzhi* [Politics of the Secret Police During the Ming Dynasty] (Beijing, 1951), p. 25.

12. Information on the Annamese envoy's visit to the Forbidden City is based on Jian Bozan et al., *Zhongwai lishinianbiao* [Comparative Historical Events of China and the World] (Beijing, 1979), p. 582; and *MS*, 56, Treatise 32, Rites 10, pp. 1423–24. Throughout the years, the names of imperial buildings had changed with subsequent reconstruction and modifications.

13. The palace layout is reconstructed from works by Sun Chengze. Sun Chengze was a supervising secretary in the Office of Scrutiny for Revenues in the later part of the last Ming reign. *Chun Ming mengyulu* (1874), juan 6, 7, 8. Also see Ray Huang, *Taxation and Governmental Finance in Sixteenth-Century Ming China* (Cambridge: Cambridge University Press, 1974), pp. 8–9; and Xu Pingfang, ed., *Ming Qing Beijingcheng kao* [A Study of the City of Beijing During the Ming-Qing Period] (Beijing, 1986).

14. Liu Ruoyu, *Zhuozhong zhi*, pp. 97, 149.

15. Ibid., pp. 135–153; also see Lü Bi, *Minggong shi* [History of the Ming Court] (Reprint Taiwan: seventeenth century blockprint edition, 1974), juan 2, p. 2. Hereafter cited as *Ming Court*.

16. Ibid., p. 3.

17. Ibid., pp. 4–5.

18. Ibid., pp. 5–6.

19. Liu Ruoyu, *Zhuozhong zhi*, pp. 201–207.

20. Lü Bi, *Ming Court*, pp. 5–6, 44–45.

21. Taisuke Mitamura, *Kangan: Sokkin Seiji no Kozo* [Eunuchs: The Structure of Intimate Politics] (Tokyo, 1963), pp. 76–78.

22. Lü Bi, *Ming Court*, p. 11.

23. Ibid., pp. 12, 29.

24. Ibid., pp. 12–13.

25. Ibid., p. 13.

26. Ibid., pp. 14, 29, 44.

27. Ray Huang, "Fiscal Administration During the Ming Dynasty," in Charles O. Hucker, ed., *Chinese Government in Ming Times* (New York: Columbia University Press, 1969), p. 90.

28. Lü Bi, *Ming Court*, pp. 15–16, 40.

29. Ibid., pp. 17–22.

30. Ibid., pp. 23, 38–39. It is to be noted that Madame Ke, Emperor Tianqi's wet nurse and Wei Zhongxian's political ally, was beaten to death in the Nursing Home Bureau in 1627.

31. Ibid., pp. 23–24.

32. "On Eunuchs," vol. 2, pp. 4021, 4031, 4035; vol. 10, p. 4391.

33. *MS*, 74, Treatise 50, Officials 3, pp. 1813–14. Professor Charles O. Hucker's translation of Shanglinyuanjian as Directorate of Imperial Parks is somewhat misleading. Judging from its broad functions in horticulture, agronomy, animal and poultry production, and so on, it should be more properly translated as the Directorate of Imperial Farms. See Hucker's invaluable work on "Governmental Organization of the Ming Dynasty," *Harvard Journal of Asiatic Studies* 21 (1958): 37. For more, see "On Eunuchs," vol. 9, pp. 3973, 4318; also see Sun Chengze, *Chun Ming mengyulu*, juan 62, p. 951.

34. Lü Bi, *Ming Court*, pp. 43–44.

35. *MS*, 74, loc. cit., p. 1812.

36. List of the herbs comes from Li Shizhen's *Materia Medica*, which was completed in 1578.

37. "On Eunuchs," vol. 5, pp. 4141–44.

38. Lü Bi, *Ming Court*, p. 25. One dou has ten shengs and one sheng is about 3.1 liters.

39. Ibid., pp. 26, 31–32.

40. Ibid., p. 27; also Liu Ruoyu, *Zhuozhong zhi*, p. 139.

41. Liu Ruoyu, ibid., p. 151.

42. Lü Bi, *Ming Court*, p. 28.

43. Ibid., pp. 22–23; also see Liu Ruoyu, *Zhuozhong zhi*, pp. 147, 195.

44. Lü Bi, ibid., pp. 32–34.

45. For an interesting account of Christianity and Ming eunuchs, see Father Jean Charbonnier's *Histoire des Chretiens de Chine* (Paris: Desclee/Begedis, 1992), pp. 133–137.

46. Lü Bi, *Ming Court*, p. 8.

47. *MS*, 74, Treatise 50, Officials 3, p. 1822.

CHAPTER IV.

EUNUCHS AND THE MING MILITARY SYSTEM

1. Wang Shizhen, "Zhongguankao" ["On Eunuchs"] in *Yanshantang bieji* (Taiwan reprint, Ming blockprint edition, 1964), vol. 1. pp. 3976–77.

2. Ibid., pp. 3975–77.

3. Ibid., 3978–79.

4. Ibid., p. 3981. Also see Zhang Tingyu et al., eds., *Ming shi* [History of Ming Dynasty] juan 92, Treatise 68, Military 4, pp. 2264–65.

5. Ibid., 89, Treatise 65, Military 1, p. 2176; 90, Treatise 66, Military 2, p. 2204; and 91, Treatise 67, Military 3, p. 2250. Also see Fu Weilin, *Ming shu* [Books on the Ming] (Reprint Shanghai: Guoxue jiben congshu, 1937), juan 72, p. 1454.

6. *MS*, 89, Treatise 65, Military 1, p. 2179.

7. For more, see Henri Bernard-Maitre, *Le Pere Mattieu Ricci et la societe chinoise de son temps (1552–1610)*, 2 vols. (Tianjin: Hautes Etudes, 1937).

Also see Jacques Gernet, *A History of Chinese Civilization* (Cambridge: Cambridge University Press, 1985), p. 431.

8. *MS*, 40, Treatise 16, Geography 1, p. 882; and 76, Treatise 52, Officials 5, pp. 1866–71. Also see Lu Rong, *Shuyuan zaji* [Miscellany from the Bean Garden] (Reprint Shanghai: Commercial Press, 1936), vol. 5, p. 49.

9. "On Eunuchs," vol. 1, p. 3984; also *MS*, 89, Treatise 65, Military 1, p. 2176.

10. Wanyou wenku, ed., *Xu wenxian tongkao* (Reprint Shanghai, 1936), 134, (ce 2), pp. 3996–97.

11. Ding Yi, *Mingdai tewu zhengzhi* [Politics of the Secret Police During the Ming Period] (Beijing, 1951), p. 258.

12. "On Eunuchs," vol. 1, pp. 3986–89.

13. Ibid., p. 3991.

14. Ibid., pp. 3991, 3994.

15. *MS*, 304, Biography 192, Eunuchs 1, pp. 7792–93; also "On Eunuchs," vol. 8, pp. 4312, 4420–21.

16. Ibid., p. 3989. The drill scene of the eunuch army is described by Mao Qiling in his *Wuzhong waiji* [Anecdotal Story of Emperor Zhengde] contained in the *Xihe wenji*, Wanyou wenkou ed., 2nd series, vol. 8.

17. *MS*, 18, Annals 18, Emperor Jiajing 2, p. 240, and 234, Biography 122, p. 6093.

18. Ibid., 222, Biography 110, pp. 5856–57.

19. Ibid., 234, Biography 122, p. 6093.

20. Ibid., p. 6094.

21. Ibid., 305, Biography 193, Eunuchs 2, pp. 7817–18.

22. Ibid., 89. Treatise 65, Military 1, p. 2175; also see Jean Charbonnier, *Histoire des Chretiens de Chine* (Paris: Desclee/Begedis, 1992), pp. 133–137.

23. For more, see the article on Nanjing in Chen Qiaoyi, ed., *Zhongguo lishi mingcheng* [Famed Cities in Chinese History] (Beijing: China Youth Publication, 1986), pp. 82–84.

24. *MS*. 40, Treatise 16, Geography 1, p. 910.

25. Ibid., 76, Treatise 52, Officials 5, p. 1865. Also see Edward L. Farmer, *Early Ming Government: The Evolution of Dual Capitals* (Cambridge,

Mass.: Harvard University Press, 1976) and *Da Ming huidian* (1511), vol. 7, pp. 25–30.

26. Shen Defu, *Yehuo bian puyi* (Reprinted 1827 Zhejiang: blockprint edition) cf. Ding Yi, *Mingdai tewu zhengzhi*, p. 301. Also see Cha Jizuo, *Zuiwei lu* [Biographical Sketches of Ming Personages] (Hangzhou: Zhejiang Ancient Books Publishing Co., 1986), vol. 4, Biography 29, pp. 2607–08.

27. *MS*, 180, Biography 68, p. 4788. Also "On Eunuchs," vol. 4, p. 4114.

28. "On Eunuchs," p. 4117.

29. Ibid., vol. 5, p. 4168; vol. 6, pp. 4243, 4247.

30. Ibid., vol. 5, p. 4154; vol. 8, pp. 4288–89.

31. Ibid., vol. 8, pp. 4290–91.

32. Xing Chengye, *Ming Nanjing chejiasu zangzhi* [The Functions of the Nanjing Bureau of Equipment During the Ming] (Shanghai: Commercial Press, 1934), pp. 4–5.

33. Ibid., pp. 40–41.

34. "On Eunuchs," vol. 7, pp. 4270–71.

35. Ibid., vol. 9, p. 4366; also see Jian Bozan et al., *Zhongwai lishinianbiao* [Comparative Historical Events of China and the World] (Beijing, 1979), p. 615.

36. "On Eunuchs," vol. 8, p. 4315; vol. 10, pp. 4390, 4407.

37. Ibid., vol. 7, pp. 4273–76; vol. 8, pp. 4325, 4311, 4380; vol. 9, p. 4427.

38. Ibid., vol. 4, p. 4138; vol. 5, p. 4163; vol. 8, p. 4316.

39. Ibid., vol. 7, pp. 4272–74; vol. 9, p. 4364.

40. Ibid., vol. 11, pp. 4436, 4449–50.

41. Ibid., vol. 5, p. 4138; vol. 7, pp. 4265–66.

42. Ibid., vol. 9, pp. 4367–68; vol. 10, p. 4376.

43. *MS*, 77, Treatise 53, pp. 1883–87; also Xie Yucai, "Mingdai weisuo zhidu xingshuai kao" [A Study of the Rise and Decline of the Ming Guard-Battalion System], *Shuowen yuekan* 2 (December 1942): 413.

44. Mitsutaka Tani, *A Study on Horse Administration in the Ming Period* (Kyoto: The Society of Oriental Research, Kyoto University, 1972), pp. 24, 29.

45. "On Eunuchs," vol. 8, pp. 4316–17, 4320–21.

46. Ibid., vol. 8, pp. 4320, 4324; vol. 10, pp. 4386–87. Also see *MS*, 89, Treatise 65, Military 1, pp. 2179–82.

47. Wang Shizhen, "Shimakao" [A Study of Horse Trade] in *Yanshantang bieji* (Reprint Taiwan: Ming blockprint edition, 1964), juan 89, pp. 3923, 3936.

48. Ibid., p. 3938–39. See also Morris Rossabi, "The Tea and Horse Trade with Inner Asia During the Ming," *Journal of Asian History* 4, no. 2 (1970): 136–168.

49. Hongwu Veritable Record 71, 1st moon of 5th year, Hongwu reign. Also *MS*, 81, Treatise 57, Economics 5, pp. 1980–83; and Mitsutaka Tani's, *Horse Administration in Ming Dynasty*, p. 7.

50. Wang Shizhen, "A Study of Horse Trade," pp. 3925, 3931.

51. Hongwu Veritable Record, 100, 5th moon of 8th year, and 217, 5th moon of 25th year, Hongwu reign. Also see "On Eunuchs," vol. 1, p. 3967.

52. Yongle Veritable Record, 56, 4th moon of 6th year, Yongle reign.

53. Xuande Veritable Record, 91, 6th moon of 7th year, and 98, 1st moon of 8th year, Xuande reign; also Zhengtong Veritable Record 133, 9th moon of 10th year, Zhengtong reign.

54. Mitsutaka Tani, *Horse Administration in Ming Dynasty*, pp. 4, 7–8.

55. Ibid., 10–13; also Lu Rong, *Shuyuan zaji*, vol. 4, p. 41.

56. "On Eunuchs," vol. 9, pp. 4360–61; vol. 10, p. 4402.

CHAPTER V. EUNUCHS AND THE MING
INTELLIGENCE–GATHERING APPARATUSES

1. Zhang Tingyu et al., eds., *Ming shi* [History of Ming Dynasty] (Taipei: Dingwen publishing edition, 1979), 95, Treatise 71, Criminal Laws 3, p. 2331. See also Robert Crawford, "Eunuch Power in the Ming Dynasty," *T'oung Pao* (1962): 131–133. Among the several Ming documents, there are conflicting dates on the establishment of the Eastern Depot. Interestingly enough, in the Veritable Records of Emperors Hongxi, Xuande, Zhengtong, and Jingtai, there is no mention about the Eastern Depot.

2. Liu Ruoyu, *Zhuozhong zhi* (Reprint Shanghai: Commercial Press, 1935), 16, pp. 104–105.

3. Ibid., pp. 103–104.

4. Ibid., also see Ding Yi, *Mingdai tewu zhengzhi* [Politics of the Secret Police During the Ming Dynasty] (Beijing, 1951), pp. 28–29.

5. *MS*, 95, loc. cit., p. 1331.

6. Chenghua Veritable Record, 196, leap 10th moon of 15th year, Chenghua reign.

7. Ibid., 228, 6th moon of 18th year, Chenghua reign.

8. Ibid., 248, 1st moon of 20th year, Chenghua reign.

9. *MS*, 304, Biography 192, Eunuchs, p. 7781; also see Cha Jizuo, *Zuiwei lu* [Biographical Sketches of Ming Personages] (Hangzhou: Zhejiang Ancient Books Publishing Co., 1986), vol. 4, Biography 29, p. 2612.

10. *MS*, 95, Treatise 71, Criminal Laws 3, p. 2331.

11. Hongzhi Veritable Record, 11, 2nd moon of 1st year, and 57, 11th moon of 4th year, Hongzhi reign.

12. *MS*, 16, Annals 16, Emperors, pp. 119–200. See, for example, Edward L. Dreyer, *Early Ming China, A Political History, 1355–1435* (Stanford, Calif.: Stanford University Press, 1982), pp. 245–46. Also see Wang Shizhen, "Zhongguankao" (On Eunuchs), in *Yanshantang bieji* (Reprint Taiwan: Ming blockprint edition, 1964), vol. 4, pp. 4204–06.

13. Zhengde Veritable Record, 18, 10th moon of 1st year, Zhengde reign; also *MS*, 304, Biography 192, Eunuchs, pp. 7786–87, and "On Eunuchs," vol. 5, p. 4161.

14. There are discrepancies on Wang Yue's successor as director of the Eastern Depot. *Ming shi* says it was Ma Yongzheng (see *MS* 304, Biography 192, p. 7789), but other documents mention Qiu Ju, see Zhengde Veritable Record, 19, 11th moon of 1st year, Zhengde reign.

15. Zhengde Veritable Record, ibid., also see *MS*, 16, Annals 16, p. 200 and 95, Treatise 71, Criminal Laws 3, p. 2331.

16. Zhengde Veritable Record, 22, leap 1st moon of 2nd year, Zhengde reign.

17. Ibid., 73, 3rd moon of 6th year, Zhengde reign.

18. Ibid., 88, leap 5th moon of 7th year, Zhengde reign; also *MS*, 95, Treatise 71, Criminal Laws 3, p. 2332.

19. Zhengde Veritable Record, 114, 7th moon of 9th year and 163, 6th moon of 13th year, Zhengde reign.

20. Jiajing Veritable Record, 1, 4th moon of 16th year, Zhengde reign.

21. Ibid., 4, 7th moon of 16th year, Zhengde reign.

22. For more on Ming judiciary functionings, see Charles O. Hucker, "Governmental Organization of the Ming Dynasty," *Harvard Journal of Asiatic Studies* 21 (1958): 55–56; and his other work, *The Censorial System of Ming China* (Stanford, Calif.: Stanford University Press, 1966), pp. 30–107.

23. For more, see Ray Huang, *1587, A Year of No Significance* (New Haven, Conn.: Yale University Press, 1981), p. 115.

24. Jiajing Veritable Record, 23, 10th moon of 2nd year and 46, 11th moon of 3rd year, Jiajing reign.

25. Ibid., 337, 6th moon of 27th year and 366, 10th moon of 29th year, Jiajing reign.

26. Ibid., 462, leap 7th moon of 37th year, Jiajing reign.

27. *MS*, 305, Biography 193, Eunuchs, pp. 7800–1. Also "On Eunuchs," vol. 11, pp. 4478–79.

28. *MS*, pp. 7801–3; also see Ray Huang, *1587*, pp. 15–16, 25; and "On Eunuchs," vol. 11, pp. 4479–80.

29. Ray Huang, ibid., pp. 34–35; also see Wanli Veritable Record, 131, 12th moon of 10th year, Wanli reign.

30. *MS*, 305, Biography 193, Eunuchs, p. 7804.

31. Ibid.

32. Ibid., 95, Treatise 71, pp. 2332–33.

33. Liu Ruoyu, *Zhuozhong zhi*, 7, p. 39.

34. Ibid., pp. 41–44; also *MS*, 95, Treatise 71, p. 2333.

35. *MS*, 305, Biography 193, Eunuchs, pp. 7813–14.

36. Ibid., p. 7814; also see Wanli Veritable Record, 390, 11th moon of 31st year, 391, 12th moon of 31st year, and 396, 5th moon of 32nd year, Wanli reign.

37. *MS*, 305, loc. cit.

38. For more, see *The Century of Tung Ch'i-ch'ang, 1555–1636* (Kansas City, Mo.: Trustees of the Nelson Gallery Foundation, 1992).

39. Wanli Veritable Record, 479, 1st moon of 39th year, Wanli reign and Tianqi Veritable Record, 5, 5th moon of 1st year, Tianqi reign.

40. *MS*, 95, Treatise 71, pp. 2333–34.

41. Chongzhen Veritable Record, 1, 1st moon of 1st year, Chongzhen reign.

42. *MS*, 95, Treatise 71, pp. 2333–34.

43. Ibid., 14, Annals 14, p. 174; also see Chenghua Veritable Record, 162, 2nd moon of 13th year, Chenghua reign.

44. Ding Yi, *Secret Police During Ming Dynasty*, p. 31.

45. Ibid., also see *MS*, 304, Biography 192, Eunuchs, pp. 7778–79; and Chenghua Veritable Record, 162, 2nd moon of 13th year, Chenghua reign.

46. *MS*, 176, Biography 64, p. 4690; also Chenghua Veritable Record, 166, 5th moon of 13th year, Chenghua reign.

47. *MS*, 176, Biography 64, p. 4691; also Chenghua Veritable Record, 167, 6th moon of 13th year, Chenghua reign.

48. *MS*, 304, Biography 192, Eunuchs, pp. 7780–81.

49. Zhengde Veritable Record, 41, 8th moon of 3rd year, Zhengde reign.

50. *MS*, 95, Treatise 71, p. 2332; also "On Eunuchs," vol. 5, pp. 4177–78.

51. Zhengde Veritable Record, 66, 8th moon of 5th year, Zhengde reign. For a more detailed discussion of the fall of Liu Jin, see "On Eunuchs," vol. 6, pp. 4192–4204.

CHAPTER VI. EUNUCHS AND MING DIPLOMACY

1. Zhang Tingyu et al., eds., *Ming shi* [History of the Ming Dynasty] (Taipei: Dingwen Publishing edition, 1979), 32, Biography 215, Foreign country 7, Tartars, p. 8466.

2. Hongwu Veritable Record, 93, 9th moon of 7th year; 120, 10th moon of 11th year, Hongwu reign.

3. For more, see L. Carrington Goodrich and Fang Chaoying, eds., *Dictionary of Ming Biography* (New York: Columbia University Press, 1976), vol. 2, p. 1036.

4. *MS*, 328, Biography 216, Foreign country 9, Oirats, p. 8498. For more, see Henry Serruys, "The Mongols in China," *Monumenta Serica* 27 (1968): 233–305.

5. Serruys, ibid.

6. Yongle Veritable Record, 105, 3rd and 4th moon of 15th year; 119, 3rd moon of 19th year, and 121, 8th moon of 19th year, Yongle reign.

7. *MS*, loc. cit., p. 8499; also see Rene Grousset, *The Empire of the Steppes: A History of Central Asia* (New Brunswick, N.J.: Rutgers University Press, 1970), p. 507.

8. Chen Qiaoyi, ed., *Zhongguo lishi mingcheng* [Famed Cities in Chinese History] (Beijing: China Youth Publication, 1986), p. 52.

9. Goodrich and Fang, *Ming Biography*, vol. 1, p. 145.

10. Zahiruddin Ahmad, *China and Tibet, 1708–1959: A Resume of Facts* (Oxford: Oxford University Press, 1960), p. 1; also Christopher I. Beckwith, *The Tibetan Empire in Central Asia: A History of the Struggle for Great Power Among Tibetans, Turks, Arabs, and Chinese During the Early Middle Ages* (Princeton, N.J.: Princeton University Press, 1987), p. 24.

11. *MS*, 304, Biography 192, Eunuchs, 1, pp. 7768–69.

12. Yongle Veritable Record, 87, 2nd moon of 11th year; 91, 1st moon of 12th year; and 114, 10th moon of 17th year, Yongle reign. Also *MS*, 331, Biography 219, p. 8586.

13. *MS*, 304, Biography 192, Eunuchs 1, p. 7769; also Goodrich and Fang, *Ming Biography*, vol. 1, pp. 522–23.

14. Hongxi Veritable Record, 2, 9th moon of 22nd year, Yongle reign; Xuande Veritable Record, 190, 3rd moon of 9th year, Xuande reign; and Zhengtong Veritable Record, 20, 7th moon of 1st year, Zhengtong reign.

15. Zhengde Veritable Record, 131, 11th moon of 10th year, Zhengde reign; also *MS*, 331, Biography 219, Western regions, 3, pp. 8573–75.

16. *MS*, 304, Biography 192, Eunuchs 1, p. 7776.

17. Yuan Lukun et al., *Taijian shihua* [Stories About Eunuchs] (Zhengzhou: Henan People's Publication, 1984), pp. 171–172.

18. Ibid., pp. 172–173. Almost all of the offices established by Yishiha fell into the hands of Jianzhou Jurchens, whose chief Nurhaci (1559–1626) founded the Qing dynasty.

19. Wang Shizhen, "Zhongguankao," or "On Eunuchs," in *Yanshantang bieji* (Reprint Taiwan: Ming blockprint edition, 1964), vol. 1, pp. 3979–80.

20. *MS*, 331, Biography 219, Western regions, 3, p. 8575.

21. For more, see Owen Lattimore, *Pivot of Asia* (Boston, 1950), pp. 15–16; and his other authoritative work, *Inner Asian Frontiers of China* (New York, 1940), pp. 170–171.

22. Goodrich and Fang, *Ming Biography*, vol. 1, pp. 144–145. For a background study of the region, see Denis Sinor, ed., *The Cambridge History of Early Inner Asia* (Cambridge: Cambridge University Press, 1990).

23. "Xiyu fanguo zhi" [Treatise on the Barbarian Countries of the Western Regions], in Yang Jianxin, ed., *Gu xixing ji* [Journey to the West in Ancient Times] (Yingchuan: Ningxia People's Publication, 1987), p. 291.

24. Ibid., p. 289; also Yongle Veritable Record, 47, 4th moon of 5th year, Yongle reign. For more on Kashghar, see H. W. Bellew, "History of Kashghar," in T. D. Forsyth, ed., *Report of a Mission to Yarkund in 1873* (Calcutta: Foreign Department Press, 1875), pp. 106–213.

25. The day by day account of the journey is based upon Chen Cheng's "Xiyu xingcheng ji" [Travel Journal to the Western Regions], a photolithographical copy collected in Yang Jianxin, ed., *Gu xixing ji*, pp. 260–295.

26. Yongle Veritable Record, 98, 10th moon of 13th year and 108, 12th moon of 15th year, Yongle reign; also see Grousset, *Empire of the Steppes*, pp. 459, 624; and Morris Rossabi, "Ming China and Turfan, 1406–1517," *Central Asiatic Journal* 16, no. 3 (1972): 206–225.

27. Hongwu Veritable Record 40, 4th moon of 2nd year, Hongwu reign.

28. Hongwu Veritable Record, 55, 1st moon of 6th year, Hongwu reign; also Yongle Veritable Record, 114, 10th moon of 17th year; 113, 6th moon of 17th year; and 126, 7th moon of 21st year, Yongle reign.

29. Yongle Veritable Record, 65, 7th moon of 7th year, 113, 6th moon of 17th year, and 126, 7th moon of 21st year, Yongle reign.

30. *MS*, 320, Biography 208, Foreign country, Korea, pp. 8284–85.

31. For a general discussion of the fifteenth century Korean culture, see James Scarth Gale, *History of the Korean People* (Seoul: Royal Asiatic Society, Korean Branch, 1983), pp. 234–251; Ki-baik Lee, *A New History of*

Korea, trans. Edward W. Wagner (Cambridge, Mass.: Harvard University Press, 1984), pp. 192–200; and William E. Henthorn, *A History of Korea* (New York: The Free Press, 1971), pp. 146–154. Also see K. T. Wu, "Ming Printing and Printers," *Harvard Journal of Asiatic Studies* 7, no. 3 (February, 1943): 203–260.

32. Hongxi Veritable Record, 5, 12th moon of 22nd year, Yongle reign; Xuande Veritable Record, 13, 1st moon of 1st year, Xuande reign; Zhengtong Veritable Record, 192, 5th moon of 1st year and 263, 2nd moon of 7th year, Jingtai reign.

33. Xuande Veritable Record, 88, 3rd moon of 7th year and 106, 9th moon of 8th year, Xuande reign. Also see Gale's *History of the Korean People*, pp. 228–229.

34. Ki-baik Lee, *A New History of Korea*, p. 189.

35. Clarence Norwood Weems, ed., *Hubert's History of Korea* (New York: Hillary House Publishers, 1962), vol. 1, p. 347.

36. Ibid., p. 348.

37. Wanli Veritable Record, 434, 3rd moon of 38th year, Wanli reign; also Henthorn's *History of Korea*, p. 154.

38. Tianqi Veritable Record, 51, 2nd moon of 5th year, Tianqi reign; and Chongzhen Veritable Record, 7, 1st moon of 7th year, Chongzhen reign.

CHAPTER VII.
EUNUCHS AND MING MARITIME ACTIVITIES

1. *Da Ming huidan* [Great Ming Administration Code], 1511 edition, juan 108, on tribute regulations.

2. Zhang Dechang, "Mingdai Guangzhou zhi haibo maoyi" [Maritime Trade of Guangzhou During the Ming Period], *Qinghua xuebao* 7, no. 2, (1932): 5–12. Professor Charles O. Hucker translates *Huitong guan* as College of Interpreters, but judging from its operations and functioning, it should be more appropriately translated as an International Inn. See Hucker's "Governmental Organization of the Ming Dynasty," *Harvard Journal of Asiatic Studies* 21 (1958): 35.

3. T'ien Ju-kang, "Cheng Ho's Voyages and the Distribution of Pepper in China," *The Journal of the Royal Asiatic Society of Great Britain and Ireland*, pt. 2 (1981): 188–189.

4. Zhang Tingyu et al., eds., *Ming shi* [History of Ming Dynasty] (Reprinted Taipei: Dingwen Publishing edition, 1979), 322, Biography 210, Foreign country 3, Japan, p. 8347.

5. Ibid., p. 8345. Also see Chen Wenshi, *Ming Hongwu Jiajing jian de haijin zhengce* [The Maritime Prohibition Policy of the Ming Between the Reign of Hongwu and the Reign of Jiajing] (Taipei, 1966), pp. 56–62.

6. *MS.*, p. 8346; also Xuande Veritable Record, 103, 6th moon of 8th year, Xuande reign.

7. *MS*, p. 8348. See also Kwan-wai So, *Japanese Piracy in Ming China During the Sixteenth Century* (East Lansing: Michigan State University Press, 1975).

8. Ibid., 322, Biography 211, Foreign country 4, Ryukyu, pp. 8361–64.

9. *Lidai baoan* [Valuable Documents of the Ryukyu Kingdom] (Taipei: National Taiwan University Reprint, 1973); also see Atsushi Kobata, *Chusei Nanto tsuko bookishi no kenkyu* [A Study of Communication and Trade History of Southern Islands During the Middle Ages] (Tokyo: Nihon Hyoronsha, 1939), pts. 2 & 3.

10. *MS*, loc. cit., p. 8365.

11. Wu Han, "Shiliu shiji qian zhi Zhongguo yu Nanyang" [China and Southeast Asia Prior to the Sixteenth Century] *Qinghua xuebao* 2, no. 1 (1936): 143.

12. Henry Yule and Henri Cordier, *The Book of Ser Marco Polo* (London, 1903), vol. 1, p. 204.

13. Henry Yule, "Ibn Battuta's Travels in Bengal and China" in *Cathay and the Way Thither* (London, 1916), vol. 4, pp. 24–25, 96.

14. *MS*, Biography 212, Foreign country 5, Champa, pp. 8383–85.

15. Ibid., also Hongwu Veritable Record, 190, 4th moon of 21st year, Hongwu reign.

16. Yongle Veritable Record, 45, 8th moon of 4th year; 52, 9th moon of 5th year, Yongle reign; also *MS*, loc. cit., p. 8386.

17. *MS*, ibid., Foreign country 5, Cambodia, pp. 8394–95.

18. Ibid.

19. Ibid., Siam, pp. 8396–97; also T'ien Ju-kang, "Cheng Ho's Voyages," p. 189.

20. *MS*, ibid., pp. 8397–98. Also Hongwu Veritable Record, 234, 12th moon of 28th year, Hongwu reign and Yongle Veritable Record, 22, 9th moon of 1st year, Yongle reign.

21. Yongle Veritable Record, 86, 12th moon of 10th year, Yongle reign; also *MS*, ibid., p. 8399.

22. *MS*, ibid., p. 8400.

23. Ibid.

24. Ibid.

25. Ibid., Malacca, pp. 8416–17.

26. Yongle Veritable Record, 20, 5th moon of 1st year and 27, 1st moon of 2nd year, Yongle reign.

27. Tien-tse Chang, *Sino-Portuguese Trade from 1514 to 1644* (Leyden: E. J. Brill Ltd., 1969), p. 33.

28. *MS*, loc. cit., Sumatra, pp. 8420–21.

29. Ibid., Borneo, pp. 8411–12.

30. Yongle Veritable Record, 60, 12th moon of 6th year and 74, 2nd moon of 9th year, Yongle reign.

31. *MS*, 324, Biography 212, Foreign country 5, Java, pp. 8402–4.

32. Yongle Veritable Record, 73, 12th moon of 8th year; 84, 7th moon of 10th year and 89, 9th moon of 11th year, Yongle reign.

33. For more, see Pin-tsun Chang, "The Chinese Maritime Trade: The Case of Sixteenth-Century Fuchien" (Ph.D. dissertation, Princeton University, 1983), pp. 90–103.

34. For more, see George Phillips, "The Seaports of India and Ceylon, Described by Chinese Voyagers of the Fifteenth Century, Together with an Account of Chinese Navigation," *Journal of the Chinese Branch of the Royal Asiatic Society* 20 (1885): 209–226; 21 (1886): 30–42; Charles Otto Blagden, "Notes on Malay History," *Journal of the Chinese Branch of the Royal Asiatie Society* 53 (1909): 153–162. J. V. G. Mills early wrote "Malaya in the Wu Pei Chih Charts," *Malayan Branch Royal Asiatic Society Journal* 15 (1937). Among J. J. L. Duyvendak's important works are: "Ma Huan Re-examined," *Verhandeling d. Koninklijke Akademie v. Wetenschappen te Amsterdam*, Afd. Letterkunde, 32, no. 3, (1933); and "The True Dates of the Chinese Maritime Expeditions in the Early Fifteenth Century," *T'oung Pao* 34 (1939): 341–412; and "Desultory Notes on the Hsi-Yang Chi," *T'oung Pao* 42

(1954): 1–35. W. W. Rockhill's study appears much earlier in the *T'oung Pao*, see "Notes on the Relations and Trade of China with the Eastern Archipelago and the Coast of the Indian Ocean During the Fourteenth Century," 16 (1915): 61–84.

35. *Yuan shi* [History of Yuan Dynasty] (Reprint Taiwan: Dingwen Publishing Co., 1979), 125, Biography 12, pp. 3063–65.

36. Cha Jizuo, *Zuiwei lu* [Biographical Sketches of Ming Personages] (Hangzhou: Zhejiang Ancient Books Publishing Co., , 1986), vol. 4, Biography 29, Eunuchs, pp. 2603–4.

37. Xuande Veritable Record, 6, 6th moon of 10th year, Xuande reign.

38. China Maritime History Society, ed., *Zheng He jiashi ziliao* [Historical Materials on Zheng He's Ancestors] (Beijing: New China Publishing Co., 1985), pp. 2–3.

39. China Maritime History Society, ed., *Zheng He xia xiyang* [Zheng He's Navigations to Western Ocean] (Beijing, 1985), pp. 28–29.

40. George Phillips, "Seaports of India and Ceylon," loc. cit.

41. Charles Otto Blagden, "Notes on Malay History," loc. cit.

42. Paul Pelliot, "Deux Itinéraires de Chine en Inde à la fin du VIIIe siècle," *Bulletin de l'Ecole Française d'Extreme-Orient* 4 (1904): 131–413; "Encore à propos des voyages de Tcheng Houo," *T'oung Pao* 32 (1936): 210–222; "Les grands voyages maritimes chinois au début du XVe siècle," *T'oung Pao* 30 (1933): 237–452, "Les Hoja et le Sayid Husain de l'histoire des Ming," *T'oung Pao* 38 (1948): 81–292; "Notes additionnelles sur Tcheng Houo et sur ses voyages," *T'oung Pao* 31 (1935): 274–314.

43. After its publication in either 1433 or 1436, *Yingyai shenglan* was amplified by a Ming scholar named Zhang Sheng.

44. See W. W. Rockhill, "Notes on the Relations and Trade of China," pp. 73–74.

45. J. J. L. Duyvendak, "True Dates of Chinese Expeditions," pp. 347–399.

46. *MS*, 304, Biography 192, Eunuchs 1, p. 7767.

47. Pelliot, "Les grands voyages maritimes chinois," pp. 446–448.

48. Laurence G. Thompson, "The Junk Passage Across the Taiwan Strait: Two Early Chinese Accounts," *Harvard Journal of Asiatic Studies* 28 (1968): 170–194.

49. Bao Zunpeng, "Zheng He xia xiyang zhi baochuan kao" [A Study of Zheng He's Ships to Western Ocean], *Dalu zazhi* 18 (1959): 9, fn. 7.

50. Ibid., p. 6.

51. L. Carrington Goodrich and Fang Chaoying, eds., *Dictionary of Ming Biography* (New York: Columbia University Press, 1976), vol. 2, p. 1365.

52. The names of the military commissioners come from Jin Yunming, "Zheng He qici xi xiyang nianyue kaozheng" [A Study of the Months and Years of Zheng He's Seven Expeditions to Western Ocean], *Fujian wenhua* 26 (December 1937): 1–48.

53. For slightly different translations of these names, see Pelliot, "Les grands voyages maritimes chinois," p. 306.

54. Wu Han, "China and Southeast Asia," p. 180. The late Professor Jung-pang Lo disputed this account. He said that the documents that Liu Daxia burned were the 1407 records of troop mobilization used by Emperor Yongle against Annam but not the sea charts used in the Zheng He expeditions. See Lo's article, "Policy Formulation and Decision-Making on Issues Respecting Peace and War," in Charles O. Hucker, ed., *Chinese Government in Ming Times* (New York: Columbia University Press, 1969), pp. 62–63.

CHAPTER VIII.
EUNUCHS' INVOLVEMENT IN THE MING ECONOMY

1. Jian Bozan, "Lun Zhongguo gudai de fengjian shehui" [On China's Past Feudal Society], in *Lishi wenti luncong (Collected Essays on Historical Issues)* (Beijing: People's Publications, 1962), p. 93. For more on the eunuchs and Ming economy, see a substantial book edited by Wang Chunyu and Du Wanyan, *Mingdai huangguan yu jingji shiliao chubian* (Beijing, 1986).

2. Zhang Tingyu et al., eds., *Ming shi* [History of Ming Dynasty] (Taipei: Dingwen Publishing edition, 1979), juan 77, Treatise 53, Economics 1, p. 1882.

3. Wang Shizhen, "Zhongguankao" ("On Eunuchs") in *Yanshantang bieji* (Reprint Taiwan: Ming blockprint edition, 1964), vol. 9, p. 4346.

4. *MS,* loc. cit., p. 1887.

5. Ibid.

6. Shi Zhengkang, "Mingdai nanfeng de Anlu huangzhuang" ["The Anlu Imperial Estate in Ming's Southern China"] in *Mingdaishi yanjiu luncong*

[*Collected Essays on Ming Historical Studies*] (Beijing: China's Academy of Social Sciences, 1985), no. 3, pp. 116–117.

7. *MS*, 77, Treatise 53, Economics 1, pp. 1888–89. Also see *Ming-Qing shi guoji xueshu taolunhui lunwenji* [Proceedings of International Scholarly Conference on Ming-Qing History] (Tianjin: People's Publishing, 1981), pp. 556–558.

8. For more on the status and roles of the Ming bond servants, see Lloyd E. Eastman, *Family, Field, and Ancestors: Constancy and Change in China's Social and Economic History, 1550–1949* (London: Oxford University Press, 1988), pp. 72–73.

9. Shi Zhengkang, "Anlu Imperial Estate," pp. 113, 116.

10. Ibid., p. 117.

11. For more, see Ding Yi, *Mingdai tewu zhengzhi* [Politics of the Secret Police During the Ming Period] (Beijing, 1951), pp. 118–119.

12. Shi Zhengkang, "Anlu Imperial Estate," pp. 118–119.

13. *MS*, 77, Treatise 53, Economics 1, p. 1889; also "On Eunuchs," vol. 7, p. 4254.

14. Jian Bozan et al., *Zhongwai lishi nianbiao* [Comparative Historical Events of China and the World] (Beijing, 1979), p. 572. Also "On Eunuchs," vol. 2, pp. 4014–15.

15. Ibid., vol. 2, pp. 4020–21.

16. Ibid., vol. 11, p. 4419; also *MS*, 77, Treatise 53, Economics 1, p. 1889; 162, Biography 50, pp. 4416–17; and 194, Biography 82, p. 5146.

17. *MS*, 81, Treatise 57, Economics 5, pp. 1974–75.

18. Ibid., pp. 1975–76.

19. Ibid., p. 1976 and 186, Biography 74, p. 4943.

20. "On Eunuchs," vol. 8, p. 4322; and vol. 1, pp. 4377–78.

21. Ibid., vol. 9, pp. 4332–33.

22. *MS*, 81, Treatise 57, Economics 5, p. 1977; 214, Biography 102, p. 5663. Also see Albert Chan, *The Glory and Fall of the Ming Dynasty* (Norman: University of Oklahoma Press, 1982), p. 114.

23. "On Eunuchs," vol. 9, pp. 4369–71.

24. Wu Han, *Dushi zhaji* [Notes from Reading History] (Beijing, 1956), pp. 301–306.

25. "On Eunuchs," vol. 8, p. 4300.

26. Liu Ruoyu, *Zhuozhong zhi* (Reprint Shanghai: Commercial Press, 1935), pp. 133–134.

27. Lu Rong, *Shuyuan zaji* [Miscellany from the Bean Garden] (Reprint Shanghai: Commercial Press, 1936), vol. 12, p. 135.

28. *MS*, 75, Treatise 51, Officials 4, pp. 1847–48.

29. "On Eunuchs," vol. 3, pp. 4062–63; vol. 4, p. 4138; and vol. 5, p. 4185.

30. Ibid., vol. 3, p. 4062; vol. 5, pp. 4151–53.

31. Ibid., vol. 3, pp. 4094–95; vol. 4, p. 4105. Also see Cha Jizuo, *Zuiwei lu* [Biographical Sketches of Ming Personages] (Hangzhou: Zhejiang Ancient Books Publishing Co., 1986), vol. 4, Biography 29, p. 2623.

32. "On Eunuchs," vol. 4, p. 4104; vol. 5, p. 4185; and vol. 8, pp. 4258–60.

33. Ibid., vol. 7, pp. 4319–20.

34. Ibid., vol. 3, p. 4062; vol. 5, pp. 4146, 4176.

35. Ibid., vol. 6, pp. 4188–89.

36. Ibid., vol. 7, p. 4277; and vol. 10, p. 4380.

37. Cf. Joseph Needham, *Science and Civilization in China* (Cambridge: Cambridge University Press, 1959), vol. 3, pp. 666–667, 675–676.

38. *MS*, 81, Treatise 57, Economics 5, P. 1970.

39. Ibid., 159, Biography 47, p. 4346.

40. Ibid., 81, Treatise 57, Economics 5, pp. 1970–71.

41. Ray Huang, "Fiscal Adminstration During the Ming Dynasty," in Charles O. Hucker, ed., *Chinese Government in Ming Times* (New York: Columbia University Press, 1969), p. 126.

42. "On Eunuchs," vol. 4, pp. 4108–10.

43. Ibid., vol. 3, pp. 4066–67.

44. Xia Xie, *Ming Tongjian* (Shanghai, 1888), juan 71, p. 6.

45. *MS*, 81, Treatise 57, Economics 5, p. 1971.

46. Ibid., 232, Biography 120, p. 6062; and 305, Biography 193, Eunuchs 2, p. 7805.

47. Ibid., 234, Biography 122, p. 6097.

48. Ibid., 81, Treatise 57, Economics 5, pp. 1971–72.

49. Ibid., 305, Biography 193, Eunuchs 2, pp. 7805–6.

50. Ibid., pp. 7806–8.

51. Ibid., pp. 7808–9.

52. Joseph Needham, *The Development of Iron and Steel Technology in China* (Cambridge: W. Heffer and Sons Ltd., 1964), pp. 14–15.

53. Zhao Yi, *Nianershi zhaji* [Notes from Twenty-Two Histories] (Reprint Taipei, 1966), juan 35, pp. 1–3.

54. Xia Xie, *Ming tongjian*, juan 16; also "On Eunuchs," vol. 2, pp. 4011–12.

55. Ibid., vol. 2, pp. 4014–15; *MS*, 161, Biography 49, p. 4380.

56. "On Eunuchs," vol. 3, pp. 4093–95; *MS*, 183, Biography 71, p. 4856; and 82, Treatise 58, Economics 6, pp. 1993–94.

57. *MS*, ibid., p. 1996.

58. Ibid., pp. 1996–97; also "On Eunuchs," vol. 11, p. 4465.

59. *MS*, 82, Treatise 58, Economics, 6, pp. 1998–99.

60. Ibid., p. 1997; also *MS*, 192, Biography 80, p. 5100.

61. For more on Chinese textile technology, see Joseph Needham, *Science and Technology in China,* (Cambridge: Cambridge University Press, 1988), vol. 5, part 9, pp. 2–3, 15–59, 285–433.

62. Ibid., p. 256: also Cha Jizuo, *Ming Personages,* Biography 29, p. 2633.

CHAPTER IX.

MISCELLANEOUS DUTIES OF THE MING EUNUCHS

1. Zhang Tingyu et al., eds., *Ming shi* [History of Ming Dynasty] (Taipei: Dingwen publishing edition, 1979), 74, Treatise 50, Officials, 3, p. 1826.

2. Zhu Yuanzhang, *Ming Taizu yuzhi wenji* [Collection of Literature Relating to the First Ming Emperor] (Taipei: Student Publishing Co., 1965), vol. 4, p. 12.

3. *MS*, 74, Treatise 50, Officials 3, pp. 1803–4.

4. Ibid., 199, Biography 87, p. 5272.

5. Cha Jizuo, *Zuiwei lu* [Biographical Sketches of Ming Personages] (Hangzhou: Zhejiang Ancient Books Publishing Co., 1986), vol. 4, Biography 30, p. 2653.

6. *MS*, 74, Treatise 50, Officials 3, pp. 1828–29.

7. Ibid., p. 1804.

8. Fang Hongren, "Mingdai zhi shangbaosi yu shangbaojian" [The Seal Office versus the Eunuch Seal Agency of the Ming Period], in *Ming shi yanjiu zuankan* (Special Issue for the Studies of Ming History) 3 (1981): 107.

9. *MS*, 74, loc. cit.

10. Sun Chengze, *Chun Ming mengyulu* (1874), in *The Complete Collection of the Four Treasures*, juan, 2, pp. 3–4.

11. Fang Hongren, "Seal Office versus the Eunuch Seal Agency," pp. 111–131.

12. Wang Shizhen, *Yanshantang bieji* (Reprint Taipei, 1965), juan 93, p. 4102; also *MS*, 305, Biography 193, p. 7823; and 306, Biography 194, p. 7839.

13. Qian Mu, *Guoshi dagang* [Outlines of Chinese History] (Chongqing, 1944), pp. 524–535.

14. *MS*, 83, Treatise 59, Rivers 1, Yellow River, pp. 2013–14.

15. Cha Jizuo, *Ming Personages*, vol. 4, Biography 29, pp. 2604–5.

16. Xuande Veritable Record, 51, 2nd moon of 4th year, Xuande reign.

17. Zhengtong Veritable Record, 20, 7th moon of 1st year, Zhengtong reign.

18. Ibid., 84, 10th moon of 6th year, Zhengtong reign.

19. Ibid., 119, 7th moon of 9th year, Zhengtong reign. More on the functioning of the locks of the Grand Canal, see Joseph Needham, *Science and Civilization in China* (Cambridge: Cambridge University Press, 1971), vol. 4, pt. 3, p. 306.

20. Cha Jizuo, *Ming Personages*, p. 2605; also *MS*, 304, Biography 192, Eunuchs, p. 7771.

21. Zhengtong Veritable Record, 175, 2nd moon of 14th year, Zhengtong reign; also see Needham, *Science and Civilization*, pp. 314–316. For more, see Ray Huang's doctoral dissertation, "The Grand Canal During the Ming Dynasty" (University of Michigan, 1964).

22. *MS*, 83, loc. cit., pp. 2015–16.

23. Ibid., p. 2016.

24. Ibid., p. 2017.

25. Jingtai Veritable Record 224, Supplement 42, 12th moon of 3rd year, Jingtai reign.

26. Needham, *Science and Civilization*, p. 320.

27. Chenghua Veritable Record 143, 7th moon of 11th year, Chenghua reign.

28. Ibid., 186, 1st moon of 15th year, Chenghua reign; also Needham, *Science and Civilization*, pp. 183–184.

29. Hongzhi Veritable Record, 29, 8th moon of 2nd year, Hongzhi reign.

30. *MS*, 83, loc. cit., pp. 2021–23. In L. Carrington Goodrich and Fang Chaoying's *Dictionary of Ming Biography* (New York: Columbia University Press, 1976), there is a favorable profile of Liu Daxia by Ray Huang, pp. 958–962.

31. Hongzhi Veritable Record, 88, 5th moon of 7th year, Hongzhi reign.

32. Ibid.

33. Ibid., 12th moon of 7th year, Hongzhi reign; also Cha Jizuo, *Ming Personages*, vol. 1, Treatise 13, Rivers, p. 756.

34. Ibid., p. 757; also see Goodrich and Fang, *Ming Biography*, pp. 1107–9.

35. Hongzhi Veritable Record, 104, 9th moon of 8th year, Hongzhi reign.

36. Zhengtong Veritable Record 44, 7th moon of 3rd year, Zhengtong reign.

37. Ibid., 79, 5th moon of 6th year, Zhengtong reign.

38. *MS* 95, Treatise 71, Criminal Laws 3, p. 2340; and 304, Biography 192, Eunuchs 1, p. 7770.

39. Ibid., also see Zhentong Veritable Record 178, 5th moon of 14th year, Zhengtong reign.

40. Wang Shizhen, "Zhongguan kao," or "On Eunuchs," in *Yanshantang bieji* (Blockprint edition, 1590), vol. 1, p. 3976. Also see Cha Jizuo, *Ming Personages*, vol. 4, p. 2606.

41. Jingtai Supplement Veritable Record 68, 2nd moon of 6th year, Jingtai reign; also see *MS*, 95, Treatise 71, Criminal Laws 3, p. 2341.

42. Chenghua Veritable Record 53, 4th moon of 4th year, Chenghua reign.

43. Ibid., 54, 5th moon of 4th year, Chenghua reign.

44. Ibid., 103, 4th moon of 8th year, Chenghua reign.

45. Ibid., 214, 4th moon of 17th year, Chenghua reign; also *MS*, loc. cit.

46. Cha Jizuo, *Ming Personages*, p. 2612.

47. Hongzhi Veritable Record 50, 4th moon of 4th year, and 161, 4th moon of 13th year, Hongzhi reign; also *MS*, loc. cit., p. 2341.

48. Zhengde Veritable Record 13, 5th moon of 1st year, Zhengde reign.

49. Ibid., 16, 8th moon of 1st year, Zhengde reign.

50. Ibid., 74, 4th moon of 6th year, Zhengde reign.

51. Ibid., 140, 8th moon of 11th year, Zhengde reign.

52. Jian Bozan et al., *Zhongwai lishinianbiao* [Comparative Historical Events of China and the World] (Beijing, 1979), pp. 614–615.

53. Jiajing Veritable Record 26, leap 4th moon of 2nd year, Jiajing reign.

54. Ibid., 125, 5th moon of 10th year, Jiajing reign.

55. Ibid., 249, 5th moon of 20th year and 435, 5th moon of 35th year, Jiajing reign. Also see "On Eunuchs," vol. 10, 4377, 4477; and vol. 11, pp. 4427–32. For more on Ming politics and judiciary, see an important work by Huai Xiaofeng, *Jiajing zhuanzhi zhengzhi yu fa-zhi* (Changsha, 1989).

56. Longqing Veritable Record 57, 5th moon of 5th year, Longqing reign.

57. Wanli Veritable Record 50, 5th moon of 4th year and 53, 8th moon of 4th year, Wanli reign.

58. Ibid., 420, 4th moon of 34th year, Wanli reign; also Chongzhen Veritable Record 10, leap 4th moon of 10th year, Chongzhen reign.

59. *MS*, loc. cit., p. 2341.

CHAPTER X. CONCLUSION

1. Gu Cheng, "Mingdai de zongsi," or "The Ming Royal Family," in *Ming-Qing shi guoji xueshu taolunhui lunwenji* (Tianjin: People's Publishing, 1981), p. 97.

2. Liu Ruoyu, *Zhuozhong zhi* (Shanghai: Commercial Press, 1935), 13, pp. 67–68 and 14, p. 75.

3. Ye Sheng, *Shuidong riji* (Ming blockprint edition, 1680), vol. 8, p. 15.

4. For more, see Wen Gongyi, *Mingdai di huangguan he chaoting* [Eunuchs and the Court During the Ming Period] (Chongqing, 1989).

BIBLIOGRAPHY

Bao Zunpeng. "Zheng He xia xiyang zhi baocuan kao" [A Study of Zheng He's Treasure Ships to the Western Ocean]. *Dalu zazhi* 18 (1959).

Beckwith, Christopher I. *The Tibetan Empire in Central Asia.* Princeton, N.J.: Princeton University Press, 1987.

Beijing University, History Department, ed. *Beijing shi* [History of Beijing]. Beijing, 1985.

Bernard-Maitre, Henri. *Le Pere Mattieu Ricci et la societe chinoise de son temps (1552–1610),* 2 vols. Tianjin: Haute Etudes, 1937.

Blagden, Charles Otto. "Notes on Malay History" *Journal of the Chinese Branch of the Royal Asiatic Society* 53 (1909).

Boxer, Charles R. *South China in the Sixteenth Century.* London, 1953.

Busch, Heinrich. "The Tung-lin Academy and Its Political and Philosophical Significance." *Monumenta Serica* 14 (1949).

Cha Jizuo. *Zuiwei lu* [Biographical Sketches of Ming Personages]. 4 vols. Reprint Hangzhou: Zhejiang Ancient Books Publishing Co., 1986.

Chan, Albert. *The Glory and Fall of the Ming Dynasty.* Norman: University of Oklahoma Press, 1982.

Chang, Pin-tsun. "The Chinese Maritime Trade: The Case of Sixteenth-Century Fuchien." Ph.D. dissertation, Princeton University, 1983.

Chang, Tien-tse. *Sino-Portuguese Trade From 1514 to 1644.* Leyden: E. J. Brill Ltd., 1934.

Charbonnier, Jean. *Histoire des Chretiens de Chine.* Paris: Desclee/Begedis 1992.

Chen Cheng. *Xiyu xingchengji* [Travel Journal to the Western Regions]. Reprint Ningxia, 1987.

Chen Qiaoyi, ed., *Zhongguo lishi mingcheng* [Famed Cities in Chinese History]. Beijing: China Youth Publications, 1986.

Chen Wenshi. *Ming Hongwu Jiajing jian de haijin zhengce* [The Maritime Prohibition Policy of the Ming Between the Reign of Hongwu and the Reign of Jiajing]. Taipei, 1966.

Chenghua Veritable Record [Xianzong shilu]. Photographic reprint, Jiangsu guoxue tushuguan quan chaoben.

China Maritime History Society, ed. *Zheng He xia xiyang* [Zheng He's Expeditions to the Western Ocean]. Beijing: New China Publishing Co., 1985.

————. ed. *Zheng He jiashi ziliao* [Historical Materials on Zheng He's Ancestors]. Beijing, 1985.

Chongzhen Veritable Record (Sizong shilu). Photographic reprint, Jiangsu guoxue tushuguan quan chaoben.

Crawford, Robert C. "The Life and Thought of Chang Chu-cheng." Ph.D. dissertation, University of Washington, 1961.

————. "Eunuch Power in the Ming Dynasty." *T'oung Pao* 49 (1966).

Da Ming huidian [Great Ming Administrative Code]. 1511 Zhengde edition (180 juan) and 1587 Wanli revised edition (228 juan). Reprint, Taipei, 1963.

de Bary, W.T., ed. *Self and Society in Ming Thought.* New York, 1970.

Ding Yi. *Mingdai tewu zhengzhi* [Politics of the Secret Police During the Ming Dynasty]. Beijing, 1951.

Dong Guo. *Taijian shengya* [Lives of the Eunuchs]. Taipei, 1985.

Dreyer, Edward. *Early Ming China, A Political History, 1355–1435.* Calif.: Stanford University Press, Stanford, 1982.

Du Naiji. *Mingdai neige zhidu* [The Grand Secretariat of the Ming Period]. Taipei, 1967.

Duyvendak, J. J. L. "The True Dates of the Chinese Maritime Expeditions in the Early Fifteenth Century." *T'oung Pao* 34 (1939).

Eastman, Lloyd E. *Family, Field, and Ancestors: Constancy and Change in China's Social and Economic History, 1550–1949.* London: Oxford University Press, 1988.

Fang Hongren. "Mingdai zhi shangbaosi yu shangbaojian," [The Seal Office versus the Eunuch Seal Directorate of the Ming Period]. *Ming shi yanjiu zuankan* (1981).

Farmer, Edward L. *Early Ming Government: The Evolution of Dual Capitals.* Cambridge, Mass.: Harvard University Press, 1976.

Fei Xin. *Xingcha shenglan* [The Overall Survey of the Starry Raft]. 1436.

Franke, Wolfgang. *Preliminary Notes on the Important Chinese Literary Sources for the History of the Ming Dynasty (1368–1644).* Chengdu, 1948.

Fu Weilin. *Ming shu* [Books on the Ming]. Reprint Shanghai: Guoxue jiben congshu, 1937.

Gale, James S. *History of the Korean People.* Seoul: Royal Asiatic Society, Korean Branch, 1983.

Gernet, Jacques. *A History of Chinese Civilization*, trans. J. R. Foster, Cambridge: Cambridge University Press, 1985.

Goodrich, Carrington L., and Fang Chaoying, eds. *Dictionary of Ming Biography.* New York: Columbia University Press, 1976.

Grimm, Tilemann. "Das Neiko der Ming-Zeit, von den Anfangen bis 1506." *Oriens Extremus* 1 (1954).

Grousset, Rene. *The Empire of the Steppes: A History of Central Asia.* New Brunswick, N.J.: Rutgers University Press, 1970.

Gu Rong and Ge Jingang. *Wuheng weiqiang: Gudai huanguan qunti de wenhua kaocha* [Fog Across the Curtain Wall: An Examination of the Collective Culture of Eunuchs in Ancient Times). Xian, 1992.

Gu Yanwu. *Rizhi lu jishi* [Notes on the Recording of Daily Learning]. Reprint Hubei: Congwen Publishing Co., 1872.

Gu Yingtai. *Ming shi jishi benmo* [Ming History Compiled According to Subjects]. 80 juan. Reprint Taipei, 1956.

Hai Rui. *Hai Rui Ji.* Beijing, 1962.

Halde, Jean Baptiste du. *Description geographique, historique, chronologigue, politique, et physique de l'Empire de la Chine*, 4 vols. Paris, 1735.

Henthorn, William E. *A History of Korea.* New York: The Free Press, 1971.

Ho Ping-ti. *The Ladder of Success in Imperial China.* New York, 1962.

Hongwu Veritable Record [Taizu shilu]. Photographic reprint, Jiangsu guoxue tushuguan guan chaoben.

Hongxi Veritable Record [Renzong shilu]. Photographic reprint, Jiangsu guoxue tushuguan quan chaoben.

Hongzhi Veritable Record [Xiaozong shilu]. Photographic reprint, Jiangsu guoxue tushuguan quan chaoben.

Huai Xiaofeng, *Jiajing zhuanzhi zhengzhi yu fa-zhi*, Changsha, 1989.

Huang, Ray. "The Grand Canal during the Ming Dynasty." Ph.D. dissertation, University of Michigan, 1964.

———. *Taxation and Governmental Finance in Sixteenth Century Ming China.* Cambridge: Cambridge University Press, 1974.

———. *1587, A Year of No Significance.* New Haven, Conn.: Yale University Press, 1981.

Huang Zhangjian, "Lun Huang Ming zuxunlu suoji Mingchu huanguan zhidu" [On the Early Ming Eunuchs System as Recorded in the Ming Emperor's Instructions]. *Academia Sinica History and Philology Institute Collections,* vol. 32. Taipei, 1960.

Huang Zongxi. *Mingru xuean.* Guoxue jiben congshu edition, 1937.

Hucker, Charles O. "Governmental Organization of the Ming Dynasty." *Harvard Journal of Asiatic Studies* 21 (1958).

———. *The Censorial System of Ming China.* Stanford, Calif.: Stanford University Press, 1966.

———. ed. *Chinese Government in Ming Times: Seven Studies.* New York: Columbia University Press, 1969.

———. *A Dictionary of Official Titles in Imperial China.* Stanford, Calif., 1985.

Hummel, Arthur W., ed. *Eminent Chinese of the Ch'ing Period.* Washington, D.C., 1943.

Jiajing Veritable Record [Shizong shilu]. Photographic reprint, Jiangsu guoxue tushuguan quan chaoben.

Jian Bozan et al., eds. *Zhongwai lishinianbiao* [Comparative Historical Events of China and the World]. Beijing, 1979.

———. *Zhongguo shi lunji* [Collected Essays on Chinese History]. Shanghai, 1947.

Jingtai Supplement Record (Jingtai fulu). Photographic reprint, Jiangsu guoxue tushuguan quan chaoben.

Jugel, Ulrike. *Politische Funktion und Soziale Stellung der Eunuchen zur Spateren Hanzeit (25–220 n. Chr.).* Weisbaden, 1976.

Kong Hualong. "Mingdai caikuang shiye de fazhan he liudu" [The Development and the Residual Poison of the Ming Mining Enterprise]. *Shihuo banyue kan* 1 (1935).

Kuwabara, Jitsuzo. "Shina no kangan" [The Eunuchs in China]. *Toyo shi setsuen* 22 (1936).

Lattimore, Owen. *Inner Asian Frontiers of China*. New York, 1940.

Lee Ki-baik. *A New History of Korea*. Cambridge, Mass.: Harvard University Press, 1984.

Leng Dong. *Bei yange de shouhu shen: huanguan yu Zhongguo zhengzhi* [Castrated Patro-Saints: Eunuchs and Chinese Politics]. Changchun, 1990.

Li Dongfang. *Xishuo Mingchao* [Detailed Narrative of the Ming Dynasty]. Taipei, 1966.

Li Jiannong. *Song Yuan Ming jingji shigao* [Draft History of the Economy of Song, Yuan and Ming Dynasties]. Beijing, 1957.

Li Shizhen. *Bencao gangmu* [Materia Medica]. Reprint Shanghai, 1977.

Liu Ruoyu. *Zhuozhong zhi*. Reprint Shanghai: Commercial Press, 1935.

Llewellyn, Bernard. *China's Court and Concubines*. London, 1956.

Long Wenbin. *Ming huiyao*. Shanghai, 1956.

Longqing Veritable Record (Muzong shilu). Photographic reprint, Jiangsu guoxue tushuguan quan chaoben.

Lü Bi. *Minggong shi* [History of the Ming Court]. Reprint Taipei: seventeenth century blockprint edition, 1974.

Lu Rong. *Shuyuan zaji* [Miscellany from the Bean Garden]. Reprint Shanghai: Commercial Press, 1936.

Ma Huan. *Yingyai shenglan* [The Overall Survey of the Ocean's Shores]. 1433.

Mammitzsch, Ulrich. "Wei Chung-hsien (1528–1628): A Reappraisal of the Eunuch and the Factional Strife at the Later Ming Court." Ph.D. Dissertation, University of Hawaii, 1968.

Mao Qiling. *Wuzhong waiji* [Anecdotal Story of Emperor Zhengde]. *Xihe wenji*, Wanyou wenku edition.

Meng Sen. *Ming shi* [History of the Ming Period]. Taipei, 1957.

Meskill, John. *Academies in Ming China, A Historical Essay*. Tucson, 1982.

Michael, Franz. *The Origins of Manchu Rule in China*. Baltimore, 1942.

Millant, Richard. *Les Eunuques: A Travers Les Ages*. Paris, 1908.

Mitamura, Taisuke. *Kangan: sokkin seiji no kozo* [Chinese Eunuchs: The Structure of Intimate Politics]. Tokyo, 1963.

Mote, Frederick W., and Denis Twitchett, eds. *The Cambridge History of China*, vol. 7, *The Ming Dynasty, 1368–1644, Part I.* Cambridge: Cambridge University Press, 1988.

———. "The Growth of Chinese Despotism, A Critique of Wittfogel's Theory of Oriental Despotism as Applied to China." *Oriens Extremus* 8 (1961).

Na Chih-liang and William Kohler. *The Emperor's Procession: Two Scrolls of the Ming Dynasty.* Taipei, 1970.

Needham, Joseph. *Science and Civilization in China*, vol. 3. Cambridge: Cambridge Unversity Press, , 1959.

———. *The Development of Iron and Steel Technology in China.* Cambridge: W. Heffer and Sons Ltd., 1964.

———. *Science and Technology in China*, vol. V, part IX. Cambridge, 1988.

Parsons, James B. *Peasant Rebellions of the Late Ming Dynasty.* Tucson, 1970.

Pelliot, Paul. "Les grands voyages maritimes chinois au début XVe siecle." *T'oung Pao* 30 (1933).

Peschel, Enid R. and Richard Peschel. "Medical Insights into the Castrati in Opera." *American Scientist*, (November–December, 1987).

Phillips, George. "The Seaports of India and Ceylon, Described by Chinese Voyagers of the Fifteenth Century, Together with an Account of Chinese Navigation" *Journal of the Chinese Branch of the Royal Asiatic Society* 28 (1885).

Qian Mu. *Guoshi dagang* [Outlines of Chinese History]. Chongqing, 1944.

———. *Zhongguo lidai zhengzhi deshi* [Political Gains and Losses of China's Past Dynasties]. Hongkong, 1952.

Ricci, Matteo. *China in the Sixteenth Century: The Journals of Matthew Ricci, 1583–1610*, trans. L. J. Gallagher. New York, 1953.

Ross, John. *The Manchus.* London, 1891.

Rossabi, Morris. "The Tea and Horse Trade with Inner Asia During the Ming." *Journal of Asian History* 4 (1970).

———. "Ming China and Turfan, 1406–1517." *Central Asiatic Journal* 16, no.3 (1972).

Samedo, C. Alvarez. *The History of That Great and Renowned Monarchy of China*, anonymously translated. London, 1655.

Serruys, Henry. "The Mongols in China." *Monumenta Serica* 27 (1968).

Shen Defu. *Yehuo bian puyi*. Reprint Zhejiang: blockprint edition, 1827.

Shen Mingzhang. *Mingdai zhengzhi shi* [Political History of the Ming Period]. Taipei, 1967.

Shi Zhengkang, "Mingdai nanfeng de Anlu huangzhuang" [The Anlu Imperial Estate in Ming's Southern China]. In *Mingdaishi yanjiu luncong*. Beijing: China's Academy of Social Sciences, 1985.

Shimizu, Taiji. "Jigu kangan no kenkyu" [A Study of Eunuch's Self-Castration]. *Shigaku zasshi* 43 (1932).

So Kwan-wai. *Japanese Piracy in Ming China During the Sixteenth Century*. East Lansing: Michigan State University Press, 1975.

Song Yingxing. *Tiangong kaiwu* [The Exploitation of the Works of Nature]. Reprint Shanghai, 1937.

Stent, Carter G. "Chinese Eunuchs." *Journal of the North China Branch of the Royal Asiatic Society* n.s. 9 (1877).

Sun Chengze. *Chun Ming mengyulu*. Blockprint, 1874.

Tani, Mitsutaka. *A Study on Horse Administration in the Ming Period*. Kyoto: The Society of Oriental Rersearch, Kyoto University, 1972.

Tianshun Veritable Record [Yingzong Shilu]. Photographic reprint, Jiangsu guoxue tushuguan quan chaoben.

Tianqi Veritable Record [Xizong shilu]. Photographic reprint, Jiangsu guoxue tushuguan quan chaoben.

Tong, James. *Disorder Under Heaven: Collective Violence in the Ming Dynasty*. Stanford, Calif., 1991.

Wang Chunyu and Du Wanyan, eds. *Mingdai huanguan yu jingji shiliao chubian* [Preliminary Edition of Historical Materials on Ming Eunuchs and Economy]. Beijing, 1986.

Wang Hongxu. *Ming shi gao* [Ming Draft History]. Blockprint edition, 1723.

Wang Gengwu. "The Opening of Relations Between China and Malacca 1403–5." In J. Bastin and R. Roolvink, eds., *Malayan and Indonesian Studies: Essays Presented to Sir Richard Winstedt*. London, 1964.

————."China and Southeast Asia 1402–1424." In J. Ch'en and N. Tarling, eds., *Studies in the Social History of China and S. E. Asia*. Cambridge, 1970.

Wang Ming-yu. "The Involvement in Recurrent Power Struggles of the Han, Tang, and Ming Eunuchs." Ph.D. dissertation, St. John's University, 1974.

Wang Shizhen. "Zhongguankao" (On Eunuchs). In *Yanshantang bieji*, 11 juan. Reprint Taipei: Ming blockprint ed., 1964.

Wang Yangming. *Instructions for Practical Living and Other Neo-Confucian Writings*, trans. Wing-tsit Chan. New York, 1963.

Wang Yi-t'ung. *Official Relations Between China and Japan, 1368–1549*, Cambridge, Mass., 1953.

Wanli Veritable Record [Shenzong shilu]. Photographic reprint, Jiangsu guoxue tushuguan quan chaoben.

Wen Gongyi. *Mingdai di huanguan he chaoting* [Eunuchs and the Court During the Ming Period]. Chongqing, 1989.

Wittfogel, Karl A. *Oriental Despotism*. New Haven, Conn., 1957.

Wu Han. "Shiliu shiji qian zhi Zhongguo yu Nanyang" [China and Southeast Asia Prior to the Sixteenth Century]. *Qinghua xuebao* 2 (1936).

———. *Zhu Yuanzhang zhuan* [Biography of the First Ming Emperor]. Shanghai, 1949.

Wu, K. T. "Ming Printing and Printers." *Harvard Journal of Asiatic Studies* 7 (1943).

Wu, Silas. "The Memorial System of the Ch'ing Dynasty (1644–1911)." *Harvard Journal of Asiatic Studies* 26 (1967).

Xia Xie. *Ming Tongjian*. Shanghai, 1888.

Xing Chengye. *Ming Nanjing chejiasu zangzhi* [The Functioning of the Nanjing Bureau of Equipment During the Ming]. Shanghai: Commercial Press, 1934.

Xu Fuyuan et. al, *Huang Ming jingshi wenbian*, Reprint Taipei: Guofeng Publishing Co., 1964.

Xu Pingfang, ed. *Ming Qing Beijingcheng kao* [A Study of the City of Beijing During the Ming-Qing Period]. Beijing, 1986.

Xuande Veritable Record [Xuanzong shilu]. Photographic reprint, Jiangsu guoxue tushuguan quan chaoben.

Yang Jianxin, ed. *Gu xixing ji* [Journey to the West in Ancient Times]. Yingchuan: Ningxia People's Publication, 1987.

Yang Li. *Yang Dahong ji*, late Qing edition.

Yang Lien-sheng. "Female Rulers in Chinese History." *Harvard Journal of Asiatic Studies* 23 (1960–61).

Ye Sheng. *Shuidong riji*. Blockprint, 1680.

Yongle Veritable Record [Taizong shilu]. Photographic reprint, Jiangsu guoxue tushuguan quan chaoben.

Yuan Lukun et al., *Taijian shihua* [Stories about Eunuchs]. Zhengzhou: Henan People's Publication, 1984.

Zhang Dechang. "Mingdai Guangzhou zhi haibo maoyi" [Maritime Trade of Guangzhou During the Ming Period]. *Qinghua xuebao* 7 (1932).

Zhang Tingyu et al., eds. *Ming shi* [History of Ming Dynasty]. Taipei: Dingwen Publishing edition, 332 juan, 1979.

Zhao Yi. *Nianershi zhaji* [Notes from Twenty-Two Histories]. Reprint Taipei, 1966.

Zhengde Veritable Record [Wuzong shilu]. Photographic reprint, Jiangsu guoxue tushuguan quan chaoben.

Zhengtong Veritable Record [Yingzong shilu]. Photographic reprint, Jiangsu guoxue tushuguan quan chaoben.

Zhou Long. "Mingdai zhi huanguan" [The Ming Eunuchs]. M.A. thesis, National Taiwan University, 1960.

Zhu Dan. *Mingji shedang yanjiu* [A Study of Factional Rivalry During the Ming Period]. Chongqing, 1945.

Zhu Dongrun. *Zhang Juzheng dazhuan* [Great Biography of Zhang Juzheng]. Shanghai, 1947.

Zhu Yuanzhang. *Ming Taizu yuzhi wenji* [Collection of Literature Relating to the First Ming Emperor]. Taipei: Student Publication Co., 1965.

INDEX